COMMENTARY

ON THE

GOSPEL ACCORDING TO JOHN.

VOLUME II.

COMMENTARY

ON THE

GOSPEL ACCORDING TO JOHN.

BY JOHN CALVIN.

A NEW TRANSLATION, FROM THE ORIGINAL LATIN,

BY THE REV. WILLIAM PRINGLE.

VOLUME SECOND.

WIPF & STOCK · Eugene, Oregon

Wipf and Stock Publishers
199 W 8th Ave, Suite 3
Eugene, OR 97401

Commentary on the Gospel According to John,
Volume 2
A New Translation, from the Original Latin
By Calvin, John and Pringle, William
Softcover ISBN-13: 978-1-6667-3305-1
Hardcover ISBN-13: 978-1-6667-2732-6
eBook ISBN-13: 978-1-6667-2733-3
Publication date 7/23/2021
Previously published by Calvin Translation Society, 1847

This edition is a scanned facsimile of
the original edition published in 1847.

NOTE BY THE TRANSLATOR.

THE TABLES and INDEX placed at the end of this Volume will, it is hoped, render material aid in consulting the Work. One of those Tables is intended to supply what some may deem an unhappy omission. Considerable progress had been made in printing the Commentary on JOHN'S GOSPEL before it was observed that *headings,* enabling the reader to find easily any chapter or verse of the text, might have been advantageously introduced. In the HARMONY, such *headings* were purposely omitted, as unsuitable to its particular arrangement; but I am authorized to state that they will be found in all the future volumes of the Commentaries issued by the CALVIN SOCIETY.

Meanwhile, it is hoped that all inconvenience will be remedied by the accompanying TABLE, which points out the volume and page where each section and verse of the Commentary begins.

The HARMONY bears on its title-page that it has been " translated from the original Latin, and collated with the Author's French version." A broad line drawn between the Latin and French copies, while no important variation of them is neglected, forms a distinguishing feature in these New Translations; and the foot-notes will exhibit, at a glance, the extent to which the collation has been carried.

W. P.

AUCHTERARDER, 31*st March* 1848.

CONTENTS OF VOLUME II.

	PAGE
TABLE OF THE CHAPTERS AND VERSES OF THE GOSPEL ACCORDING TO JOHN, SHOWING WHERE THE EXPOSITION OF THEM WILL BE FOUND, . . .	ix
COMMENTARY, ...	9
TABLE I. OF PASSAGES OF SCRIPTURE ILLUSTRATED, .	303
TABLE II. OF GREEK WORDS EXPLAINED, . . .	315
TABLE III. OF HEBREW WORDS EXPLAINED, . .	317
INDEX, ...	319

TABLE OF THE CHAPTERS AND VERSES OF THE GOSPEL OF JOHN, SHOWING WHERE THE EXPOSITION OF THEM WILL BE FOUND.

Chap	Ver	Vol	Page	Chap	Ver	Vol	Page
i	1—5	i	25		30—32	i.	210
	6—13	i.	35		33—36	i.	212
	14	i.	44		37—40	i.	216
	15—18	i.	48		41—47	i.	219
	19—23	i.	55	vi.	1—13	i.	226
	24—28	i.	59		14—21	i.	233
	29—34	i.	63		22—25	i.	237
	35—39	i.	69		26—29	i.	239
	40—42	i	71		30—33	i.	245
	43—46	i.	74		34—40	i.	248
	47—51	i	77		41—45	i	255
ii.	1—11	i.	81		46—51	i.	259
	12—17	i	90		52—58	i.	263
	18—22	i.	95		59—64	i.	270
	23—25	i	100		65—71	i	275
iii.	1—6	i	103	vii.	1—8	i.	281
	7—12	i.	114		9—13	i	285
	13—18	i.	120		14—19	i	288
	19—21	i.	128		20—24	i	294
	22—28	i.	130	vii	25—30	i.	297
	29—24	i.	133		31—36	i.	301
	35, 36	i	140		37—39	i.	306
iv	1—9	i.	143		40—44	i.	310
	10—15	i.	147		45—53	i.	313
	16—21	i.	152	viii.	1—11	i.	318
	22—26	i.	159		12—14	i.	324
	27—34	i	166		15—20	i.	327
iv.	35—38	i.	170		21—24	i.	330
	39—45	i.	175		25—29	i.	334
	46—54	i	179		30—38	i.	340
v	1—9	i.	184		39—42	i.	346
	10—16	i.	191		43—45	i.	349
	17—19	i.	195		46—50	i.	353
	20—24	i.	199		51—55	i	356
	25—29	i	205		56—59	i	360

VOL. II.

TABLE.

Chap	Ver	Vol	Page	Chap.	Ver	Vol	Page
ix.	1—5	i.	363	xv.	7—11	ii.	111
	6—12	i.	369		12—15	ii.	115
	13—17	i	373		16—21	ii.	118
	18—23	i.	378		22—27	ii.	126
	24—33	i	382	xvi.	1—7	ii	132
	34—41	i	386		8—15	ii.	137
x	1—6	i.	394		16—20	ii.	147
	7—10	i	397		21—24	ii	150
	11—15	i.	400		25—28	ii	155
	16—18	i	406		29—33	ii.	159
	19—30	i.	410	xvii.	1—5	ii	163
	31—36	i.	417		6—11	ii	169
	37—42	i.	421		12, 13	ii	175
xi.	1—10	i.	424		14—19	ii.	178
	11—17	i	429		20—23	ii	181
	18—27	i	132		24—26	ii.	186
	28—38	i.	437	xviii.	1—6	ii.	189
	39—44	i.	443		7—9	ii.	192
	45—52	i.	447		10—14	ii.	194
	53—57	i.	455		15—18	ii	198
xii.	1—8	ii.	9		19—24	ii.	200
	9—15	ii	15		25—27	ii.	203
	16—19	ii.	23		28—32	ii.	204
xii.	20—26	ii.	25		33—36	ii.	208
	27—33	ii.	31		37—40	ii.	211
	34—36	ii.	37	xix.	1—6	ii.	214
	37—41	ii.	40		7—11	ii.	216
	42—46	ii.	44		12—16	ii.	222
	47—50	ii	50		17—22	ii.	225
xiii.	1—7	ii	53		23, 24	ii.	229
	8—11	ii.	56		25—27	ii.	230
	12—17	ii.	60		28—30	ii.	233
	18—20	ii.	63		31—37	ii.	237
	21—29	ii.	68		38—42	ii.	243
	30—35	ii.	72	xx.	1—9	ii.	247
xiv.	1—7	ii.	79		10—15	ii.	253
	8—14	ii.	86		16—18	ii.	253
	15—18	ii.	91		19—23	ii.	263
	19, 20	ii.	94		24—29	ii.	273
	21—24	ii.	96		30, 31	ii.	280
	25—28	ii.	99	xxi.	1—14	ii.	283
	29—31	ii.	103		15—19	ii.	287
xv	1—6	ii.	106		20—25	ii.	295

COMMENTARY

ON THE

HOLY GOSPEL OF JESUS CHRIST

ACCORDING TO JOHN.

CHAPTER XII.

1. Jesus therefore, six days before the passover, came to Bethany, where Lazarus was, who had been dead, whom he had raised from the dead 2. There therefore they made him a banquet, and Martha served,[1] and Lazarus was one of those who sat at table with him. 3. Then Mary took a pound of ointment of costly spikenard, and anointed the feet of Jesus, and wiped his feet with her hair, and the house was filled with the odour of the ointment. 4. Then one of his disciples, Judas Iscariot, the son of Simon, who was to betray him, saith, 5 Why was not this ointment sold for three hundred denarii, and given to the poor? 6 Now he said this, not because he cared for the poor, but because he was a thief, and had the purse, and carried what was put into it 7. Jesus therefore said, Let her alone, for the day of my burial she hath kept it. 8. For the poor you have always with you, but me you have not always

1. *Jesus came to Bethany.* We see that they judged too rashly who thought that Christ *would not come to the feast,*[2] (John xi. 56;) and this reminds us that we ought not to be so hasty as not to wait patiently and quietly, till the season

---

[1] " Et Marthe servoit à table; "—" and Martha waited at table "
[2] " Ne viendroit point à la feste "

arrive, which is unknown to us. Now *Jesus came* first *to Bethany,* that thence he might go three days afterwards to Jerusalem. Meanwhile, he intended to give Judas a fit time and place for betraying him, that he might present himself, ready to be sacrificed, at the appointed time; for he is not ignorant of what is to take place, but willingly comes forward to be sacrificed.

Having *come to Bethany six days before the passover,* he remained there four days; which may easily be inferred from Matthew and Mark. On what day the banquet was made for him, at which he was anointed by Mary, John does not state; but it seems probable that it took place not long after he had arrived. There are some who think that the anointing mentioned by Matthew (xxvi. 7) and Mark (xiv. 3) is different from what is mentioned here; but they are mistaken. They have been led to adopt this view by a calculation of time, because the two Evangelists, (Matth. xxvi. 2; Mark xiv. 1,) before relating that Christ was anointed, speak of *two days* as having elapsed. But the solution is easy, and may be given in two ways. For John does not say that Christ was anointed on the first day after his arrival; so that this might happen even when he was preparing to depart. Yet, as I have already said, there is another conjecture which is more probable, that he was anointed one day, at least, or two days, before his departure; for it is certain that Judas had made a bargain with the priests, before Christ sent two of his disciples to make ready the passover.[1] Now, at the very least, one day must have intervened. The Evangelists add, that he *sought a convenient opportunity for betraying Christ,* (Matth. xxvi. 16,) after having received the bribe. When, therefore, after mentioning *two days,* they add the history of the anointing, they place last in the narrative what happened first. And the reason is, that after having related the words of Christ, *You know that after two days the Son of man shall be betrayed,* (Matth. xxvi. 2,) they now add—what had been formerly omitted—in what manner and on what occasion he was betrayed by his disciple. There is thus a

---

[1] " Pour faire apprester la Pasque "

perfect agreement in the account of his having been anointed at Bethany.

2. *There therefore they made him a banquet.* Matthew (xxvi. 7) and Mark (xiv. 3) say that he then supped at the house of Simon the leper. John does not mention the house, but shows plainly enough, that it was in some other place than the house of Lazarus and Martha that he supped; for he says that *Lazarus was one of those who sat at table with him,* that is, one who had been invited along with Christ. Nor does it involve any contradiction, that Matthew and Mark relate that the *head* of Christ was anointed, while John relates that his *feet* were anointed. The usual practice was the anointing of *the head,* and on this account Pliny reckons it an instance of excessive luxury, that some anointed the ankles. The three Evangelists agree in this, that Mary did not anoint Christ sparingly, but poured on him a large quantity of ointment. What John speaks, about *the feet,* amounts to this, that the whole body of Christ, down to the feet, was anointed. There is an amplification in the word *feet,* which appears more fully from what follows, when he adds, that Mary *wiped his feet with her hair.*

3. *And the house was filled with the odour of the ointment.* It was not a simple liquor extracted from *spikenard,* but a compound of many odoriferous substances; and therefore it is not wonderful that *the* whole *house was filled with the odour.*

4. *One of his disciples, therefore, saith.* Next follows the murmuring of Judas, which Matthew (xxvi. 8) attributes to *the disciples* indiscriminately, and Mark (xiv. 4) to *some* of them; but it is customary in Scripture to apply to many, by way of synecdoche, what belongs to one or to a few. Yet I think it is probable, that the murmuring proceeded from Judas alone, and that the rest were induced to give him their assent, as murmurings, by fanning a flame, easily kindle in us a variety of dispositions; and more especially, as we are too prone to form unfavourable judgments, slanders are readily embraced by us. But the credulity which the Spirit of God

reproves in the Apostles is a warning to us not to be too easy and credulous in listening to calumnious statements.

5. *Why was not this ointment sold for three hundred denarii?* A pound of ordinary ointment, Pliny tells us, cost not more than ten denarii; but the same Pliny says, that the highest price of the best ointment was three hundred and ten denarii. Now the Evangelists agree, that this was the most costly ointment, and therefore Judas is correct in valuing a pound of it at *three hundred denarii,*—a sum which, according to the computation of Budæus, amounts to fifty *livres* of French money. And as almost every kind of luxury involves excess and superfluity, the greater the waste of money, the more plausible reason had Judas for murmuring; as if he had said, " Had Mary spent little, there would have been some excuse for her; but now, since, in a matter of no importance, she has wasted a vast sum of money, has she not done an injury to *the poor,* who might have obtained from such a sum great relief? What she has done, therefore, admits of no apology."

6. *Because he was a thief.* The rest of the Apostles, not from any bad disposition, but thoughtlessly, condemn Mary. But Judas resorts to a plausible pretext for his wickedness, when he brings forward *the poor,* though he cared nothing about them. We are taught by this instance what a frightful beast the desire of possessing is; the loss which Judas thinks that he has sustained, by the loss of an opportunity for stealing, excites him to such rage that he does not hesitate to betray Christ. And probably, in what he said about *the poor* having been defrauded, he did not only speak falsely to others, but likewise flattered himself inwardly, as hypocrites are wont to do; as if the act of betraying Christ were a trivial fault, by which he endeavoured to obtain compensation for the loss which he had sustained. He had but one reason, indeed, for betraying Christ; and that was, to regain in some way the prey which had been snatched from his hands; for it was the indignation excited in him, by the gain which he had lost, that drove him to the design of betraying Christ.

It is wonderful that Christ should have chosen, as a steward, a person of this description, whom he knew to be *a thief*. For what else was it than to put into his hands a rope for strangling himself? Mortal man can give no other reply than this, that the judgments of God are a deep gulf. Yet the action of Christ ought not to be viewed as an ordinary rule, that we should commit the care of the poor, or any thing sacred, to a wicked and ungodly man. For God has laid down to us a law, who they are that ought to be called to the government of the Church, and to other offices; and this law we are not at liberty to violate. The case was otherwise with Christ, who, being the eternal Wisdom of God, furnished an opportunity for his secret predestination in the person of Judas.

7. *Let her alone.* When Christ bids them *let* Mary *alone*, he shows that they act improperly and unjustly who disturb their neighbours without a good reason, and raise a disturbance about nothing. Christ's reply, as given by the other Evangelists, is longer; but the meaning is the same. The *anointing*, which Judas finds fault with, is defended on this ground, that it will serve for his burial. Christ, therefore, does not approve of it as an ordinary service, or one which ought to be commonly used in the Church; for if he had intended that an office of this sort should be performed daily, he could have said something else instead of speaking of it as connected with his burial. God certainly does not approve of outward display. Nay, more, perceiving that the mind of man is too prone to carnal observances, He frequently enjoins us to be sober and moderate in the use of them. Those persons, therefore, are absurd interpreters, who infer from Christ's reply, that costly and magnificent worship is pleasing to God; for he rather excuses Mary on the ground of her having rendered to him an extraordinary service, which ought not to be regarded as a perpetual rule for the worship of God.

For the day of my burial she hath kept it. When he says, that the ointment was *kept*, he means that it was not poured unseasonably, but with a due regard to the time when it occurred; for a thing is said to be *kept*, which is reserved in store to be brought out at a fit time and place. It is certain that, if any person, at a former period, had burdened him

with costly delicacies, he would not have endured it. But
he affirms that Mary did not do this as a customary matter,
but in order to discharge her last duty towards him. Besides,
the anointing of bodies was not at that time a useless ceremony, but rather a spiritual symbol, to place before their eyes
the hope of a resurrection. The promises were still obscure;
Christ had not risen, who is justly designated *the first-fruits
of them that rise,* (1 Cor. xv. 20.) Believers, therefore, needed
such aids to direct them to Christ, who was still absent; and,
accordingly, the *anointing* of Christ was not at that time
superfluous, for he was soon to be buried, and he was *anointed*
as if he were to be laid in the tomb. The disciples were not yet
aware of this, and Mary unquestionably was suddenly moved
to do, under the direction of the Spirit of God, what she had
not previously intended. But Christ applies to the hope of
his resurrection what they so greatly disapproved, in order
that the usefulness, which he pointed out to them in this
action,[1] might lead them to renounce the fretful and wicked
opinion which they had formed respecting it. As it was the
will of God that the childhood of his ancient people should
be guided by such exercises, so, in the present day, it would
be foolish to attempt the same thing; nor could it be done
without offering an insult to Christ, who has driven away
such shadows by the brightness of his coming. But as his
resurrection had not yet brought the fulfilment of the shadows
of the Law, it was proper that his burial should be adorned
by an outward ceremony. The odour of his resurrection has
now sufficient efficacy, without spikenard and costly oint-
ments, to quicken the whole world. But let us remember
that, in judging of the actions of men, we ought to abide by
the decision of Christ alone, at whose tribunal we must one
day stand.

8. *For the poor you have always with you.* We must observe
what I have already pointed out, that a distinction is here
drawn expressly between the extraordinary action of Mary,
and the daily service which is due to Christ. Those persons,

---

[1] "A fin que l'utilité laquelle il leur monstre en ce faict les retire du jugement chagrin et pervers qu'ils en faisoyent."

therefore, are apes, and not imitators, who are desirous to serve Christ by costly and splendid display ; as if Christ approved of what was done once, and did not rather forbid that it should be done afterwards.

But me you have not always. When he says, that he will not always be with his disciples, this ought to be referred to that kind of presence to which carnal worship and costly honours are suitable. For as to his presence with us by the grace and power of his Spirit, his dwelling in us, and also feeding us with his flesh and blood, this has nothing to do with bodily observances. Of all the pompous ceremonies which the Papists have contrived for the worship of Christ, in vain do they tell us that they have bestowed them upon him, for he openly rejects them. When he says, that *the poor will always be with us,* though, by this saying, he reproves the hypocrisy of the Jews, yet we may learn from it a profitable doctrine ; namely, that alms, by which the wants of the poor are relieved, are sacrifices acceptable, and of sweet savour, to God, and that any other kind of expense in the worship of God is improperly bestowed.

9. Then a great multitude of the Jews knew that he was there, and came, not on account of Jesus only, but that they might see Lazarus also, whom he had raised from the dead. 10. Now the chief priests consulted, that they might put Lazarus also to death , 11. For many of the Jews on his account went away, and believed on Jesus. 12. Next day, a great multitude, who had come to the feast, when they heard that Jesus was come to Jerusalem, 13 Took branches of palm-trees, and went out to meet him, and shouted, Hosanna, Blessed be the King of Israel, that cometh in the name of the Lord 14 And Jesus, having found a young ass, sat upon it, as it is written, Fear not, daughter of Zion, because thy King cometh sitting on the foal of an ass.

9. *Then a great multitude of the Jews knew that he was there.* The more nearly the time of the death of Christ approached, it became the more necessary that his name should be universally celebrated, in order that it might be a preparation for stronger faith after his death. More especially, the Evangelist relates that the recent miracle of the resurrection of Lazarus had acquired great celebrity : and as Christ showed in it a remarkable proof of his Divinity, God intended that it should have many witnesses. When he says that

they came not on account of Jesus only, but also for the sake of Lazarus, he does not mean that they came out of regard to Lazarus, as if they bestowed this mark of honour on him in particular, but that they might behold the astonishing display of the power of Christ in Lazarus.

10. *Now the chief priests consulted.* It certainly was worse than insane fury to endeavour to put to death one who had manifestly been raised from the dead by divine power. But such is the spirit of giddiness with which Satan torments the wicked, so that there is no end of their madness, even though God should bring heaven, and earth, and sea, to oppose them. For this wicked consultation is thus described, for the purpose of informing us that the enemies of Christ were led to so great obstinacy, not by mistake or folly, but by furious wickedness, so that they did not even shrink from making war against God; and also for the purpose of informing us that the power of God was not dimly seen in the resurrection of Lazarus, since ungodliness could contrive no other method of banishing it from remembrance than by perpetrating a base and shocking murder on an innocent man. Besides, since Satan labours with his utmost strength utterly to bury, or at least in some measure to obscure, the works of God, it is our duty to devote ourselves diligently to continual meditation on them.

12. *The next day, a great multitude.* This entrance of Christ is more copiously related (Matth. xxi. 1; Mark xi. 1; Luke xix. 29) by the other Evangelists; but John here embraces the leading points. In the first place, we ought to remember Christ's design, which was, that he came to Jerusalem of his own accord, to offer himself to die; for it was necessary that his death should be voluntary, because the wrath of God could be appeased only by a sacrifice of obedience. And, indeed, he well knew what would be the result; but before he is dragged to the cross, he wishes to be solemnly acknowledged by the people as their King; nay, he openly declares that he commences his reign by advancing to death. But though his approach was celebrated by a vast crowd of

people, still he remained unknown to his enemies until, by the fulfilment of prophecies, which we shall afterwards see in their own place, he proved that he was the true Messiah; for he wished to omit nothing that would contribute to the full confirmation of our faith.

A great multitude, which came to the feast. Thus strangers were more ready to discharge the duty of paying respect to the Son of God than the citizens of Jerusalem, who ought rather to have been an example to all others. For they had sacrifices daily; the temple was always before their eyes, which ought to have kindled in their hearts the desire of seeking God; these too were the highest teachers of the Church, and *there* was the sanctuary of the divine light. It is therefore a manifestation of excessively base ingratitude in them that, after they have been trained to such exercise from their earliest years, they reject or despise the Redeemer who had been promised to them. But this fault has prevailed in almost every age, that the more nearly and the more familiarly God approached to men, the more daringly did men despise God.

In other men who, having left their homes, assembled to celebrate the feast, we observe much greater ardour, so that they eagerly inquire about Christ; and when they hear that he is coming into the city, they go out to meet and congratulate him. And yet it cannot be doubted that they were aroused by a secret movement of the Spirit to meet him. We do not read that this was done on any former occasion. But as earthly princes summon their subjects by the sound of a trumpet or by the public crier, when they go to take possession of their kingdom, so Christ, by a movement of his Spirit, assembled this people, that they might hail him as their king. When the multitudes wished to make him a king, while he was in the wilderness, (John vi. 15,) he withdrew secretly into the mountain; for at that time they dreamed of no other kingdom than one under which they might be well fattened, in the same manner as cattle. Christ could not therefore grant and comply with their foolish and absurd wish, without denying himself, and renouncing the office which the Father had bestowed upon him. But now he claims for himself such a kingdom as he had received from the Father. I readily acknowledge that the people who went out to meet him were not well acquainted with the nature of this kingdom; but Christ looked to the future. Meanwhile, he permitted nothing to be done that was not suitable to his spiritual kingdom.

13. *Took branches of palm-trees.* The *palm* was the emblem of victory and peace among the ancients; but they were wont to employ *branches of palm-trees,* when they bestowed kingly power on any one, or when they humbly supplicated the favour of a conqueror. But those persons appear to have taken into their hands *branches of palm-trees,* as a token of gladness and rejoicing at receiving a new king.

Shouted, Hosanna. By this phrase they testified that they acknowledged Jesus Christ to be the Messiah, who had anciently been promised to the fathers, and from whom redemption and salvation were to be expected. For the Psalm (cxviii. 25) from which that exclamation is taken was composed in reference to the Messiah for this purpose, that all the saints might continually desire and ardently long for his coming, and might receive him with the utmost reverence, when he was manifested. It is therefore probable, or rather it may be inferred with certainty, that this prayer was frequently used by the Jews, and, consequently, was in every man's mouth; so that the Spirit of God put words into the mouths[1] of those men, when they wished a prosperous arrival to the Lord Jesus; and they were chosen by him as heralds to attest that Christ was come.

The word *Hosanna* is composed of two Hebrew words, and means, *Save, I beseech you.* The Hebrews, indeed, pronounce it differently, (הוֹשִׁיעָה־נָא,) *Hoshiana ;*[2] but it usually happens that the pronunciation of words is corrupted, when they are transferred to a foreign language. Yet the Evangelists, though they wrote in Greek, purposely retained the Hebrew word, in order to express more fully that the multitude employed the ordinary form of prayer, which was first employed

---

[1] "Et pourtant le Sainct Esprit mettoit les mots en la bouche des hommes, quand ils ont ainsi souhaitté heureuse venue au Seigneur Jesus."
[2] See *Harmony of the Evangelists,* vol. ii. p. 451.

by David, and afterwards throughout an uninterrupted succession of ages, received by the people of God, and peculiarly consecrated for the purpose of blessing the kingdom of the Messiah.[1] To the same purpose are the words which immediately follow, *Blessed be the King of Israel, who cometh in the name of the Lord;* for this is also a joyful prayer for the happy and prosperous success of that kingdom, on which the restoration and prosperity of the Church of God depended.

But as David appears to speak of himself rather than of Christ in that psalm, we must first of all solve this difficulty; nor will the task be hard. We know for what purpose the kingdom was established in the hand of David and of his posterity; and that purpose was, that it might be a sort of prelude of the everlasting kingdom which was to be manifested at the proper time. And, indeed, it was not necessary that David should confine his attention to himself; and the Lord, by the prophets, frequently commands all the godly to turn their eyes to a different person from David.[2] So then all that David sung about himself is justly referred to that king who, according to the promise, was to arise from the seed of David to be the Redeemer.

But we ought to derive from it a profitable admonition; for if we are members of the Church, the Lord calls upon us to cherish the same desire which he wished believers to cherish under the Law; that is, that we should wish with our whole heart that the kingdom of Christ should flourish and prosper; and not only so, but that we should demonstrate this by our prayers. In order to give us greater courage in prayer, we ought to observe that he prescribes to us the words. Woe then to our slothfulness, if we extinguish by our coldness, or quench by indifference, that ardour which God excites. Yet let us know that the prayers which we offer by the direction and authority of God will not be in vain. Provided that we be not indolent or grow weary in praying, He will be a faithful guardian of his kingdom, to defend it by his invincible power and protection. True, indeed, though we re-

---

[1] " Le royaume du Messias "
[2] " De jetter leurs yeux ailleurs qu'à David."

main drowsy and inactive,[1] the majesty of his kingdom will be firm and sure; but when—as is frequently the case—it is less prosperous than it ought to be, or rather falls into decay, as we perceive it to be, at the present day, fearfully scattered and wasted, this unquestionably arises through our fault. And when but a small restoration, or almost none, is to be seen, or when at least it advances slowly, let us ascribe it to our indifference. We daily ask from God *that his kingdom may come,* (Matth. vi. 10,) but scarcely one man in a hundred earnestly desires it. Justly, therefore, are we deprived of the blessing of God, which we are weary of asking.

We are also taught by this expression, that it is God alone who preserves and defends the Church; for He does not claim for himself, or command us to give him, anything but what is his own. Since, therefore, while He guides our tongues, we pray that he may preserve the kingdom of Christ, we acknowledge that, in order that this kingdom may remain in a proper state, God himself is the only bestower of salvation. He employs, indeed, the labours of men for this purpose, but of men whom his own hand has prepared for the work. Besides, while he makes use of men for advancing or maintaining the kingdom of Christ, still everything is begun and completed, through their agency, by God alone, through the power of his Spirit.

Who cometh in the name of the Lord. We must first understand what is meant by this phrase, *to come in the name of the Lord.* He who does not rashly put himself forward, or falsely assume the honour, but, being duly called, has the direction and authority of God for his actions, *cometh in the name of God.* This title belongs to all the true servants of God. A Prophet who, guided by the Holy Spirit, honestly delivers to men the doctrine which he has received from heaven,— *cometh in the name of God.* A King, by whose hand God governs his people, *cometh in* the same *name.* But as the Spirit of the Lord rested on Christ, and he is *the Head of all things,* (Eph. i. 22,) and all who have ever been ordained to rule over the Church are subject to his sway, or rather, are

---

[1] "Endormis et oisifs."

streams flowing from him as the fountain, he is justly said to have *come in the name of God.* Nor is it only by the high rank of his authority that he surpasses others, but because God manifests himself to us fully in him; for *in him dwelleth the fulness of the Godhead bodily,* as Paul says, (Col. ii. 9,) and he is *the lively image* of God, (Heb. i. 3,) and, in short, is the true *Immanuel,* (Matth. i. 23.) It is therefore by a special right that he is said to have *come in the name of the Lord,* because by him God has manifested himself fully, and not partially, as he had formerly done by the Prophets. We ought therefore to begin with him as the Head, when we wish to bless the servants of God.

Now, since the false prophets arrogantly boast of *the name of God,* and shelter themselves under this false pretence, we ought to supply an opposite clause in the prayer, that the Lord may scatter and utterly destroy them. Thus we cannot bless Christ without cursing the Pope and that sacrilegious tyranny which he has raised up against the Son of God.[1] He hurls his excommunications against us, indeed, with great violence, as if they were thunderbolts, but they are mere air-bladders,[2] and therefore we ought boldly to despise them. On the contrary, the Holy Spirit here dictates to us an awful curse, that it may sink the Pope to the lowest hell, with all his pomp and splendour. Nor is it necessary that there should be any Bishop or Pontiff[3] to pronounce the curse against him, since Christ at one time bestowed this authority on *children,* when he approved of their *crying in the temple, and saying, Hosanna to the Son of David,* as the other Evangelists relate, (Matth. xxi. 15, 16.)

14. *And Jesus having found a young ass.* This part of the history is more minutely related by the other Evangelists, who tell us, that Christ *sent two of his disciples* to bring an ass, (Matth. xxi. 1; Mark xi. 1; Luke xix. 29.) John, who was the latest writer of all the Evangelists, reckoned it enough to notice briefly the substance of what had been stated by

[1] " Contre le Fils de Dieu "
[2] " Vessies pleines de vent."
[3] " Quelque Evesque ou Pontiffe."

the rest; and, on this account, he leaves out many circumstances. An apparent contradiction, by which many persons are perplexed, is very easily removed. When Matthew says, that Christ sat upon *a she-ass and her colt,* we ought to view it as a synecdoche.¹ Some imagine that he sat first on the she-ass, and afterwards on her colt; and out of this conjecture they frame an allegory, that he first sat on the Jewish people, who had been long accustomed to bear the yoke of the Law, and afterwards subdued the Gentiles, like an untrained *young ass* which had never carried a rider.² But the plain truth is, that Christ rode on an ass which had been brought along with its mother; and to this agree the words of the Prophet, who, by a repetition very frequent among the Hebrews, expresses the same thing twice by different words. *On an ass,* he says, *and on the colt of an ass which was under the yoke,* (ὑποζυγίου.) Our Evangelist, who studies brevity, leaves out the former clause, and quotes only the latter.

The Jews themselves are constrained to expound the prediction of Zechariah, (ix. 9,) which was at that time fulfilled, as referring to the Messiah; but, at the same time, they ridicule us for being led astray by *the shadow of an ass,*³ so as to give the honour of the Messiah to the son of Mary. But far different are the testimonies on which our faith rests. And, indeed, when we say that Jesus is the Messiah, we do not begin by saying, that he entered into Jerusalem sitting on an ass; for there was displayed in him a glory, such as belonged to the Son of God, as we have seen under the first chapter of this Gospel;⁴ and it was chiefly in his resurrection that his Divine power was illustriously displayed. But we ought not to despise this confirmation, that God, by his wonderful Providence, exhibited on that entrance, as on a public stage, the fulfilment of that which Zechariah had foretold.

---

¹ " C'est une façon de parler qui comprend quelques fois le tout pour une partie, ou une partie pour le tout "—"It is a mode of expression which sometimes puts the whole for a part, or a part for the whole."

² See *Harmony of the Evangelists,* vol. ii. p. 448.

³ *The shadow of an ass,* ὄνου σκιά, *asini umbra,* was a proverbial phrase among the Greeks and Romans.—*Ed.*

⁴ Vol. i. p. 47.

Fear not. In these words of the Prophet, as the Evangelist quotes them, we ought to observe, first, that never is tranquillity restored to our minds, or fear and trembling banished from them, except by knowing that Christ reigns amongst us. The words of the Prophet, indeed, are different; for he exhorts believers to gladness and rejoicing. But the Evangelist has here described the manner in which our hearts exult with true joy. It is, when that fear is removed, with which all must be tormented, until, being reconciled to God, they obtain that peace which springs from faith, (Rom. v. 1.) This benefit, therefore, comes to us through Christ, that, freed from the tyranny of Satan, the yoke of sin being broken, guilt cancelled, and death abolished, we freely boast, relying on the protection of our King, since they who are placed under his guardianship ought not to fear any danger. Not that we are free from fear, so long as we live in the world, but because confidence, founded on Christ, rises superior to all fear. Though Christ was still at a distance, yet the Prophet exhorted the godly men of that age to be glad and joyful, because Christ was to come. *Behold,* said he, *thy King will come; therefore fear not.* Now that he is come, in order that we may enjoy his presence, we ought more vigorously to contend with fear, that, freed from our enemies, we may peacefully and joyfully honour our King.

Daughter of Zion. The Prophet addressed *Zion* in his own time, because that was the habitation and abode of the Church. God has now, indeed, collected a Church for himself out of the whole world; but this promise is peculiarly addressed to believers, who submit to Christ, that he may reign in them. When he describes Christ as *riding on an ass,* the meaning is, that his kingdom will have nothing in common with the pomp, splendour, wealth, and power of the world; and it was proper that this should be made known by an outward manifestation, that all might be fully assured that it is spiritual.

16. These things his disciples did not understand at first; but when Jesus was glorified, then they remembered that these things had been written concerning him, and that they had done these things to him. 17. And the multitude, which were with him, gave their testimony that he

had called Lazarus out of the tomb, and had raised him from the dead. 18. For this reason the multitude met him, because they had heard that he had performed this miracle. 19 The Pharisees therefore said among themselves, Perceive you not that you gain nothing? Behold, the world is gone after him

16. *These things his disciples did not understand at first.* As the seed does not spring up as soon as it is thrown into the earth, so the result of the works of God is not immediately seen. The Apostles are the servants of God to fulfil the prophecy, but they do not understand what they are doing. They hear the shout of the multitude, which was no confused noise, but a distinct salutation of Christ as King; but they do not perceive what is the object of it, or what it means. To them, therefore, it is an unmeaning exhibition, until the Lord, after his glorious resurrection, opens their eyes.

When it is said, that they at length *remembered that these things had been written concerning him,* the Evangelist points out the cause of such gross ignorance, by which their knowledge was preceded. It was because they had not the Scripture at that time as their guide and instructor, to direct their minds to just and accurate views; for we are blind, unless the word of God go before our steps, and it is not even enough that the word of God shine on us, if the Spirit do not also enlighten our eyes, which otherwise would be blind amidst the clearest light. This grace Christ bestowed on his disciples after his resurrection, because the full time, when the Spirit should bestow his riches in great abundance, was not come, until he was received into the heavenly glory, as we have seen under chap. vii. 39.[1]

Taught by this example, let us learn to form our judgment of every thing that relates to Christ, not by our own carnal feelings, but by the Scripture. Besides, let us remember that it is a special favour of the Holy Spirit to instruct us in a gradual manner, that we may not be stupid in considering the works of God.

That these things had been written concerning him, and that they had done these things to him. I interpret that clause in

[1] Vol i. p. 310.

this manner: "*Then*, for the first time, did it occur to the disciples that Christ did not do these things rashly, and that those men were not employed in idle amusement; but that the whole of this transaction had been regulated by the providence of God, because those things which *had been written* must necessarily be fulfilled;" so that the words may be thus arranged: "They did these things to him, as they had been written concerning him."

17. *The multitude gave their testimony.* He again repeats what he had said, that many persons, aroused by the report of so great a miracle, came to meet Christ. The reason why they go out in crowds is, that the rumour, respecting Lazarus who had been restored to life, was widely spread. They had good reason, therefore, for ascribing to the son of Mary the honour of the Messiah, since he was known to possess such extraordinary power.

19. *Do you not see that you gain nothing?* By these words they urge themselves to greater rage; for it may be regarded as a reproach of their slothfulness, as if they had said, that the reason why the people revolted and followed Christ was their own excessive indolence and cowardice. This is the way in which desperate men are wont to talk, when they are making themselves ready for attempting any extreme measures. And if the enemies of God persevere so obstinately in what is evil, we ought to be far more steady in a just undertaking.

20. Now there were some Greeks among these who had come up to worship at the feast. 21. These therefore went to Philip, who was of Bethsaida of Galilee, and asked him, saying, Sir, we wish to see Jesus. 22. Philip cometh and telleth Andrew, and again Andrew and Philip tell Jesus. 23. And Jesus answered them, saying, The hour is come, when the Son of man must be glorified. 24 Verily, verily, I say to you, Unless a grain of wheat, having fallen into the ground, die, it remaineth alone; but if it die, it bringeth forth much fruit. 25. He who loveth his soul shall destroy it; and he who hateth his soul in this world shall keep it to eternal life. 26. If any man serves me, let him follow me; and where I am, there also shall my servant be. And if any man shall serve me, my Father will honour him.

20. *Now there were some Greeks.* I do not think that they

were Gentiles or uncircumcised, because immediately afterwards it follows that they came *to worship*. Now it was strictly prohibited by the Roman laws, and severely punished by the Proconsuls and other magistrates, if any person was discovered to have left the worship of his native country and passed over to the Jewish religion. But Jews, who were scattered throughout Asia and Greece, were allowed to cross the sea for the purpose of offering sacrifices in the temple. Besides, the Jews were not permitted to associate with them in the solemn worship of God, because they thought that the temple, and the sacrifices, and themselves, would in that way be polluted. But though they were the descendants of Jews, yet as they resided at a great distance beyond the sea, we need not wonder that the Evangelist introduces them as strangers and unacquainted with the occurrences which took place at that time in Jerusalem and in places adjacent. The meaning therefore is, that Christ was received as King, not only by the inhabitants of Judea, who had come from villages and towns *to the feast*, but that the report had also reached men who lived beyond the sea, and who had come from distant countries.

To worship. They might have done this also in their own country; but John describes here solemn *worship*, which was accompanied by sacrifices. For though religion and the fear of God were not confined to the temple, yet in no other place were they permitted to offer sacrifices to God, nor had they any where else the Ark of the Testimony, which was the token of the presence of God. Every man worshipped God daily at his own house in a spiritual manner; but the saints under the Law were likewise bound to make profession of outward worship and obedience,[1] such as was prescribed by Moses, by appearing in the temple in the presence of God. Such was the design for which the feasts were appointed. And if those men undertook so long a journey at great expense, with great inconvenience, and not without personal risk, that they might not treat with indifference the external profession of their piety, what apology can we now offer, if we do not

---

[1] "De service et obeissance exterieure."

testify, in our own houses, that we worship the true God? The worship which belonged to the Law has indeed come to an end; but the Lord has left to his Church Baptism, the Lord's Supper, and public prayer, that in those exercises believers may be employed. If we despise them, therefore, it proves that our desire of godliness is excessively cold.

21. *These men therefore went to Philip.* It is an indication of reverence, that they do not address Christ, but are desirous to obtain access through *Philip;* for reverence always begets modesty. The inference which the Papists draw from this, that we ought to call on departed saints,[1] that they may be our advocates with Christ and with the Father, is so ridiculous that it does not need refutation. The Greeks address *Philip,* while he is present; and, pray, where is the resemblance to those who address their prayers to departed saints, from whom they are separated?[2] But such are the fruits of human presumption, when it has once permitted itself to go beyond the limits of the word of God. Invocation of the saints has been rashly fabricated by the Papists out of their own brain; and now, in order to shelter themselves under a false pretence borrowed from the word of God, they corrupt the Scripture, and tear it to pieces, and do not scruple to expose it to shameful taunts.

23. *The hour is come.* Many explain this as referring to the death of Christ, because by it the glory of Christ was manifested; so that, in their opinion, Christ now declares that the time of his death is at hand. But I rather view it as referring to the publication of the gospel; as if he had said, that the knowledge of him would soon be spread through every region of the world. Thus he wished to meet the astonishment which his death might excite in his disciples; for he shows that there is no reason why their courage should fail, because the doctrine of the gospel will nevertheless be proclaimed throughout the whole world. Again, that this

---

[1] "Les saincts trespassez."
[2] "Qui addressent leurs oraisons aux saincts trespassez, desquels ils sont separez."

contemplation of his glory may not soon afterwards vanish, when he shall be condemned to death, hung on the cross, and finally buried, he gives them early information and warning that the ignominy of his death is no obstruction to his glory. For this purpose he employs a most appropriate comparison.

24. *Unless a grain of wheat, having fallen into the ground, die, it remaineth alone.* If a grain of wheat do not die or putrify, it continues to be dry and unfruitful; but the death of the seed has the beneficial effect of quickening it, that it may yield fruit. In short, Christ compares his death to sowing, which appears to tend to the destruction of the *wheat,* but yet is the cause of far more abundant increase. Though this admonition was especially necessary at that time, yet it is of continual use in the Church. And, first, we ought to begin with the Head. That dreadful appearance of disgrace and cursing, which appears in the death of Christ, not only obscures his glory, but removes it altogether from our view. We must not, therefore, confine our attention to his death alone, but must likewise consider the fruit which has been yielded by his glorious resurrection.[1] Thus there will be nothing to prevent his glory from being every where displayed. From him we must next come to the members; for not only do we think that we perish in death, but our life also is a sort of continual death, (Col. iii. 3.) We shall therefore be undone, unless we be supported by that consolation which Paul holds out: *if our outward man decays, the inward man is renewed from day to day,* (2 Cor. iv. 16.) When, therefore, the godly are distressed by various afflictions, when they are pressed hard by the difficulties of their situation, when they suffer hunger, or nakedness, or disease, when they are assailed by reproaches, when it appears as if they would every hour be almost overwhelmed by death, let them unceasingly consider that this is a *sowing* which, in due time, will yield fruit.

25. *He who loveth his soul shall destroy it.* To doctrine

---

[1] "Sa resurrection glorieuse."

Christ joins exhortation; for if we must *die* in order that we may bring forth *fruit,* we ought patiently to permit God to mortify us. But as he draws a contrast between the love of life and the hatred of it, we ought to understand what it is to *love* and *hate life.* He who, under the influence of immoderate desire of the present life, cannot leave the world but by constraint, is said to *love life;* but he who, despising *life,* advances courageously to death, is said to *hate life.* Not that we ought absolutely to *hate life,* which is justly reckoned to be one of the highest of God's blessings; but because believers ought cheerfully to lay it down, when it retards them from approaching to Christ; just as a man, when he wishes to make haste in any matter, would shake off from his shoulders a heavy and disagreeable burden. In short, to love this life is not in itself wrong, provided that we only pass through it as pilgrims, keeping our eyes always fixed on our object. For the true limit of *loving life* is, when we continue in it as long as it pleases God, and when we are prepared to leave it as soon as he shall order us, or—to express it in a single word—when we carry it, as it were, in our hands, and offer it to God as a sacrifice. Whoever carries his attachment to the present life beyond this limit, *destroys his life;* that is, he consigns it to everlasting ruin. For the word *destroy* (ἀπολέσει) does not signify *to lose,* or to sustain the loss of something valuable, but to devote it to destruction.

His soul. It frequently happens that the word ψυχή, *soul,* is put for *life.* Some consider it as denoting, in this passage, the seat of the affections; as if Christ had said, " He who too much indulges the desires of his flesh destroys his soul." But that is a forced interpretation, and the other is more natural, that he who disregards his own life takes the best method of enjoying it eternally.

In this world. To make the meaning still more clear, the phrase *in this world,* which is but once expressed, ought to be twice repeated, so that the meaning may be, " They do not take the proper method of preserving their life who love it *in this world,* but, on the other hand, they truly know how to preserve their life who despise it *in this world."* And, indeed, whoever is attached to the world does, of his own accord, deprive himself of the heavenly life, of which we cannot be heirs in any other way than by being strangers and foreigners *in the world*. The consequence is, that the more anxious any person is about his own safety, the farther does he remove himself from the kingdom of God, that is, from the true life.

He who hateth his soul.[1] I have already suggested that this expression is used comparatively; because we ought to despise *life,* so far as it hinders us from living to God; for if meditation on the heavenly life were the prevailing sentiment in our hearts, the world would have no influence in detaining us. Hence, too, we obtain a reply to an objection that might be urged. " Many persons, through despair, or for other reasons, and chiefly from weariness of life, kill themselves; and yet we will not say that such persons provide for their own safety, while others are hurried to death by ambition, who also rush down to ruin." [2] But here Christ speaks expressly of that hatred or contempt of this fading life, which believers derive from the contemplation of a better life. Consequently, whoever does not look to heaven, has not yet learned in what way life must be preserved. Besides, this latter clause was added by Christ, in order to strike terror into those who are too desirous of the earthly life; for if we are overwhelmed by the love of the world, so that we cannot easily forget it, it is impossible for us to go to heaven. But since the Son of God[3] arouses us so violently, it would be the height of folly to sleep a mortal sleep.

26. *If any man serve me.* That death may not be exceedingly bitter and disagreeable to us, Christ invites us by his example to submit to it cheerfully; and certainly we shall be ashamed to refuse the honour of being his disciples. But on no other condition does he admit us into their number, except that we follow the path which he points out. He leads the

[1] " Qui odit animam suam."—" Qui hait sa vie;"—" he who hateth his life."
[2] " Lesquels se precipitent bas à une ruine eternelle par leur ambition;" —" who throw themselves down to eternal ruin by their ambition."
[3] " Le Fils de Dieu."

way to us to suffer death. The bitterness of death is therefore mitigated, and is in some measure rendered agreeable, when we have in common with the Son of God the condition of submitting to it. So far is it from being proper that we should shrink from Christ on account of the cross, that we ought rather to desire death for his sake. To the same purpose is the statement which immediately follows:

And where I am, there shall also my servant be. For he demands that his servants should not refuse to submit to death, to which they see him go before them as an example; for it is not right that the servant should have any thing separate from his lord. The future tense, *shall be,* (ἔσται,) is put for *let him be,* according to the custom of the Hebrew language. Others regard it as a consolation, as if Christ promised to those who should not be unwilling to die along with him, that they would be partakers of his resurrection. But the former view, as I have said, is more probable; for he afterwards adds the consolation, that the Father will not leave without reward the servants of Christ, who shall have been his companions both in life and in death.

27. Now is my soul troubled, and what shall I say? Father, save me from this hour, but for this cause came I into this hour. 28. Father, glorify thy name. Then came a voice from heaven, I have both glorified it, and will glorify it again. 29. Therefore the multitude, who were there, and heard it, said that it thundered. Others said, An angel spoke to him. 30. Jesus answered and said, This voice came not for my sake, but for yours. 31. Now is the judgment of this world; now is the prince of this world cast out. 32. And I, if I be lifted up from the earth, will draw all men to me. 33. Now this he said, intimating by what death he should die.

27. *Now is my soul troubled.* This statement appears at first to differ widely from the preceding discourse. He had displayed extraordinary courage and magnanimity by exhorting his disciples not only to suffer death, but willingly and cheerfully to desire it, whenever it is necessary; and now, by shrinking from death, he confesses his cowardice. Yet there is nothing in this passage that is not in perfect harmony, as every believer knows by his own experience. If scornful men laugh at it, we need not wonder; for it cannot be understood but by practice.

Besides, it was highly useful, and even necessary for our salvation, that the Son of God should have experience of such feelings. In his death we ought chiefly to consider his atonement, by which he appeased the wrath and curse of God, which he could not have done, without taking upon himself our guilt. The death which he underwent must therefore have been full of horror, because he could not render satisfaction for us, without feeling, in his own experience, the dreadful judgment of God; and hence we come to know more fully the enormity of sin, for which the Heavenly Father exacted so dreadful a punishment from his only-begotten Son. Let us therefore know, that death was not a sport and amusement to Christ, but that he endured the severest torments on our account.

Nor was it unsuitable that the Son of God should be troubled in this manner; for the Divine nature, being concealed, and not exerting its force, may be said to have reposed, in order to give an opportunity of making expiation. But Christ himself was clothed, not only with our flesh, but with human feelings. In him, no doubt, those feelings were voluntary; for he feared, not through constraint, but because he had, of his own accord, subjected himself to fear. And yet we ought to believe, that it was not in pretence, but in reality, that he feared; though he differed from other men in this respect, that he had all his feelings regulated in obedience to the righteousness of God, as we have said elsewhere.

There is also another advantage which it yields to us. If the dread of death had occasioned no uneasiness to the Son of God,[1] which of us would have thought that his example was applicable to our case? For it has not been given to us to die without a feeling of regret; but when we learn that He had not within him a hardness like stone or iron,[2] we summon courage to follow him, and the weakness of the flesh, which makes us tremble at death, does not hinder us from becoming the companions of our General in struggling with it.

And what shall I say? Here we see, as it were, before our

---

[1] "Le Fils de Dieu"
[2] "Une durete de pierre et de fer."

eyes, how much our salvation cost the Son of God, when he was reduced to such extremity of distress, that he found neither words to express the intensity of his sorrow, nor yet resolution as man. He betakes himself to prayer, which is his only remaining resource, and asks to be delivered from death. Again, perceiving also that, by the eternal purpose of God, he has been appointed to be a sacrifice for sins, he suddenly corrects that wish which his prodigious sorrow had wrung from him, and puts forth his hand, as it were, to pull himself back, that he may entirely acquiesce in the will of his Father.

In this passage we ought to observe five steps. For, first, there is the complaint, which breaks out from vehement sorrow. Secondly, he feels that he needs a remedy, and, in order that he may not be overwhelmed with fear, he puts the question to himself, what he ought to do. Thirdly, he goes to the Father, and entreats him to deliver him. Fourthly, he recalls the wish which he knows to be inconsistent with his calling, and chooses rather to suffer anything than not to fulfil what his Father has enjoined upon him. Lastly, he is satisfied with the glory of God alone, forgets all things else, and reckons them of no value.

But it may be thought, that it is unbecoming in the Son of God rashly to utter a wish which he must immediately retract, in order to obey his Father. I readily admit, that this is the folly of the cross, which gives offence to proud men; but the more the Lord of glory humbled himself, so much the more illustrious is the manifestation of his vast love to us. Besides, we ought to recollect what I have already stated, that the human feelings, from which Christ was not exempt, were in him pure and free from sin. The reason is, that they were guided and regulated in obedience to God; for there is nothing to prevent Christ from having a natural dread of death, and yet desiring to obey God. This holds true in various respects: and hence he corrects himself by saying,

For this cause came I into this hour. For though he may lawfully entertain a dread of death, yet, considering why he was sent, and what his office as Redeemer demands from him, he presents to his Father the dread which arose out of his natural disposition, in order that it may be subdued, or rather, having subdued it, he prepares freely and willingly to execute the command of God. Now, if the feelings of Christ, which were free from all sin, needed to be restrained in this manner, how earnestly ought we to apply to this object, since the numerous affections which spring from our flesh are so many enemies to God in us! Let the godly, therefore, persevere in doing violence to themselves, until they have denied themselves.

It must also be observed, that we ought to restrain not only those affections which are directly contrary to the will of God, but those which hinder the progress of our calling, though, in other respects, they are not wicked or sinful. To make this more fully evident, we ought to place in the first rank the will of God; in the second, the will of man pure and entire, such as God gave to Adam, and such as was in Chiist: and, lastly, our own, which is infected by the contagion of sin. The will of God is the rule, to which every thing that is inferior ought to be subjected. Now, the pure will of nature will not of itself rebel against God; but man, though he were wholly formed to righteousness, would meet with many obstructions, unless he subject his affections to God. Christ, therefore, had but one battle to fight, which was, to cease to fear what he naturally feared, as soon as he perceived that the pleasure of God was otherwise. We, on the other hand, have a twofold battle; for we must struggle with the obstinacy of the flesh. The consequence is, that the most valiant combatants never vanquish without being wounded.

Father, save me. This is the order which ought to be maintained, whenever we are either distressed by fear, or oppressed with grief. Our hearts ought instantly to be raised up to God. For there is nothing worse, or more injurious, than to nourish inwardly what torments us; as we see a great part of the world consumed by hidden torments, and all who do not rise to God are justly punished for their indolence by never receiving any alleviation.

28. *Father, glorify thy name.* By these words he testifies, that he prefers the *glory* of *the Father* to all things else, and even neglects and disregards his own life. And the true regulation of all our desires is, to seek the glory of God in such a manner that all other things shall give way to it; for it ought to be reckoned by us an abundant recompense, leading us to endure patiently all that is vexatious or irksome.

I have both glorified it. It is as if he had said, "I will finish what I have begun;" for *God never leaveth the work of his hands imperfect,* as it is said, Ps. cxxxviii. 8. But as it is the purpose of God to prevent the offence of the cross, he not only promises that the death of Christ will be glorious, but also mentions with commendation the numerous ornaments with which he had already adorned it.

29. *That it thundered.* It was truly monstrous, that the assembled multitude were unmoved by so evident a miracle. Some are so deaf, that they hear as a confused sound what God had distinctly pronounced. Others are less dull of hearing, but yet take away much from the majesty of the Divine voice, by pretending that *it was an angel who spoke.* But the same thing is practised every day; for God speaks plainly enough in the Gospel, in which is also displayed the power and energy of the Spirit, which ought to shake heaven and earth; but many are as little affected by the doctrine, as if it only proceeded from a mortal man, and others consider the word of God to be confused and barbarous, as if it were nothing else than thunder.

But a question arises: Did that voice sound from heaven without any profit or advantage? I reply, what the Evangelist here ascribes to the multitude belongs only to a part of them; for there were some besides the Apostles who did not interpret it so badly. But the Evangelist intended to point out briefly what is commonly done in the world; and that is, that the greater part of men, while they hear God, do not hear him though he speak plainly and distinctly.

30. *This voice came not for my sake.* Had Christ no need of being strengthened, or did the Father care less for him than for us? But we must attend to this principle. As it was on our account that Christ clothed himself with flesh, so all the blessings which he received from the Father were bestowed on our account. Again, it is also true, that *the voice came from heaven* FOR THE SAKE of the people; for he had no need of an outward miracle. Besides, there is here an indirect reproof, that the Jews are deaf like stones to the voice of God; for since God speaks *for their sake,* there can be no excuse for their ingratitude, when they do not lend their ears.

31. *Now is the judgment of this world.* The Lord now, as if he had already succeeded in the contest, boasts of having obtained a victory not only over fear, but over death; for he describes, in lofty terms, the advantage of his death, which might have struck his disciples with consternation. Some view the word *judgment* (*κρίσις*) as denoting *reformation,* and others, as denoting *condemnation.* I rather agree with the former, who explain it to mean, that *the world* must be restored to a proper order; for the Hebrew word משפט, *mishpat,* which is translated *judgment,* means a well-ordered state. Now we know, that out of Christ there is nothing but confusion in *the world;* and though Christ had already begun to erect the kingdom of God, yet his death was the commencement of a well-regulated condition, and the full restoration of the world.

Yet it must also be observed, that this proper arrangement cannot be established in *the world,* until the kingdom of Satan be first destroyed, until the flesh, and every thing opposed to the righteousness of God, be reduced to nothing. Lastly, the renovation of *the world* must be preceded by mortification. Accordingly, Christ declares:

Now shall the prince of this world be cast out; for the confusion and deformity arise from this, that while Satan usurps tyrannical dominion, iniquity everywhere abounds. When Satan has been *cast out,* therefore, *the world* is brought back from its revolt, and placed under obedience to the government of God. It may be asked, how was Satan *cast out* by the death of Christ, since he does not cease to make war continually? I reply, this *casting out* must not be limited to any short period of time, but is a description of that remarkable effect of the death of Christ which is daily manifested.

32. *If I be lifted up.* Next follows the method by which *the judgment* shall be conducted; namely, Christ, being *lifted up* on the cross, shall gather all men to himself, in order that he may raise them from earth to heaven. The Evangelist says, that Christ pointed out the manner of his death; and, therefore, the meaning undoubtedly is, that the cross will be, as it were, a chariot, by which he shall raise all men, along with himself, to his Father. It might have been thought, that at that time he was carried away from the earth, so as no longer to have any interests in common with men; but he declares, that he will go in a very different manner, so as to *draw* upwards to himself those who were fixed on the earth. Now, though he alludes to the form of his death, yet he means generally, that his death will not be a division to separate him from men, but that it will be an additional means of *drawing* earth upwards towards heaven.

I will draw all men to myself. The word *all,* which he employs, must be understood to refer to the children of God, who belong to his flock. Yet I agree with Chrysostom, who says that Christ used the universal term, *all,* because the Church was to be gathered equally from among Gentiles and Jews, according to that saying, *There shall be one shepherd, and one sheepfold,* (John x. 16.) The old Latin translation has, *I will draw* ALL THINGS *to me;* and Augustine maintains that we ought to read it in that manner; but the agreement of all the Greek manuscripts ought to have greater weight with us.

34. The multitude answered, We have heard from the law, that Christ remaineth for ever; and how sayest thou, that the Son of man must be lifted up? Who is that Son of man? 35. Jesus therefore said to them, Yet a little while you have the light with you. Walk while you have the light, lest darkness overtake you; for he who walketh in darkness knoweth not whither he goeth. 36. While you have the light, believe in the light, that you may be the children of light. These things spoke Jesus, and went away, and hid himself from them.

34. *We have heard from the law.* Their intention undoubtedly was, to carp malignantly at the words of Christ; and

therefore their malice blinds them, so that they perceive
nothing amidst the clearest light. They say that Jesus ought
not to be regarded as the Christ, because he said that he
would die, while *the Law* ascribes perpetuity to the Messiah;
as if both statements had not been expressly made in *the Law*
that Christ will die, and that afterwards his kingdom will
flourish to the end of the world. But they seize on the second
clause, and make it a ground of calumny. The origin of their
error was, that they judged of the splendour of Messiah's
kingdom according to their carnal views; in consequence of
which, they reject Christ because he does not correspond to
their foolish notion. Under the term *the Law* they embrace
also the Prophets, and the present tense—*remaineth*—is used,
agreeably to the Hebrew idiom, instead of the future tense,
will remain.

Who is that Son of man? This is a reproachful question, as
if that short refutation vanquished Christ so completely that
he had nothing more to say.[1] This shows how haughty
their ignorance was; for it is as if they had said, "Go now,
and boast that thou art the Christ, since thine own confession proves that thou hast nothing to do with the Messiah."

35. *Yet a little while the light is with you.* Though in this
reply the Lord gently admonishes them, yet at the same
time he reproves them sharply; for he charges them with
shutting their eyes against *the light,* and at the same time
threatens that ere long *the light* will be taken away from them.
When he says that *yet a little while* there is some remaining
light, he confirms what he had already said about his death;
for though by *the light* he does not mean his bodily presence,
but his Gospel, yet he alludes to his departure; as if he had
said, When I shall have gone away, I will not cease to be *the
light,* and thus my glory will not be diminished through your
darkness. When he says that *the light is with them,* he indirectly reproves them for closing their eyes and shutting out
the light; and thus he declares that they do not deserve an
answer to their objection, because of their own accord they
seek an opportunity of falling into error.

[1] "Comme si Christ demeuroit confus, sans avoir plus que dire."

Walk while you have the light, lest darkness overtake you. This statement, that *the light* does not continue to shine on them but for *a little while,* applies equally to all unbelievers; for Scripture promises that to the children of God *the Sun of righteousness* (Mal. iv. 2) will rise, and will never go down. *The sun shall no longer be your light by day, nor the moon by night, but the Lord shall be your everlasting light,* (Isa. lx. 19.) But all ought to *walk* cautiously, because contempt of *the light* is followed by darkness. This, too, is the reason why a night so thick and dark sat down on the world for many centuries. It was because there were few who deigned to walk in the brightness of heavenly wisdom; for Christ enlightens us by his Gospel, in order that we may follow the way of salvation, which he points out to us. For this reason, they who do not avail themselves of the grace of God extinguish, as far as lies in their power, the light which is offered to them.

And he who walketh in darkness knoweth not where he goeth. To strike them with still deeper alarm, he reminds them how wretched is the condition of those who, being destitute of light, do nothing but wander throughout the whole course of their life. For they cannot move a step without the risk of falling or even of destruction. But now Christ declares that we are *in darkness,* unless he shine upon us. Hence infer what is the value of the sagacity of the human mind, when it is the sole guide and instructor, apart from Christ.

36. *Believe in the light.* He exhorts them to retain by faith the possession of *the light,* for he gives the appellation, *children of light,* to those who, like true heirs, enjoy it to the end.

These things spoke Jesus. We might have wondered why he withdrew himself from them, when they were so eager to receive him; but from the other Evangelists it may easily be inferred that what is here said relates to adversaries, who burned with envy on account of the godly zeal of good and sincere disciples. For the strangers, who had gone out to meet Christ, followed him even to the temple, where he met with the saints and with the multitude of the inhabitants of the town.

37. And though he had done so many signs in their presence, they believed not in him: 38. That the saying of Isaiah the prophet might be fulfilled, which he spoke, Lord, who hath believed our report?[1] and to whom hath the arm of the Lord been revealed? 39. Therefore they could not believe, because Isaiah saith again, 40 He hath blinded their eyes, and hardened their heart, lest they should see with their eyes, and understand with their heart, and be converted, and I should heal them. 41. These things said Isaiah, when he saw his glory, and spoke of him.

37. *And though he had done so many signs.* That no man may be disturbed or perplexed at seeing that Christ was despised by the Jews, the Evangelist removes this offence, by showing that he was supported by clear and undoubted testimonies, which proved that credit was due to him and to his doctrine; but that the blind did not behold the glory and power of God, which were openly displayed in his miracles. First, therefore, we ought to believe that it was not owing to Christ that the Jews did not place confidence in him, because by many miracles he abundantly testified who he was, and that it was therefore unjust and highly unreasonable that their unbelief should diminish his authority. But as this very circumstance might lead many persons to anxious and perplexing inquiry how the Jews came to be so stupid, that the power of God, though visible, produced no effect upon them, John proceeds further, and shows that faith does not proceed from the ordinary faculties of men, but is an uncommon and extraordinary gift of God, and that this was anciently predicted concerning Christ, that very few would believe the Gospel.

38. *That the saying of Isaiah the prophet might be fulfilled.* John does not mean that the prediction laid a necessity on the Jews; for Isaiah (liii. 1; Rom. x. 16) uttered nothing but what the Lord revealed to him from the secret treasures of his purpose. Indeed, it must have happened, though the prophet had not spoken of it; but as men would not have known what should take place, if God had not testified by the mouth of the prophet, the Evangelist places before our eyes in the prediction, as in a mirror, what would otherwise have appeared to men obscure and almost incredible.

[1] "Qui a creu a nostre ouye, *ou, parole?*"—"Who hath believed our report, *or, speech?*"

Lord, who hath believed? This sentence contains two clauses. In the former, Isaiah, having begun to speak of Christ, foreseeing that all that he proclaims concerning Christ, and all that shall afterwards be made known by the Apostles, will be generally rejected by the Jews, exclaims, as if in astonishment at something strange and monstrous, *Lord, who shall believe our report,* or, *our speech?*[1]

To whom hath the arm of the Lord been revealed? In this second clause he assigns the reason why they are few; and that reason is, that men do not attain it by their own strength, and God does not illuminate all without distinction, but bestows the grace of his Holy Spirit on very few.[2] And if among the Jews the obstinate unbelief of many ought not to have been an obstacle to believers, though they were few in number, the same argument ought to persuade us, at the present day, not to be ashamed of the Gospel, though it has few disciples. But we ought first to observe the reason which is added, that what makes men believers is not their own sagacity, but the revelation of God. The word *arm*, it is well known, denotes *power*. The prophet declares that *the arm of God*, which is contained in the doctrine of the Gospel, lies hid until it is *revealed*, and at the same time testifies that all are not indiscriminately partakers of this *revelation*. Hence it follows, that many are left in their blindness destitute of inward light, because *hearing they do not hear,* (Matth. xiii. 13.)

39. *Therefore they could not believe.* This is somewhat more harsh; because, if the words be taken in their natural meaning, the way was shut up against the Jews, and the power of believing was taken from them, because the prediction of the prophet adjudged them to blindness, before they determined what choice they should make. I reply, there is no absurdity in this, if nothing could happen different from what God had foreseen. But it ought to be observed, that the mere foreknowledge of God is not in itself the cause of

---

[1] " Qui croira à nostre ouye, ou, a nostre parole ? "
[2] " A bien peu de gens."

events; though, in this passage, we ought to consider not so much the foreknowledge of God as his justice and vengeance. For God declares not what he beholds from heaven that men will do, but what He himself will do; and that is, that he will strike wicked men with giddiness and stupidity, and thus will take vengeance on their obstinate wickedness. In this passage he points out the nearer and inferior cause why God intends that his word, which is in its own nature salutary and quickening, shall be destructive and deadly to the Jews. It is because they deserved it by their obstinate wickedness.

This punishment it was impossible for them to escape, because God had once decreed to give them over to a reprobate mind, and to change the light of his word, so as to make it darkness to them. For this latter prediction differs from the former in this respect, that in the former passage the prophet testifies that none believe but those whom God, of his free grace, enlightens for his own good pleasure, the reason of which does not appear; for since all are equally ruined, God, of his mere good pleasure, distinguishes from others those whom he thinks fit to distinguish. But, in the latter passage, he speaks of the hardness by which God has punished the wickedness of an ungrateful people. They who do not attend to these steps mistake and confound passages of Scripture, which are quite different from each other.

40. *He hath blinded their eyes, and hardened their heart.* The passage is taken from Isaiah, (vi. 9,) where the Lord forewarns the prophet, that the labour which he spends in instructing will lead to no other result than to make the people worse. First then he says, Go, and tell this people, *Hearing, hear and do not hear;* as if he had said, " I send thee to speak to the deaf." He afterwards adds, *Harden the heart of this people, &c.* By these words he means, that he intends to make his word a punishment to the reprobate, that it may render them more thoroughly blind, and that their blindness may be plunged in deeper darkness. It is indeed a dreadful judgment of God, when He overwhelms men by the light of doctrine, in such a manner as to deprive them of all under-

standing; and when, even by means of that which is their only light, he brings darkness upon them.

But it ought to be observed, that it is accidental to the word of God, that it *blinds* men; for nothing can be more inconsistent than that there should be no difference between truth and falsehood, that the bread of life should become a deadly poison, and that medicine should aggravate a disease. But this must be ascribed to the wickedness of men, which turns life into death. It ought also to be observed, that sometimes the Lord, by himself, blinds the minds of men, by depriving them of judgment and understanding; sometimes by Satan and false prophets, when he maddens them by their impostures; sometimes too by his ministers, when the doctrine of salvation is injurious and deadly to them. But provided that prophets labour faithfully in the work of instruction, and commit to the Lord the result of their labour, though they may not succeed to their wish, they ought not to give way or despond. Let them rather be satisfied with knowing that God approves of their labour, though it be useless to men: and that even *the savour* of doctrine, which wicked men render deadly to themselves, *is good and pleasant to God*, as Paul testifies, (2 Cor. ii. 15.)

The heart is sometimes in Scripture put for the seat of the affections; but here, as in many other passages, it denotes what is called the intellectual part of the soul. To the same purpose Moses speaks: *God hath not given you a heart to understand*, (Deut. xxix. 4.)

Lest they should see with their eyes. Let us remember that the prophet speaks of unbelievers who had already rejected the grace of God. It is certain that all would continue to be such by nature, if the Lord did not form to obedience to him those whom he has elected. At first, therefore, the condition of men is equal and alike, but when reprobate men have, of their own accord, and by their own wickedness, rebelled against God, they subject themselves to this vengeance, by which, being given up to a reprobate mind, they continually rush forward more and more to their own destruction. It is their own fault, therefore, if God does not choose to convert them, because they were the cause of their own despair. We are briefly instructed also, by these words of the prophet, what is the beginning of our conversion to God. It is when he enlightens the hearts, which must have been turned away from him, so long as they were held by the darkness of Satan; but, on the contrary, such is the power of Divine light, that it attracts us to itself, and forms us to the image of God.

And I should heal them. He next adds the fruit of conversion, that is, *healing.* By this word the prophet means the blessing of God and a prosperous condition, and likewise deliverance from all the miseries which spring from the wrath of God. Now, if this happens to the reprobate, contrary to the nature of the word, we ought to attend to the contrast implied in the opposite use of it; namely, that the purpose for which the word of God is preached is, to enlighten us in the true knowledge of God, to turn us to God, and reconcile us to him, that we may be happy and blessed.

41. *These things spoke Jesus.* Lest readers should think that this prediction was inappropriately quoted, John expressly states, that the prophet was not sent as a teacher to a single age, but, on the contrary, that the glory of Christ was exhibited to him, that he might be a witness of those things which should take place under his reign. Now the Evangelist takes for granted, that Isaiah saw the glory of Christ; and hence he infers, that Isaiah accommodates his instruction to the future state of Christ's kingdom.

42. Nevertheless, many of the rulers believed on him, but on account of the Pharisees they did not confess it, lest they should be cast out of the synagogue. 43. For they loved the glory of men more than the glory of God. 44. And Jesus stood, and said, He who believeth on me, believeth not on me, but on him who sent me; 45. And he who seeth me seeth him that sent me. 46. I am come into the world as a light, that whosoever believeth on me may not remain in darkness.

Nevertheless, many even of the rulers believed on him. The murmuring and fierceness of the Jews, in rejecting Christ, having risen to such a height of insolence, it might have been thought that all the people, without exception, conspired against him. But the Evangelist says that, amidst the general madness of the nation, there were *many* who were of a sound mind. A striking instance, truly, of the grace of

God; for, when ungodliness has once prevailed, it is a sort of universal plague, which infects with its contagion every part of the body. It is therefore a remarkable gift, and special grace of God, when, amidst a people so corrupt, there are some who remain untainted. And yet we now perceive in the world the same grace of God; for though ungodliness and contempt of God abound everywhere, and though a vast multitude of men make furious attempts to exterminate utterly the doctrine of the Gospel, yet it always finds some places of retreat; and thus faith has—what may be called—its harbours or places of refuge, that it may not be entirely banished from the world.

The word *even* is emphatic; for in the order of *the rulers*, there existed so deep and inveterate a hatred of the Gospel, that it could scarcely be believed that a single believer could be found amongst them. So much the greater admiration was due to the power of the Spirit of God, which entered where no opening was made; though it was not a vice, peculiar to a single age, that *rulers* were rebellious and disobedient to Christ; for honour, and wealth, and high rank, are usually accompanied by pride. The consequence is, that they who, swelled with arrogance, scarcely acknowledge themselves to be men, are not easily subdued by voluntary humility. Whoever, then, holds a high station in the world, will, if he is wise, look with suspicion on his rank, that it may not stand in his way. When the Evangelist says that there were *many*, this must not be understood as if they were the majority or the half; for, as compared with others who were vastly numerous, they were few, but yet they were *many*, when viewed in themselves.

On account of the Pharisees. It may be thought that he speaks incorrectly, when he separates faith from *confession;* for *with the heart we believe to righteousness, and with the mouth confession is made unto salvation,* (Rom. x. 10;) and it is impossible that the faith, which has been kindled in the heart, shall not put forth its flame. I reply, he points out here how weak was the faith of those men who were so lukewarm, or rather cold. In short, John means that they embraced the doctrine of Christ, because they knew that it had come from God, but that they had not a lively faith, or a faith so vigorous as it ought to have been; for Christ does not grant to his followers a spirit of fear, but of firmness, that they may boldly and fearlessly *confess* what they have learned from him. Yet I do not think that they were altogether silent; but as their *confession* was not sufficiently open, the Evangelist, in my opinion, simply declares that they did not make profession of their faith; for the proper kind of profession was, openly to declare that they were the disciples of Christ. Let no man, therefore, flatter himself who, in any respect, conceals or dissembles his faith for fear of incurring the hatred of men; for however hateful the name of Christ may be, that cowardice which compels us to turn aside, in the smallest degree, from the confession of him, admits of no excuse.

It must also be observed, that *rulers* have less vigour and firmness, because ambition almost always reigns in them, which is the most slavish of all dispositions; and, to express it in a single word, earthly honours may be said to be golden fetters, which bind a man, so that he cannot perform his duty with freedom. On this account, persons who are placed in a low and mean condition ought to bear their lot with the greater patience, for they are, at least, delivered from many very bad snares. Yet the great and noble ought to struggle against their high rank, that it may not hinder them from submitting to Christ.

John says that they were afraid of *the Pharisees;* not that the other scribes and priests freely permitted any man to call himself a disciple of Christ, but because, under the semblance of zeal, cruelty burned in them with greater fierceness. Zeal, in defending religion, is, indeed, an excellent virtue; but if hypocrisy be added to it, no plague can be more dangerous. So much the more earnestly ought we to entreat the Lord to guide us by the unerring rule of his Spirit.

Lest they should be thrown out of the synagogue. This was what hindered them, the fear of disgrace; for they would have been *thrown out of the synagogue.* Hence we see how great is the perversity of men, which not only corrupts and debases the best of God's ordinances, but turns them into destructive tyranny. Excommunication ought to have been the sinew of holy discipline, that punishment might be ready to be inflicted, if any person despised the Church. But matters had come to such a pitch, that any one who confessed that he belonged to Christ was banished from the society of believers. In like manner, at the present day, the Pope, in order to exercise the same kind of tyranny, falsely pretends to a right of excommunicating, and not only thunders with blind rage against all the godly, but endeavours to cast down Christ from his heavenly throne; and yet he does not hesitate impudently to hold out the right of sacred jurisdiction, with which Christ has adorned his Church.

43. *For they loved the glory of men.* The Evangelist expressly states that those men were not guided by any superstition, but only endeavoured to avoid disgrace among men; for if ambition had greater influence over them than the fear of God, it follows, that it was no vain scruple of conscience that gave them uneasiness. Now, let the reader observe how great ignominy is incurred before God, by the cowardice of those who, from the fear of being hated, dissemble their faith before men. Can any thing be more foolish, or rather, can any thing be more beastly, than to prefer the silly applauses of men to the judgment of God? But he declares that all who shrink from the hatred of men, when the pure faith ought to be confessed, are seized with this kind of madness. And justly; for the apostle, in applauding the unshaken steadiness of Moses, says that *he remained firm, as if he had seen him who is invisible,* (Heb. xi. 27.) By these words he means that, when any person has fixed his eyes on God, his heart will be invincible, and utterly incapable of being moved.

Whence, therefore, comes the effeminacy[1] which causes us to give way to treacherous hypocrisy, but because, at the sight of the world, all our senses grow dull? For a true sight of God would instantly chase away all the mists of wealth and honours. Away with those who look upon an indirect denial of Christ as some trivial offence, or, as they call it, a venial sin! For, on the contrary, the Holy Spirit declares that it is more base and monstrous than if heaven and earth were mingled.

[1] "D'où vient donc la delicatesse?"

To love the glory of men means, in this passage, to desire to enjoy reputation among men. The Evangelist, therefore, means, that those men were so much devoted to the world, that they were more desirous to please men than to please God. Besides, when he accuses of this crime those who denied Christ, he, at the same time, shows that the excommunication, which the priests abused, contrary to all that was right and lawful, had no value or efficacy. Let us know, therefore, that all the excommunications which the Pope now mutters against us are mere bugbears to frighten children,[1] since we are fully convinced, in our own consciences, that he aims at nothing else than to lead us away from Christ.

44. *And Jesus cried.* The object of Christ, in this statement, is to encourage his followers to a proper and unshaken stedfastness of faith; but it contains also an implied reproof, by which he intended to correct that perverse fear. The *cry* is expressive of vehemence; for it is not a simple doctrine, but an exhortation intended to excite them more powerfully. The statement amounts to this, that faith in Christ does not rely on any mortal man, but on God; for it finds in Christ nothing but what is divine, or rather, it beholds God in his face. Hence he infers, that it is foolish and unreasonable for faith to be wavering or doubtful; for it is impossible to offer a greater insult to God, than not to rely on his truth. Who is it then that has duly profited by the Gospel? It is he who, relying on this confidence, that he does not believe men but God, quietly and steadily contends against all the machinations of Satan. If, then, we would render to God the honour due to him, we must learn to remain firm in faith, not only though the world were shaken, but even though Satan should disturb and overturn all that is under heaven.

He that believeth on me believeth not on me, but on him that sent me. Believers are said *not to believe on Christ,* when they do not fix their whole attention on his human countenance. Comparing himself with the Father, he bids us look at the power of God; for the weakness of the flesh has no firmness in

---

[1] " Ne sont qu'espouvantemens de petits enfants "

itself. When we shall, afterwards, find him exhorting the disciples to *believe on him*, it will be in a different sense; for, in that passage, God is not contrasted with man, but Christ is brought forward with all his gifts and graces,[1] which ought to be sufficient for upholding our faith.

45. *And he who seeth me.* The word *see* is here taken for *knowledge;* for, in order to give true and thorough tranquillity to our consciences, which would otherwise have been constantly liable to various agitations, he sends us to the Father. The reason why the stability of faith is firm and secure is, that it is stronger than the world, and is above the world.[2] Now, when Christ is truly known, the glory of God shines in him, that we may be fully persuaded that the faith which we have in him does not depend on man, but that it is founded on the eternal God; for it rises from the flesh of Christ to his Divinity. And, if it be so, not only must it be fixed perpetually in our hearts, but it must likewise show itself boldly in the tongue, when it is necessary.

46. *I am come into the world as a light.* In order to render his disciples more bold and persevering, he proceeds still farther in maintaining the certainty of faith. And, first, he testifies that *he came into the world to be a light,* by which men might be delivered from darkness and errors; and, at the same time, he points out the means of obtaining so great a benefit, when he says, *that whosoever believeth in me may not remain in darkness.* Besides, he accuses of ingratitude all who, after having been taught by the Gospel, do not separate themselves from unbelievers: for the higher the excellence of this benefit, of being called from darkness to *light,* the less excusable are they who, through their indolence or carelessness, quench *the light* that had been kindled in them.

The words, *I am come into the world as a light,* are highly emphatic; for though Christ was *a light* from the beginning, yet there is a good reason why he adorns himself with this

---

[1] " Avec toutes ses graces et dons."
[2] " Pource qu'elle est plus forte que le monde, et pardessus le monde."

title, that he has come to perform the part of *a light*. That we may perceive distinctly the various steps, he shows, first, that he is *a light* to others rather than to himself; secondly, that he is *a light*, not only to angels, but also to men; thirdly, that he was manifested in the flesh, in order that he might shine with full brightness.

The term, *whosoever*, appears to have been added on purpose, partly, that all believers, without exception, may enjoy this benefit in common, and partly, to show that the reason why unbelievers perish in darkness is, that, of their own accord, they forsake *the light*. Now, if the whole wisdom of the world were collected into one mass, not a single ray of the true *light* would be found in that vast heap; but, on the contrary, it will be a confused chaos; for it belongs to Christ alone to deliver us from darkness.

47. And if any man hear my words, and do not believe them,[1] I do not judge him; for I came not to judge the world, but to save the world. 48. He who rejecteth me, and receiveth not my words, hath one who judgeth him The word which I have spoken shall judge him at the last day 49. For I have not spoken from myself; but the Father who hath sent me hath given me a commandment what to say and what to speak 50 And I know that his commandment is eternal life those things, therefore, which I speak, I speak as my Father hath told me.

47. *If any man hear my words.* After having spoken concerning his grace, and exhorted his disciples to steady faith, he now begins to strike the rebellious, though even here he mitigates the severity due to the wickedness of those who deliberately—as it were—reject God; for he delays to pronounce *judgment* on them, because, on the contrary, he has come for the salvation of all. In the first place, we ought to understand that he does not speak here of all unbelievers without distinction, but of those who, knowingly and willingly, reject the doctrine of the Gospel which has been exhibited to them. Why then does Christ not choose to condemn them? It is because he lays aside for a time the office of a *judge*, and offers salvation to all without reserve, and stretches out his arms to embrace all, that all may be the more encouraged to repent. And

---

[1] "Et ne les croit point."

yet there is a circumstance of no small moment, by which he points out the aggravation of the crime, if they reject an invitation so kind and gracious, for it is as if he had said, "Lo, I am here to invite all, and, forgetting the character of a judge, I have this as my single object, to persuade all, and to rescue from destruction those who are already twice ruined." No man, therefore, is condemned on account of having despised the Gospel, except he who, disdaining the lovely message of salvation, has chosen of his own accord to draw down destruction on himself.

The word *judge*, as is evident from the word *save*, which is contrasted with it, here signifies to *condemn*. Now this ought to be understood as referring to the office which properly and naturally belongs to Christ; for that unbelievers are not more severely *condemned* on account of the Gospel is accidental, and does not arise from its nature, as we have said on former occasions.

48. *He who rejecteth me.* That wicked men may not flatter themselves as if their unbounded disobedience to Christ would pass unpunished, he adds here a dreadful threatening, that though he were to do nothing in this matter, yet his doctrine alone would be sufficient to condemn them, as he says elsewhere, that there would be no need of any other judge than Moses, in whom they boasted, (John v. 45.) The meaning, therefore, is: "Burning with ardent desire to promote your salvation, I do indeed abstain from exercising my right to condemn you, and am entirely employed in saving what is lost; but do not think that you have escaped out of the hands of God; for though I should altogether hold my peace, *the word* alone, which you have despised, is sufficient to *judge* you."

And receiveth not my words. This latter clause is an explanation of the former; for since hypocrisy is natural to men, nothing is easier for them than to boast in words that they are ready to receive Christ; and we see how common this boasting is even amongst the most wicked men. We must therefore attend to this definition, that Christ is *rejected* when we do not embrace the pure doctrine of the Gospel.

Loudly do the Papists, indeed, proclaim this word which Christ uttered; but as soon as his pure truth is brought forward, nothing is more hateful to them. Such persons kiss Christ in the same manner as Judas kissed him, (Matth. xxvi. 49.) Let us therefore learn to receive him along with *his word*, and to render to him that homage and obedience which he demands as his sole right.

The word which I speak shall judge you at the last day. It is impossible to give a nobler or more magnificent title to the Gospel than to ascribe to it the power of *judging;* for, according to these words, the last judgment shall be nothing else than an approbation or ratification[1] of the doctrine of the Gospel. Christ himself will indeed ascend the tribunal, but he declares that he will pronounce the sentence according to *the word* which is now preached. This threatening ought to strike deep terror into the ungodly, since they cannot escape the *judgment* of that doctrine which they now so haughtily disdain.

But when Christ mentions the last judgment, he means that they are now destitute of understanding; for he reminds them that the punishment which they now treat with mockery will then be openly displayed. On the other hand, it yields to the godly an invaluable consolation, that to whatever extent they may be now condemned by the world, still they do not doubt that they are already acquitted in heaven; for, wherever the faith of the Gospel has its seat, the tribunal of God is erected to save. Relying on this right, we need not trouble ourselves about Papists or their absurd decisions; for our faith rises even above angels.

49. *For I do not speak from myself.* That the outward appearance of man may not lessen the majesty of God, Christ frequently sends us to the Father. This is the reason why he so often mentions the Father; and, indeed, since it would be unlawful to transfer to another a single spark of the Divine glory, *the word,* to which *judgment* is ascribed, must have proceeded from God. Now Christ here distinguishes himself

---

[1] " Une approbation ou ratification."

from the Father, not simply as to his Divine Person, but rather as to his flesh; lest the doctrine should be judged after the manner of men, and, therefore, should have less weight. But if consciences were subject to the laws and doctrine of men, this argument of Christ would not apply, "My word (he says) will judge, because it has not proceeded from man;" according to that saying, *There is one lawgiver, who is able to save and to destroy*, (James iv. 12.) We may likewise infer from it, how monstrous is the sacrilege of the Pope in daring to bind souls by his inventions; for in this way he claims more for himself than the Son of God does, who declares that he does not speak but by the commandment of his Father.

50. *And I know that his commandment is eternal life.* He again applauds the fruit of his doctrine, that all may more willingly yield to it; and it is reasonable that wicked men should feel the vengeance of God, whom they now refuse to have as the Author of life.

CHAPTER XIII.

1 Before the feast of the passover, Jesus, knowing that his hour was come, that he should remove out of this world to the Father, having loved his own, who were in the world, he loved them to the end. 2. And after supper,[1] the devil having already put it into the heart of Judas Iscariot, the son of Simon, to betray him, 3 Jesus, knowing that the Father had given all things into his hands, and that he had come from God, and was going to God, 4 Riseth from supper, and layeth aside his garments, and, taking a towel, he girdeth himself 5. Then he poureth water into a basin, and began to wash the feet of his disciples, and to wipe them with the towel with which he was girded. 6. He cometh, therefore, to Simon Peter, who saith to him, Lord, dost thou wash my feet? 7. Jesus answered and said to him, What I do thou knowest not now, but thou shalt know hereafter.

1. *Before the feast of the passover.* John intentionally passes by many things which, he knew, had been related by Matthew and others. He undertakes to explain those circumstances which they had left out, one of which was the

---

[1] " Et apres avoir souppé ; "—" and after having supped."

narrative of the *washing of feet*. And though he will afterwards explain more clearly for what purpose Christ *washed the feet* of his disciples, yet, before doing so, he states, in a single word, that the Lord testified, by this visible sign, that the love with which he embraced them was firm and lasting; that, though they were deprived of his presence, they might still be convinced that death itself would not quench this love. This conviction ought now to be fixed also in our hearts.

The words are, that Christ *loved even to the end his own, who were in the world.* Why does he employ this circumlocution in describing the Apostles, but in order to inform us that, in consequence of their being engaged, as we are, in a hazardous and difficult warfare, Christ regarded them with so much the greater solicitude? And, therefore, though we think that we are at a distance from Christ, yet we ought to know that he is looking at us; for *he loveth his own, who are in the world;* for we have no reason to doubt that he still bears the same affection which he retained at the very moment of his death.

To remove from this world to the Father. This phrase is worthy of notice; for it refers to the knowledge of Christ, that he knew that his death was a *passage* to the heavenly kingdom of God. And if, while he was hastening thither, he did not cease to regard *his own* with his wonted love, there is no reason why we should now think that his affection is changed. Now, since he is the first-born from the dead, this definition of death applies to the whole body of the Church, that it is an opening or passage to go to God, from whom believers are now absent.[1]

2. *After supper.*[2] We shall afterwards take into consideration, at the proper place, the whole of Christ's design in *washing the feet* of his disciples, and the advantage to be derived from this narrative. Let us now attend to the connection of the words. The Evangelist says that this was done, while

---

[1] " Que c'est une ouverture ou passage pour aller à Dieu "
[2] " Et apres avoir souppé."—" And after having supped."

Judas already resolved to betray Christ, not only to show the wonderful patience of Christ, who could endure to *wash the feet* of such a wicked and detestable traitor; but also that he purposely selected the time when he was near death, for performing what may be regarded as the last act of his life.

The devil having already put it into the heart of Judas. When the Evangelist says that Judas had been impelled by *the devil* to form the design of *betraying* Christ, this tends to show the enormity of the crime; for it was dreadful and most atrocious wickedness, in which the efficacy of Satan was openly displayed. There is no wickedness, indeed, that is perpetrated by men, to which Satan does not excite them, but the more hideous and execrable any crime is, the more ought we to view in it the rage of *the devil,* who drives about, in all possible directions,[1] men who have been forsaken by God. But though the lust of men is kindled into a fiercer flame by Satan's fan, still it does not cease to be a furnace; it contains the flame kindled within itself, it receives with avidity the agitation of the fan, so that no excuse is left for wicked men.

3. *Jesus, knowing that the Father had given all things into his hands.* I am of opinion that this was added for the purpose of informing us whence Christ obtained such a well-regulated composure of mind. It was because, having already obtained a victory over death, he raised his mind to the glorious triumph which was speedily to follow. It usually happens, that men seized with fear are greatly agitated. The Evangelist means, that no agitation of this sort was to be found in Christ, because, though he was to be immediately betrayed by Judas, still he knew that *the Father had given all things into his hand.* It may be asked, How then was he reduced to such a degree of sadness that he sweat blood? I reply, both were necessary. It was necessary that he should have a dread of death, and it was necessary that, notwith-

---

[1] "*Sursum ac deorsum.*"—"Up and down."

standing of this, he should fearlessly discharge every thing that belonged to the office of the Mediator.

4. *And layeth aside his garments.* The meaning is, that he laid aside his *upper garment,* not his *coat;* for we know that the inhabitants of Eastern countries wore long *garments.*

5. *And began to wash the feet of his disciples.* These words express the design of Christ, rather than the outward act; for the Evangelist adds, that he began with Peter.

6. *Lord, dost thou wash my feet?* This speech expresses strong dislike of the action as foolish and unsuitable; for by asking what Christ is doing, he puts out his hand, as it were, to push him back. The modesty would be worthy of commendation, were it not that obedience is of greater value in the sight of God than any kind of honour or service, or rather, if this were not the true and only rule of humility, to yield ourselves in obedience to God, and to have all our senses regulated by his good pleasure, so that every thing which he declares to be agreeable to Him shall also be approved by us, without any scruple. We ought, therefore, above all, to observe this rule of serving God, that we shall be always ready to acquiesce, without delay, as soon as he issues any command.

7. *What I do.* We are taught by these words, that we ought simply to obey Christ, even though we should not perceive the reason why he wishes this or that thing to be done. In a well-regulated house, one person, the head of the family, has the sole right to say what ought to be done; and the servants are bound to employ their hands and feet in his service. That man, therefore, is too haughty, who refuses to obey the command of God, because he does not know the reason of it. But this admonition has a still more extensive meaning, and that is, that we should not take it ill to be ignorant of those things which God wishes to be hidden from us for a time; for this kind of ignorance is more learned than any other kind of knowledge, when we permit God to be wise above us.

8. Peter saith to him, Thou shalt never wash my feet. Jesus answered him, If I wash thee not, thou shalt have no part with me. 9. Simon Peter saith to him, Lord, not my feet only, but also my hands and my head. 10. Jesus saith to him, He who is washed needeth not to wash more than his feet, but is altogether clean; and you are clean, but not all. 11. For he knew who it was that should betray him;[1] therefore he said, You are not all clean.

8. *Thou shalt never wash my feet.* Hitherto Peter's modesty was excusable, though it was not free from blame; but now he errs more grievously, when he has been corrected, and yet does not yield.[2] And, indeed, it is a common fault, that ignorance is closely followed by obstinacy. It is a plausible excuse, no doubt, that the refusal springs from reverence for Christ; but since he does not absolutely obey the injunction, the very desire of showing his respect for Christ loses all its gracefulness. The true wisdom of faith, therefore, is to approve and embrace with reverence whatever proceeds from God, as done with propriety and in good order; nor is there any other way, indeed, in which his name can be sanctified by us; for if we do not believe that whatever he does is done for a very good reason, our flesh, being naturally stubborn, will continually murmur, and will not render to God the honour due to him, unless by constraint. In short, until a man renounce the liberty of judging as to the works of God, whatever exertions he may make to honour God, still pride will always lurk under the garb of humility.

If I wash thee not. This reply of Christ does not yet explain the reason why he resolved to *wash the feet of his disciples;* only by a comparison drawn from the soul to the body, he shows that, in washing the feet of his disciples, he does nothing that is unusual or inconsistent with his rank. Meanwhile, the reply points out the folly of Peter's wisdom. The same thing will always happen to us, whenever the Lord begins to contend with us. So long as he remains silent, men imagine that they have a good right to differ from him: but nothing is easier for him than to refute, by a single word, all the plausible arguments which they employ. As Christ

---

[1] " Lequel c'estoit qui le trahiroit "
[2] " Neantmoins il ne se deporte pas de contredire;"—" yet, notwithstanding, he does not cease to contradict him."

is Lord and Master, Peter thinks it inconsistent that Christ should wash his feet. But the evil is,[1] that, in refusing such a service, he rejects the principal part of his own salvation. There is also a general doctrine contained in this statement, that we are all filthy and abominable in the sight of God, until Christ *wash* away our stains. Now, since he claims for himself the exclusive right of *washing*, let every man present himself to be cleansed from his pollution, that he may obtain a place among the children of God.

But before proceeding farther, we must understand what is the meaning of the word *wash*. Some refer it to the free pardon of sins; others, to newness of life; while a third class extends it to both, and this last view I cheerfully admit. For Christ *washes* us when he removes the guilt of our sins by his atoning sacrifice, that they may not come into judgment before God; and, on the other hand, he *washes* us when he takes away, by his Spirit, the wicked and sinful desires of the flesh. But as it will shortly afterwards be evident from what follows, that he speaks of the grace of regeneration, I do not absolutely maintain the opinion that he included here the *washing* of pardon.

9. *Lord, not my feet only.* When Peter heard that he was ruined, if he did not accept the cleansing which was offered to him by Christ, this necessity proved, at length, to be a sufficient instructor to tame him. He therefore lays aside opposition and yields, but wishes to be entirely washed, and, indeed, acknowledges that, for his own part, he is altogether covered with pollution, and, therefore, that it is doing nothing, if he be only *washed* in one part. But here too he goes wrong through thoughtlessness, in treating, as a thing of no value, the benefit which he had already received; for he speaks as if he had not yet obtained any pardon of sins, or any sanctification by the Holy Spirit. On this account, Christ justly reproves him, for he recalls to his recollection what he had formerly bestowed on him; at the same time, reminding all his disciples in the person of one man, that, while they re-

---

[1] "Mais voyci le mal."

membered the grace which they had received, they should consider what they still needed for the future.

10. *He who is washed needeth not to wash more than his feet, but is altogether clean.* First, he says that believers are *altogether clean;* not that they are in every respect pure, so that there no longer remains in them any stain, but because they are cleansed in their chief part; that is, when sin is deprived of its kingly power, so that the righteousness of God holds the superiority; just as if we were to say, that a body was altogether healthy, because it was not infected with any universal disease. It is by newness of life, therefore, that we must testify ourselves to be the disciples of Christ, for he declares that he is the Author of purity in all his followers.

Again, the other comparison was also applied to the case in hand, that Peter might not set aside the washing of *the feet* as foolish; for, as Christ washes from the head to *the feet,* those whom he receives as his disciples, so, in those whom he has cleansed, the lower part remains to be daily cleansed. The children of God are not altogether regenerated on the first day, so as to aim at nothing but the heavenly life; but, on the contrary, the remains of the flesh continue to dwell in them, with which they maintain a continued struggle throughout their whole life. The term *feet,* therefore, is metaphorically applied to all the passions and cares by which we are brought into contact with the world; for, if the Holy Spirit occupied every part of us, we would no longer have anything to do with the pollutions of the world; but now, by that part in which we are carnal, we creep on the ground, or at least fix our feet in the clay, and, therefore, are to some extent unclean. Thus Christ always finds in us something to cleanse. What is here spoken of is not the forgiveness of sins, but the renewal, by which Christ, by gradual and uninterrupted succession, delivers his followers entirely from the sinful desires of the flesh.

And you are clean. This proposition may be said to be the minor in the syllogism, and hence it follows that *the washing of the feet* applies to them with strict propriety.

But not all. This exception is added, that every one may examine himself, if Judas may perhaps be moved by a feeling of repentance; though he intended by it to take an early opportunity of fortifying the rest of the disciples, that they might not be perplexed by the atrocity of the crime, which was soon afterwards to be made known. Yet he purposely abstains from naming him, that he may not shut against him the gate of repentance. As that hardened hypocrite[1] was utterly desperate, the warning served only to aggravate his guilt; but it was of great advantage to the other disciples, for by means of it the Divinity of Christ was more fully made known to them, and they likewise perceived that purity is no ordinary gift of the Holy Spirit.

12. After then he had washed their feet, and had taken his garments, sitting down again at table,[2] he saith to them, Know ye what I have done to you? 13 You call me Master and Lord; and you say well, for so I am 14 If I then, who am the Lord and Master, have washed your feet, you ought also to wash one another's feet 15. For I have given you an example, that, as I have done to you, you should do also. 16. Verily, verily, I tell you, the servant is not greater than his lord, nor the ambassador[3] greater than he who sent him. 17. If you know these things, happy are you if you do them.

12. *When then he had washed their feet.* Christ at length explains what was his intention in *washing the feet* of his disciples; for what he had said about the spiritual washing was a sort of digression from his main design. Had it not been for the opposition made by Peter, Christ would not have spoken on that subject. Now, therefore, he discloses the reason of what he had done; namely, that he *who is the Master and Lord of all gave an example* to be followed by all the godly, that none might grudge to descend to do a service to his brethren and equals, however mean and low that service might be. For the reason why the love of the brethren is despised is, that every man thinks more highly of himself than he ought, and despises almost every other person. Nor did he intend merely to inculcate modesty, but likewise to lay down this

[1] " Cest hypocrite effronté "
[2] " Et (apres) qu'il se fut rassis à table ,"—" and (after) that he had sat down again at table."
[3] " Apostolus ,"—" l'ambassadeur."

rule of brotherly love, that they should serve one another; for there is no brotherly love where there is not a voluntary subjection in assisting a neighbour.

Know you what I have done? We see that Christ, for a short time, concealed his intention from his disciples, but that, after having tried their obedience, he seasonably revealed to them that which it was not expedient for them previously to know. Nor does he now wait till they ask, but of his own accord anticipates them. The same thing will be experienced by us also, provided that we suffer ourselves to be guided by his hand, even through unknown ways.

14. *If then I, who am your Lord and Master.* This is an argument from the greater to the less. Pride hinders us from maintaining that equality which ought to exist amongst us. But Christ, who is far exalted above all others, stoops down, that he may make the proud men ashamed, who, forgetting their station and rank, look upon themselves as not bound to hold intercourse with the brethren. For what does a mortal man imagine himself to be, when he refuses to bear the burdens of brethren, to accommodate himself to their customs, and, in short, to perform those offices by which the unity of the Church is maintained? In short, he means that the man who does not think of associating with weak brethren, on the condition of submitting mildly and gently even to offices which appear to be mean, claims more than he has a right to claim, and has too high an opinion of himself.[1]

15. *For I have given you an example.* It deserves our attention that Christ says that he *gave an example;* for we are not at liberty to take all his actions, without reserve, as subjects of imitation. The Papists boast that, by Christ's example, they observe the forty days' fast, or Lent. But we ought first to see whether or not he intended to lay down his fast as an example, that the disciples might conform to it as a rule. We read nothing of this sort, and, therefore, the imitation of it is not less wicked than if they attempted to

[1] " Cestuy-là s'attribue plus qu'il ne faut, et fait trop grand conte de soy "

fly to heaven. Besides, when they ought to have followed Christ, they were not imitators, but apes. Every year they have a fashion of washing some people's feet, as if it were a farce which they were playing on the stage;[1] and so, when they have performed this idle and unmeaning ceremony, they think that they have fully discharged their duty, and reckon themselves at liberty to despise their brethren during the rest of the year.[2] But—what is far worse[3]—after having washed the feet of twelve men, they subject every member of Christ to cruel torture, and thus spit in Christ's face. This display of buffoonery, therefore, is nothing else than a shameful mockery of Christ. At all events, Christ does not here enjoin an annual ceremony, but bids us be ready, throughout our whole life, to wash the feet of our brethren and neighbours.[4]

16. *Verily, verily, I tell you.* These are indeed proverbial sayings, which admit of a far more extensive application, but which ought to be accommodated to the case in hand. In my opinion, therefore, they are mistaken who suppose them to have a general acceptation, as if Christ were now exhorting his disciples to bear the cross; for it is more correct to say that he employed them to serve his purpose.

17. *If you know these things.* He declares that they *are happy, if they* KNOW *and* DO *these things ;* for *knowledge* is not entitled to be called true, unless it produce such an effect on believers as to lead them to conform themselves to their Head. On the contrary, it is a vain imagination, when we look upon Christ, and the things which belong to Christ, as separate from ourselves. We may infer from this that, until a man has learned to yield to his brethren, he does not *know* if Christ be *the Master.* Since there is no man who performs his duty to his brethren in all respects, and since there are many who are careless and sluggish in brotherly offices, this shows us

---

[1] "Comme s'ils jouyoient une farce sur des eschaffauts."
[2] "Tout le reste de l'an."   [3] "Il y a bien pis."
[4] "De nos freres et prochains."

that we are still at a great distance from the full light of faith.

18. I speak not of you all; I know whom I have chosen; but that the Scripture may be fulfilled, He who eateth bread with me hath lifted up his heel against me 19. I tell you this now, before it happen, that when it shall have happened, you may believe that I am.[1] 20 Verily, verily, I tell you, if I send any one, he who receiveth him receiveth me; and he who receiveth me receiveth him who sent me.

18. *I speak not of you all.* He again declares that there is one among the disciples who, in reality, is the very reverse of a disciple; and he does so, partly for the sake of Judas, in order to render him the more inexcusable, and partly for the sake of the others, that they may not be overpowered by the ruin of Judas. Not only does he encourage them still to persevere in their calling when Judas falls away; but as the happiness which he speaks of is not common to all, he exhorts them to desire it with so much the greater eagerness, and to adhere to it the more firmly.

I know whom I have chosen. This very circumstance—that they will persevere—he ascribes to their *election;* for the virtue of men, being frail, would tremble at every breeze, and would be laid down by the feeblest stroke, if the Lord did not uphold it by his hand. But as he governs those whom he has *elected,* all the engines which Satan can employ will not prevent them from persevering to the end with unshaken firmness. And not only does he ascribe to election their perseverance, but likewise the commencement of their piety. Whence does it arise that one man, rather than another, devotes himself to the word of God? It is, because he was elected. Again, whence does it arise that this man makes progress, and continues to lead a good and holy life, but because the purpose of God is unchangeable, to complete the work which was begun by his hand? In short, this is the source of the distinction between the children of God and unbelievers, that the former are drawn to salvation by the Spirit of adoption, while the latter are hurried to destruction by their flesh, which is under no restraint. Otherwise Christ

---

[1] " Que ce suis-je;"—" that I am he."

might have said, "I know what kind of person each of you will be;" but that they may not claim anything for themselves, but, on the contrary, may acknowledge that, by the grace of God alone, and not by their own virtue, they differ from Judas, he places before them that election by free grace on which they are founded. Let us, therefore, learn that every part of our salvation depends on election.

In another passage he includes Judas in the number of the elect. *Have not I chosen* (or, *elected*) *you twelve, and one of you is a devil?*[1] (John vi. 70.) But in that passage the mode of expression, though different, is not opposite; for there the word denotes a temporal *election*, by which God appoints us to any particular work; in the same manner as Saul, who was *elected* to be a king, and yet was a reprobate. But here Christ speaks of the eternal *election*, by which we become the children of God, and by which God predestinated us to life before the creation of the world. And, indeed, the reprobate are sometimes endued by God with the gifts of the Spirit, to execute the office with which he invests them. Thus, in Saul, we perceive, for a time, the splendour of royal virtues, and thus Judas also was distinguished by eminent gifts, and such as were adapted to an apostle of Christ. But this is widely different from the sanctification of the Holy Spirit, which the Lord bestows on none but his own children; for he renews them in understanding and heart, that they may be holy and unblameable in his sight. Besides, that sanctification has a deep root in them, which cannot be removed; because the adoption of God is without repentance. Meanwhile, let us regard it as a settled point, that it results from the election of God, when, having embraced by faith the doctrine of Christ, we also follow it during our life; and that this is the only cause of our happiness, by which we are distinguished from the reprobate; for they, being destitute of the grace of the Spirit, miserably perish, while we have Christ for our guardian, who guides us by his hand, and upholds us by his power.

Besides, Christ gives here a clear proof of his Divinity;

---

[1] See vol. i. p. 280.

first, when he declares that he does not judge after the manner of men; and, secondly, when he pronounces himself to be the Author of *election.* For when he says, *I know,* the *knowledge,* of which he speaks, belongs peculiarly to God; but the second proof—contained in the words, *whom I have chosen*—is far more powerful, for he testifies that they who were *elected* before the creation of the world were *elected* by himself. So remarkable a demonstration of his Divine power ought to affect us more deeply, than if the Scripture had called him God a hundred times.

That the Scripture may be fulfilled. It might have been thought improper that one should have been *elected* to so honourable a rank, who yet did not possess true piety; for it might readily have been objected, Why did not Christ *elect* one whom he intended to admit into the number of the Apostles? or rather, Why did he appoint a man to be an Apostle, who, he well knew, would become so wicked? He explains that this must have happened, because it was foretold; or, at least, that it was no new occurrence, for David had experienced the same thing. For some think that it is a prediction quoted, which properly applies to Christ; while others think that it is merely a comparison, that, as David was basely betrayed by a private enemy, so a similar condition awaits the children of God. According to the latter, the meaning would be: "That one of my disciples wickedly betrays his Master, is not the first instance of treachery that has taken place in the world; but, on the contrary, we now experience what Scripture declares to have happened in ancient times." But, as in David there was shadowed out what was afterwards to be seen more fully in Christ, I readily agree with the former expositors, who think that this was strictly the fulfilment of that which David, by the Spirit of prophecy, had foretold, (Ps. xli. 9.) Besides, some are of opinion that the clause under consideration does not contain a complete sense, and needs to have the principal verb supplied. But if we read it continuously, *That the Scripture may be fulfilled, he who eateth bread with me lifteth up his heel against me,* there will be nothing wanting.

To lift up the heel is a metaphorical expression, and means, to attack a person in an unperceived manner, under the pretence of friendship, so as to gain an advantage over him, when he is not on his guard. Now what Christ suffered, who is our Head and our Pattern, we, who are his members, ought to endure patiently. And, indeed, it has usually happened in the Church in almost every age, that it has had no enemies more inveterate than the members of the Church; and, therefore, that believers may not have their minds disturbed by such atrocious wickedness, let them accustom themselves early to endure the attacks of traitors.

19. *I tell you this now, before it happen.* By this statement he reminds his disciples that, when one of their number becomes a reprobate, this is so far from being a good reason for their being discouraged, that it ought to be a more full confirmation of their faith. For if we did not see before our eyes, in the Church, what has been foretold about her distresses and struggles, a doubt might justly arise in our minds, Where are the prophecies? But when the truth of Scripture agrees with our daily experience,[1] then do we perceive more clearly, that God takes care of us, and that we are governed by his providence.

That you may believe that I am.[2] By the phrase, *that I am,* he means that he is that Messiah who had been promised; not that the conduct of Judas, as a traitor, was the first event that led the disciples to the exercise of faith, but because their faith made greater progress, when they arrived at the experience of those things which they had formerly heard from the mouth of Christ. Now this may be explained in two ways; either that Christ says that they will believe after the event has happened, because there was nothing which was hidden from him, or that nothing will be wanting in him of all that the Scripture testifies concerning Christ. As the two in-

[1] " Avec l'expérience qui se présente aujourdhui devant nos yeux ;"—" with the experience which is exhibited before our eyes at the present day."

[2] " A fin que vous croyez que ce suis-je ;"—" that you may believe that I am he."

terpretations agree well enough together, I leave my readers at liberty to choose which of them they will prefer.

20. *Verily, verily, I tell you.* In these words either the Evangelist relates a discourse on a different subject, and in a broken and imperfect state, or, Christ intended to meet the offence which was likely to arise from the crime of Judas; for the Evangelists do not always exhibit the discourses of Christ in unbroken succession, but sometimes throw together, in heaps, a variety of statements. It is more probable, however, that Christ intended to provide against this scandal. There is too good evidence that we are very ready to be wounded by bad examples; for, in consequence of this, the revolt of one man inflicts a deadly wound on two hundred others, while the steadiness of ten or twenty pious men hardly edifies a single individual. On this account, while Christ was placing such a monster before the eyes of his disciples, it was also necessary that he should stretch out his hand to them, lest, struck by the novelty, they should fall back. Nor was it only on their account that he said this, but he also consulted the advantage of those who should come after; for, otherwise, the remembrance of Judas might, even at the present day, do us grievous injury. When the devil cannot estrange us from Christ by hatred of his doctrine, he excites either dislike or contempt of the ministers themselves.

Now this admonition of Christ shows that it is unreasonable that the impiety of any whose conduct is wicked or unbecoming their office, should at all diminish the apostolical authority. The reason is, we ought to contemplate God, the Author of the ministry, in whom, certainly, we find nothing which we have a right to despise; and next, we ought to contemplate Christ, who, having been appointed by the Father to be the only Teacher, speaks by his apostles. Whoever, then, does not deign to receive the ministers of the Gospel, rejects Christ in them, and rejects God in Christ.

The Papists act a foolish and ridiculous part, when they endeavour to obtain this applause for themselves, in order exhibit their tyranny. For, in the first place, they adorn themselves with begged and borrowed feathers, having no resemblance to the apostles of Christ; and, secondly, granting that they are apostles, nothing was farther from Christ's intention, in this passage, than to transfer his own right to men; for what else is it to receive those whom Christ sends, but to give place to them, that they may fulfil the office which has been committed to them?

21. When Jesus had said these words, he was troubled in spirit, and testified, and said, Verily, verily, I tell you, that one of you will betray me. 22. The disciples, therefore, looked on one another, doubting of whom he spoke. 23. And one of the disciples, whom Jesus loved, was lying at table in Jesus' bosom. 24. Therefore Simon Peter made a sign to him, to ask who it was of whom he spoke. 25. Lying on the breast of Jesus, therefore, he saith to him, Lord, who is he? 26. Jesus answered, It is he to whom I shall give the dipped sop; and when he had dipped the sop, he gave it to Judas Iscariot, the son of Simon. 27. And after the sop, Satan entered into him. Then said Jesus to him, What thou doest, do quickly. 28. And no one of those who were at table knew why he said this to him. 29. For some thought, because Judas had the purse, that Jesus said to him, Buy the things which we need for the feast; or, that he should give something to the poor.

21. *When Jesus had said these words.* The more sacred the apostolic office is, and the higher its dignity, the more base and detestable was the treachery of Judas. A crime so monstrous and detestable struck Christ himself with horror, when he saw how the incredible wickedness of one man had polluted that sacred order in which the majesty of God ought to have shone with brightness. To the same purpose is what the Evangelist adds, that he *testified.* His meaning is, the action was so monstrous that the bare mention of it could not be immediately believed.

He was troubled in spirit. The Evangelist says that Christ *was troubled in spirit,* in order to inform us that he did not merely, in countenance and language, assume the appearance of a man who was *troubled,* but that he was deeply moved in his mind. *Spirit* here denotes the understanding, or, the soul; for I do not assent to the opinion of some who explain it, as if Christ had been driven by a violent impulse of the Holy *Spirit* to break out into these words. I readily acknowledge that all the affections of Christ were guided by the Holy *Spirit;* but the meaning of the Evangelist is different, namely, that this suffering of Christ was inward, and was not feigned; and it is of great importance for us to know this, because his zeal is held out for our imitation, that we may be moved with deep horror by those monsters which overturn the sacred order of God and of his Church.

22. *The disciples, therefore, looked on one another.* They who are not conscious of any crime are rendered uneasy by what Christ has said: Judas alone is so stupid amidst his malice, that he remains unmoved. The authority of Christ was held in so great estimation by the disciples, that they were fully convinced that he said nothing without a good reason; but Satan had expelled from the heart of Judas all reverence, so that it was harder than a rock to reject every admonition. And though Christ appears to be somewhat unkind in inflicting this torture, for a time, on those who were innocent, yet as anxiety of this kind was profitable to them, Christ did them no injury. It is proper that, when the children of God have heard the sentence of the ungodly, they should themselves feel uneasiness, that they may sift themselves, and guard against hypocrisy; for this gives them an opportunity of examining themselves and their life.

This passage shows that we ought sometimes to reprove the ungodly in such a manner as not instantly to point the finger to them, until God, by his own hand, drag them forth to the light. For it frequently happens that there are secret diseases in the Church, which we are not at liberty to disguise; and yet the wickedness of men is not so ripe as to be capable of being laid open. In such cases we ought to take this middle path.

23. *Whom Jesus loved.* The peculiar *love* with which Christ *loved* John plainly testifies that, if we *love* some more than others, this is not always inconsistent with brotherly love; but all lies in this, that our love shall be directed towards God, and that every man, in proportion as he excels in the gifts of God, shall share in it the more largely. From this end Christ never turned aside in the smallest degree; but with us the case is widely different, for such is the vanity

of our mind, that there are few who, in loving men, approach more nearly to God. And yet the love of men towards each other will never be properly regulated, unless it be directed to God.

Lay at table in Jesus' bosom. What is here related by John might be regarded in the present day as indecorous; but such was, at that time, the manner of being placed at table; for they did not *sit*, as we do, *at table*, but, after having put off their shoes, *lay* half-stretched out, *reclining* on small cushions.

26. *To whom I shall give the dipped sop.* It may be asked, what purpose did it serve to give *a dipped sop*, for discovering the traitor, when Christ might have openly pointed him out by name, if he wished to make him known? I answer, the sign was of such a nature, that it discovered Judas to one person only, and did not immediately bring him forward to the view of all. But it was advantageous that John should be witness of this fact, in order that he might afterwards reveal it to others at the proper time; and Christ intentionally delayed to make Judas publicly known, that, when hypocrites are concealed, we may more patiently bear, till they are dragged forth to the light. We see Judas sitting amongst the others, and yet condemned by the mouth of the Judge. In no respect better is the condition of those who hold a place among the children of God.

27. *Satan entered into him.* As it is certain that it was only at the instigation of Satan that Judas formed the design of committing so heinous a crime, why is it now said, for the first time, that *Satan entered into him*, who had already held the throne in his heart? But as they who are more fully confirmed in the faith which they formerly possessed are often said to *believe*, and thus an increase of their faith is called *faith*, so now that Judas is utterly given up to Satan, so as to be hurried on, by vehement impetuosity, to every extremity of evil, *Satan* is said to have *entered into him*. For as the saints make gradual progress, and in proportion to the new gifts by which they are continually enlarged, they are said to be filled with the Holy Spirit; so, in proportion

as wicked men provoke the anger of God against themselves by their ingratitude, the Lord deprives them of his Spirit, of all light of reason, and, indeed, of all human feeling, and delivers them unreservedly to *Satan.* This is a dreadful vengeance of God, when men are *given up to a reprobate mind,* (Rom. i. 28,) so that they scarcely differ at all from the brutes, and—what is worse—fall into horrid crimes from which the brutes themselves would shrink. We ought, therefore, to walk diligently in the fear of the Lord, lest, if we overpower his goodness by our wickedness, he at length give us up to the rage of Satan.

By giving *the sop,* Christ did not give an opportunity to Satan, but rather Judas, *having received the sop,* gave himself up entirely to Satan. It was, indeed, the occasion, but not the cause. His heart, which was harder than iron, ought to have been softened by so great kindness showed to him by Christ; and now his desperate and incurable obstinacy deserves that God, by his just judgment, should harden his heart still more by Satan. Thus, when, by acts of kindness to enemies, we *heap coals of fire on their heads,* (Rom. xii. 20,) if they are utterly incurable, they are the more enraged and inflamed[1] to their destruction. And yet no blame is due, on this account, to our kindness, by which their hearts ought to have been inflamed to love us.

Augustine was wrong in thinking that this *sop* was an emblem of the body of Christ, since it was not during the Lord's Supper that it was given to Judas. It is also a very foolish dream to imagine that the devil entered essentially— as the phrase is—into Judas; for the Evangelist speaks only of the power and efficacy of Satan. This example reminds us what a dreadful punishment awaits all those who profane the gifts of the Lord by abusing them.

What thou doest, do quickly. The exhortation addressed by Christ to Judas is not of such a nature that he can be regarded as exciting him to do the action: it is rather the language of one who views the crime with horror and detes-

---

[1] "Ils se despitent et enflamment davantage."

tation.¹ Hitherto he had endeavoured, by various methods, to bring him back, but to no purpose. Now he addresses him as a desperate man, " Go to destruction, since you have resolved to go to destruction ;" and, in doing so, he performs the office of a judge, who condemns to death not those whom he, of his own accord, desires to ruin, but those who have already ruined themselves by their own fault. In short, Christ does not lay Judas under the necessity of perishing, but declares him to be what he had formerly been.

28. *Not one of those who were at table.* Either John had not yet related to others what Christ had told him, or they were so much struck by it, that they lost their presence of mind; and, indeed, it is probable, that John himself was almost out of his senses. But what then happened to the disciples, we frequently see taking place in the Church, that few of the believers discern the hypocrites whom the Lord loudly condemns.

29. *Or that he should give something to the poor.* It is plain enough from other passages how great was Christ's poverty, and yet, out of the little that he had, he *gave something to the poor,* in order to lay down a rule for us; for the Apostles would not have conjectured that he had spoken about *the poor,* if it had not been their usual custom to relieve *the poor.*

30. When, therefore, he had received the sop, he went immediately out; and it was night. 31. When, therefore, he was gone out, Jesus said, Now is the Son of man glorified, and God is glorified in him. 32. If God is glorified in him, God will also glorify him in himself, and will immediately glorify him. 33. Little children, but a little while am I yet with you. You shall seek me; and as I said to the Jews, that whither I go, you cannot come, so now I say to you. 34. A new commandment I give you, That you love one another ; as I have loved you, that you also love one another. 35 By this will all men know that you are my disciples, if you have love one to another.

31. *Now is the Son of man glorified.* The last hour was at hand ; Christ knew that the minds of his disciples were very

¹ " C'est plustost la parole d'un homme qui a en horreur et detestation quelque forfait."

weak, and, therefore, he endeavoured, by every possible method, to support them, that they might not give way. Even at the present day, the remembrance of the cross of Christ is sufficient to make us tremble, were we not instantly met by the consolation, that he triumphed in the cross, having obtained a victory over Satan, sin, and death. What, then, might have happened to the Apostles, when they saw the Lord soon dragged to the cross, loaded with every kind of reproaches? Might not an exhibition so melancholy and revolting have overwhelmed them a hundred times? Christ, therefore, provides against this danger, and withdraws them from the outward aspect of death to its spiritual fruit. Whatever ignominy, then, may be seen in the cross, fitted to confound believers, yet Christ testifies that the same cross brings glory and honour to him.[1]

And God is glorified in him. This clause, which immediately follows the other, is added for confirmation; for it was a paradoxical statement, that *the glory of the Son of man* arose from a death which was reckoned ignominious among men, and was even accursed before God. He shows, therefore, in what manner he would obtain glory to himself from such a death. It is, because by it[2] he glorifies God the Father; for in the cross of Christ, as in a magnificent theatre, the inestimable goodness of God is displayed before the whole world. In all the creatures, indeed, both high and low, the glory of God shines, but nowhere has it shone more brightly than in the cross, in which there has been an astonishing change of things, the condemnation of all men has been manifested, sin has been blotted out, salvation has been restored to men; and, in short, the whole world has been renewed, and every thing restored to good order.

In him. Though the preposition (ἐν) *in* is often used instead of the Hebrew ב, and, in such cases, is equivalent to *by*, yet I have preferred translating it simply, that *God is glorified* IN *the Son of man;* because I considered that phrase to be more emphatic. When he says, AND *God is glorified,* the meaning, I apprehend, is, FOR *God is glorified.*

---

[1] "Luy est glorieuse et honorable."   [2] "Par icelle."

32. *If God is glorified.* Christ concludes that he will obtain a *glorious* triumph by his death; because his sole design in it is, to *glorify* his Father; for the Father did not seek his *glory* from the death of his Son in such a manner as not to make the Son a partaker of that *glory.* He promises, therefore, that when the ignominy which he shall endure for a short time has been effaced, illustrious honour will be displayed in his death. And this too was accomplished; for the death of the cross, which Christ suffered, is so far from obscuring his high rank, that in that death his high rank is chiefly displayed, since there his amazing love to mankind, his infinite righteousness in atoning for sin and appeasing the wrath of God, his wonderful power in conquering death, subduing Satan, and, at length, opening heaven, blazed with full brightness. This doctrine is now extended also to all of us; for though the whole world should conspire to cover us with infamy, yet if we sincerely and honestly endeavour to promote the glory of God, we ought not to doubt that God will also glorify us.

And will immediately glorify him. Christ heightens the consolation by arguments drawn from the shortness of the time, when he promises that it will take place *immediately.* And though this glory began at the day of his resurrection, yet what is chiefly described here is the extension of it, which followed *immediately* afterwards, when, raising the dead by the power of the Gospel and of his Spirit, he created a new people for himself; for the honour which peculiarly belongs to the death of Christ, is the fruit which sprung from it for the salvation of men.

33. *Little children, yet a little while am I with you.* As it was impossible that the disciples should not be deeply grieved at their Master's departure, so he gives them early warning that he will no longer be with them, and, at the same time, exhorts them to patience. Lastly, to remove unseasonable eagerness of desire, he declares that they cannot immediately follow him. In calling them *little children,* he shows, by that gentle appellation, that his reason for departing from them is not that he cares little about their welfare, for he loves them very tenderly. True, the object which he had in view in

clothing himself with our flesh was, that he might be our brother, but by that other name he expresses more strongly the ardour of his love.

As I said to the Jews. When he says, that he repeats to them what he had formerly *said to the Jews*, this is true as to the words, but there is a wide difference in the meaning; for he declares that they cannot follow him, in order that they may endure patiently his temporary absence, and—so to speak —bridles them in, that they may remain in their office, till they have finished their warfare on earth; so that he does not perpetually exclude them, as Jews, from the kingdom of God, but only bids them wait patiently, till he bring them, along with himself, into the heavenly kingdom.

34. *A new commandment I give you.* To the consolation he adds an exhortation, *that they should love one another;* as if he had said, " Yet while I am absent from you in body, testify, by mutual love, that I have not taught you in vain; let this be your constant study, your chief meditation." Why does he call it *a new commandment?* All are not agreed on this point. There are some who suppose the reason to be, that, while the injunction formerly contained in the Law about brotherly love was literal and external, Christ wrote it anew by his Spirit on the hearts of believers. Thus, according to them, the Law is *new*, because he publishes it in a *new* manner, that it may have full vigour. But that is, in my opinion, far-fetched, and at variance with Christ's meaning. The exposition given by others is, that, though the Law directs us to the exercise of *love*, still, because in it the doctrine of brotherly love is encumbered by many ceremonies and appendages, it is not so clearly exhibited; but, on the other hand, that perfection in *love* is laid down in the Gospel without any shadows. For my own part, though I do not absolutely reject this interpretation, I consider what Christ said to be more simple; for we know that laws are more carefully observed at the commencement, but they gradually slip out of the remembrance of men, till at length they become obsolete. In order to impress more deeply, therefore, on the minds of his disciples the doctrine of brotherly love,

Christ recommends it on the ground of novelty; as if he had said, "I wish you continually to remember this commandment, as if it had been a law but lately made."

In short, we see that it was the design of Christ, in this passage, to exhort his disciples to brotherly love, that they might never permit themselves to be withdrawn from the pursuit of it, or the doctrine of it to slip out of their minds. And how necessary this admonition was, we learn by daily experience; for, since it is difficult to maintain brotherly love, men lay it aside, and contrive, for themselves, new methods of worshipping God, and Satan suggests many things for the purpose of occupying their attention. Thus, by idle employments, they in vain attempt to mock God, but they deceive themselves. Let this title of novelty, therefore, excite us to the continual exercise of brotherly love. Meanwhile, let us know that it is called *new*, not because it now began, for the first time, to please God, since it is elsewhere called *the fulfilling of the law*, (Rom. xiii. 10.)

That you love one another. Brotherly *love* is, indeed, extended to strangers, for we are all of the same flesh, and are all created after the image of God; but because the image of God shines more brightly in those who have been regenerated, it is proper that the bond of love, among the disciples of Christ, should be far more close. In God brotherly love seeks its cause, from him it has its root, and to him it is directed. Thus, in proportion as it perceives any man to be a child of God, it embraces him with the greater warmth and affection. Besides, the mutual exercise of love cannot exist but in those who are guided by the same Spirit. It is the highest degree of brotherly love, therefore, that is here described by Christ; but we ought to believe, on the other hand, that, as the goodness of God extends to the whole world, so we ought to love all, even those who hate us.

As I have loved you. He holds out his own example, not because we can reach it, for we are at a vast distance behind him, but that we may, at least, aim at the same end.

35. *By this all men will know.* Christ again confirms what he had formerly said, that they who mutually love one

another have not been in vain taught in his school; as if he had said, " Not only will you know that you are my disciples, but your profession will also be acknowledged by others to be sincere." Since Christ lays down this mark for distinguishing between his disciples and strangers, they who lay aside brotherly love, and adopt new and invented modes of worship, labour in vain; and folly of this kind prevails at this day in Popery. Nor is it superfluous that Christ dwells so largely on this subject. There is no greater agreement between the love of ourselves, and the love of our neighbour, than there is between fire and water. Self-love keeps all our senses bound in such a manner that brotherly love is altogether banished; and yet we think that we fully discharge our duty, because Satan has many enticements to deceive us, that we may not perceive our faults.[1] Whoever, then, desires to be truly a disciple of Christ, and to be acknowledged by God, let him form and direct his whole life to love the brethren, and let him pursue this object with diligence.

36. Simon Peter saith to him, Lord, whither goest thou? Jesus answered him, Whither I go, thou canst not follow me now; but thou shalt follow me afterwards. 37. Peter saith to him, Lord, why cannot I follow thee now? I will lay down my life for thee. 38. Jesus answered him, Wilt thou lay down thy life for me? Verily, verily, I tell thee, The cock will not crow until thou hast denied me thrice.

36. *Lord, whither goest thou?* This question is founded on that saying of Christ, *I said to the Jews, that whither I go you cannot come, so now I say to you,* (ver. 33.) From this it is evident how ignorant Peter was, who, after having been so frequently warned about Christ's departure, was as greatly perplexed as if he had heard something new. Yet in this respect we are too like him; for we hear daily from the mouth of Christ all that is fitted for usefulness in life, and all that is necessary to be known, and, when we come to practice, we are as much astonished as apprentices to whom not a word had ever been spoken. Besides, Peter shows that he is under the influence of an immoderate desire of Christ's bodily presence; for he reckons it absurd that, while he remains, Christ shall go elsewhere.

Whither I go. By these words Christ restrains Peter's

---

[1] "A ce que nous n'appercevions nos fautes."

excessive desire. His language is concise, as becomes a Master, but immediately softens the hardness of his statement. He shows that it will only be for a time that he shall be separated from his disciples. We are taught by this passage to subject all our desires to God, that they may not go beyond their proper bounds; and if at any time they become extravagant and foolish, let us at least submit to be held in by this bridle. That we may not lose courage, let us avail ourselves of the consolation which is immediately added, when Christ promises that we shall one day be gathered to him.

But thou shalt follow me afterwards. He means that Peter is not yet ripe for bearing the cross, but, like corn still in the blade, must be formed and strengthened by the progress of time, that he may *follow*. We ought therefore to pray to God to carry forward to a higher degree of excellence what he has begun in us. In the meantime, we must creep, till we are able to run more swiftly. Now as Christ bears with us, while we are tender and delicate, so let us learn not to reject weak brethren, who are still very far from the goal. It is desirable, indeed, that all should run with the greatest eagerness, and we ought to encourage all to quicken their pace; but if there are any who walk more slowly, we ought to hope well concerning them, provided that they keep the road.

37. *Why cannot I follow thee now?* By these words Peter declares that he was dissatisfied with Christ's answer. He is aware that he has been warned of his own weakness, from which he concludes that it is his own fault that hinders him from following Christ immediately; but he is not at all convinced of it, for mankind are naturally puffed up with confidence in their own virtue. This expression of Peter shows the opinion which we entertain from our very birth, which is, that we attribute more to our own strength than we ought to do. The consequence is, that they who can do nothing venture to attempt every thing, without imploring the assistance of God.

38. *Wilt thou lay down thy life for me?* Christ did not choose to debate with Peter, but wished that he should grow wise

by his own experience, like fools, who never grow wise till they have received a stroke. Peter promises unshaken firmness, and indeed expresses the sincere conviction of his mind; but his confidence is full of rashness, for he does not consider what strength has been given to him. Now since this example belongs to us, let each of us examine his own defects, that he may not be swelled with vain confidence. We cannot indeed make too large promises about the grace of God; but what is here reproved is the arrogant presumption of the flesh, for faith rather produces fear and anxiety.

The cock will not crow. As presumption and rashness proceed from ignorance of ourselves, Peter is blamed for pretending to be a valiant soldier, while he is beyond arrow-shot; for he has not yet made trial of his strength, and imagines that he could do any thing. He was afterwards punished, as he deserved, for his arrogance. Let us learn to distrust our own strength, and to betake ourselves early to the Lord, that he may support us by his power.

CHAPTER XIV.

1. Let not your heart be troubled · you believe in God, believe also in me. 2. In my Father's house are many dwellings, and if it were not so, I would have told you: I go to prepare a place for you. 3. And if I go away and prepare a place for you,[1] I will return again, and receive you to myself; that where I am, you may be also 4. And whither I go you know, and you know the way. 5. Thomas saith to him, Lord, we know not whither thou goest, and how can we know the way? 6. Jesus saith to him, I am the way, and the truth, and the life. No man cometh to the Father but by me. 7. If you had known me, you would have known my Father also ; and henceforth you know him, and have seen him.

1. *Let not your heart be troubled.* Not without good reason does Christ confirm his disciples by so many words, since a contest so arduous and so terrible awaited them; for it was no ordinary temptation, that soon afterwards they would see him hanging on the cross; a spectacle in which nothing was to be seen but ground for the lowest despair. The season of

---

[1] " *Ou, Et quand je m'en seray allé, et vous auray preparé le lieu;* "— " *or,* And when I shall have gone away, and prepared the place for you."

so great distress being at hand, he points out the remedy, that they may not be vanquished and overwhelmed; for he does not simply exhort and encourage them to be stedfast, but likewise informs them where they must go to obtain courage; that is, by faith, when he is acknowledged to be the Son of God, who has in himself a sufficiency of strength for maintaining the safety of his followers.

We ought always to attend to the time when these words were spoken, that Christ wished his disciples to remain brave and courageous, when they might think that every thing was in the greatest confusion; and therefore we ought to employ the same shield for warding off such assaults. It is impossible for us, indeed, to avoid feeling various emotions, but though we are shaken, we must not fall down. Thus it is said of believers, that they *are not troubled*, because, relying on the word of God, though very great difficulties press hard upon them, still they remain stedfast and upright.

You believe in God. It might also be read in the imperative mood, *Believe in God, and believe in me;* but the former reading agrees better, and has been more generally received. Here he points out the method of remaining stedfast, as I have already said; that is, if our faith rest on Christ, and view him in no other light than as being present and stretching out his hand to assist us. But it is wonderful that faith in the Father is here placed first in order, for he ought rather to have told his disciples that they ought to *believe in God*, since they had *believed in Christ;* because, as Christ is the lively image of the Father, so we ought first to cast our eyes on him; and for this reason, too, he descends to us, that our faith, beginning with him, may rise to God. But Christ had a different object in view, for all acknowledge that we ought to *believe in God*, and this is an admitted principle to which all assent without contradiction; and yet there is scarce one in a hundred who actually believes it, not only because the naked majesty of God is at too great a distance from us, but also because Satan interposes clouds of every description to hinder us from contemplating God. The consequence is, that our faith, seeking God in his heavenly glory and inaccessible light, vanishes away; and even the flesh, of its own accord, suggests a thousand imaginations, to turn away our eyes from beholding God in a proper manner. The Son of God, then, who is Jesus Christ,[1] holds out himself as the object to which our faith ought to be directed, and by means of which it will easily find that on which it can rest; for he is the true Immanuel, who answers us within, as soon as we seek him by faith. It is one of the leading articles of our faith, that our faith ought to be directed to Christ alone, that it may not wander through long windings; and that it ought to be fixed on him, that it may not waver in the midst of temptations. And this is the true proof of faith, when we never suffer ourselves to be torn away from Christ, and from the promises which have been made to us in him. When Popish divines dispute, or, I should rather say, chatter, about the object of faith, they mention God only, and pay no attention to Christ. They who derive their instruction from the notions of such men, must be shaken by the slightest gale of wind that blows. Proud men are ashamed of Christ's humiliation, and, therefore, they fly to God's incomprehensible Divinity. But faith will never reach heaven unless it submit to Christ, who appears to be a low and contemptible God, and will never be firm if it do not seek a foundation in the weakness of Christ.

2. *In my Father's house are many dwellings.* As the absence of Christ was a cause of grief, he declares that he does not go away in such a manner as to remain separate from them, since there is room for them also in the heavenly kingdom. For it was proper that he should remove the suspicion from their minds, that, when Christ ascended to the Father, he left his disciples on earth without taking any farther notice of them. This passage has been erroneously interpreted in another sense, as if Christ taught that there are various degrees of honour in the heavenly kingdom; for he says, that the *mansions* are *many,* not that they are different or unlike, but that there are enough of them for a great number of persons; as if he had said, that there is room not only for himself, but also for all his disciples.

[1] " Le Fils de Dieu donc, qui est Jesus Christ."

And if it were not so, I would have told you. Here commentators differ. Some read these words as closely connected with what goes before: "If the dwellings had not been already prepared, I would have said that I go before you to prepare them." But I rather agree with those who render it thus: "If the heavenly glory had awaited me only, I would not have deceived you. I would have told you that there was no room for any one but myself in my Father's house. But the case is widely different; for I go before, to prepare a place for you." The context, in my opinion, demands that we read it in this manner; for it follows immediately afterwards, *If I go to prepare a place for you.* By these words Christ intimates that the design of his departure is, to prepare a place for his disciples. In a word, Christ did not ascend to heaven in a private capacity, to dwell there alone, but rather that it might be the common inheritance of all the godly, and that in this way the Head might be united to his members.

But a question arises, What was the condition of the fathers after death, before Christ ascended to heaven? For the conclusion usually drawn is, that believing souls were shut up in an intermediate state or prison, because Christ says that, by his ascension into heaven, *the place will be prepared.* But the answer is easy. This *place* is said to be *prepared* for the day of the resurrection; for by nature mankind are banished from the kingdom of God, but the Son, who is the only heir of heaven, took possession of it in their name, that through him we may be permitted to enter; for in his person we already possess heaven by hope, as Paul informs us, (Eph. i. 3.) Still we will not enjoy this great blessing, until he come from heaven the second time. The condition of the fathers after death, therefore, is not here distinguished from ours; because Christ has *prepared* both for them and for us a *place*, into which he will receive us all at the last day. Before reconciliation had been made, believing souls were, as it were, placed on a watch-tower, looking for the promised redemption, and now they enjoy a blessed rest, until the redemption be finished.

3. *And if I go away.* The conditional term, *if,* ought to be interpreted as an adverb of time; as if it had been said, "AFTER THAT *I have gone away, I will return to you again.*" This *return* must not be understood as referring to the Holy Spirit, as if Christ had manifested to the disciples some new presence of himself by the Spirit. It is unquestionably true, that Christ dwells with us and in us by his Spirit; but here he speaks of the last day of judgment, when he will, at length, come to assemble his followers. And, indeed, if we consider the whole body of the Church, he every day *prepares a place* for us; whence it follows, that the proper time for our entrance into heaven is not yet come.

4. *And whither I go you know.* As we need no ordinary fortitude, that we may patiently endure to be so long separated from Christ, he adds another confirmation, that the disciples *know* that his death is not a destruction, but a passage to the Father; and next, that they *know the way* which they must *follow,* that they may arrive at the participation of the same glory. Both clauses ought to be carefully observed. First, we must see Christ, by the eyes of faith, in the heavenly glory and a blessed immortality; and, secondly, we ought to know that he is the first-fruits of our life, and that *the way* which was closed against us has been opened by him.

5. *Thomas saith to him.* Though, at first sight, the reply of *Thomas* appears to contradict what Christ had said, yet he did not intend to give the lie to his Master. But it may be asked, In what sense does he deny what Christ asserted? I reply, the knowledge possessed by the saints is sometimes confused, because they do not understand the manner or the reason of those things which are certain, and which have been explained to them. For example, the Prophets foretold the calling of the Gentiles with a true perception of faith, and yet Paul declares that it was a *mystery hidden* from them, (Eph. iii. 2, 4.) In like manner, when the Apostles believed that Christ was departing to the Father, and yet *did not know* in what way he would obtain the kingdom, *Thomas* justly replies, that they *do not know whither he is going.* Hence he

concludes that they *know* still less about *the way*; for before we enter into a road, we must know where we intend to go.

6. *I am the way.* Though Christ does not give a direct reply to the question put to him, yet he passes by nothing that is useful to be known. It was proper that Thomas' curiosity should be checked; and, therefore, Christ does not explain what would be his condition when he should have departed out of this world to go to the Father,[1] but dwells on a subject far more necessary. Thomas would gladly have heard what Christ intended to do in heaven, as we never become weary of those intricate speculations; but it is of greater importance to us to employ our study and labour in another inquiry, how we may become partakers of the blessed resurrection. The statement amounts to this, that whoever obtains Christ is in want of nothing; and, therefore, that whoever is not satisfied with Christ alone, strives after something beyond absolute perfection.

The way, the truth, and the life. He lays down three degrees, as if he had said, that he is the beginning, and the middle, and the end; and hence it follows that we ought to begin with him, to continue in him, and to end in him. We certainly ought not to seek for higher wisdom than that which leads us to eternal *life*, and he testifies that this *life* is to be found in him. Now the method of obtaining *life* is, to become new creatures. He declares, that we ought not to seek it anywhere else, and, at the same time, reminds us, that *he is the way*, by which alone we can arrive at it. That he may not fail us in any respect, he stretches out the hand to those who are going astray, and stoops so low as to guide sucking infants. Presenting himself as a leader, he does not leave his people in the middle of the course, but makes them partakers of *the truth*. At length he makes them enjoy the fruit of it, which is the most excellent and delightful thing that can be imagined.

As Christ is *the way*, the weak and ignorant have no reason

---

[1] " Quand il seroit parti hors de ce monde pour aller à son Pere."

to complain that they are forsaken by him; and as he is *the truth and the life,* he has in himself also what is fitted to satisfy the most perfect. In short, Christ now affirms, concerning happiness, what I have lately said concerning the object of faith. All believe and acknowledge that the happiness of man lies in God alone ; but they afterwards go wrong in this respect, that, seeking God elsewhere than in Christ, they tear him—so to speak—from his true and solid Divinity.

The truth is supposed by some to denote here the saving light of heavenly wisdom, and by others to denote the substance of *life* and of all spiritual blessings, which is contrasted with shadows and figures ; as it is said, *grace and truth came by Jesus Christ,* (John i. 17.) My opinion is, that *the truth* means here the perfection of faith, as *the way* means its beginning and first elements. The whole may be summed up thus : " If any man turn aside from Christ, he will do nothing but go astray; if any man do not rest on him, he will feed elsewhere on nothing but wind and vanity ; if any man, not satisfied with him alone, wishes to go farther,[1] he will find death instead of life."

No man cometh to the Father. This is an explanation of the former statement ; for he is *the way,* because he leads us *to the Father,* and he is *the truth* and *the life,* because in him we perceive *the Father.* As to calling on God, it may indeed be said, with truth, that no prayers are heard but through the intercession of Christ; but as Christ does not now speak about prayer, we ought simply to understand the meaning to be, that men contrive for themselves true labyrinths, whenever, after having forsaken Christ, they attempt *to come to God.* For Christ proves that he is *the life,* because God, *with whom is the fountain of life,* (Ps. xxxvi. 9,) cannot be enjoyed in any other way than in Christ. Wherefore all theology, when separated from Christ, is not only vain and confused, but is also mad, deceitful, and spurious ; for, though the philosophers sometimes utter excellent sayings, yet they

---

[1] " Si quel qu'un ne se contentant point de luy seul, veut passer outre. '

have nothing but what is short-lived, and even mixed up with wicked and erroneous sentiments.

7. *If you had known me.* He confirms what we have just now said, that it is a foolish and pernicious curiosity, when men, not satisfied with him, attempt to go to God by indirect and crooked paths.¹ They admit that there is nothing better than the knowledge of God; but when he is near them, and speaks to them familiarly, they wander through their own speculations, and seek above the clouds him whom they do not deign to acknowledge as present. Christ, therefore, blames the disciples for not acknowledging that the fulness of the Godhead was manifested in him. "I see," (says he,) "that hitherto you have not known me in a right and proper manner, because you do not yet acknowledge the lively image of *the Father* which is exhibited in me."

And henceforth you know him, and have seen him. He adds this, not only to soften the severity of the reproof, but likewise to accuse them of ingratitude and slothfulness, if they do not consider and inquire what has been given to them; for he said this rather for the purpose of commending his doctrine than of extolling their faith. The meaning therefore is, that God is now plainly exhibited to them if they would but open their eyes. The word *see* expresses the certainty of faith.

8. Philip saith to him, Lord, show us the Father, and it sufficeth us. 9. Jesus saith to him, Have I been so long time with you, and hast thou not known me, Philip? He who hath seen me hath seen the Father; and how sayest thou, Show us the Father? 10. Believest thou not that I am in the Father, and the Father in me? The words which I speak to you I speak not from myself; but my Father who dwelleth in me, he doeth the works. 11. Believe me, that I am in the Father, and the Father in me; but if not, believe me on account of the works themselves. 12. Verily, verily, I tell you, He who believeth in me shall himself also do the works which I do, and shall do greater works than these, because I go to my Father 13. And whatever you ask in my name, that I will do, that the Father may be glorified in the Son. 14. If you shall ask any thing in my name, I will do it.

8. *Show us the Father.* It appears to be very absurd that the Apostles should offer so many objections to the Lord; for

¹ " Par voyes obliques et tortues."

why did he speak but to inform them on that point about which *Philip* puts the question? Yet there is not one of their faults that is here described that may not be charged on us as well as on them. We profess to be earnest in seeking God; and when he presents himself before our eyes, we are blind.

9. *Have I been so long time with you?* Christ justly reproves Philip for not having the eyes of his faith pure. He had God present in Christ, and yet he did not behold him. What prevented him but his own ingratitude? Thus, in the present day, they who, in consequence of not being satisfied with Christ alone, are hurried into foolish speculations, in order to seek God in them, make little progress in the Gospel. This foolish desire springs from the meanness of Christ's low condition; and this is very unreasonable, for by that humiliation he exhibits the infinite goodness of God.

10. *That I am in the Father, and the Father in me.* I do not consider these words to refer to Christ's Divine essence, but to the manner of the revelation; for Christ, so far as regards his hidden Divinity, is not better known to us than *the Father.* But he is said to be the lively Image, or Portrait, of God,[1] because in him God has fully revealed himself, so far as God's infinite goodness, wisdom, and power, are clearly manifested in him. And yet the ancient writers do not take an erroneous view of this passage, when they quote it as a proof for defending Christ's Divinity; but as Christ does not simply inquire what he is in himself, but what we ought to acknowledge him to be, this description applies to his power rather than to his essence. *The Father,* therefore, is said *to be in Christ,* because full Divinity dwells in him, and displays its power; and Christ, on the other hand, is said *to be in the Father,* because by his Divine power he shows that he is one with *the Father.*

The words which I speak to you. He proves from the effect that we ought not to seek God anywhere else than in him; for he maintains that his doctrine, being heavenly and truly

---

[1] "La vive Image, ou Pourtraict, de Dieu."

Divine, is a proof and a bright mirror of the presence of God. If it be objected, that all the Prophets ought to be accounted sons of God, because they speak divinely from the inspiration of the Spirit, and because God was the Author of their doctrine, the answer is easy. We ought to consider what their doctrine contains; for the Prophets send their disciples to another person, but Christ attaches them to himself. Besides, we ought to remember what the apostle declares, that now *God speaketh from heaven* (Heb. xii. 25) by the mouth of his Son, and that, when he spoke by Moses, he spoke, as it were, from the earth.

I do not speak from myself; that is, as a man only, or after the manner of men; because *the Father*, exhibiting the power of his Spirit in Christ's doctrine, wishes his Divinity to be recognized in him.

The Father himself doeth the works. This must not be confined to miracles; for it is rather a continuation of the former statement, that the majesty of God is clearly exhibited in Christ's doctrine; as if he had said, that his doctrine is truly a work of God, from which it may be known with certainty that God dwelleth in him. By *the works*, therefore, I understand a proof of the power of God.

Believe me that I am in the Father, and the Father in me. He first demands from the disciples to give credit to his testimony, when he asserts that he is the Son of God; but as they had hitherto been too lazy, he indirectly reproves their indolence. "If my assertion," says he, "does not produce conviction, and if you have so mean an opinion of me, that you do not think that you ought to believe my words, consider, at least, that power which is a visible image of the presence of God." It is very absurd in them, indeed, not to believe, entirely, the words which proceed from the mouth of the Lord Jesus,[1] since they ought to have embraced, without any hesitation, every thing that he expressed, even by a single word. But here Christ reproves his disciples for having made so little progress, though they had received so many admonitions on the same subject. He does not explain what

[1] "De ne croire point entierement aux paroles qui procedent de la bouche du Seigneur Jesus."

is the nature of faith, but declares that he has what is even sufficient for convicting unbelievers.

The repetition of the words, *I am in the Father, and the Father in me,* is not superfluous; for we know too well, by experience, how our nature prompts us to foolish curiosity. As soon as we have gone out of Christ, we shall have nothing else than the idols which we have formed, but *in Christ,* there is nothing but what is divine, and what keeps us *in God.*

12. *Verily, verily, I tell you.* All that he had hitherto told his disciples about himself, so far as it regarded them, was temporal; and, therefore, if he had not added this clause, the consolation would not have been complete; particularly since our memory is so short, when we are called to consider the gifts of God. On this subject it is unnecessary to go to others for examples; for, when God has loaded us with every kind of blessings, if he pause for fourteen days, we fancy that he is no longer alive. This is the reason why Christ not only mentions his present power, which the Apostles, at that time, beheld with their eyes, but promises an uninterrupted conviction of it for the future. And, indeed, not only was his Divinity attested, so long as he dwelt on the earth, but after he had gone to the Father, striking proofs of it were enjoyed by believers. But either our stupidity or our malice hinders us from perceiving God in his works, and Christ in the works of God.

And shall do greater works than these. Many are perplexed by the statement of Christ, that the Apostles *would do greater works than he had done.* I pass by the other answers which have been usually given to it, and satisfy myself with this single answer. First, we must understand what Christ means; namely, that the power by which he proves himself to be the Son of God, is so far from being confined to his bodily presence, that it must be clearly demonstrated by many and striking proofs, when he is absent. Now the ascension of Christ was soon afterwards followed by a wonderful conversion of the world, in which the Divinity of Christ was more powerfully displayed than while he dwelt among men. Thus, we see that the proof of his Divinity was not confined to the person of Christ, but was diffused through the whole body of the Church.

Because I go to the Father. This is the reason why the disciples would do greater things than Christ himself. It is because, when he has entered into the possession of his kingdom, he will more fully demonstrate his power from heaven. Hence it is evident that his glory is in no degree diminished, because, after his departure, the Apostles, who were only his instruments, performed more excellent works. What is more, in this manner it became evident that he sitteth at the right hand of the Father, *that every knee may bow before him,* (Philip. ii. 10.)

13. *And whatever you ask in my name, that I will do.* By these words he plainly declares that he will be the Author of all that shall be done by the hands of the Apostles. But it may be asked, Was he not even then the Mediator in whose name men ought to pray to the Father? I reply, he plainly discharged the office of Mediator, ever since he entered into the heavenly sanctuary; as we shall afterwards repeat at the proper place.

That the Father may be glorified in the Son. This passage agrees with what Paul says, *That every tongue may confess that Jesus Christ is Lord, to the glory of God the Father,* (Philip. ii. 11.) The end of all things is the sanctification of the name of God; but here the true method of sanctifying it is declared; that is, *in the Son,* and *by the Son.* For, though the majesty of God be in itself hidden from us, it shines *in Christ;* though his hand be concealed, we have it visible *in Christ.* Consequently, in the benefits which the Father bestows upon us, we have no right to separate *the Father* from *the Son,* according to that saying, *He that honoureth not the Son honoureth not the Father,* (John vi. 23.)

14. *If you shall ask any thing in my name, I will do it.* This is not a useless repetition. All see and feel that they are unworthy to approach God; and yet the greater part of men burst forward, as if they were out of their senses, and rashly and haughtily address God; and afterwards, when

that unworthiness, of which I have spoken, comes to their recollection, every man contrives for himself various expedients. On the other hand, when God invites us to himself, he holds out to us one Mediator only, by whom he is willing to be appeased and reconciled. But here again the wickedness of the human mind breaks out; for the greater part do not cease to forsake the road, and to pass through many windings. The reason why they do so is, that they have but a poor and slender perception of the power and goodness of God in Christ. To this is added a second error, that we do not consider that we are justly excluded from approaching God, until he calls us, and that we are called only through the Son. And if one passage has not sufficient weight with us, let us know that, when Christ repeats, a second time, that we must pray to the Father in his name, he lays his hand on us, as it were, that we may not lose our pains by fruitlessly seeking other intercessors.

15. If you love me, keep my commandments. 16. And I will pray to the Father, and he will give you another Comforter, that he may abide with you for ever, 17. The Spirit of truth, whom the world cannot receive, because it seeth him not, and knoweth him not, but you know him; for he dwelleth with you, and shall be in you. 18. I will not leave you orphans, I come to you [1]

15. *If you love me.* The *love* with which the disciples *loved* Christ was true and sincere, and yet there was some superstition mixed with it, as is frequently the case with ourselves; for it was very foolish in them to wish to keep him in the world. To correct this fault, he bids them direct their love to another end; and that is, to employ themselves in *keeping the commandments* which he had given them. This is undoubtedly a useful doctrine, for of those who think that they *love* Christ, there are very few who honour him as they ought to do; but, on the contrary, after having performed small and trivial services, they give themselves no farther concern. The true *love* of Christ, on the other hand, is regulated by the observation of his doctrine as the only rule. But we are likewise reminded how sinful our affections are, since even the love which we bear to Christ is not without fault, if it be not directed to a pure obedience.

[1] " Je viendrai à vous ;"—" I will come to you."

16. *And I will pray to the Father.* This was given as a remedy for soothing the grief which they might feel on account of Christ's absence; but at the same time, Christ promises that he will give them strength *to keep his commandments;* for otherwise the exhortation would have had little effect. He therefore loses no time in informing them that, though he be absent from them in body, yet he will never allow them to remain destitute of assistance; for he will be present with them by his Spirit.

Here he calls the Spirit the gift of *the Father,* but a gift which he will obtain by his prayers; in another passage he promises that he will give the Spirit. *If I depart,* says he, *I will send him to you,* (John xvi. 7.) Both statements are true and correct; for in so far as Christ is our Mediator and Intercessor, he obtains from *the Father* the grace of the Spirit, but in so far as he is God, he bestows that grace from himself. The meaning of this passage therefore is: " I was given to you by *the Father* to be *a Comforter,* but only for a time; now, having discharged my office, I will pray to him to give another *Comforter,* who will not be for a short time, but will remain always with you."

And he will give you another Comforter. The word *Comforter* is here applied both to Christ and to the Spirit, and justly; for it is an office which belongs equally to both of them, to *comfort* and exhort us, and to guard us by their protection. Christ was the Protector of his disciples, so long as he dwelt in the world: and afterwards he committed them to the protection and guardianship of the Spirit. It may be asked, Are we not still under the protection of Christ? The answer is easy. Christ is a continual Protector, but not in a visible way. So long as he dwelt in the world, he openly manifested himself as their Protector; but now he guards us by his Spirit.

He calls the Spirit ANOTHER *Comforter,* on account of the difference between the blessings which we obtain from both. The peculiar office of Christ was, to appease the wrath of God by atoning for the sins of the world, to redeem men from death, to procure righteousness and life; and the peculiar office of the Spirit is, to make us partakers not only of

Christ himself, but of all his blessings. And yet there would be no impropriety in inferring from this passage a distinction of Persons; for there must be some peculiarity in which the Spirit differs from the Son so as to be *another* than the Son.

17. *The Spirit of truth.* Christ bestows on the Spirit another title, namely, that he is the Master or Teacher of truth.[1] Hence it follows, that until we have been inwardly instructed by him, the understandings of all of us are seized with vanity and falsehood.

Whom the world cannot receive. This contrast shows the peculiar excellence of that grace which God bestows on none but his elect; for he means that it is no ordinary gift of which the world is deprived. In this sense, too, Isaiah says, "Lo, the darkness shall cover the earth, and thick darkness the people; but the Lord shall arise on thee, O Jerusalem!"[2] For the mercy of God towards the Church deserves so much the higher praise, when he exalts the Church, by a distinguished privilege, above the whole world. And yet Christ exhorts the disciples, that they must not be puffed up, as the world is wont to be, by carnal views, and thus drive away from themselves the grace of the Spirit. All that Scripture tells us about the Holy Spirit is regarded by earthly men as a dream; because, trusting to their own reason, they despise heavenly illumination. Now, though this pride abounds everywhere, which extinguishes, so far as lies in our power, the light of the Holy Spirit; yet, conscious of our own poverty, we ought to know, that whatever belongs to sound understanding proceeds from no other source. Yet Christ's words show that nothing which relates to the Holy Spirit can be learned by human reason, but that He is known only by the experience of faith.

The world, he says, *cannot receive the Spirit, because it knoweth him not; but you know him, because he dwelleth with you.* It is the Spirit alone, therefore, who, by *dwelling in us,* makes himself to be known by us; for, otherwise, he is unknown and incomprehensible.

[1] "A scavoir qu'il est Maistre ou Docteur de la verité."
[2] "Sur toy, O Jerusalem!"

18. *I will not leave you orphans.* This passage shows what men are, and what they can do, when they have been deprived of the protection of the Spirit. They are *orphans*, exposed to every kind of fraud and injustice, incapable of governing themselves, and, in short, unable of themselves to do any thing. The only remedy for so great a defect is, if Christ govern us by his Spirit, which he promises that he will do. First, then, the disciples are reminded of their weakness, that, distrusting themselves, they may rely on nothing else than the protection of Christ; and, secondly, having promised a remedy, he gives them good encouragement; for he declares that he will *never leave them.* When he says, *I will come to you,* he shows in what manner he dwells in his people, and in what manner he fills all things. It is, by the power of his Spirit; and hence it is evident, that the grace of the Spirit is a striking proof of his Divinity.

19. Yet a little while, and the world shall see me no more; but you see me. because I live, you also shall live. 20 At that day you shall know that I am in my Father, and you in me, and I in you.

19. *Yet a little while.* He continues the commendation of special grace, which ought to have been sufficient for alleviating, and even for removing the grief of the disciples. " When I shall have withdrawn," says he, " from the view of the world, still I shall be present with you." That we may enjoy this secret beholding of Christ, we must not judge of his presence or his absence according to carnal perception, but we must earnestly employ the eyes of faith for contemplating his power. Thus believers always have Christ present by his Spirit, and behold him, though they be distant from him in body.

Because I live. This statement may be explained in two ways. Either it may be viewed as a confirmation of the former clause, *because I live, and you shall live;* or, it may be read separately, *because I live, you also shall live;* and then the meaning will be, that believers *will live, because Christ liveth.* I willingly embrace the former opinion, and yet we may draw from it the other doctrine, that the life of Christ is the cause of our life. He begins by pointing out the cause of the difference, why he shall be *seen* by his disciples, and *not by the world.* It is, because Christ cannot be *seen* but according to the spiritual life, of which the world is deprived. *The world seeth not* Christ; this is not wonderful, for the death of blindness is the cause; but as soon as any man begins to live by the Spirit, he is immediately endued with eyes to see Christ. Now, the reason of this is, that our life is closely connected with the life of Christ, and proceeds from it as from its source; for we are dead in ourselves, and the life with which we flatter ourselves is a very bad death. Accordingly, when the question is, how we are to obtain life, our eyes must be directed to Christ, and his life must be conveyed to us by faith, that our consciences may be fully convinced, that, so long as Christ lives, we are free from all danger of destruction; for it is an undoubted truth, that *his life* would be nothing, when his members were dead.

20. *At that day.* Some refer this to *the day* of Pentecost; but it rather denotes the uninterrupted course, as it were, of a single day, from the time when Christ exerted the power of his Spirit till the last resurrection. From that time they began to *know*, but it was a sort of feeble beginning, because the Spirit had not yet wrought so powerfully in them. For the object of these words is, to show that we cannot, by indolent speculation, *know* what is the sacred and mystical union between us and him, and again, between him and *the Father;* but that the only way of knowing it is, when he diffuses his life in us by the secret efficacy of the Spirit; and this is the trial of faith, which I lately mentioned.

As to the manner in which this passage was formerly abused by the Arians, to prove that Christ is God only by participation and by grace, it is easy to refute their sophistry. For Christ does not speak merely of his eternal essence, but of that Divine power which was manifested in him. As *the Father* has laid up in the Son all fulness of blessings, so, on the other hand, the Son has conveyed himself entirely into us. He is said *to be in us,* because he plainly shows, by the efficacy of his Spirit, that he is the Author and the cause of our life.

21. He who hath my commandments, and keepeth them, is he that loveth me; and he that loveth me will be loved by my Father; and I will love him, and will manifest myself to him. 22. Judas (not Iscariot) saith to him, Lord, why is it¹ that thou wilt manifest thyself to us, and not to the world? 23. Jesus answered and said to him, If any one love me, he will keep my word; and my Father will love him, and we will come to him, and make our abode with him. 24. He who loveth me not keepeth not my words; and the word which you have heard is not mine, but that of the Father who sent me.

21. *He who hath my commandments.* He again repeats the former statement, that the undoubted proof of our love to him lies in our *keeping his commandments;* and the reason why he so frequently reminds the disciples of this is, that they may not turn aside from this object; for there is nothing to which we are more prone than to slide into a carnal affection, so as to love something else than Christ under the name of Christ. Such is also the import of that saying of Paul, *Though we have known Christ after the flesh, yet henceforth we know him no longer in this manner. Let us therefore be a new creature,* (2 Cor. v. 16, 17.) To HAVE *his commandments* means to be properly instructed in them; and *to* KEEP *his commandments* is to conform ourselves and our life to their rule.

And he that loveth me will be loved by my Father. Christ speaks as if men loved God before he loved them; which is absurd, for, *when we were enemies, he reconciled us to him,* (Rom. v. 10;) and the words of John are well known, *Not that we first loved him, but he first loved us,* (1 John iv. 10.) But there is no debate here about cause or effect; and therefore there is no ground for the inference, that the love with which we love Christ comes in order before the love which God has toward us; for Christ meant only, that all who *love him* will be happy, because they will also *be loved by him and by the Father;* not that God then begins to *love* them, but because they have a testimony of his love to them, as a Father, engraven on their hearts. To the same purpose is the clause which immediately follows:—

And I will manifest myself to him. Knowledge undoubtedly goes before love; but Christ's meaning was, "I will grant to those who purely observe my doctrine, that they shall

---

¹ "D'où vient?"—" Whence comes it?"

make progress from day to day in faith;" that is, " I will cause them to approach more nearly and more familiarly to me." Hence infer, that the fruit of piety is progress in the knowledge of Christ; for he who promises that he will give himself to him who has it rejects hypocrites, and causes all to make progress in faith who, cordially embracing the doctrine of the Gospel, bring themselves entirely into obedience to it. And this is the reason why many fall back, and why we scarcely see one in ten proceed in the right course; for the greater part do not deserve that he should *manifest himself to them.* It ought also to be observed, that a more abundant knowledge of Christ is here represented as an extraordinary reward of our love to Christ; and hence it follows that it is an invaluable treasure.

22. *Judas (not Iscariot) saith to him.* It is not without reason that he asks why Christ does not cause his light to be imparted[1] to more than a few persons; since he is *the Sun of Righteousness,* (Mal. iv. 2,) by whom the whole world ought to be enlightened; and, therefore, it is unreasonable that he should enlighten but a few, and not shed his light everywhere without distinction. Christ's reply does not solve the whole question; for it makes no mention of the first cause, why Christ, *manifesting himself* to a few, conceals himself from the greater part of men; for certainly he finds all men at first alike, that is, entirely alienated from him; and, therefore, he cannot choose any person who loves him, but he chooses from among his enemies those whose hearts he bends to the love of him. But he did not intend, at present, to take any notice of that distinction, which was far from the object he had in view. His design was, to exhort his disciples to the earnest study of godliness, that they might make greater progress in faith; and, therefore, he is satisfied with distinguishing them from the world by this mark, that they keep the doctrine of the Gospel.

Now, this mark comes after the commencement of faith, for it is the effect of their calling. In other passages, Christ had reminded the disciples of their being called by free grace,

---

[1] "Pourquoy Christ fera que sa lumiere sera manifestee."

and he will afterwards bring it to their recollection. At present, he only enjoins them to observe his doctrine, and to maintain godliness. By these words, Christ shows in what manner the Gospel is properly obeyed. It is, when our services and outward actions proceed from the love of Christ; for in vain do the arms, and the feet, and the whole body toil, if the love of God do not reign in the heart, to govern the outward members. Now, since it is certain that we *keep the commandments* of Christ only in so far as we *love* him, it follows that a perfect *love* of him can nowhere be found in the world, because there is no man who *keeps his commandments* perfectly; yet God is pleased with the obedience of those who sincerely aim at this end.

23. *And my Father will love him.* We have already explained that the love of God to us is not placed in the second rank, as if it came after our piety as the cause of that love, but that believers may be fully convinced that the obedience which they render to the Gospel is pleasing to God, and that they may continually expect from him fresh additions of gifts.

And we will come to him who loveth me; that is, he will feel that the grace of God dwelleth in him, and will every day receive additions to the gifts of God. He therefore speaks, not of that eternal love with which he loved us, before we were born, and even before the world was created, but since the time when he seals it on our hearts by making us partakers of his adoption. Nor does he even mean the first illumination, but those degrees of faith by which believers must continually advance, according to that saying, *Whosoever hath, it shall be given to him,* (Matth. xiii. 12.)

The Papists therefore are wrong in inferring from this passage that there are two kinds of love with which we love God. They falsely maintain that we naturally love God, before he regenerates us by his Spirit, and even that by this preparation we merit the grace of regeneration; as if Scripture did not everywhere teach, and as if experience also did not loudly proclaim, that we are altogether alienated from God, and that we are infected and filled with hatred of him, until he change our hearts. We must therefore keep in view the design of Christ, that *he and the Father will come*, to confirm believers, in uninterrupted confidence in his grace.

24. *He who loveth me not keepeth not my words.* As believers are mixed with unbelievers in the world, and as they must be agitated by various storms, as in a troubled sea, Christ again confirms them by this admonition, that they may not be drawn away by bad examples. As if he had said, " Do not look upon the world so as to depend on it; for there will always be some who despise me and my doctrine; but as for you, preserve constantly to the end the grace which you have once received." Yet he likewise intimates that the world is justly punished for its ingratitude, when it perishes in its blindness, since, by despising true righteousness, it manifests a wicked hatred towards Christ.

And the word which you hear. That the disciples may not be discouraged or waver on account of the obstinacy of the world, he again procures credit to his doctrine, by testifying that it is from God, and that it was not contrived by men on the earth. And, indeed, the strength of our faith consists in our knowing that God is our leader, and that we are founded on nothing else than his eternal truth. Whatever then may be the rage and madness of the world, let us follow the doctrine of Christ, which rises far above heaven and earth. When he says that *the word is not his*, he accommodates himself to the disciples; as if he had said that it is not human, because he teaches faithfully what has been enjoined on him by the Father. Yet we know that, in so far as he is the eternal Wisdom of God, he is the only fountain of all doctrine, and that all the prophets who have been from the beginning spoke by his Spirit.

25. These things I have spoken to you, while I remain with you. 26. But the Comforter, (who is[1]) the Holy Spirit, whom the Father will send in my name, he will teach you all things, and will bring to your remembrance all things that I have said to you. 27. Peace I leave with you, my peace I give to you. not as the world giveth, give I it to you.[2] Let not your heart be troubled, and let it not be afraid. 28. You heard

[1] " (Qui est) le Sainct Esprit."
[2] " Et je ne la vous donne point, comme le monde la donne;"—" and I give it not to you, as the world giveth it."

that I said to you, I go away, and come to you. If you loved me, you would certainly rejoice that I said, I go to the Father, for the Father is greater than I.

25. *These things I have spoken to you.* He adds this, that they may not despair, though they may have profited less than they ought to have done; for at that time he scattered a seed of doctrine, which lay hidden, and, as it were, suffocated in the disciples. He therefore exhorts them to entertain good hopes, until fruit be yielded by the doctrine which might now appear to be useless. In short, he testifies that in the doctrine which they had heard they have abundant ground of consolation, and that they ought not to seek it anywhere else. And if they do not immediately see it, he bids them be of good courage, until the Holy Spirit, who is the inward Teacher, speak the same thing in their hearts. This admonition is highly useful to all; for, if we do not immediately understand what Christ teaches, we begin to grow weary, and grudge to bestow unprofitable labour on what is obscure. But we must bring an eager desire to receive instruction; we must lend our ears and give attention, if we desire to make due proficiency in the school of God; and especially we need patience, until the Holy Spirit enable us to understand what we thought that we had often read or heard to no purpose. That the desire of learning may not be weakened in us, or that we may not fall into despair, when we do not immediately perceive the meaning of Christ speaking to us, let us know that this is spoken to us all,

The Holy Spirit will bring to your remembrance all things that I have said to you. It is indeed a punishment threatened by Isaiah against unbelievers, that the Word of God shall be to them *as a book that is sealed,* (Isa. xxix. 11;) but in this manner, also, the Lord frequently humbles his people. We ought, therefore, to wait patiently and mildly for the time of revelation, and must not, on that account, reject the word. When Christ testifies that it is the peculiar office of the Holy Spirit to teach the apostles what they had already learned from his mouth, it follows that the outward preaching will be vain and useless, if it be not accompanied by the teaching of the Spirit. God has therefore two ways of teaching; for, *first*, he sounds in our ears by the mouth of men; and, *secondly*, he addresses us inwardly by his Spirit; and he does this either at the same moment, or at different times, as he thinks fit.

But observe what are *all these things* which he promises that the Spirit will teach. *He will suggest*, he says, *or bring to your remembrance,* ALL THAT I HAVE SAID. Hence it follows, that he will not be a builder of new revelations. By this single word we may refute all the inventions which Satan has brought into the Church from the beginning, under the pretence of the Spirit. Mahomet and the Pope agree in holding this as a principle of their religion, that Scripture does not contain a perfection of doctrine, but that something loftier has been revealed by the Spirit. From the same point the Anabaptists and Libertines, in our own time, have drawn their absurd notions. But the spirit that introduces any doctrine or invention apart from the Gospel is a deceiving spirit, and not the Spirit of Christ. What is meant by *the Spirit being sent by the Father in the name of Christ,* I have already explained.

27. *Peace I leave with you.* By the word *peace* he means prosperity, which men are wont to wish for each other when they meet or part; for such is the import of the word *peace* in the Hebrew language. He therefore alludes to the ordinary custom of his nation; as if he had said, *I leave you my Farewell.* But he immediately adds, that this *peace* is of far greater value than that which is usually to be found among men, who generally have the word *peace* but coldly in their mouth, by way of ceremony, or, if they sincerely wish *peace* for any one, yet cannot actually bestow it. But Christ reminds them that *his peace* does not consist in an empty and unavailing wish, but is accompanied by the effect. In short, he says that he goes away from them in body, but that *his peace* remains with the disciples; that is, that they will be always happy through his blessing.

Let not your heart be troubled. He again corrects the alarm which the disciples had felt on account of his departure. It is no ground for alarm, he tells them; for they want only his bodily presence, but will enjoy his actual presence through the Spirit. Let us learn to be always satisfied with this kind of presence, and let us not give a loose rein to the flesh, which always binds God by its outward inventions.

28. *If you loved me you would rejoice.* The disciples unquestionably *loved* Christ, but not as they ought to have done; for some carnal affection was mixed with their *love,* so that they could not endure to be separated from him; but if they had *loved* him spiritually, there was nothing which they would have had more deeply at heart, than his return to the Father.

For the Father is greater than I. This passage has been tortured in various ways. The Arians, in order to prove that Christ is some sort of inferior God, argued that *he is less than the Father.* The orthodox Fathers, to remove all ground for such a calumny, said that this must have referred to his human nature; but as the Arians wickedly abused this testimony, so the reply given by the Fathers to their objection was neither correct nor appropriate; for Christ does not now speak either of his human nature, or of his eternal Divinity, but, accommodating himself to our weakness, places himself between God and us; and, indeed, as it has not been granted to us to reach the height of God, Christ descended to us, that he might raise us to it. *You ought to have rejoiced,* he says, *because I return to the Father;* for this is the ultimate object at which you ought to aim. By these words he does not show in what respect he differs in himself from the Father, but why he descended to us; and that was, that he might unite us to God; for until we have reached that point, we are, as it were, in the middle of the course. We too imagine to ourselves but a half-Christ, and a mutilated Christ, if he do not lead us to God.

There is a similar passage in the writings of Paul, where he says that Christ *will deliver up the kingdom to God his Father, that God may be all in all,* (1 Cor. xv. 24.) Christ certainly reigns, not only in human nature, but as he is God manifested in the flesh. In what manner, therefore, will he lay aside the kingdom? It is, because the Divinity which is now beheld in Christ's face alone, will then be openly visible in him. The only point of difference is, that Paul there describes the highest perfection of the Divine brightness, the rays of which began to shine from the time when Christ ascended to heaven. To make the matter more clear, we must use still greater plainness of speech. Christ does not here make a comparison between the Divinity of the Father and his own, nor between his own human nature and the Divine essence of the Father, but rather between his present state and the heavenly glory, to which he would soon afterwards be received; as if he had said, "You wish to detain me in the world, but it is better that I should ascend to heaven." Let us therefore learn to behold Christ humbled in the flesh, so that he may conduct us to the fountain of a blessed immortality; for he was not appointed to be our guide, merely to raise us to the sphere of the moon or of the sun, but to make us one with God the Father.

29. And I have told you now, before it take place, that, when it shall take place, you may believe. 30. Henceforth I will not talk much with you. for the prince of this world cometh, and hath nothing in me. 31. But that the world may know that I love the Father, and that I do as the Father hath commanded me. Arise, let us go hence.

29. *And I have told you now.* It was proper that the disciples should be frequently admonished on this point; for it was a secret far exceeding all human capacity. He testifies that he *foretells what shall happen, that, when it has happened, they may believe;* for it was a useful confirmation of their faith, when they brought to recollection the predictions of Christ, and saw accomplished before their eyes what they had formerly heard from his mouth. Yet it appears to be a sort of concession, as if Christ had said, "Because you are not yet capable of comprehending so deep a mystery, I bear with you till the event has happened, which will serve as an interpreter to explain this doctrine." Although for a time he seemed to speak to the deaf, yet it afterwards appeared that his words were not scattered in vain, or, as we may say, in the air, but that it was a seed thrown into the earth. Now, as Christ speaks here about his word and the accomplishment

of events, so his death, and resurrection, and ascension to heaven, are combined with doctrine, that they may produce faith in us.

30. *Henceforth I will not talk much with you.* By this word he intended to fix the attention of the disciples on himself, and to impress his doctrine more deeply on their minds; for abundance generally takes away the appetite, and we desire more eagerly what we have not in our possession, and delight more in the enjoyment of that which is speedily to be taken from us. In order, therefore, to make them more desirous of hearing his doctrines, he threatens that he will very soon go away. Although Christ does not cease to teach us during the whole course of our life, yet this statement may be applied to our use; for, since the course of our life is short, we ought to embrace the present opportunity.

For the prince of this world cometh. He might have said, in direct language, that he would soon die, and that the hour of his death was at hand; but he makes use of a circumlocution, to fortify their minds beforehand, lest, terrified by a kind of death so hideous and detestable, they should faint; for to believe in him crucified, what is it but to seek life in hell? First, he says that his power will be given to Satan; and next he adds, that he will go away, not because he is compelled to do so, but in order to obey the Father.

The devil is called *the prince of this world,* not because he has a kingdom separated from God, (as the Manicheans imagined,) but because, by God's permission, he exercises his tyranny over the world. Whenever, therefore, we hear this designation applied to the devil, let us be ashamed of our miserable condition; for, whatever may be the pride of men, they are the slaves of the devil, till they are regenerated by the Spirit of Christ; for under the term *world* is here included the whole human race. There is but one Deliverer who frees and rescues us from this dreadful slavery. Now, since this punishment was inflicted on account of the sin of the first man, and since it daily grows worse on account of new sins, let us learn to hate both ourselves and our sins. While we are held captives under the dominion of Satan, still this slavery does not free us from blame, for it is voluntary. It ought also to be observed, that what is done by wicked men is here ascribed to the devil; for, since they are impelled by Satan, all that they do is justly reckoned his work.

*And hath nothing in me.*¹ It is in consequence of the sin of Adam that Satan holds the dominion of death, and, therefore, he could not touch Christ, who is pure from all the pollution of sin, if he had not voluntarily subjected himself. And yet I think that these words have a wider meaning than that in which they are usually explained; for the ordinary interpretation is, " Satan hath found nothing in Christ, for there is nothing in him that deserves death, because he is pure from every stain of sin." But, in my opinion, Christ asserts here not only his own purity, but likewise his Divine power, which was not subject to death; for it was proper to assure the disciples that he did not yield through weakness, lest they should think less highly of his power. But in this general statement the former is also included, that, in enduring death, he was not compelled by Satan. Hence we infer, that he was substituted in our room, when he submitted to death.

31. *But that the world may know.* Some think that these words should be read as closely connected with the words, *Arise, let us go hence,* so as to make the sense complete. Others read the former part of the verse separately, and suppose that it breaks off abruptly. As it makes no great difference in regard to the meaning, I leave it to the reader to give a preference to either of these views. What chiefly deserves our attention is, that the decree of God is here placed in the highest rank; that we may not suppose that Christ was dragged to death by the violence of Satan, in such a

---

¹ This is the literal rendering of καὶ ἐν ἐμοὶ οὐκ ἔχει οὐδὲν, and corresponds to other modern versions, as, for example, the German, **und hat nichts an mir;** though Wolfius quotes a marginal reading of a German translation, **an mir wird er nicht nichts finden,**—*he will find nothing in me.* The latter agrees with a Greek reading, καὶ ἐν ἐμοὶ οὐχ εὑρήσει οὐδὲν, *and will* FIND *nothing in me;* and with another reading, καὶ ἐν ἐμοὶ οὐκ ἔχει οὐδὲν εὑρεῖν, *and hath nothing to* FIND *in me.—Ed.*

manner that anything happened contrary to the purpose of God. It was God who appointed his Son to be the Propitiator, and who determined that the sins of the world should be expiated by his death. In order to accomplish this, he permitted Satan, for a short time, to treat him with scorn; as if he had gained a victory over him. Christ, therefore, does not resist Satan, in order that he may obey the decree of his Father, and may thus offer his obedience as the ransom of our righteousness.

Arise, let us go hence. Some think that Christ, after he said these things, changed his place, and that what follows was spoken by him on the road; but as John afterwards adds, that Christ went away with his disciples beyond the brook Kedron,[1] it appears more probable that Christ intended to exhort the disciples to render the same obedience to God, of which they beheld in him so illustrious an example, and not that he led them away at that moment.

CHAPTER XV.

1. I am the true Vine, and my Father is the Husbandman. 2 Every branch in me that beareth not fruit he will take away, and every branch that beareth fruit he will prune, that it may bear more fruit. 3. You are already clean, on account of the word which I have spoken to you. 4. Abide in me, and I in you. As the branch cannot bear fruit of itself, unless it abide in the vine, so neither can you, unless you abide in me. 5. I am the Vine, you are the branches. He who abideth in me, and I in him, beareth much fruit, for without me you can do nothing. 6. If any one abide not in me, he shall be cast out, and wither as a branch; and men shall gather it, and cast it into the fire, and it shall be burned.

1. *I am the true Vine.* The general meaning of this comparison is, that we are, by nature, barren and dry, except in so far as we have been ingrafted into Christ, and draw from him a power which is new, and which does not proceed from ourselves. I have followed other commentators in rendering ἄμπελος by *vitis,* (*a vine,*) and κλήματα by *palmites,* (*branches.*) Now, *vitis (a vine)* strictly denotes the plant itself, and not a

---

[1] " Que Christ s'en alla avec ses disciples outre le torrent de Cedron."

field planted with *vines,* which the Latin writers call *vinea,* (*a vineyard;*) although it is sometimes taken for *vinea* a vineyard; as, for example, when Cicero mentions in the same breath, *pauperum agellos et* VITICULAS, *the small fields and* SMALL VINEYARDS *of the poor. Palmites (branches)* are what may be called the *arms* of the tree, which it sends out above the ground. But as the Greek word κλῆμα sometimes denotes *a vine,* and ἄμπελος, *a vineyard,* I am more disposed to adopt the opinion, that Christ compares himself to a field planted with *vines,* and compares us to the plants themselves. On that point, however, I will not enter into a debate with any person; only I wish to remind the reader, that he ought to adopt that view which appears to him to derive greater probability from the context.

First, let him remember the rule which ought to be observed in all parables; that we ought not to examine minutely every property of *the vine,* but only to take a general view of the object to which Christ applies that comparison. Now, there are three principal parts; first, that we have no power of doing good but what comes from himself; secondly, that we, having a root in him, are dressed and pruned by the Father; thirdly, that he removes the unfruitful branches, that they may be thrown into the fire and burned.

There is scarcely any one who is ashamed to acknowledge that every thing good which he possesses comes from God; but, after making this acknowledgment, they imagine that a universal grace has been given to them, as if it had been implanted in them by nature. But Christ dwells principally on this, that the vital sap—that is, all life and strength[1]—proceeds from himself alone. Hence it follows, that the nature of man is unfruitful and destitute of everything good; because no man has the nature of a *vine,* till he be implanted in him. But this is given to the elect alone by special grace. So then, the Father is the first Author of all blessings, who plants us with his hand; but the commencement of life is in Christ, since we begin to take root in him. When he calls himself *the* TRUE *vine,* the meaning is, *I am* TRULY *the vine,* and

---

[1] " C'est à dire, toute la vie et vigueur."

therefore men toil to no purpose in seeking strength anywhere else, for from none will useful fruit proceed but from *the branches* which shall be produced by me.

2. *Every branch in me that beareth not fruit.* As some men corrupt the grace of God, others suppress it maliciously, and others choke it by carelessness, Christ intends by these words to awaken anxious inquiry, by declaring that all *the branches* which shall be unfruitful will be cut off from *the vine.* But here comes a question, Can any one who is ingrafted into Christ be without fruit? I answer, many are supposed to be *in the vine,* according to the opinion of men, who actually have no root *in the vine.* Thus, in the writings of the prophets, the Lord calls the people of Israel *his vine,* because, by outward profession, they had the name of The Church.

And every branch that beareth fruit he pruneth. By these words, he shows that believers need incessant culture, that they may be prevented from degenerating; and that they produce nothing good, unless God continually apply his hand; for it will not be enough to have been once made partakers of adoption, if God do not continue the work of his grace in us. He speaks of *pruning* or *cleansing*,[1] because our flesh abounds in superfluities and destructive vices, and is too fertile in producing them, and because they grow and multiply without end, if we are not *cleansed* or *pruned*[2] by the hand of God. When he says that vines are *pruned, that they may yield more abundant fruit,* he shows what ought to be the progress of believers in the course of true religion.[3]

3. *You are already clean, on account of the word.* He reminds them that they have *already* experienced in themselves what he had said; that they have been planted in him, and have also been *cleansed* or *pruned.* He points out the means of *pruning,* namely, doctrine; and there can be no doubt that he speaks of outward preaching, for he expressly mentions *the word,* which they had heard from his mouth. Not that

---

[1] " Il parle de tailler ou purger " [2] " Repurgez et taillez."
[3] " Des fideles au cours de la vraye religion."

the word proceeding from the mouth of a man has so great efficacy, but, so far as Christ works in the heart by the Spirit, *the word* itself is the instrument of *cleansing*. Yet Christ does not mean that the apostles are pure from all sin, but he holds out to them their experience, that they may learn from it that the continuance of grace is absolutely necessary. Besides, he commends to them the doctrine of the gospel from the fruit which it produces, that they may be more powerfully excited to meditate on it continually, since it resembles the vine-dresser's knife to take away what is useless.

4. *Abide in me.* He again exhorts them to be earnest and careful in keeping the grace which they had received, for the carelessness of the flesh can never be sufficiently aroused. And, indeed, Christ has no other object in view than to keep us *as a hen keepeth her chickens under her wings,* (Matth. xxiii. 37,) lest our indifference should carry us away, and make us fly to our destruction. In order to prove that he did not begin the work of our salvation for the purpose of leaving it imperfect in the middle of the course, he promises that his Spirit will always be efficacious in us, if we do not prevent him. *Abide in me,* says he; *for I am ready to abide in you.* And again, *He who abideth in me beareth much fruit.* By these words he declares that all who have a living root in him are fruit-bearing *branches.*

5. *Without me you can do nothing.* This is the conclusion and application of the whole parable. So long as we are separate from him, we bear no fruit that is good and acceptable to God, for we are unable to do anything good. The Papists not only extenuate this statement, but destroy its substance, and, indeed, they altogether evade it; for, though in words they acknowledge that *we can do nothing without Christ,* yet they foolishly imagine that they possess some power, which is not sufficient in itself, but, being aided by the grace of God, co-operates, (as they say,) that is, works along with it;[1] for they cannot endure that man should be

---

[1] " Cooperent, (comme ils disent,) c'est à dire, besongne avec icelle."

so much annihilated as to do nothing of himself. But these words of Christ are too plain to be evaded so easily as they suppose. The doctrine invented by the Papists is, that we can do nothing without Christ, but that, aided by him, we have something of ourselves in addition to his grace. But Christ, on the other hand, declares that we can do nothing of ourselves. *The branch*, he says, *beareth not fruit of itself;* and, therefore, he not only extols the aid of his co-operating grace, but deprives us entirely of all power but what he imparts to us. Accordingly, this phrase, *without me*, must be explained as meaning, *except from me.*

Next follows another sophism; for they allege that *the branch* has something from nature, for if another *branch*, which is not fruit-bearing, be ingrafted in *the vine*, it will produce nothing. But this is easily answered; for Christ does not explain what the *branch* has naturally, before it become united to the vine, but rather means that we begin to become *branches* at the time when we are united to him. And, indeed, Scripture elsewhere shows that, before we are in him, we are dry and useless wood.

6. *If any one abide not in me.* He again lays before them the punishment of ingratitude, and, by doing so, excites and urges them to perseverance. It is indeed the gift of God, but the exhortation to fear is not uncalled for, lest our flesh, through too great indulgence, should root us out.

He is cast out, and withered, like a branch. Those who are cut off from Christ are said to *wither* like a dead branch; because, as the commencement of strength is from him, so also is its uninterrupted continuance. Not that it ever happens that any one of the elect is *dried up*, but because there are many hypocrites who, in outward appearance, flourish and are green for a time, but who afterwards, when they ought to yield fruit, show the very opposite of that which the Lord expects and demands from his people.[1]

[1] "Lesquels puis apres quand il faut rendre le fruict, monstrent tout le contraire de ce que le Seigneur attend et requiert des siens."

7. If you abide in me, and my words abide in you, you shall ask what you will,[1] and it shall be done for you 8. In this my Father is glorified, that you bear much fruit, and become my disciples 9. As the Father hath loved me, so have I loved you; abide in my love. 10. If you keep my commandments, you will abide in my love, as I also have kept my Father's commandments, and abide in his love 11. These things I have spoken to you, that my joy may abide in you, and that your joy may be full.

7. *If you abide in me.* Believers often feel that they are starved, and are very far from that rich fatness which is necessary for yielding abundant fruit. For this reason it is expressly added, Whatever those who are in Christ may need, there is a remedy provided for their poverty, as soon as they ask it from God. This is a very useful admonition; for the Lord often suffers us to hunger, in order to train us to earnestness in prayer. But if we fly to him, we shall never want what we ask, but, out of his inexhaustible abundance, he will supply us with every thing that we need, (1 Cor. i. 5.)

If my words abide in you. He means that we take root in him by faith; for as soon as we have departed from the doctrine of the Gospel, we seek Christ separately from himself. When he promises that he will grant whatever we wish, he does not give us leave to form wishes according to our own fancy. God would do what was ill fitted to promote our welfare, if he were so indulgent and so ready to yield to us; for we know well that men often indulge in foolish and extravagant desires. But here he limits the wishes of his people to the rule of praying in a right manner, and that rule subjects, to the good pleasure of God, all our affections. This is confirmed by the connection in which the words stand; for he means that his people *will* or *desire* not riches, or honours, or any thing of that nature, which the flesh foolishly desires, but the vital sap of the Holy Spirit, which enables them to bear fruit.

8. *In this my Father is glorified.* This is a confirmation of the former statement; for he shows that we ought not to

---

[1] " Demandez tout ce que vous voudrez;"—" ask whatever you will."

doubt that God will listen to the prayers of his people, when they desire to be rendered fruitful; for this contributes very greatly to his glory. But by this end or effect he likewise kindles in them the desire of doing good; for there is nothing which we ought to value more highly than that the name of God may be glorified by us. To the same effect is the latter clause, *that you may become my disciples;* for he declares that he has no one in his flock who does not *bear fruit* to the *glory* of God.

9. *As the Father hath loved me.* He intended to express something far greater than is commonly supposed; for they who think that he now speaks of the sacred *love* of God the Father, which he always had towards the Son, philosophise away from the subject; for it was rather the design of Christ to lay, as it were, in our bosom a sure pledge of God's *love* towards us. That abstruse inquiry, as to the manner in which the Father always *loved* himself in the Son, has nothing to do with the present passage. But the *love* which is here mentioned must be understood as referring to us, because Christ testifies that *the Father loves* him, as he is the Head of the Church. And this is highly necessary for us; for he who, without a Mediator, inquires how he is *loved* by God, involves him in a labyrinth, in which he will neither discover the entrance, nor the means of extricating himself. We ought therefore to cast our eyes on Christ, in whom will be found the testimony and pledge of the love of God; for the love of God was fully poured out on him, that from him it might flow to his members. He is distinguished by this title, that he is *the beloved Son*, in whom the will of the Father is satisfied, (Matth. iii. 17.) But we ought to observe the end, which is, that God may accept us in him. So, then, we may contemplate in him, as in a mirror, God's paternal love towards us all; because he is not *loved* apart, or for his own private advantage, but that he may unite us with him to the Father.

Abide in my love. Some explain this to mean, that Christ demands from his disciples mutual *love;* but others explain it better, who understand it to mean the *love* of Christ towards us. He means that we should continually enjoy that love with which he once loved us, and, therefore, that we ought to take care not to deprive ourselves of it; for many reject the grace which is offered to them, and many throw away what they once had in their hands. So, then, since we have been once received into the grace of Christ, we must see that we do not fall from it through our own fault.

The conclusion which some draw from these words, that there is no efficacy in the grace of God, unless it be aided by our stedfastness, is frivolous. For I do not admit that the Spirit demands from us no more than what is in our own power, but he shows us what we ought to do, that, if our strength be deficient, we may seek it from some other quarter. In like manner, when Christ exhorts us, in this passage, to perseverance, we must not rely on our own strength and industry, but we ought to pray to him who commands us, that he would confirm us in his love.

10. *If you keep my commandments.* He points out to us the method of perseverance. It is, to follow where he calls; for, as Paul says, *They who are in Christ walk not according to the flesh, but according to the Spirit,* (Rom. viii. 1.) For these two things are continually united, that faith which perceives the undeserved love of Christ toward us, and a good conscience and newness of life. And, indeed, Christ does not reconcile believers to the Father, that they may indulge in wickedness without reserve, and without punishment; but that, governing them by his Spirit, he may keep them under the authority and dominion of his Father. Hence it follows, that the love of Christ is rejected by those who do not prove, by true obedience, that they are his disciples.

If any one object that, in that case, the security of our salvation depends on ourselves, I reply, it is wrong to give such a meaning to Christ's words; for the obedience which believers render to him is not the cause why he continues his love toward us, but is rather the effect of his love. For whence comes it that they answer to their calling, but because they are led by the Spirit of adoption of free grace?

But again, it may be thought that the condition imposed

on us is too difficult, that we should *keep the commandments* of Christ, which contain the absolute perfection of righteousness,—a perfection which far exceeds our capacity,—for hence it follows, that the love of Christ will be useless, if we be not endued with angelical purity. The answer is easy; for when Christ speaks of the desire of living a good and holy life, he does not exclude what is the chief article in his doctrine, namely, that which alludes to righteousness being freely imputed, in consequence of which, through a free pardon, our duties are acceptable to God, which in themselves deserved to be rejected as imperfect and unholy. Believers, therefore, are reckoned as *keeping the commandments* of Christ when they apply their earnest attention to them, though they be far distant from the object at which they aim; for they are delivered from that rigorous sentence of the law, *Cursed be he that hath not confirmed all the words of this law to do them*, Deut. xxvii. 26.

As I also have kept my Father's commandments. As we have been elected in Christ, so in him the image of our calling is exhibited to us in a lively manner; and therefore he justly holds himself out to us as a pattern, to the imitation of which all the godly ought to be conformed. "In me," says he, "is brightly displayed the resemblance of those things which I demand from you; for you see how sincerely I am devoted to obedience to *my Father,* and how I persevere in this course. *My Father,* too, hath loved me, not for a moment, or for a short time, but his love toward me is constant." This conformity between the Head and the members ought to be always placed before our eyes, not only that believers may form themselves after the example of Christ, but that they may entertain a confident hope that his Spirit will every day form them anew to be better and better, that they may walk to the end in newness of life.

11. *These things I have spoken to you.* He adds, that his love is far from being unknown to the godly, but that it is perceived by faith, so that they enjoy blessed peace of conscience; for the *joy* which he mentions springs from that peace with God which is possessed by all that have been

justified by free grace. As often, then, as God's fatherly love towards us is preached, let us know that there is given to us ground for true *joy*, that, with peaceable consciences, we may be certain of our salvation.

My joy and your joy. It is called *Christ's joy* and *our joy* in various respects. It is *Christ's*, because it is given to us by him; for he is both the Author and the Cause of it. I say that he is the *Cause* of it, because we were freed from guilt, when *the chastisement of our peace was laid on him,* (Isa. liii. 5.) I call him also the Author of it, because by his Spirit he drives away dread and anxiety in our hearts, and then arises that calm cheerfulness. It is said to be *ours* for a different reason; because we enjoy it since it has been given to us. Now since Christ declares that *he spake these things, that the disciples might have joy,* we conclude from these words, that all who have duly profited by this sermon have something on which they can rest.

That my joy may abide in you. By the word *abide* he means, that it is not a fleeting or temporary *joy* of which he speaks, but a *joy* which never fails or passes away. Let us therefore learn that we ought to seek in the doctrine of Christ the assurance of salvation, which retains its vigour both in life and in death.

That your joy may be full. He adds, that this *joy* will be solid and *full;* not that believers will be entirely free from all sadness, but that the ground for *joy* will be far greater, so that no dread, no anxiety, no grief, will swallow them up; for those to whom it has been given to glory in Christ will not be prevented, either by life, or by death, or by any distresses, from bidding defiance to sadness.

12. This is my commandment, That you love one another, as I have loved you. 13. Greater love hath no one than this, that one should lay down his life for his friends. 14. You are my friends, if you do the things that I command you [1] 15. Henceforth I will not call you servants, for the servant knoweth not what his lord doeth, but I have called you friends, because I have made known to you all things that I have heard from my Father.

12. *This is my commandment.* Since it is proper that we

[1] " Tout ce que je vous commande;"—" all that I command you."

regulate our life according to the *commandment* of Christ, it is necessary, first of all, that we should understand what it is that he *wills* or *commands*. He now therefore repeats what he had formerly said, that it is his will, above all things, that believers should cherish *mutual love* among themselves. True, the love and reverence for God comes first in order, but as the true proof of it is *love* toward our neighbours, he dwells chiefly on this point. Besides, as he formerly held himself out for a pattern in maintaining the general doctrine, so he now holds himself out for a pattern in a particular instance; for he loved all his people, that they may love each other. Of the reason why he lays down no express rule, in this passage, about loving unbelievers, we have spoken under the former chapter.

13. *Greater love hath no one than this.* Christ sometimes proclaims the greatness of his love to us, that he may more fully confirm our confidence in our salvation; but now he proceeds further, in order to inflame us, by his example, to love the brethren. Yet he joins both together; for he means that we should taste by faith how inestimably delightful his goodness is, and next he allures us, in this way, to cultivate brotherly love. Thus Paul writes: *Walk in love, as Christ also hath loved us, and hath given himself for us an offering and sacrifice to God of a sweet-smelling savour,* (Eph. v. 2.) God might have redeemed us by a single word, or by a mere act of his will, if he had not thought it better to do otherwise for our own benefit, that, by not sparing his own well-beloved Son, he might testify in his person how much he cares for our salvation. But now our hearts, if they are not softened by the inestimable sweetness of Divine love, must be harder than stone or iron.

But a question is put, How did Christ die for friends, since *we were enemies, before he reconciled us,* (Rom. v. 10;) for, by expiating our sins through the sacrifice of his death, he destroyed the enmity that was between God and us? The answer to this question will be found under the third chapter, where we said that, in reference to us, there is a state of variance between us and God, till our sins are blotted out by the death of Christ; but that the cause of this grace, which has been manifested in Christ, was the perpetual love of God, with which he loved even those who were his enemies.[1] In this way, too, Christ laid down his life for those who were strangers, but whom, even while they were strangers, he loved, otherwise he would not have died for them.

14. *You are my friends.* He does not mean that we obtain so great an honour by our own merit, but only reminds them of the condition on which he receives us into favour, and deigns to reckon us among his friends; as he said a little before, *If you keep my commandments, you will abide in my love,* (ver. 10.) *For the grace of God our Saviour hath appeared, teaching us that, denying ungodliness and worldly desires, we should live soberly, and righteously, and piously, in this world,* (Titus ii. 11.) But ungodly men, who, through wicked contempt of the Gospel, wantonly oppose Christ, renounce his friendship.

15. *Henceforth I will not call you servants.* By another argument he shows his love toward the disciples, which was, that he opened his mind fully to them, as familiar communication is maintained among *friends.* "I have condescended," he says, "far more to you than a mortal man is wont to condescend to his *servants.* Let this be regarded by you, therefore, as a pledge of my love toward you, that I have, in a kind and friendly manner, explained to you the secrets of heavenly wisdom which I had heard from the Father." It is indeed a noble commendation of the Gospel, that we have the heart of Christ opened (so to speak) in it, so that we can no longer doubt of it or perceive it slightly. We have no reason for desiring to rise above the clouds, or to penetrate into the deep, (Rom. x. 6, 7,) to obtain the certainty of our salvation. Let us be satisfied with this testimony of his love toward us which is contained in the Gospel, for it will never deceive us. Moses said to the ancient people, *What nation under heaven is so highly favoured as to have God near to them, as God talketh with you this day?* (Deut. iv. 7.) But far higher is the distinction which God hath conferred on us,

---

[1] See vol. i. p. 123.

since God hath entirely conveyed himself to us in his Son. So much the greater is the ingratitude and wickedness of those who, not satisfied with the admirable wisdom of the Gospel, fly with proud eagerness to new speculations.

All that I have heard from my Father. It is certain that the disciples did not know all that Christ knew, and indeed it was impossible that they should attain to so great a height; and because the wisdom of God is incomprehensible, he distributed to each of them a certain measure of knowledge, according as he judged to be necessary. Why then does he say that he revealed *all things?* I answer, this is limited to the person and office of the Mediator. He places himself between God and us, having received out of the secret sanctuary of God those things which he should deliver to us—as the phrase is—from hand to hand. Not one of those things, therefore, which related to our salvation, and which it was of importance for us to know, was omitted by Christ in the instructions given to his disciples. Thus, so far as he was appointed to be the Master and Teacher of the Church, he heard nothing from the Father which he did not faithfully teach his disciples. Let us only have an humble desire and readiness to learn, and we shall feel that Paul has justly called the Gospel *wisdom to make men perfect,* (Col. i. 28.)

16. You have not chosen me, but I have chosen you; and I have ordained you to go and bear fruit, and that your fruit should continue; that whatever you shall ask from the Father in my name he may give you. 17. These things I command you, that you may love one another. 18 If the world hate you, you know that it hated me before it hated you. 19. If you were of the world, the world would love what was its own; but because you are not of the world, but I have chosen you out of the world, therefore the world hateth you 20. Remember the word which I said to you, The servant is not greater than his master. If they have persecuted me, they will also persecute you; if they have kept my word, they will keep yours also. 21. But all these things they will do to you on account of my name, because they know not him who sent me.

16. *You have not chosen me.* He declares still more clearly that it must not be ascribed to their own merit, but to his grace, that they have arrived at so great an honour; for when he says that *he was not chosen by them,* it is as if he had said, that whatever they have they did not obtain by

their own skill or industry. Men commonly imagine some kind of concurrence to take place between the grace of God and the will of man; but that contrast, *I chose you, I was not chosen by you,* claims, exclusively, for Christ alone what is usually divided between Christ and man; as if he had said, that a man is not moved of his own accord to seek Christ, until he has been sought by him.

True, the subject now in hand is not the ordinary *election* of believers, by which they are adopted to be the children of God, but that special *election*, by which he set apart his disciples to the office of preaching the Gospel. But if it was by free gift, and not by their own merit, that they were *chosen* to the apostolic office, much more is it certain that the *election*, by which, from being the children of wrath and an accursed seed, we become the children of God, is of free grace. Besides, in this passage Christ magnifies his grace, by which they had been *chosen* to be Apostles, so as to join with it that former election by which they had been ingrafted into the body of the Church; or rather, he includes in these words all the dignity and honour which he had conferred on them. Yet I acknowledge that Christ treats expressly of the apostleship; for his design is, to excite the disciples to execute their office diligently and faithfully.[1]

He takes, as the ground of his exhortation, the undeserved favour which he had bestowed on them; for the greater our obligations to the Lord, the more earnest ought we to be in performing the duties which he demands from us; otherwise it will be impossible for us to avoid the charge of base ingratitude. Hence it appears that there is nothing which ought more powerfully to kindle in us the desire of a holy and religious life, than when we acknowledge that we owe every thing to God, and that we have nothing that is our own; that both the commencement of our salvation, and all the parts which follow from it, flow from his undeserved mercy. Besides, how true this statement of Christ is, may be clearly perceived from the fact, that Christ *chose* to be his apostles those who might have been thought to be the

---

[1] "Diligemment et fidelement."

most unfit of all for the office; though in their person he intended to preserve an enduring monument of his grace. For, as Paul says, (1 Cor. ii. 16,) who among men shall be found fit for discharging the embassy by which God reconciles mankind to himself? Or rather, what mortal is able to represent the person of God? It is Christ alone who makes them fit by his election. Thus Paul ascribes his *apostleship* to *grace*, (Rom. i. 5,) and again mentions that *he had been separated from his mother's womb*, (Gal. i. 15.) Nay more, since we are altogether useless servants, those who appear to be the most excellent of all will not be fit for the smallest calling, till they have been *chosen*. Yet the higher the degree of honour to which any one has been raised, let him remember that he is under the deeper obligations to God.

And I have appointed you. The election is hidden till it is actually made known, when a man receives an office to which he had been appointed; as Paul, in the passage which I quoted a little ago, where he says that *he had been separated from his mother's womb*, adds, that he was created an apostle, because *it so pleased God*. His words are: *When it pleased God, who separated me from my mother's womb, and called me by his grace*, (Gal. i. 15.) Thus also the Lord testifies that he *knew* Jeremiah *before he was in his mother's womb*, (Jer. i. 5,) though he calls him to the prophetical office at the proper and appointed time. It may happen, no doubt, that one who is duly qualified enters into the office of teaching; or rather, it usually happens in the Church that no one is called till he be endued and furnished with the necessary qualifications. That Christ declares himself to be the Author of both is not wonderful; since it is only by him that God acts, and he acts along with the Father. So then, both election and ordination belong equally to both.

That you may go. He now points out the reason why he mentioned his grace. It was, to make them apply more earnestly to the work. The apostleship was not a place of honour without toil, but they had to contend with very great difficulties; and therefore Christ encourages them not to shrink from labours, and annoyances, and dangers. This argument is drawn from the end which they ought to have in view; but Christ reasons from the effect, when he says,

That you may bear fruit; for it is hardly possible that any one would devote himself earnestly and diligently to the work, if he did not expect that the labour would bring some advantage. Christ, therefore, declares that their efforts will not be useless or unsuccessful, provided that they are ready to obey and follow when he calls them.[1] For he not only enjoins on the apostles what their calling involves and demands, but promises to them also prosperity and success, that they may not be cold or indifferent. It is hardly possible to tell how great is the value of this consolation against those numerous temptations which daily befall the ministers of Christ. Whenever, then, we see that we are losing our pains, let us call to remembrance that Christ will, at length, prevent our exertions from being vain or unproductive; for the chief accomplishment of this promise is at the very time when there is no appearance of *fruit.* Scorners, and those whom the world looks upon as wise men, ridicule our attempts as foolish, and tell us that it is in vain for us to attempt to mingle heaven and earth; because the *fruit* does not yet correspond to our wishes. But since Christ, on the contrary, has promised that the happy result, though concealed for a time, will follow, let us labour diligently in the discharge of our duty amidst the mockeries of the world.

And that your fruit may abide. A question now arises, why does Christ say that this *fruit* will be perpetual? As the doctrine of the Gospel obtains souls to Christ for eternal salvation, many think that this is the perpetuity of *the fruit.* But I extend the statement much farther, as meaning that the Church will last to the very end of the world; for the labour of the apostles yields *fruit* even in the present day, and our preaching is not for a single age only, but will enlarge the Church, so that new *fruit* will be seen to spring up after our death.

When he says, *your fruit,* he speaks as if it had been obtained by their own industry, though Paul teaches that *they*

---

[1] "A obeir et suyvre où il les appellera."

who plant or water are nothing, (1 Cor. iii. 7.) And, indeed, the formation of the Church is so excellent a work of God, that the glory of it ought not to be ascribed to men. But as the Lord displays his power by the agency of men, that they may not labour in vain, he is wont to transfer to them even that which belongs peculiarly to himself. Yet let us remember that, when he so graciously commends his disciples, it is to encourage, and not to puff them up.

That your Father may give you all that you ask in my name. This clause was not added abruptly, as many might suppose; for, since the office of teaching far exceeds the power of men, there are added to it innumerable attacks of Satan, which never could be warded off but by the power of God. That the apostles may not be discouraged, Christ meets them with the most valuable aid; as if he had said, "If the work assigned to you be so great that you are unable to fulfil the duties of your office, my Father will not forsake you; for I have appointed you to be ministers of the Gospel on this condition, that my Father will have his hand stretched out to assist you, whenever you pray to him, *in my name*, to grant you assistance." And, indeed, that the greater part of teachers either languish through indolence, or utterly give way through despair, arises from nothing else than that they are sluggish in the duty of prayer.

This promise of Christ, therefore, arouses us to call upon God; for whoever acknowledges that the success of his work depends on God alone, will offer his labour to him with fear and trembling. On the other hand, if any one, relying on his own industry, disregard the assistance of God, he will either throw away his spear and shield, when he comes to the trial, or he will be busily employed, but without any advantage. Now, we must here guard against two faults, pride and distrust; for, as the assistance of God is fearlessly disregarded by those who think that the matter is already in their own power, so many yield to difficulties, because they do not consider that they fight through the power and protection of God, under whose banner they go forth to war.

17. *These things I command you.* This, too, was appropri-

ately added, that the Apostles might know that mutual love among ministers is demanded above all things, that they may be employed, with one accord, in building up the Church of God; for there is no greater hinderance than when every one labours apart, and when all do not direct their exertions to the common good. If, then, ministers do not maintain brotherly intercourse with each other, they may possibly erect some large heaps, but utterly disjointed and confused; and, all the while, there will be no building of a Church.

18. *If the world hate you.* After having armed the Apostles for the battle, Christ exhorts them likewise to patience; for the Gospel cannot be published without instantly driving the world to rage. Consequently, it will never be possible for godly teachers to avoid the hatred of the world. Christ gives them early information of this, that they may not be instances of what usually happens to raw recruits, who, from want of experience, are valiant before they have seen their enemies, but who tremble as soon as the battle is commenced. And not only does Christ forewarn his disciples, that nothing may happen to them which is new and unexpected, but likewise confirms them by his example; for it is not reasonable that Christ should be *hated by the world*, and that we, who represent his person, should have the world on our side, which is always like itself.

You know. I have translated the verb γινώσκετε in the indicative mood, *you know;* but if any one prefer to translate it in the imperative mood, *know ye,* I have no objection, for it makes no change in the meaning. There is greater difficulty in the phrase which immediately follows, πρῶτον ὑμῶν, *before you;* for when he says that he is *before* the disciples, this may be referred either to *time* or to *rank.* The former exposition has been more generally received, namely, that Christ *was hated by the world* BEFORE *the Apostles were hated.* But I prefer the second exposition, namely, that Christ, who is far exalted above them, was not exempted from the hatred of the world, and therefore his ministers ought not to refuse the same condition; for the phraseology is the same as that which we have seen twice before, in the 27th and 30th verses of the first chapter of this book, *He who cometh after me is preferred to me,* (ὅτι πρῶτός μου ἦν,) *for he was before me.*

19. *If you were of the world.* This is another consolation, that the reason why they are *hated by the world* is, that they have been separated from it. Now, this is their true happiness and glory, for in this manner they have been rescued from destruction.

But I have chosen you out of the world. To choose means here *to separate.* Now, if they were *chosen out of the world*, it follows that they were a part *of the world*, and that it is only by the mercy of God that they are distinguished from the rest who perish. Again, by the term, *the world*, Christ describes, in this passage, all who have not been regenerated by the Spirit of God; for he contrasts the Church with *the world*, as we shall see more fully under the seventeenth chapter. And yet this doctrine does not contradict the exhortation of Paul, *Be at peace with all men, as far as lieth in you,* (Rom. xii. 18;) for the exception which he adds amounts to saying, that we ought to see what is right and proper for us to do, that no man, by seeking to please *the world*, may give himself up to its corruptions.

But there is still another objection that may be urged; for we see that it commonly happens that wicked men, who are *of the world*, are not only *hated*, but accursed by others. In this respect, certainly, *the world loveth* not *what is its own.* I reply, earthly men, who are regulated by the perception of their flesh, never have a true hatred of sin, but only so far as they are affected by the consideration of their own convenience or injury. And yet the intention of Christ was not to deny that *the world* foams and rages within itself by internal quarrels. He only intended to show, that *the world hates* nothing in believers but what is of God. And hence, too, it plainly appears how foolish are the dreams of the Anabaptists, who conclude from this single argument that they are the servants of God, because they displease the greater part of men. For it is easy to reply, that many who are *of the world* favour their doctrine, because they are delighted at the thought of having every thing in shameful confusion; while many who are *out of the world* hate it, because they are desirous that the good order of the state should remain unbroken.

20. *Remember the word.* It might also be read in the indicative mood, *You remember the word*, and the meaning is not very different; but I think that it is more suitable to read it in the imperative mood, *Remember the word.* It is a confirmation of what Christ had spoken immediately before, when he said that he was hated by the world, though he was far more excellent than his disciples; for it is unreasonable that the condition of *the servant* should be better than that of *his master.* Having spoken of persons, he likewise makes mention of doctrine.

If they have kept my word, they will keep yours also. Nothing gives greater uneasiness to the godly than when they see the doctrine, which is of God, haughtily despised by men; for it is truly shocking and dreadful, and the sight of it might shake the stoutest heart. But when we remember, on the other hand, that not less obstinate resistance was manifested against the Son of God himself, we need not wonder that the doctrine of God is so little reverenced among men. When he calls it *his doctrine* and *their doctrine*, this refers to the ministry. Christ is the only Teacher of the Church; but he intended that *his doctrine,* of which he had been the first Teacher, should be afterwards preached by the apostles.

21. *But all these things they will do to you.* As the fury of the world is monstrous, when it is so enraged against the doctrine of its own salvation, Christ assigns the reason to be, that it is hurried on by blind ignorance to its own destruction; for no man would deliberately engage in battle against God. It is blindness and ignorance of God, therefore, that hurries on the world, so that it does not hesitate to make war with Christ. We ought, then, always to observe the cause of this conduct, and the true consolation consists in nothing else than the testimony of a good conscience. It should also excite gratitude in our minds, that, while the world perishes in its blindness, God hath given to us his light. Yet let it

be understood that hatred of Christ arises from stupidity of mind, when God is not known; for, as I have often said, unbelief is blind; not that wicked men do not understand or know anything, but because all the knowledge that they have is confused, and quickly vanishes away. On this subject I have elsewhere treated more largely.

22. If I had not come and spoken to them, they would not have sin, but now they have no excuse for their sin. 23. He who hateth me hateth my Father also. 24 If I had not done among them the works which no other man did, they would not have had sin; but now have they both seen and hated both me and my Father. 25. But that the word may be fulfilled which is written in their law, They have hated me without a cause. 26. But when the Comforter is come, whom I will send to you from the Father, the Spirit of truth, who proceedeth from the Father, will testify of me 27. And you also will bear testimony, *(or, are witnesses,)* because from the beginning you are with me.

22. *If I had not come.* He had said that the Jews regarded the Gospel with hatred, because they did not know God. Lest any one should think that this tended to alleviate their guilt, he adds, that it is through malice that they are blind, just as if one were to shut his eyes, that he might not be compelled to see the light. For otherwise it might have been brought as an objection against Christ, "If they do not know thy Father, how comes it that thou dost not cure their ignorance? Why didst thou not at least make trial whether they were altogether incapable of being taught, or not?" He replies, that he has performed the duty of a good and faithful Teacher, but without success, because their malice would not suffer them to acquire soundness of mind. In the person of those men he intended to strike terror into all who reject the truth of God, when it is offered to them, or intentionally fight against it, when it is known. And though a dreadful vengeance awaits them, still Christ, in this passage, looks chiefly to his own disciples, to animate them by the confident and well-grounded expectation of victory, lest, at any time, they should yield to the malice of wicked men; for when we learn that such will be the issue, we may already triumph, as if we were in the midst of the battle.

They would not have sin. It may be thought that Christ intended by these words to say, that there is no other sin but unbelief; and there are some who think so. Augustine speaks more soberly, but he approaches to that opinion; for, since faith forgives and blots out all sins, he says, that the only sin that damns a man is unbelief. This is true, for unbelief not only hinders men from being delivered from the condemnation of death, but is the source and cause of all evils. But the whole of that reasoning is inapplicable to the present passage; for the word *sin* is not taken in a general sense, but as related to the subject which is now under consideration; as if Christ had said, that their ignorance is utterly inexcusable, because in his person they maliciously rejected God; just as if we were to pronounce a person to be innocent, just, and pure, when we wished merely to acquit him of a single crime of which he had been accused. Christ's acquittal of them, therefore, is confined to one kind of *sin*, because it takes away from the Jews every pretence of ignorance in this *sin*[1] of despising and hating the Gospel.

But there is still another question that arises: "Was not unbelief sufficient to condemn men before the coming of Christ?" There are fanatics who reason inconclusively from this passage, that all who died before the coming of Christ died without faith, and remained in a state of doubt and suspense till Christ manifested himself to them; as if there were not many passages of Scripture which testify that their conscience alone was sufficient to condemn them. *Death*, says Paul, *reigned in the world even to Moses*, (Rom. v. 14.) And again he declares, that *they who have sinned without law shall perish without law*, (Rom. ii. 12.)

What, then, does Christ mean? There is undoubtedly an admission made in these words, by which he means that the Jews have nothing more to offer in extenuation of their guilt, since they knowingly and wilfully rejected the life which was offered to them. Thus the excuse which he makes for them does not free them from all blame, but only extenuates the heinousness of their crime, according to that saying, *The servant, who knoweth the will of his master, and despiseth it, shall be severely punished.*[2] For it was not the intention of Christ

---

[1] "En ce peché."
[2] The Author quotes, as he often does, from memory; but the passage

here to promise pardon to any, but to hold his enemies convicted, who had obstinately rejected the grace of God, that it might be fully evident that they were unworthy of all pardon and mercy.

If I had not come, and SPOKEN TO THEM. It ought to be observed, that he does not speak of his coming, as viewed by itself, but as connected with his doctrine; for they would not have been held guilty of so great a crime on account of his bodily presence alone, but the contempt of the doctrine made them utterly inexcusable.

23. *He who hateth me hateth my Father also.* This is a remarkable passage, which teaches us that no man can hate the doctrine of the Gospel without manifesting his impiety against God. There are many, indeed, who profess differently in words; for, though they abhor the Gospel, still they wish to be thought very good servants of God; but it is false, for a contempt of God is concealed within. In this manner Christ discovers the hypocrisy of many by the light of his doctrine; and on this subject we have spoken more largely under that passage, *Whosoever doeth what is evil hateth the light*,[1] (John iii. 20,) and under that passage, *He who honoureth not the Son honoureth not the Father*,[2] (John v. 23.)

24. *If I had not done among them the works.* Under the word *works* he includes, in my opinion, all the proofs which he gave of his Divine glory; for by miracles, and by the power of the Holy Spirit, and by other demonstrations, he clearly proved that he was the Son of God, so that in him was plainly seen the majesty *of the Only-begotten Son,* as we have seen under the 14th verse of the first chapter.[3] It is commonly objected, that he did not perform more miracles or greater miracles than Moses and the Prophets. The answer is well known, that Christ is more eminent in miracles in this respect, that he was not merely a minister, like the rest, but

stands thus · *That servant, who knew his master's will, and did not make himself ready, nor did according to his will, shall be beaten with many stripes,* (Luke xii. 47.)—*Ed.*

[1] See vol. i. p. 128.   [2] See vol. i. p. 199.   [3] See vol. i. p. 47.

was strictly the Author of them; for he employed his own name, his own authority, and his own power, in performing miracles. But, as I have said, he includes in general all the testimonies of heavenly and spiritual power by which his Divinity was displayed.

They have seen and hated. He concludes that his enemies cannot escape by any shifts to which they may have recourse, since they despised his power, which evidently was altogether Divine; for God had openly manifested his Divinity in the Son; and therefore it would serve no purpose for them to say that they had only to do with a mortal man. This passage reminds us to consider attentively the works of God, in which, by displaying his power, he wishes us to render the honour which is due to him. Hence it follows, that all who obscure the gifts of God, or who contemptuously overlook them, are ungrateful to God, and malicious.

25. *But that the word may be fulfilled.* What is contrary to nature appears to be incredible. But nothing is more contrary to reason than to hate God; and, therefore, Christ says that so great was the malice with which their minds were envenomed, that *they hated him without a cause.* Christ quotes a passage from Ps. xxxv. 19, which, he says, is now *fulfilled.* Not that the same thing did not happen, formerly, to David, but to reprove the obstinate malice of the nation, which reigned perpetually from age to age, being continued from grandfathers to grandchildren in unbroken succession; as if he had said, that they were in no respect better than their fathers, who *hated* David *without a cause.*

Which is written in their Law. By the word *Law,* he means the Psalms; for the whole doctrine of the Prophets was nothing else than an appendage to *the Law;* and we know that the ministry of Moses lasted till the time of Christ. He calls it THEIR *Law,* not as an expression of respect for them, but to wound them more deeply by a designation which was well known among them; as if he had said, "They have *a Law* transmitted to them by hereditary right, in which they see their morals painted to the life."

26. *But when the Comforter is come.* After having explained to the apostles that the Gospel ought not to be less highly valued by them, because it has many adversaries, even within the Church itself; Christ now, in opposition to the wicked fury of those men, produces the testimony of the Spirit, and if their consciences rest on this testimony, they will never be shaken; as if he had said, " True, the world will rage against you; some will mock, and others will curse your doctrine; but none of their attacks will be so violent as to shake the firmness of your faith, when *the Holy Spirit* shall have been given to you to establish you by his testimony." And, indeed, when the world rages on all sides, our only protection is, that the truth of God, sealed by the Holy Spirit on our hearts, despises and defies all that is in the world; for, if it were subject to the opinions of men, our faith would be overwhelmed a hundred times in a day.

We ought, therefore, to observe carefully in what manner we ought to remain firm among so many storms. It is because *we have received, not the spirit of the world, but the Spirit which is of God, that we may know the things which have been given to us by God,* (1 Cor. ii. 12.) This single Witness powerfully drives away, scatters, and overturns, all that the world rears up to obscure or crush the truth of God. All who are endued with this Spirit are so far from being in danger of falling into despondency on account of the hatred or contempt of the world, that every one of them will obtain a glorious victory over the whole world. Yet we must beware of relying on the good opinion of men; for so long as faith shall wander in this manner, or rather, as soon as it shall have gone out of the sanctuary of God, it must become involved in miserable uncertainty. It must, therefore, be brought back to the inward and secret testimony of the Spirit, which, believers know, has been given to them from heaven.

The Spirit is said *to testify of Christ,* because he retains and fixes our faith on him alone, that we may not seek elsewhere any part of our salvation. He calls him also the *Comforter,* that, relying on his protection, we may never be alarmed; for by this title Christ intended to fortify our faith, that it may not yield to any temptations. When he calls him *the Spirit of truth,* we must apply the term to the matter in hand; for we must presuppose a contrast to this effect, that, when they have not this Witness, men are carried about in various ways, and have no firm resting-place, but, wherever he speaks, he delivers the minds of men from all doubt and fear of being deceived.

When he says that *he will send him from the Father*, and, again, that *he proceedeth from the Father*, he does so in order to increase the weight of his authority; for the testimony of *the Spirit* would not be sufficient against attacks so powerful, and against efforts so numerous and fierce, if we were not convinced that *he proceedeth from God*. So then it is Christ who sends the Spirit, but it is from the heavenly glory, that we may know that it is not a gift of men, but a sure pledge of Divine grace. Hence it appears how idle was the subtilty of the Greeks, when they argued, on the ground of these words, that the Spirit does not *proceed* from the Son; for here Christ, according to his custom, mentions *the Father*, in order to raise our eyes to the contemplation of his Divinity.

27. *And you also bear testimony.* Christ means that the testimony of *the Spirit* will not be of such a nature that the apostles shall have it for their private advantage, or that they alone shall enjoy it, but that by them it will be widely diffused, because they will be organs of the Holy Spirit, as, indeed, he spoke by their mouth. We now see in what way *faith is by hearing*, (Rom. x. 17,) and yet it derives its certainty from the *seal* and *earnest of the Spirit*, (Eph. i. 13, 14.) Those who do not sufficiently know the darkness of the human mind imagine that faith is formed naturally by hearing and preaching alone;[1] and there are many fanatics who disdain the outward preaching, and talk in lofty terms about secret revelations and inspirations, (ἐνθουσιασμοὺς.) But we see how Christ joins these two things together; and, therefore, though there is no faith till the Spirit of God seal our minds and hearts, still we must not go to seek visions or oracles in the clouds; but the word, *which is neár us, in our mouth and heart*, (Rom. x. 8,) must keep all our senses bound and fixed

[1] "De la seule ouye et predication."

on itself, as Isaiah says beautifully : *My Spirit that is upon thee, and my words which I have put in thy mouth, shall not depart out of thy mouth, nor out of the mouth of thy seed, nor out of the mouth of thy seed's seed, saith the Lord, from henceforth and for ever,* (Isa. lix. 21.)

Because you are with me from the beginning. This clause was added in order to inform us that so much the greater credit is due to the apostles on this ground, that they were eye-witnesses of what they relate; as John says, *what we have heard, what we have seen, what our hands have handled, we declare to you,* (1 John i. 1;) for thus the Lord intended to provide for our welfare in every possible way, that nothing might be wanting for a full confirmation of the Gospel.

CHAPTER XVI.

1. These things I have spoken to you, that you may not be offended. 2. They will drive you out of the synagogues; yea, the time cometh, that whosoever shall kill you will think that he offereth service to God. 3 And they will do these things to you, because they have not known the Father, nor me 4 But these things I have spoken to you, that, when the time shall come, you may remember that I told you of them. And I told you not these things at the beginning, because I was with you. 5. And now I go to him who sent me, and none of you asketh me, Whither goest thou? 6. But because I have told you these things, sorrow hath filled your hearts. 7. But I tell you the truth, It is expedient for you that I go away · for if I go not away, the Comforter will not come to you; but if I shall go away, I will send him to you

1. *These things I have spoken to you.* He again states that none of *those things which he has spoken* are superfluous; for, since wars and contests await them, it is necessary that they should be provided beforehand with the necessary arms. Yet he also means that, if they meditate deeply on this doctrine, they will be fully prepared for resistance. Let us remember that what he then said to the disciples is also spoken to us. And, first, we ought to understand that Christ does not send his followers into the field unarmed, and, therefore, that, if any man fail in this warfare, his own indolence alone is to blame. And yet we ought not to wait till the struggle be actually commenced, but ought rather to endeavour to become

well acquainted with these discourses of Christ, and to render them familiar to our minds, so that we may march into the field of battle, as soon as it is necessary; for we must not doubt that the victory is in our hands, so long as those admonitions of Christ shall be deeply imprinted on our minds. For, when he says, THAT YOU MAY NOT *be offended*, he means that there is no danger, lest anything turn us aside from the right course. But how few there are that learn this doctrine in a proper manner, is evident from this fact, that they who think that they know it by heart when they are beyond arrow-shot, are no sooner obliged to enter into actual combat than they give way, as if they were utterly ignorant, and had never received any instruction.[1] Let us, therefore, accustom ourselves to use this armour in such a manner that it may never drop out of our hands.

2. *They will drive you out of the synagogues.* This was no light offence to disturb their minds, that they were to be banished like wicked men from the assembly of the godly, or, at least, of those who boasted that they were the people of God, and gloried in the title of *The Church;* for believers are subject not only to persecutions, but to ignominy and reproaches, as Paul tells us, (1 Cor. iv. 12, 13.) But Christ bids them stand firm against this attack; because, though they be *banished from the synagogues,* still they remain within the kingdom of God. His statement amounts to this, that we ought not to be dismayed by the perverse judgments of men, but ought to endure boldly the reproach of the cross of Christ, satisfied with this single consideration, that our cause, which men unjustly and wickedly condemn, is approved by God.

Hence too we infer, that the ministers of the Gospel not only are ill treated by the avowed enemies of the faith, but sometimes also endure the greatest reproaches from those who appear to belong to the Church, and who are even regarded as its pillars. The scribes and priests, by whom the apostles were condemned, boasted that they were appointed

---

[1] " Et que jamais ils n'en eussent ouy parler."

by God to be judges of the Church; and, indeed, the ordinary government of the Church was in their hands, and the office of judging was from God, and not from men. But by their tyranny, they had corrupted the whole of that order which God had appointed. The consequence was, that the power which had been given to them for edification, was nothing else than a cruel oppression of the servants of God; and excommunication, which ought to have been a medicine for purifying the Church, was turned to an opposite purpose, for driving away from it the fear of God.

Since the apostles knew this by experience, in their own age, we have no reason to be greatly alarmed at the Pope's excommunications, with which he thunders against us on account of the testimony of the Gospel; for we ought not to fear that they will do us any more injury than those ancient excommunications which were made against the apostles. Nay more, nothing is more desirable than to be driven out of that assembly from which Christ is banished. Yet let us observe that, though the abuse of excommunication was so gross, still it did not effect the destruction of that discipline which God had appointed in his Church from the beginning; for, though Satan devotes his utmost efforts to corrupt all the ordinances of God, we must not yield to him, so as to take away, on account of corruptions, what God has appointed to be perpetual. Excommunication, therefore, not less than Baptism and the Lord's Supper, must be brought back, by the correction of abuses, to its pure and lawful use.

But the hour cometh. Christ dwells still more largely on this *offence,* that the enemies of the Gospel lay claim to so much authority, that they think they are offering sacrifices to God when they slay believers. It is sufficiently hard in itself, that innocent people should be cruelly tormented, but it is far more grievous and distressing that those outrages, which wicked men commit against the children of God, should be reckoned punishments justly due to them on account of their crimes. But we ought to be so fully assured of the protection of a good conscience, as to endure patiently to be oppressed for a time, till Christ appear from heaven, to defend his cause and ours.

It may be thought strange, however, that the enemies of the truth, though they are conscious of their own wickedness, not only impose on men, but even in the presence of God lay claim to praise for their unjust cruelty. I reply, hypocrites, though their conscience accuses them, always resort to flatteries to deceive themselves. They are ambitious, cruel, and proud, but they cover all these vices with the cloak of zeal, that they may indulge in them without restraint. To this is added what may be called a furious drunkenness, after having tasted the blood of martyrs.

3. *And they will do these things.* Not without good reason does Christ frequently remind the apostles of this consideration, that there is only one reason why unbelievers are so greatly enraged against them. It is, because they do not know God. And yet this is not said for the purpose of extenuating their guilt, but that the apostles may boldly despise their blind fury; for it often happens that the authority which wicked men possess, and the lustre which shines in them, shake modest and pious minds. But Christ, on the other hand, enjoins his followers to rise with holy magnanimity, to despise their adversaries, who are impelled by nothing else than error and blindness; for this is our wall of brass, when we are fully persuaded that God is on our side, and that they who oppose us are destitute of reason. Again, these words remind us, what a serious evil it is not to know God, since it leads even those who have murdered their own parents to expect praise and approbation for their wickedness.

4. *That when the hour cometh, you may remember.* He repeats what he had already said, that this is not a philosophy fitted only for a season of leisure, but that it is adapted to practice and use, and that he now discourses on these matters, that they may actually demonstrate that they have not been taught in vain. When he says, *that you may remember,* he enjoins them, first, to lay up in their minds what they have heard; secondly, to remember them, when they shall be re-

quired to put them in practice; and, lastly, he declares that no small importance attaches to the fact, that he utters predictions of future events.

And I told you not these things at the beginning. As the apostles were still weak and tender, so long as Christ conversed with them in the flesh, their singularly good and indulgent Master spared them, and did not suffer them to be urged beyond what they were able to bear. At that time, therefore, they had no great need of confirmation, while they enjoyed leisure and freedom from persecution; but now he tells them that they must change their mode of life, and as a new condition awaits them, he likewise exhorts them to prepare for a conflict.

5. *And now I go to him who sent me.* By a very excellent consolation he assuages the grief which they might feel on account of his departure, and this was highly necessary. They who had hitherto been allowed to remain at their ease, were called to severe and arduous battles for the future. What, then, would have become of them, if they had not known that Christ was in heaven, as the guardian of their salvation? For *to go to the Father* is nothing else than to be received into the heavenly glory, in order to possess the highest authority. This is held out to them, therefore, as a solace and remedy of grief, that, though Christ be absent from them in body, yet he will sit at the right hand of the Father, to protect believers by his power.

Here Christ reproves the apostles for two faults; first, that they were too much attached to the visible presence of his flesh; and, secondly, that, when this had been taken away, they were seized with grief, and did not lift their eyes to a higher region. The same thing happens to us; for we always hold Christ bound by our senses, and then, if he do not appear to us according to our desire, we contrive for ourselves a ground of despair.

And none of you asketh me, Whither goest thou? It may appear to be an unfounded charge against the apostles, that they *did not ask whither* their Master *was going;* for they had formerly inquired at him on this subject with great earnestness. But the answer is easy. When they inquired, they did not raise their minds to confidence, and this was the chief duty which they were bound to perform. The meaning therefore is, "As soon as you hear of my departure, you become alarmed, and do not consider *whither I am going,* or for what purpose I go away."

7. *Yet I tell you the truth.* That they may no longer wish to have him present before their eyes, he testifies that his absence will be advantageous, and makes use of a sort of oath; for we are carnal, and consequently nothing is more difficult than to tear from our minds this foolish inclination, by which we attempt to draw down Christ from heaven to us. He explains where the advantage lies, by saying, that the Holy Spirit could not be given to them, if he did not leave the world. But far more advantageous and far more desirable is that presence of Christ, by which he communicates himself to us through the grace and power of his Spirit, than if he were present before our eyes. And here we must not put the question, "Could not Christ have drawn down the Holy Spirit while he dwelt on earth?" For Christ takes for granted all that had been decreed by the Father; and, indeed, when the Lord has once pointed out what he wishes to be done, to dispute about what is possible would be foolish and pernicious.

8 And when he is come, he will convince the world of sin, and of righteousness, and of judgment 9. Of sin, because they believe not in me · 10. Of righteousness, because I go to my Father, and you see me no more: 11. Of judgment, because the prince of this world hath been judged. 12. I have yet many things to say to you, but you cannot bear them now. 13 But when he, the Spirit of truth, is come, he will lead you into all truth, for he will not speak from himself, but will speak all that he has heard, and will declare to you the things that are to come. 14. He will glorify me, for he will take of what is mine, and will declare it to you. 15. All things that the Father hath are mine; therefore I said to you, He will take of what is mine, and will declare it to you.

8. *And when he is come.* Passing by the diversity of expositions, which we have received in consequence of the obscurity of the passage, I shall only state what appears to me to be in accordance with Christ's true meaning. He had promised his *Spirit* to the disciples; and now he praises the excellence of the gift from its effect, because this *Spirit* will not only guide,

support, and protect them in private, but will extend more widely his power and efficacy.

He will convince the world; that is, he will not remain shut up in you, but his power will go forth from you to be displayed to the whole world. He therefore promises to them a *Spirit,* who will be the Judge of the world, and by whom their preaching will be so powerful and efficacious, that it will bring into subjection those who formerly indulged in unbounded licentiousness, and were restrained by no fear or reverence.

It ought to be observed, that in this passage Christ does not speak of secret revelations, but of the power of the Spirit, which appears in the outward doctrine of the Gospel, and in the voice of men. For how comes it that the voice proceeding from the mouth of a man[1] penetrates into the hearts, takes root there, and at length yields fruit, changing hearts of stone into hearts of flesh, and renewing men, but because the Spirit of Christ quickens it? Otherwise it would be a dead letter and a useless sound, as Paul says in that beautiful passage, in which he boasts of being *a minister of the Spirit,* (2 Cor. iii. 6,) because God wrought powerfully in his doctrine. The meaning therefore is, that, though the Spirit had been given to the apostles, they would be endued with a heavenly and Divine power, by which they would exercise jurisdiction over the whole world. Now, this is ascribed to the Spirit rather than to themselves, because they will have no power of their own, but will be only ministers and organs, and the Holy Spirit will be their director and governor.[2]

Under the term *world* are, I think, included not only those who would be truly converted to Christ, but hypocrites and reprobates. For there are two ways in which *the Spirit convinces* men by the preaching of the Gospel. Some are moved in good earnest, so as to bow down willingly, and to assent willingly to the *judgment* by which they are condemned. Others, though they are convinced of guilt and cannot escape, yet do not sincerely yield, or submit themselves to the authority and jurisdiction of the Holy Spirit, but, on the contrary,

---

[1] "La voix sortant de la bouche d'un homme."
[2] "Leur conducteur et gouverneur."

being subdued they groan inwardly, and, being overwhelmed with confusion, still do not cease to cherish obstinacy within their hearts.

We now perceive in what manner the Spirit was to CONVINCE *the world* by the apostles. It was, because God revealed his *judgment* in the Gospel, by which their consciences were struck, and began to perceive their evils and the grace of God. For the verb ἐλέγχειν here signifies *to convince* or *convict;* and, for understanding this passage, not a little light will be obtained from the words of the Apostle Paul, when he says, *If all shall prophesy, and an unbeliever or unlearned man enter, he is* CONVICTED *by all, he is judged by all, and thus shall the secrets of his heart be made manifest,* (1 Cor. xiv. 23.) In that passage Paul speaks particularly of one kind of *conviction,* that is, when the Lord brings his elect to repentance by the Gospel; but this plainly shows in what manner *the Spirit* of God, by the sound of the human voice, constrains men, who formerly were not accustomed to his yoke, to acknowledge and submit to his authority.

A question now arises, For what purpose did Christ say this? Some think that he points out the cause of the hatred which he had mentioned; as if he had said, that the reason why they will be hated by *the world* is, that *the Spirit,* on the other hand, will earnestly solicit *the world* by means of them. But I rather agree with those who tell us that the design of Christ was different, as I stated briefly at the commencement of the exposition of this verse; for it was of great importance that the apostles should know that the gift of *the Spirit,* which had been promised to them, was of no ordinary value. He therefore describes its uncommon excellence, by saying that God will, in this way, erect his tribunal for *judging* the whole *world.*

9. *Of sin.* It now remains that we see what it is to *convince of sin.* Christ appears to make unbelief the only cause *of sin,* and this is tortured by commentators in various ways; but, as I have already said, I do not intend to detail the opinions which have been held and advanced. First, it ought to be observed, that the *judgment of the Spirit* commences with

the demonstration *of sin;* for the commencement of spiritual instruction is, that men born in *sin* have nothing in them but what leads to *sin.* Again, Christ mentioned *unbelief,* in order to show what is the nature of men in itself; for, since faith is the bond by which he is united to us, until we believe in him, we are out of him and separated from him. The import of these words is as if he had said, " *When the Spirit is come,* he will produce full conviction that, apart from me, *sin* reigns in *the world;*" and, therefore, unbelief is here mentioned, because it separates us from Christ, in consequence of which nothing is left to us but *sin.* In short, by these words he condemns the corruption and depravity of human nature, that we may not suppose that a single drop of integrity is in us without Christ.

10. *Of righteousness.* We must attend to the succession of steps which Christ lays down. He now says that *the world* must be *convinced* OF RIGHTEOUSNESS; for men will never hunger and thirst for *righteousness,* but, on the contrary, will disdainfully reject all that is said concerning it, if they have not been moved by a conviction *of sin.* As to believers particularly, we ought to understand that they cannot make progress in the Gospel till they have first been humbled; and this cannot take place, till they have acknowledged their sins. It is undoubtedly the peculiar office of the Law to summon consciences to the judgment-seat of God, and to strike them with terror; but the Gospel cannot be preached in a proper manner, till it lead men from *sin* to *righteousness,* and from death to life; and, therefore, it is necessary to borrow from the Law that first clause of which Christ spoke.

By *righteousness* must here be understood that which is imparted to us through the grace of Christ. Christ makes it to consist in his ascension to the Father, and not without good reason; for, as Paul declares that he *rose for our justification,* (Rom. iv. 25,) so he now sits at the right hand of the Father in such a manner as to exercise all the authority that has been given to him, and thus to *fill all things,* (Eph. iv. 10.) In short, from the heavenly glory he fills the world with the sweet savour of his *righteousness.* Now, *the Spirit* declares, by the Gospel, that this is the only way in which we are accounted *righteous.* Next to the conviction *of sin,* this is the second step, that *the Spirit* should *convince the world* what true *righteousness* is; namely, that Christ, by his ascension to heaven, has established the kingdom of life, and now sits at the right hand of the Father, to confirm true *righteousness.*

11. *Of judgment.* Those who understand the word (κρίσεως) *judgment* as signifying *condemnation,* have some argument on their side; for Christ immediately adds, that *the prince of this world hath been judged.* But I prefer a different opinion, namely, that, the light of the Gospel having been kindled, *the Spirit* manifests that the world has been brought into a state of good order by the victory of Christ, by which he overturned the authority of Satan; as if he had said, that this is a true restoration, by which all things are reformed, when Christ alone holds the kingdom, having subdued and triumphed over Satan. *Judgment,* therefore, is contrasted with what is confused and disordered, or, to express it briefly, it is the opposite (τῆς ἀταξίας) of *confusion,* or, we might call it *righteousness,* a sense which it often bears in Scripture. The meaning therefore is, that Satan, so long as he retains the government, perplexes and disturbs all things, so that there is an unseemly and disgraceful confusion in the works of God; but when he is stripped of his tyranny by Christ, then the world is restored, and good order is seen to reign. Thus *the Spirit convinces the world of judgment;* that is, having vanquished the prince of wickedness, Christ restores to order those things which formerly were torn and decayed.

12. *I have still many things to say to you.* Christ's discourse could not have so much influence over his disciples, as to prevent their ignorance from still keeping them in perplexity about *many things;* and not only so, but they scarcely obtained a slight taste of those things which ought to have imparted to them full satisfaction, had it not been for the obstruction arising from the weakness of the flesh. It was, therefore, impossible but that the consciousness of their poverty should oppress them with fear and anxiety. But

Christ meets it by this consolation, that, when they have received the Spirit, they will be new men, and altogether different from what they were before.

But you are not able to bear them now. When he says that, were he to tell them anything more, or what was loftier, they would *not be able to bear it*, his object is to encourage them by the hope of better progress, that they may not lose courage; for the grace which he was to bestow on them ought not to be estimated by their present feelings, since they were at so great a distance from heaven. In short, he bids them be cheerful and courageous, whatever may be their present weakness. But as there was nothing else than doctrine on which they could rely, Christ reminds them that he had accommodated it to their capacity, yet so as to lead them to expect that they would soon afterwards obtain loftier and more abundant instruction; as if he had said, "If what you have heard from me is not yet sufficient to confirm you, have patience for a little; for ere long, having enjoyed the teaching of the Spirit, you will need nothing more; he will remove all the ignorance that now remains in you."

Now arises a question, What were those things which the apostles *were not yet able* to learn? The Papists, for the purpose of putting forward their inventions as the oracles of God, wickedly abuse this passage. "Christ," they tell us, "promised to the apostles new revelations; and, therefore, we must not abide solely by Scripture, for something beyond Scripture is here promised by him to his followers." In the first place, if they choose to talk with Augustine, the solution will be easily obtained. His words are, "Since Christ is silent, which of us shall say that it was this or that? Or, if he shall venture to say so, how shall he prove it? Who is so rash and insolent, even though he say what is true, as to affirm, without any Divine testimony, that those are the things which the Lord at that time did not choose to say?" But we have a surer way of refuting them, taken from Christ's own words, which follow.

13. *But when he is come, the Spirit of truth.* The *Spirit*, whom Christ promised to the apostles, is declared to be a

perfect Master or Teacher[1] *of truth.* And why was he promised, but that they might deliver from hand to hand the wisdom which they had received from him? *The Spirit* was given to them, and under his guidance and direction they discharged the office to which they had been appointed.

He will lead you into all truth. That very *Spirit* had *led them into all truth,* when they committed to writing the substance of their doctrine. Whoever imagines that anything must be added to their doctrine, as if it were imperfect and but half-finished, not only accuses the apostles of dishonesty, but blasphemes against *the Spirit.* If the doctrine which they committed to writing had proceeded from mere learners or persons imperfectly taught, an addition to it would not have been superfluous; but now that their writings may be regarded as perpetual records of that revelation which was promised and given to them, nothing can be added to them without doing grievous injury to the Holy Spirit.

When they come to determine what those things actually were, the Papists act a highly ridiculous part, for they define those mysteries, which the apostles were *unable to bear,* to be certain childish fooleries, the most absurd and stupid things that can be imagined. Was it necessary that the Spirit should come down from heaven that the apostles might learn what ceremony must be used in consecrating cups with their altars, in baptizing church-bells, in blessing the holy water, and in celebrating Mass? Whence then do fools and children obtain their learning, who understand all those matters most thoroughly? Nothing is more evident than that the Papists mock God, when they pretend that those things came from heaven, which resemble as much the mysteries of Ceres or Proserpine as they are at variance with the pure wisdom of the Holy Spirit.

If we do not wish to be ungrateful to God, let us rest satisfied with that doctrine of which the writings of the apostles declare them to be the authors, since in it the highest perfection of heavenly wisdom is made known to us, fitted *to*

---

[1] "Maistre ou Docteur."

make the man of God perfect, (2 Tim. iii. 17.) Beyond this let us not reckon ourselves at liberty to go; for our *height,* and *breadth,* and *depth,* consist in *knowing the love of God,* which is manifested to us in Christ. This *knowledge,* as Paul informs us, *far exceeds all learning,* (Eph. iii. 18;) and when he declares that *all the treasures of wisdom and knowledge are hidden in Christ,* (Col. ii. 3,) he does not contrive some unknown Christ, but one whom by his preaching he painted to the life, so that, as he tells the Galatians, *we see him, as it were, crucified before our eyes,* (Gal. iii. 1.) But that no ambiguity may remain, Christ himself afterwards explains by his own words what those things are which the apostles *were not yet able to bear.*

He will tell you things which are to come. Some indeed limit this to the Spirit of prophecy; but, in my opinion, it denotes rather the future condition of his spiritual kingdom, such as the apostles, soon after his resurrection, saw it to be, but were at that time utterly unable to comprehend. He does not therefore promise them prophecies of things that would happen after their death, but means only that the nature of his kingdom will be widely different, and its glory far greater than their minds are now able to conceive. The Apostle Paul, in the Epistle to the Ephesians, from the first chapter to the close of the fourth, explains the treasures of this *hidden wisdom,* which the heavenly angels learn with astonishment from the Church; and therefore we need not go to seek them from the archives or repositories of the Pope.

For he will not speak from himself. This is a confirmation of the clause, *he will lead you into all truth.* We know that God is the fountain of *truth,* and that out of Him there is nothing that is firm or sure; and, therefore, that the apostles may safely place full confidence in the oracles of the Spirit, Christ declares that they will be divine oracles; as if he had said, that every thing which the Holy Spirit shall bring proceeds from God himself. And yet these words take nothing away from the majesty of the Spirit, as if he were not God, or as if he were inferior to the Father, but are accommodated to the capacity of our understanding; for the reason why his Divinity is expressly mentioned is, because, on account of the veil that is between us, we do not sufficiently understand with what reverence we ought to receive what the Spirit reveals to us. In like manner, he is elsewhere called *the earnest,* by which God ratifies to us our salvation, and *the seal,* by which he *seals* to us its certainty, (Eph. i. 13, 14.) In short, Christ intended to teach that the doctrine of the Spirit would not be of this world, as if it were produced in the air, but that it would proceed from the secret places of the heavenly sanctuary.

14. *He will glorify me.* Christ now reminds them that the Spirit will not come to erect any new kingdom, but rather to confirm the *glory* which has been given to him by the Father. For many foolishly imagine that Christ taught only so as to lay down the first lessons, and then to send the disciples to a higher school. In this way they make the Gospel to be of no greater value than *the Law,* of which it is said that it was *a schoolmaster* of the ancient people, (Gal. iii. 24.)

This error is followed by another equally intolerable, that, having bid adieu to Christ, as if his reign were terminated, and he were now nothing at all, they substitute the Spirit in his place. From this source the sacrileges of Popery and Mahometanism have flowed; for, though those two Antichrists differ from each other in many respects, still they agree in holding a common principle; and that is, that in the Gospel we receive the earliest instructions to lead us into the right faith,[1] but that we must seek elsewhere the perfection of doctrine, that it may complete the course of our education. If Scripture is quoted against the Pope, he maintains that we ought not to confine ourselves to it, because the Spirit is come, and has carried us above Scripture by many additions. Mahomet asserts that, without his Alcoran, men always remain children. Thus, by a false pretence of the Spirit, the world was bewitched to depart from the simple purity of Christ; for, as soon as the Spirit is separated from the word of Christ, the door is open to all kinds of delusions and impostures. A similar method of deceiving has been attempted,

---

[1] " Les premieres instructions pour estre amenez à la droite foy."

in the present age, by many fanatics. The written doctrine appeared to them to be literal, and, therefore, they chose to contrive a new theology that would consist of revelations.

We now see that the information given by Christ, that he would be *glorified* by the Spirit whom he should send, is far from being superfluous; for it was intended to inform us, that the office of the Holy Spirit was nothing else than to establish the kingdom of Christ, and to maintain and confirm for ever all that was given him by the Father. Why then does he speak of the Spirit's teaching? Not to withdraw us from the school of Christ, but rather to ratify that word by which we are commanded to listen to him, otherwise he would diminish the glory of Christ. The reason is added. Christ says,

For he will take of what is mine. By these words he means that we receive the Spirit in order that we may enjoy Christ's blessings. For what does he bestow on us? That we may be washed by the blood of Christ, that sin may be blotted out in us by his death, that *our old man may be crucified,* (Rom. vi. 6,) that his resurrection may be efficacious in forming us again to *newness of life,* (Rom. vi. 4;) and, in short, that we may become partakers of his benefits. Nothing, therefore, is bestowed on us by the Spirit apart from Christ, but he takes it from Christ, that he may communicate it to us. We ought to take the same view of his doctrine; for he does not enlighten us, in order to draw us away in the smallest degree from Christ, but to fulfil what Paul says, that *Christ is made to us wisdom,* (1 Cor. i. 30,) and likewise to display *those treasures which are hidden in Christ,* (Col. ii. 3.) In a word, the Spirit enriches us with no other than the riches of Christ, that he may display his glory in all things.

15. *All things that the Father hath are mine.* As it might be thought that Christ took away from the Father what he claimed for himself, he acknowledges that he has received from the Father all that he communicates to us by the Spirit. When he says that *all things that the Father hath are his,* he speaks in the person of the Mediator, for we must draw *out of his fulness,* (John i. 16.) He always keeps his eye on us, as we have said. We see, on the other hand, how the greater

part of men deceive themselves; for they pass by Christ, and go out of the way to seek God by circuitous paths.

Other commentators explain these words to mean, that *all that the Father hath* belongs equally to the Son, because he is the same God. But here he does not speak of his hidden and intrinsic power, as it is called, but of that office which he has been appointed to exercise toward us. In short, he speaks of his riches, that he may invite us to enjoy them, and reckons the Spirit among the gifts which we receive from the Father by his hand.

16 A little while, and you do not see me:[1] and again a little while, and you will see me; because I go to the Father. 17. Then said some of his disciples among themselves, What is this that he saith to us, A little while, and you do not see me: and again a little while, and you will see me and, Because I go to the Father? 18 They said, therefore, What is this that he saith, A little while? We know not what he saith. 19. Jesus, therefore, knew that they wished to ask him, and he said to them, You ask among yourselves about what I said, A little while, and you do not see me: and again a little while, and you will see me. 20. Verily, verily, I tell you, That you will weep and lament, but the world will rejoice; and you will be sorrowful, but your sorrow will be turned into joy.

16. *A little while, and you do not see me.* Christ had often forewarned the apostles of his departure, partly that they might bear it with greater courage, partly that they might desire more ardently the grace of the Spirit, of which they had no great desire, so long as they had Christ present with them in body. We must, therefore, guard against becoming weary of reading what Christ, not without cause, repeats so frequently. First, he says that he will very soon be taken from them, that, when they are deprived of his presence, on which alone they relied, they may continue to be firm. Next, he promises what will compensate them for his absence, and he even testifies that he will quickly be restored to them, after he has been removed, but in another manner, that is, by the presence of the Holy Spirit.

And again a little while, and you will see me. Yet some explain this second clause differently: "You will see me when I shall have risen from the dead, but only for a short time; for

---

[1] " Et vous ne me verrez point ; "—" and you will not see me."

I shall very soon be received into heaven." But I do not think that the words will bear that meaning. On the contrary, he mitigates and soothes their sorrow for his absence, by this consolation, that it will not last long; and thus he magnifies the grace of the Spirit, by which he will be continually present with them; as if he had promised that, after a short interval, he would return, and that they would not be long deprived of his presence.

Nor ought we to think it strange when he says that he is *seen,* when he dwells in the disciples by the Spirit; for, though he is not *seen* with the bodily eyes,[1] yet his presence is known by the undoubted experience of faith. What we are taught by Paul is indeed true, that believers, *so long as they remain on earth, are absent from the Lord, because they walk by faith, and not by sight,* (2 Cor. v. 6, 7.) But it is equally true that they may justly, in the meantime, glory in having Christ dwelling in them by faith, in being united to him as members to the Head, in possessing heaven along with him by hope. Thus the grace of the Spirit is a mirror, in which Christ wishes to be seen by us, according to the words of Paul, *Though we have known Christ according to the flesh, yet we know him no more; if any man be in Christ, let him be a new creature,* (2 Cor. v. 16, 17.)

Because I go to the Father. Some explain these words as meaning that Christ will no longer be seen by the disciples, because he will be in heaven, and they on earth. For my part, I would rather refer it to the second clause, *" You will soon see me;* for my death is not a destruction to separate me from you, but a passage into the heavenly glory, from which my divine power will diffuse itself even to you." He intended, therefore, in my opinion, to teach what would be his condition after his death, that they might rest satisfied with his spiritual presence, and might not think that it would be any loss to them that he no longer dwelt with them as a mortal man.

19. *Jesus, therefore, knew that they wished to ask him.* Though

---

[1] " Combien qu'il ne soit point veu des yeux corporels."

sometimes the Lord appears to speak to the deaf, he, at length, cures the ignorance of his disciples, that his instruction may not be useless. Our duty is to endeavour that our slowness of apprehension may not be accompanied by either pride or indolence, but that, on the contrary, we show ourselves to be humble and desirous to learn.

20. *You will weep and lament.* He shows for what reason he foretold that his departure was at hand, and, at the same time, added a promise about his speedy return. It was, that they might understand better that the aid of the Spirit was highly necessary. "A hard and severe temptation," says he, "awaits you; for, when I shall be removed from you by death, the world will proclaim its triumphs over you. You will feel the deepest anguish. The world will pronounce itself to be happy, and you to be miserable. I have resolved, therefore, to furnish you with the necessary arms for this warfare." He describes the interval that elapsed between his death and the day when the Holy Spirit was sent;[1] for at that time their faith, so to speak, lay prostrate and exhausted.

Your sorrow will be turned into joy. He means the *joy* which they felt after having received the Spirit; not that they were afterwards free from all *sorrow,* but that all the sorrow which they would endure was swallowed up by spiritual *joy.* We know that the apostles, so long as they lived, sustained a severe warfare, that they endured base reproaches, that they had many reasons for *weeping and lamenting;* but, renewed by the Spirit, they had laid aside their former consciousness of weakness, so that, with lofty heroism, they nobly trampled under foot all the evils that they endured. Here then is a comparison between their present weakness and the power of the Spirit, which would soon be given to them; for, though they were nearly overwhelmed for a time, yet afterwards they not only fought bravely, but obtained a glorious triumph in the midst of their struggles. Yet it ought also to be observed, that he points out not only the interval that

---

[1] "Et le jour que le S. Esprit fut envoyé."

elapsed between the resurrection of Christ and the death of the apostles, but also the period which followed afterwards; as if Christ had said, "You will lie prostrate, as it were, for a short time; but when the Holy Spirit shall have raised you up again, then will begin a new *joy*, which will continue to increase, until, having been received into the heavenly glory, you shall have perfect *joy*."

21. A woman, when she is in labour, hath sorrow, because her hour is come; but when she hath brought forth a child, she remembereth no more her anguish, on account of the joy that a man is born into the world. 22. And you therefore have sorrow now; but I will see you again, and your heart will rejoice, and your joy no man shall take from you. 23. And in that day you will ask me nothing. Verily, verily, I tell you, That whatever you shall ask from the Father in my name, he will give to you. 24. Hitherto you have asked nothing in my name: ask, and receive, that your joy may be full.

21. *A woman, when she is in labour.* He employs a comparison to confirm the statement which he had just now made, or rather, he expresses his meaning more clearly, that not only will *their sorrow be turned into joy*, but also that it contains in itself the ground and occasion of *joy*. It frequently happens that, when adversity has been followed by prosperity, men forget their former grief, and give themselves up unreservedly to *joy*, and yet the grief which came before it is not the cause of the *joy*. But Christ means that the *sorrow* which they shall endure for the sake of the Gospel will be profitable. Indeed, the result of all griefs cannot be otherwise than unfavourable, unless when they are blessed in Christ. But as the cross of Christ always contains in itself the victory, Christ justly compares the grief arising from it to *the sorrow of a woman in labour*, which receives its reward when the mother is cheered by the birth of the child. The comparison would not apply, if *sorrow* did not produce *joy* in the members of Christ, when they become partakers of his sufferings, just as the *labour* in the woman is the cause of the birth. The comparison must also be applied in this respect, that though the *sorrow* of *the woman* is very severe, it quickly passes away. It was no small solace to the apostles, therefore, when they learned that their *sorrow* would not be of long duration.

We ought now to appropriate the use of this doctrine to

ourselves. Having been regenerated by the Spirit of Christ, we ought to feel in ourselves such a joy as would remove every feeling of our distresses. We ought, I say, to resemble *women in labour,* on whom the mere sight of *the child born* produces such an impression, that their pain gives them pain no longer. But as we have received nothing more than the first-fruits, and these in very small measure, we scarcely taste a few drops of that spiritual gladness, to soothe our grief and alleviate its bitterness. And yet that small portion clearly shows that they who contemplate Christ by faith are so far from being at any time overwhelmed by grief, that, amidst their heaviest sufferings, they rejoice with exceeding great joy.

But since it is an obligation laid *on all creatures to labour till the last day of redemption,* (Rom. viii. 22, 23,) let us know that we too must groan, until, having been delivered from the incessant afflictions of the present life, we obtain a full view of the fruit of our faith. To sum up the whole in a few words, believers are like *women in labour,* because, having been born again in Christ, they have not yet entered into the heavenly kingdom of God and a blessed life; and they are like pregnant women who are in childbirth, because, being still held captive in the prison of the flesh, they long for that blessed state which lies hidden under hope.

22. *Your joy no man shall take from you.* The value of the *joy* is greatly enhanced by its perpetuity; for it follows that the afflictions are light, and ought to be patiently endured, because they are of short duration. By these words Christ reminds us what is the nature of true *joy.* The world must unavoidably be soon deprived of its *joys,* which it seeks only in fading things; and, therefore, we must come to the resurrection of Christ, in which there is eternal solidity.

But I will see you again. When he says that he *will see* his disciples, he means that he will visit them again by the grace of his Spirit, that they may continually enjoy his presence.

23. *And in that day you will ask me nothing.* After having promised to the disciples that they would derive *joy* from their unshaken firmness and courage, he now speaks of another

grace of the Spirit which would be given to them, that they would receive so great light of understanding as would rasie them on high to heavenly mysteries. They were at that time so slow that the slightest difficulty of any kind made them hesitate; for as children who are learning the alphabet cannot read a single verse without pausing frequently, so almost every word of Christ gave them some sort of offence, and this hindered their progress. But soon afterwards, having been enlightened by the Holy Spirit, they no longer had any thing to prevent them from becoming familiarly acquainted with the wisdom of God, so as to move amidst the mysteries of God without stumbling.

True, the apostles did not cease to *ask* at the mouth of Christ, even when they had been elevated to the highest degree of wisdom, but this is only a comparison between the two conditions; as if Christ had said that their ignorance would be corrected, so that, instead of being stopped—as they now were—by the smallest obstructions, they would penetrate into the deepest mysteries without any difficulty. Such is the import of that passage in Jeremiah, *No longer shall every man teach his neighbour, saying, Know the Lord; for all shall know me, from the least to the greatest, saith the Lord,* (Jer. xxxi. 34.) The prophet assuredly does not take away or set aside instruction, which must be in its most vigorous state in the kingdom of Christ; but he affirms that, when all shall be taught by God, no room will be any longer left for this gross ignorance, which holds the minds of men, till Christ, *the Sun of Righteousness,* (Mal. iv. 2,) shall enlighten them by the rays of his Spirit. Besides, though the apostles were exceedingly like children, or rather, were more like stocks of wood than men, we know well what they suddenly became, after having enjoyed the teaching of the Holy Spirit.

Whatever you shall ask the Father in my name. He shows whence they will obtain this new faculty. It is because they will have it in their power to draw freely from God, the fountain of wisdom, as much as they need; as if he had said, "You must not fear that you will be deprived of the gift of understanding; for *my Father* will be ready, with all the abundance of blessings, to enrich you bountifully." Besides, by these words he informs them that the Spirit is not promised in such a manner that they to whom He is promised may wait for him in sloth and inactivity, but, on the contrary, that they may be earnestly employed in seeking the grace which is offered. In short, he declares that he will at that time discharge the office of Mediator, so that *whatever they shall ask* he will obtain for them from the Father abundantly, and beyond their prayers.

But here arises a difficult question: Was this the first time that men began to call on God *in the name* of Christ? for never could God be reconciled to men in any other way than for the sake of the Mediator. Christ describes the future time, when the Heavenly Father will give to the disciples *whatever they shall ask in his name.* If this be a new and unwonted favour, it would seem that we may infer from it that, so long as Christ dwelt on earth, he did not yet exercise the office of Advocate, that through him the prayers of believers might be acceptable to God. This is still more clearly expressed by what immediately follows:

24. *Hitherto you have asked nothing in my name.* It is probable that the apostles kept the rule of prayer which had been laid down in the Law. Now we know that the fathers were not accustomed to pray without a Mediator; for God had trained them, by so many exercises, to such a form of prayer. They saw the high priest enter into the holy place in the name of the whole people, and they saw sacrifices offered every day, that the prayers of the Church might be acceptable before God. It was, therefore, one of the principles of faith, that prayers offered to God, when there was no Mediator, were rash and useless. Christ had already testified to his disciples plainly enough that he was the Mediator, but their knowledge was so obscure, that they were not yet able to form their prayers *in his name* in a proper manner.

Nor is there any absurdity in saying that they prayed to God, with confidence in the Mediator, according to the injunction of the Law, and yet did not clearly and fully understand what that meant. The veil of the temple was still stretched out, the majesty of God was concealed under the shadow of the cherubim, the true High Priest had not yet entered into the heavenly sanctuary to intercede for his people, and had not yet consecrated the way by his blood. We need not wonder, therefore, if he was not acknowledged to be the Mediator as he is, now that he appears for us in heaven before the Father, reconciling Him to us by his sacrifice, that we, miserable men, may venture to appear before him with boldness; for truly Christ, after having completed the satisfaction for sin, was received into heaven, and publicly showed himself to be the Mediator.

But we ought to attend to the frequent repetition of this clause, that we must pray *in the name* of Christ. This teaches us that it is a wicked profanation of the name of God, when any one, leaving Christ out of view, ventures to present himself before the judgment-seat of God. And if this conviction be deeply impressed on our minds, that God will willingly and abundantly give to us *whatever we shall ask in the name* of his Son, we will not go hither and thither to call to our aid various advocates, but will be satisfied with having this single Advocate, who so frequently and so kindly offers to us his labours in our behalf. We are said *to pray in the name* of Christ when we take him as our Advocate, to reconcile us, and make us find favour with his Father,[1] though we do not expressly mention his name with our lips.

Ask, and receive. This relates to the time of his manifestation, which was to take place soon afterwards. So much the less excusable are those who, in the present day, obscure this part of doctrine by the pretended intercessions of the Saints. The people, under the Old Testament,[2] had to turn their eyes to the high priest, (who was given to them to be a figure and shadow,[3]) and to the sacrifices of beasts, whenever they wished to pray. We are, therefore, worse than ungrateful, if we do not keep our senses fixed on the true High Priest, who is exhibited to us as our Propitiator, that

---

[1] "A fin qu'il nous reconcile, et nous face trouver grace envers son Pere."
[2] " Le peuple sous l'Ancien Testament."
[3] " Qui luy estoit donné pour figure et ombre."

by him we may have free and ready access to the throne of the glory of God. He adds, lastly,

That your joy may be full. By this he means that nothing will be wanting which could contribute to a perfect abundance of all blessings, to the accomplishment of our desires, and to calm satisfaction, provided that we ask from God, *in his name,* whatever we need.

25. These things I have spoken to you in proverbs; but the time cometh when I shall no longer speak to you in parables, but will tell you plainly about the Father. 26. In that day you shall ask in my name: and I do not say that I will pray the Father for you; 27. For the Father himself loveth you, because you have loved me, and have believed that I came out from God. 28. I came out from the Father, and am come into the world: again, I leave the world, and go to the Father.

25. *These things I have spoken to you in proverbs.* The intention of Christ is, to give courage to his disciples, that, entertaining good hopes of making better progress, they may not think that the instruction to which they now listen is useless, though there be but little of it that they comprehend; for such a suspicion might lead them to suppose that Christ did not wish to be understood, and that he purposely kept them in suspense. He declares, therefore, that they will soon perceive the fruit of this doctrine, which, by its obscurity, might produce disgust in their minds. The Hebrew word משל (*mashal*) sometimes denotes a *proverb;* but as *proverbs* most commonly contain tropes and figures, this is the reason why the Hebrews give the name of משלים (*meshalim*) to enigmas or remarkable sayings, which the Greeks call (ἀποφθέγματα) *apophthegms,* which have almost always some ambiguity or obscurity. The meaning therefore is, "You think that I now speak to you figuratively, and not in plain and direct language; but I will soon speak to you in a more familiar manner, in order that there may be nothing puzzling or difficult to you in my doctrine."

We now see what I mentioned a little ago, that this is intended to encourage the disciples by holding out to them the expectation of making greater progress, that they may not reject the doctrine, because they do not yet understand what it means; for, if we are not animated by the hope of profiting, the desire of learning must, unavoidably, be cooled. The fact, however, clearly shows that Christ did not employ terms purposely obscure, but addressed his disciples in a simple and even homely style: but such was their ignorance that they hung on his lips with astonishment. That obscurity, therefore, did not lie so much in the doctrine as in their understandings; and, indeed, the same thing happens to us in the present day, for not without good reason does the word of God receive this commendation, that it is our *light,* (Ps. cxix. 105; 2 Pet. i. 19;) but its brightness is so obscured by our darkness, that what we hear we reckon to be pure allegories. For, as he threatens by the prophet, that he will be a barbarian to the unbelievers and reprobate, as if he had *a stammering tongue,* (Isa. xxviii. 11;) and Paul says that *the Gospel is hidden from such persons, because Satan hath blinded their understandings,* (2 Cor. iv. 3, 4;) so to the weak and ignorant it commonly appears to be something so confused that it cannot be understood. For, though their understandings are not completely darkened, like those of unbelievers, still they are covered, as it were, with clouds. Thus God permits us to be stupified for a time, in order to humble us by a conviction of our own poverty; but those whom he enlightens by his Spirit he causes to make such progress, that the word of God is known and familiar to them. Such, too, is the import of the next clause:

But the time cometh; that is, *the time* will soon *come, when I shall no more speak to you* in figurative language. The Holy Spirit, certainly, did not teach the apostles anything else than what they had heard from the mouth of Christ himself, but, by enlightening their hearts, he drove away their darkness, so that they heard Christ speak, as it were, in a new and different manner, and thus they easily understood his meaning.

But will tell you plainly about the Father. When he says that he *will tell them about the Father,* he reminds us that the design of his doctrine is to lead us to God, in whom true happiness lies. But another question remains: How does he say, elsewhere, that *it was given to the disciples to know the mysteries of the kingdom of heaven?* (Matth. xiii. 11.) For here he acknowledges that he has spoken to them in obscure language, but there he lays down a distinction between them and the rest of the people, that *he speaketh to the people in parables*, (Matth. xiii. 13.) I reply, the ignorance of the apostles was not so gross that they had not, at least, a slight perception of what their Master meant, and, therefore, it is not without reason that he excludes them from the number of the blind. He now says that his discourses have hitherto been allegorical, in comparison of that clear light of understanding which he would soon give to them by the grace of his Spirit. Both statements are therefore true, that the disciples were far above those who had no relish for the word of the Gospel, and yet they were still like children learning the alphabet, in comparison of the new wisdom which was bestowed on them by the Holy Spirit.

26. *In that day you shall ask in my name.* He again repeats the reason why the heavenly treasures were then to be so bountifully opened up. It is, because *they ask in the name of Christ* whatever they need, and God will refuse nothing that shall be asked *in the name* of his Son. But there appears to be a contradiction in the words; for Christ immediately adds, that it will be unnecessary for him *to pray to the Father.* Now, what purpose does it serve to pray *in his name*, if he does not undertake the office of Intercessor? In another passage John calls him *our Advocate*, (1 John ii. 1.) Paul also testifies that Christ now *intercedes for us*, (Rom. viii. 34;) and the same thing is confirmed by the author of the Epistle to the Hebrews, who declares that Christ *always liveth to make intercession for us*, (Heb. vii. 25.) I reply, Christ does not absolutely say, in this passage, that he will not be Intercessor, but he only means, that *the Father* will be so favourably disposed towards the disciples, that, without any difficulty, he will give freely whatever they shall ask. " *My Father*," he says, " will meet you, and, on account of the great love which he bears towards you, will anticipate the Intercessor, who, otherwise, would speak on your behalf."

Besides, when Christ is said to intercede with *the Father* for us, let us not indulge in carnal imaginations about him, as if he were on his knees before *the Father*, offering humble supplication in our name. But the value of his sacrifice, by which he once pacified God toward us, is always powerful and efficacious; the blood by which he atoned for our sins, the obedience which he rendered, is a continual intercession for us. This is a remarkable passage, by which we are taught that we have the heart of the Heavenly Father,[1] as soon as we have placed before Him *the name* of his Son.

27. *Because you have loved me.* These words remind us that the only bond of our union with God is, to be united to Christ; and we are united to him by a faith which is not feigned, but which springs from sincere affection, which he describes by the name of *love;* for no man believes purely in Christ who does not cordially embrace him, and, therefore, by this word he has well expressed the power and nature of faith. But if it is only when we have loved Christ that God begins to love us, it follows that the commencement of salvation is from ourselves, because we have anticipated the grace of God. Numerous passages of Scripture, on the other hand, are opposed to this statement. The promise of God is, *I will cause them to love me;* and John says, *Not that we first loved Him,*[2] (1 John iv. 10.) It would be superfluous to collect many passages; for nothing is more certain than this doctrine, that the Lord *calleth those things which are not*, (Rom. iv. 17,) *raises the dead*, (Luke vii. 22,) unites himself to those who were *strangers* to him, (Eph. ii. 12,) makes *hearts of flesh* out of *hearts of stone*, (Ezek. xxxvi. 26,) manifests himself to *those who do not seek him*, (Isa. lxv. 1; Rom. x. 20.) I reply, God loves men in a secret way, before they are called, if they are among the elect; for he loves his own before they are created; but, as they are not yet reconciled, they are justly accounted *enemies* of God, as Paul speaks, *When we were* ENEMIES, *we were reconciled to God by the death of his Son,*

---

[1] " Le cœur du Pere celeste."
[2] Quoting from memory, our Author has mingled two passages. The first is, *Herein is love, not that we loved God, but that he loved us,* (1 John iv. 10;) and the second is, *We love him, because he first loved us,* (1 John iv. 19.)—*Ed.*

(Rom. v. 10.) On this ground it is said that we are *loved by God,* when we *love Christ;* because we have the pledge of the fatherly love of Him from whom we formerly recoiled as our offended Judge.

28. *I came out from the Father.* This mode of expression draws our attention to the Divine power which is in Christ. Our faith in him would not be steady, if it did not perceive his Divine power; for his death and resurrection, the two pillars of faith, would be of little avail to us, if heavenly power were not connected with them. We now understand in what manner we ought to *love* Christ. Our *love* ought to be of such a nature that our faith shall contemplate the purpose and power of God, by whose hand he is offered to us. For we must not receive coldly the statement that *he came out from God,* but must also understand for what reason and for what purpose *he came out,* namely, that he might be *to us wisdom, and righteousness, and sanctification, and redemption,* (1 Cor. i. 30.)

Again, I leave the world, and go to the Father. By this second clause he points out to us that this power is perpetual: for the disciples might have thought that it was a temporary blessing, that he was sent into the world to be a Redeemer. He therefore said that *he returns to the Father,* that they may be fully persuaded that none of those blessings which he brought are lost by his departure, because from his heavenly glory he sheds on the world the power and efficacy of his death and resurrection. He therefore *left the world* when, laying aside our weaknesses, he was received into heaven; but his grace toward us is still in all its force, because he is seated at the right hand of the Father, that he may sway the sceptre of the whole world.[1]

29. His disciples say to him, Lo, now thou speakest openly, and speakest no proverb. 30. Now we know that thou knowest all things, and needest not that any one should ask thee; by this we believe that thou camest out from God. 31. Jesus answered them, Do you now believe? 32. Behold, the hour cometh, and is now come, when you shall be scattered, every one to his own, and shall leave me alone; yet I am not alone,

---

[1] " A fin d'estre Empereur et Dominateur de tout le monde ;"—in order to be the Emperor and Ruler of the whole world."

because the Father is with me. 33. These things I have spoken to you, that you may have peace in me. In the world you will have tribulation; but be of good courage; I have overcome the world.

29. *His disciples say to him.* This shows how great was the efficacy of that consolation, for it suddenly brought into a state of great cheerfulness those minds which formerly were broken and cast down. And yet it is certain that *the disciples* did not yet understand fully the meaning of Christ's discourse; but though they were not yet capable of this, the mere odour of it refreshed them. When they exclaim that their Master *speaketh openly,* and without a figure, their language is certainly extravagant, and yet they state honestly what they feel. The same thing falls within our own experience in the present day; for he who has only tasted a little of the doctrine of the Gospel is more inflamed, and feels much greater energy in that small measure of faith, than if he had been acquainted with all the writings of Plato. Not only so, but the *groans* which the Spirit of God produces in the hearts of the godly are sufficient proofs that God worketh in a secret manner beyond their capacity; for otherwise Paul would not call them *groans that cannot be uttered*, (Rom. viii. 26.)

Thus we ought to understand that the apostles were conscious of having made some progress, so that they could say with truth, that they did not now find the words of Christ to be altogether obscure; but that they were deceived in this respect, that they thought they understood more than they did. Now the source of their mistake was, that they did not know what the gift of the Holy Spirit would be. They therefore give themselves up to joy before the time, just as if a person should think himself rich with a single gold piece. They conclude, from certain signs, that Christ *came out from God,* and they glory in it, as if nothing more were needed. Yet still they were far from that knowledge, so long as they did not understand what Christ would be to them in future.

31. *Do you now believe?* As the disciples were too highly pleased with themselves, Christ reminds them that, remembering their weakness, they ought rather to confine themselves within their own little capacity. Now, we never are fully aware of what we want, and of our great distance from the

fulness of faith, till we come to some serious trial; for then the fact shows how weak our faith was, which we imagined to be full. Christ recalls the attention of the disciples to this matter, and declares that they will ere long forsake him; for persecution is a touchstone to try faith, and when its smallness becomes evident, they who formerly were swelled with pride begin to tremble and to draw back.

The question put by Christ is therefore ironical; as if he had said, "Do you boast as if you were full of faith? But the trial is at hand, which will disclose your emptiness." In this manner we ought to restrain our foolish confidence, when it indulges itself too freely. But it might be thought, either that the disciples had no faith at all, or that it was extinguished, when they had forsaken Christ, and were scattered in all directions. I reply, though their faith was weakened, and had almost given way, still something was left, from which fresh branches might afterwards shoot forth.

32. *Yet I am not alone.* This correction is added, in order to inform us that, when Christ is forsaken by men, he loses nothing of his dignity. For since his truth and his glory are founded on himself, and do not depend on what the world believes, if it happen that he is forsaken by the whole world, still he is in no degree impaired, because he is God, and needs not any assistance from another.

Because my Father is with me. When he says that *the* FATHER *will be with him,* the meaning is, that God will be on his side, so that he will have no need to borrow anything from men. Whoever shall meditate on this in a proper manner will remain firm, though the whole world should be shaken, and the revolt of all men will not overturn his faith; for we do not render to God the honour which is due to him, if we are not satisfied with having God alone.

33. *These things I have spoken to you.* He again repeats how necessary those consolations are which he had addressed to them; and he proves it by this argument, that numerous distresses and *tribulations* await them *in the world.* We ought to attend, first, to this admonition, that all believers ought

to be convinced that their life is exposed to many afflictions, that they may be disposed to exercise patience. Since, therefore, *the world* is like a troubled sea, true *peace* will be found nowhere but in Christ. Next, we ought to attend to the manner of enjoying that *peace*, which he describes in this passage. He says that they will have *peace*, if they make progress in this doctrine. Do we wish then to have our minds calm and easy in the midst of afflictions? Let us be attentive to this discourse of Christ, which in itself will give us *peace*.

But be of good courage. As our sluggishness must be corrected by various afflictions, and as we must be awakened to seek a remedy for our distress, so the Lord does not intend that our minds shall be cast down, but rather that we shall fight keenly, which is impossible, if we are not certain of success; for if we must fight, while we are uncertain as to the result, all our zeal will quickly vanish. When, therefore, Christ calls us to the contest, he arms us with assured confidence of victory, though still we must toil hard.

I have overcome the world. As there is always in us much reason for trembling, he shows that we ought to be confident for this reason, that he has obtained a *victory* over *the world*, not for himself individually, but for our sake. Thus, though in ourselves almost overwhelmed, if we contemplate that magnificent glory to which our Head has been exalted, we may boldly despise all the evils which hang over us. If, therefore, we desire to be Christians, we must not seek exemption from the cross, but must be satisfied with this single consideration, that, fighting under the banner of Christ, we are beyond all danger, even in the midst of the combat. Under the term *World*, Christ here includes all that is opposed to the salvation of believers, and especially all the corruptions which Satan abuses for the purpose of laying snares for us.

CHAPTER XVII.

1. These words spake Jesus, and lifted up his eyes to heaven, and said, Father, the hour is come; glorify thy Son, that thy Son also may glorify thee: 2. As thou hast given him power over all flesh, that he may give eternal life to all whom thou hast given to him. 3. And this is eternal life, that they may know thee, the only true God, and him whom thou hast sent, Jesus Christ. 4. I have glorified thee on the earth; I have finished the work which thou gavest me to do. 5. And now, O Father, glorify thou me with thyself, with the glory which I had with thee before the world was.

1. *These words spake Jesus.* After having preached to the disciples about bearing the cross, the Lord exhibited to them those consolations, by relying on which they would be enabled to persevere. Having promised the coming of the Spirit, he raised them to a better hope, and discoursed to them about the splendour and glory of his reign. Now he most properly betakes himself to prayer; for doctrine has no power, if efficacy be not imparted to it from above. He, therefore, holds out an example to teachers, not to employ themselves only in sowing the word, but, by mingling their prayers with it, to implore the assistance of God, that his blessing may render their labour fruitful. In short, this passage of the Lord Jesus[1] Christ might be said to be the seal of the preceding doctrine, both that it might be ratified in itself, and that it might obtain full credit with the disciples.

And lifted up his eyes to heaven. This circumstance related by John, that Christ prayed, *lifting up his eyes to heaven,* was an indication of uncommon ardour and vehemence; for by this attitude Christ testified that, in the affections of his mind, he was rather in heaven than in earth, so that, leaving men behind him, he conversed familiarly with God. He looked towards *heaven,* not as if God's presence were confined to *heaven,* for *he filleth also the earth,* (Jer. xxiii. 24,) but because it is there chiefly that his majesty is displayed. Another reason was, that, by looking towards *heaven,* we are reminded that the majesty of God is far exalted above all creatures. It is with the same view that the hands are lifted up in prayer;

---

[1] " Du Seigneur Jesus."

for men, being by nature indolent and slow, and drawn downwards by their earthly disposition, need such excitements, or I should rather say, chariots, to raise them to *heaven*.

Yet if we desire actually to imitate Christ, we must take care that outward gestures do not express more than is in our mind, but that the inward feeling shall direct the eyes, the hands, the tongue, and every thing about us. We are told, indeed, that *the publican*, with downcast eyes, prayed aright to God, (Luke xviii. 13,) but that is not inconsistent with what has now been stated; for, though he was confused and humbled on account of his sins, still this self-abasement did not prevent him from seeking pardon with full confidence. But it was proper that Christ should pray in a different manner, for he had nothing about him of which he ought to be ashamed; and it is certain that David himself prayed sometimes in one attitude, and sometimes in another, according to the circumstances in which he was placed.

Father, the hour is come. Christ asks that his kingdom may be glorified, in order that he also may advance the glory of the Father. He says that *the hour is come*, because though, by miracles and by every kind of supernatural events, he had been manifested to be the Son of God, yet his spiritual kingdom was still in obscurity, but soon afterwards shone with full brightness. If it be objected, that never was there any thing less glorious than the death of Christ, which was then at hand, I reply, that in that death we behold a magnificent triumph which is concealed from wicked men; for there we perceive that, atonement having been made for sins, the world has been reconciled to God, the curse has been blotted out, and Satan has been vanquished.

It is also the object of Christ's prayer, that his death may produce, through the power of the Heavenly Spirit, such fruit as had been decreed by the eternal purpose of God; for he says that *the hour is come*, not an hour which is determined by the fancy of men, but an hour which God had appointed. And yet the prayer is not superfluous, because, while Christ depends on the good pleasure of God, he knows that he ought to desire what God promised would certainly take place. True, God will do whatever he has decreed, not only though the whole world were asleep, but though it were opposed to him; but it is our duty to ask from him whatever he has promised, because the end and use [1] of promises is to excite us to prayer.

That thy Son also may glorify thee. He means that there is a mutual connection between the advancement of his glory and of the glory of his Father; for why is Christ manifested, but that he may lead us to the Father? Hence it follows, that all the honour which is bestowed on Christ is so far from diminishing the honour of the Father, that it confirms it the more. We ought always to remember under what character Christ speaks in this passage; for we must not look only at his eternal Divinity, because he speaks as God manifested in the flesh, and according to the office of Mediator.

2. *As thou hast given him.* He again confirms the statement, that he asks nothing but what is agreeable to the will of the Father; as it is a constant rule o prayer not to ask more than God would freely bestow; for nothing is more contrary to reason, than to bring forward in the presence of God whatever we choose.

Power over all flesh means the authority which was given to Christ, when the Father appointed him to be King and Head; but we must observe the end, which is, *to give eternal life* to all his people. Christ receives authority, not so much for himself as for the sake of our salvation; and, therefore, we ought to submit to Christ, not only that we may obey God, but because nothing is more lovely than that subjection, since it brings to us eternal life.

To all whom thou hast given me. Christ does not say that he has been made Governor over the whole world, in order to bestow *life* on all without any distinction; but he limits this grace to those who *have been given to him.* But how were they *given to him?* For the Father has subjected to him the reprobate. I reply, it is only the elect who belong to his peculiar flock, which he has undertaken to guard as a Shepherd. So then, the kingdom of Christ extends, no doubt, to

---

[1] "La fin et l'usage."

all men; but it brings salvation to none but the elect, who with voluntary obedience follow the voice of the Shepherd; for the others are compelled by violence to obey him, till at length he utterly bruise them with his iron sceptre.

3. *And this is eternal life.* He now describes the manner of bestowing *life*, namely, when he enlightens the elect in the true knowledge of God; for he does not now speak of the enjoyment of *life* which we hope for, but only of the manner in which men obtain *life*. And that this verse may be fully understood, we ought first to know that we are all in death, till we are enlightened by God, who alone is *life*. Where he has shone, we possess him by faith, and, therefore, we also enter into the possession of *life;* and this is the reason why the *knowledge* of him is truly and justly called saving, or bringing salvation.[1] Almost every one of the words has its weight; for it is not every kind of knowledge that is here described, but that knowledge which forms us anew into the image of God from faith to faith, or rather, which is the same with faith, by which, having been ingrafted into the body of Christ, we are made partakers of the Divine adoption, and heirs of heaven.[2]

To know thee, and Jesus Christ whom thou hast sent. The reason why he says this is, that there is no other way in which God is *known* but in the face of *Jesus Christ*, who is the bright and lively image of Him. As to his placing the Father first, this does not refer to the order of faith, as if our minds, after having known God, afterwards descend to Christ; but the meaning is, that it is by the intervention of a Mediator that God is known.

The only true God. Two epithets are added, *true* and *only*, because, in the first place, faith must distinguish God from the vain inventions of men, and embracing him with firm conviction, must never change or hesitate; and, secondly, believing that there is nothing defective or imperfect in God, faith must

---

[1] "Salutaire, ou apportant salut."
[2] "Nous sommes faits participans de l'adoption Divine, qui nous fait enfans et heritiers du royaume des cieux;"—"we are made partakers of the Divine adoption, which makes us children and heirs of the kingdom of heaven."

be satisfied with him alone. Some explain it, *That they may know thee, who alone art God;* but this is a poor interpretation. The meaning therefore is, *That they may know thee alone to be the true God.*

But it may be thought that Christ disclaims for himself the right and title of Divinity. Were it replied, that the name of God is quite as applicable to Christ as to the Father, the same question might be raised about the Holy Spirit; for if only the Father and the Son are God, the Holy Spirit is excluded from that rank, which is as absurd as the former. The answer is easy, if we attend to that manner of speaking which Christ uniformly employs throughout the Gospel of John, of which I have already reminded my readers so frequently, that they must have become quite accustomed to it. Christ, appearing in the form of a man, describes, under the person of the Father, the power, essence, and majesty of God. So then the Father of Christ is *the only* true *God;* that is, he is *the one God,* who formerly promised a Redeemer to the world; but in Christ the *oneness* and *truth* of Godhead will be found, because Christ was humbled, in order that he might raise us on high. When we have arrived at this point, then his Divine majesty displays itself; then we perceive that he is wholly in the Father, and that the Father is wholly in him. In short, he who separates Christ from the Divinity of the Father, does not yet acknowledge Him who is *the only true God,* but rather invents for himself a strange god. This is the reason why we are enjoined *to know God, and Jesus Christ whom he hath sent,* by whom, as it were, with outstretched hand, he invites us to himself.

As to the opinion entertained by some, that it would be unjust, if men were to perish solely on account of their ignorance of God, it arises from their not considering that there is no fountain of *life* but in God alone, and that all who are alienated from him are deprived of *life.* Now, if there be no approach to God but by faith, we are forced to conclude, that unbelief keeps us in a state of death. If it be objected, that persons otherwise righteous and innocent are unjustly treated, if they are condemned, the answer is obvious, that nothing right or sincere is found in men, so long as they remain in their natural state. Now, Paul informs us that *we are renewed in the image of God by the knowledge of him,* (Col. iii. 10.)

It will be of importance for us now to bring into one view those three articles of faith; first, that the kingdom of Christ brings *life* and salvation; secondly, that all do not receive *life* from him, and it is not the office of Christ to *give life* to all, but only to the elect whom the Father has committed to his protection; and, thirdly, that this life consists in faith, and Christ bestows it on those whom he enlightens in the faith of the Gospel. Hence we infer that the gift of illumination and heavenly wisdom is not common to all, but peculiar to the elect. It is unquestionably true that the Gospel is offered to all, but Christ speaks here of that secret and efficacious manner of teaching by which the children of God only are drawn to faith.

4. *I have glorified thee.* His reason for saying this is, that God had been made known to the world both by the doctrine of Christ, and by his miracles; and the *glory* of God is, when we know what he is. When he adds, *I have finished the work which thou gavest me to do,* he means that he has completed the whole course of his calling; for the full time was come when he ought to be received into the heavenly *glory.* Nor does he speak only of the office of teaching, but includes also the other parts of his ministry; for, though the chief part of it still remained to be accomplished, namely, the sacrifice of death, by which he was to take away the iniquities of us all, yet, as the hour of his death was already at hand, he speaks as if he had already endured it. The amount of his request, therefore, is, that the Father would put him in possession of the kingdom; since, having completed his course, nothing more remained for him to do, than to display, by the power of the Spirit, the fruit and efficacy of all that he had done on earth by the command of his Father, according to the saying of Paul, *He humbled and annihilated himself,*[1] *by taking the form of a servant. Wherefore God hath highly exalted him,*

---

[1] "Il s'est humilié et aneanti soy-mesme"

and given him a name which is above every name, (Philip. ii. 7, 10.)

5. *The glory which I had with thee.* He desires to be *glorified* WITH THE FATHER, not that the Father may *glorify* him secretly, without any witnesses, but that, having been received into heaven, he may give a magnificent display of his greatness and power, *that every knee may bow to him*, (Philip. ii. 10.) Consequently, that phrase in the former clause, *with the Father*, is contrasted with earthly and fading glory, as Paul describes the blessed immortality of Christ, by saying that *he died to sin once, but now he liveth to God*, (Rom. vi. 10.)

The glory which I had with thee before the world was. He now declares that he desires nothing that does not strictly belong to him, but only that he may appear in the flesh, such as he was before the creation of the world; or, to speak more plainly, that the Divine majesty, which he had always possessed, may now be illustriously displayed in the person of the Mediator, and in the human flesh with which he was clothed. This is a remarkable passage, which teaches us that Christ is not a God who has been newly contrived, or who has existed only for a time; for if his *glory* was eternal, himself also has always been. Besides, a manifest distinction between the person of Christ and the person of the Father is here expressed; from which we infer, that he is not only the eternal God, but also that he is the eternal Word of God, begotten by the Father before all ages.

6. I have manifested thy name to the men whom thou hast given me out of the world, thine they were, and thou hast given them to me, and they have kept thy word. 7. Now they have known that all things which thou hast given me are from thee, 8. For I have given to them the words which thou gavest me, and they have received them, and have known truly that I came out from thee, and have believed that thou hast sent me. 9 I pray for them; I do not pray for the world, but for those whom thou hast given me, for they are thine; 10. And all that is mine is thine, and thine is mine,[1] and I am glorified in them. 11 And I am no longer in the world, but these are in the world, and I come to thee. Holy Father, keep in thy name those whom thou hast given me, that they may be one, as we are.

---

[1] " Et tout ce qui est mien est tien, et ce qui est tien est mien,"—
" And all that is mine is thine, and what is thine is mine "

6. *I have manifested thy name.* Here Christ begins to pray to the Father for his disciples, and, with the same warmth of love with which he was immediately to suffer death for them, he now pleads for their salvation. The first argument which he employs on their behalf is, that they have embraced the doctrine which makes men actually children of God. There was no want of faith or diligence on the part of Christ, to call all men to God, but among the elect only was his labour profitable and efficacious. His preaching, which *manifested the name* of God, was common to all, and he never ceased to maintain the glory of it even among the obstinate. Why then does he say that it was only to a small number of persons that he *manifested the name* of his Father, but because the elect alone profit by the grace of the Spirit, who teaches inwardly?[1] Let us therefore infer that not all to whom the doctrine is exhibited are truly and efficaciously taught, but only those whose minds are enlightened. Christ ascribes the cause to the election of God; for he assigns no other difference as the reason why he *manifested the name* of the Father to some, passing by others, but because they were *given to him.* Hence it follows that faith flows from the outward predestination of God, and that therefore it is not given indiscriminately to all, because all do not belong to Christ.[2]

Thine they were, and thou hast given them to me. By adding these words, he points out, first, the eternity of election; and, secondly, the manner in which we ought to consider it. Christ declares that the elect always belonged to God. God therefore distinguishes them from the reprobate, not by faith, or by any merit, but by pure grace; for, while they are alienated from him to the utmost, still he reckons them as his own in his secret purpose. The certainty of that election by free grace[3] lies in this, that he commits to the guardianship of his Son all whom he has elected, that they may not perish; and this is the point to which we should turn our eyes, that we may be fully certain that we belong to the rank of the child-

[1] "Pourquoy donc dit-il qu'il a manifesté le nom de son Pere seulement à quelque petit nombre de gens, sinon d'autant qu'il n'y a que les eleus qui profitent par la grace de l'Esprit qui les enseigne au dedans?"
[2] "Au Fils de Dieu;"—"to the Son of God."
[3] "La certitude de ceste election gratuite."

ren of God; for the predestination of God is in itself hidden, but it is manifested to us in Christ alone.

And they have kept thy word. This is the third step; for the first is, the election by free grace, and the second is, that gift by which we enter into the guardianship of Christ. Having been received by Christ, we are gathered by faith into the fold. The word of God flows out to the reprobate, but it takes root in the elect, and hence they are said to *keep* it.

7. *Now they have known.* Here our Lord expresses what is the chief part in faith, which consists in our believing in Christ in such a manner, that faith does not rest satisfied with beholding the flesh, but perceives his Divine power. For, when he says, *They have known that all things which thou hast given me are from thee,* he means, that believers feel that all that they possess is heavenly and divine. And, indeed, if we do not perceive God in Christ, we must remain continually in a state of hesitation.

8. *And they have received them.* He expresses the manner of this knowledge. It is, because they have received the doctrine which he taught them. But that no one may think that his doctrine is human or is earthly in its origin, he declares that God is the Author of it, when he says, *The words which thou gavest me I have given to them.* He speaks according to his ordinary custom, in the person of the Mediator or servant of God, when he says that he taught nothing but what he had received from the Father; for, since his own condition was still mean, while he was in the flesh, and since his Divine majesty was concealed under the form of a servant, under the person of the Father he simply means God. Yet we must hold by the statement which John made at the beginning of his Gospel, that, in so far as Christ was the Eternal Word of God, he was always one God with the Father. The meaning therefore is, that Christ was a faithful witness of God to the disciples, so that their faith was founded exclusively on the truth of God, since the Father himself spoke in the Son. The *receiving,* of which he speaks,

arose from his having efficaciously manifested to them the name of his Father by the Holy Spirit.

And have known truly. He now repeats in other words what he had formerly mentioned; for that Christ *came out from the Father*, and *was sent* by him, has the same meaning with what went before, that *all things which he has are from the Father*. The meaning amounts to this, that faith ought to cast its eyes direct on Christ, yet so as to form no conception of him that is earthly or mean, but to be carried upwards to his Divine power, so as to believe firmly that he has perfectly in himself God, and all that belongs to God.

And have believed. Let it be observed, also, that in the former clause he employs the verb *know*, and now he employs the verb *believe;* for thus he shows that nothing which relates to God can be known aright but by *faith*, but that in *faith* there is such certainty that it is justly called *knowledge*.

9. *I pray for them.* Hitherto Christ has brought forward what might procure for the disciples favour with the Father. He now forms the prayer itself, in which he shows that he asks nothing but what is agreeable to the will of the Father, because he pleads with the Father in behalf of those only whom the Father himself willingly loves. He openly declares that he *does not pray for the world*, because he has no solicitude but about his own flock, which he received from the hand of the Father. But this might be thought to be absurd; for no better rule of prayer can be found than to follow Christ as our Guide and Teacher. Now, we are commanded to *pray for all*, (1 Tim. ii. 1,) and Christ himself afterwards prayed indiscriminately for all, *Father, forgive them; for they know not what they do*, (Luke xxiii. 34.) I reply, the prayers which we offer for all are still limited to the elect of God. We ought to pray that this man, and that man, and every man, may be saved, and thus include the whole human race, because we cannot yet distinguish the elect from the reprobate; and yet, while we desire the coming of the kingdom of God, we likewise pray that God may destroy his enemies.

There is only this difference between the two cases, that we pray for the salvation of all whom we know to have been created after the image of God, and who have the same nature with ourselves; and we leave to the judgment of God those whom he knows to be reprobate. But in the prayer which is here related there was some special reason, which ought not to be produced as an example; for Christ does not now pray from the mere impulse of faith and of love towards men, but, entering into the heavenly sanctuary, he places before his eyes the secret judgments of the Father, which are concealed from us, so long as we walk by faith.

Besides, we learn from these words, that God chooses out of the world those whom he thinks fit to choose to be heirs of life, and that this distinction is not made according to the merit of men, but depends on his mere good-pleasure. For those who think that the cause of election is in men must begin with faith. Now, Christ expressly declares that they who *are given to him* belong to *the Father;* and it is certain that they are *given* so as to believe, and that faith flows from this act of *giving*. If the origin of faith is this act of giving, and if election comes before it in order and time, what remains but that we acknowledge that those whom God wishes to be saved out of the world are elected by free grace? Now, since Christ prays for the elect only, it is necessary for us to believe the doctrine of election, if we wish that he should plead with the Father for our salvation. A grievous injury, therefore, is inflicted on believers by those persons who endeavour to blot out the knowledge of election from the hearts of believers, because they deprive them of the pleading and intercession of the Son of God.[1] These words serve also to expose the stupidity of those who, under the pretence of election, give themselves up to indolence, whereas it ought rather to arouse us to earnestness in prayer, as Christ teaches us by his example.

10. *And all things that are mine are thine.* The object of the former clause is to show that the Father will assuredly listen to him. "I do not," says he, "plead with thee for any but those whom thou acknowledgest to be *thine*, for I have

---

[1] "D'autant qu'ils les privent de la recommandation et intercession du Fils de Dieu."

nothing separated from thee, and therefore I shall not meet with a refusal." In the second clause, *and thine are mine*, he shows that he has good reason for caring about the elect; for they are *his* in consequence of their being *his Father's*. All these things are spoken for the confirmation of our faith. We must not seek salvation anywhere else than in Christ. But we shall not be satisfied with having Christ, if we do not know that we possess God in him. We must therefore believe that there is such a unity between the Father and the Son as makes it impossible that they shall have anything separate from each other.

And I am glorified in them. This is connected with the second clause of the verse, *and thine are mine;* for it follows that it is reasonable that he, for his part, should promote their salvation; and this is a most excellent testimony for confirming our faith, that Christ never will cease to care for our salvation, since he *is glorified in us.*

11. *And I am no longer in the world.* He assigns another reason why he prays so earnestly for the disciples, namely, because they will very soon be deprived of his bodily presence, under which they had reposed till now. So long as he dwelt with them, he cherished them, *as a hen gathereth her chickens under her wings,* (Matth. xxiii. 37;) but now that he is about to depart, he asks that the Father will guard them by his protection. And he does so on their account; for he provides a remedy for their trembling, that they may rely on God himself, to whose hands, as it were, he now commits them. It yields no small consolation to us, when we learn that the Son of God becomes so much the more earnest about the salvation of his people, when he leaves them as to his bodily presence; for we ought to conclude from it, that, while we are labouring under difficulties in the world, he keeps his eye on us, to send down, from his heavenly glory, relief from our distresses.

Holy Father. The whole prayer is directed to this object, that the disciples may not lose courage, as if their condition were made worse on account of the bodily absence of their Master. For Christ, having been appointed by the Father to be their guardian for a time, and having now discharged the duties of that office, gives them back again, as it were, into the hands of the Father, that henceforth they may enjoy his protection, and may be upheld by his power. It amounts therefore to this, that, when the disciples are deprived of Christ's bodily presence, they suffer no loss, because God receives them under his guardianship, the efficacy of which shall never cease.

That they may be one. This points out the way in which they shall be kept; for those whom the Heavenly *Father* has decreed to *keep*, he brings together in a *holy* unity of faith and of the Spirit. But as it is not enough that men be agreed in some manner, he adds, *As we are.* Then will our unity be truly happy, when it shall bear the image of God the Father and of Christ, as the wax takes the form of the seal which is impressed upon it. But in what manner the Father, and Jesus Christ [1] his Son, *are one*, I shall shortly afterwards explain.

12. While I was with them in the world, I kept them in thy name. Those whom thou hast given to me I have kept, and none of them is lost, but the son of perdition, that the Scripture might be fulfilled 13. And now I come to thee, and speak those things in the world, that they may have my joy fulfilled in themselves.

12. *While I was with them in the world.* Christ says that he hath kept them in the name of his Father; for he represents himself to be only a servant, who did nothing but by the power, and under the protection, of God. He means, therefore, that it were most unreasonable to suppose that they would now perish, as if by his departure the power of God had been extinguished or dead. But it may be thought very absurd that Christ surrenders to God the office of keeping them, as if, after having finished the course of his life, he ceased to be the guardian of his people. The reply is obvious. He speaks here of visible guardianship only, which ended at the death of Christ; for, while he dwelt on earth, he needed not to borrow power from another, in order to *keep* his dis-

---

[1] "Le Pere, et Jesus Christ son Fils."

ciples; but all this relates to the person of the Mediator, who appeared, for a time, under the form of a servant. But now he bids the disciples, as soon as they have begun to be deprived of the external aid, to raise their eyes direct towards heaven. Hence we infer that Christ keeps believers in the present day not less than he formerly did, but in a different manner, because Divine majesty is openly displayed in him.

Whom thou hast given me. He again employs the same argument, that it would be highly unbecoming that the Father should reject those whom his Son, by his command, has *kept* to the very close of his ministry; as if he had said, "What thou didst commit to me I have faithfully executed, and I took care that *nothing was lost* in my hands; and when thou now receivest what thou hadst intrusted to me, it belongs to thee to see that it continue to be safe and sound."

But the son of perdition. Judas is excepted, and not without reason; for, though he was not one of the elect and of the true flock of God, yet the dignity of his office gave him the appearance of it; and, indeed, no one would have formed a different opinion of him, so long as he held that exalted rank. Tried by the rules of grammar,[1] the exception is incorrect; but if we examine the matter narrowly, it was necessary that Christ should speak thus, in accommodation to the ordinary opinion of men. But, that no one might think that the eternal election of God was overturned by the damnation of Judas, he immediately added, that he was *the son of perdition.* By these words Christ means that his ruin, which took place suddenly before the eyes of men, had been known to God long before; for *the son of perdition,* according to the Hebrew idiom, denotes a man who is ruined, or devoted to destruction.

That the Scripture might be fulfilled. This relates to the former clause. Judas fell, *that the Scripture might be fulfilled.* But it would be a most unfounded argument, if any one were to infer from this, that the revolt of Judas ought to be ascribed to God rather than to himself, because the prediction

---

[1] " Selon la reigle de grammaire."

laid him under a necessity. For the course of events ought not to be ascribed to prophecies, because it was predicted in them; and, indeed, the prophets threaten nothing but what would have happened, though they had not spoken of it. It is not in the prophecies, therefore, that we must go to seek the cause of events. I acknowledge, indeed, that nothing happens but what has been appointed by God; but the only question now is, Do those things which it has foretold, or predicted, lay men under a necessity? which I have already demonstrated to be false.

Nor was it the design of Christ to transfer to Scripture the cause of the ruin of Judas, but he only intended to take away the occasion of stumbling, which might shake weak minds.[1] Now the method of removing it is, by showing that the Spirit of God had long ago testified that such an event would happen; for we commonly startle at what is new and sudden. This is a highly useful admonition, and admits of extensive application. For how comes it that, in our own day, the greater part of men give way on account of offences, but because they do not remember the testimonies of Scripture, by which God has abundantly fortified his people, having foretold early all the evils and distresses which would come before their eyes?

13. *And these things I speak in the world.* Here Christ shows that the reason why he was so earnest in praying for his disciples was, not that he was anxious about their future condition, but rather to provide a remedy for their anxiety. We know how prone our minds are to seek external aids; and if these present themselves, we eagerly seize them, and do not easily suffer ourselves to be torn from them. Christ, therefore, prays to his Father in the presence of his disciples, not because he needed any words, but to remove from them all doubt. *I speak in the world,* says he; that is, within their hearing, or, in their presence,[2] that their minds may be calm;

---

[1] "Les consciences infirmes,"—"weak consciences."
[2] "En leur presence"

for their salvation already was in no danger, having been placed by Christ in the hands of God.

That they may have my joy fulfilled. He calls it HIS *joy*, because it was necessary that the disciples should obtain it from him; or, if you choose to express it more briefly, he calls it *his*, because he is the Author, Cause, and Pledge of it; for in us there is nothing but alarm and uneasiness, but in Christ alone there is peace and joy.

> 14. I have given them thy word, and the world hath hated them; because they are not of the world, even as I am not of the world. 15. I ask not that thou shouldest take them out of the world, but that thou shouldest keep them from the evil. 16. They are not of the world, even as I am not of the world. 17. Sanctify them by thy truth. thy word is truth. 18. As thou hast sent me into the world, I also have sent them into the world. 19 And for their sakes I sanctify myself, that they also may be sanctified by the truth.

14. *I have given them thy word.* He employs a different argument in pleading with the Father on behalf of the disciples. It is, because they need his assistance on account of *the hatred of the world.* He likewise declares the cause of that *hatred* to be, that they have embraced *the word* of God, which the world cannot receive; as if he had said, "It belongs to thee to protect those who, on account of *thy word,* are *hated by the world."* We must now keep in remembrance what we have lately heard, that the end of this prayer is, *that Christ's joy may be fulfilled in us.* As often, therefore, as the rage of the world is kindled against us to such an extent that we think we are very near destruction, let us learn suddenly to ward it off by this shield, that God will never forsake those who labour in defence of the Gospel.

Because they are not of the world. He says that his disciples *are not of the world,* because all those whom he regenerates by his Spirit are separated *from the world.* God will not suffer his sheep to wander among wolves, without showing himself to be their shepherd.

15. *I ask not that thou shouldest take them out of the world.* He shows in what the safety of believers[1] consists; not that

---

[1] "Des fideles."

they are free from every annoyance, and live in luxury and at their ease, but that, in the midst of dangers, they continue to be safe through the assistance of God. For he does not admonish the Father of what is proper to be done, but rather makes provision for their weakness, that, by the method which he prescribes, they may restrain their desires, which are apt to go beyond all bounds. In short, he promises to his disciples the grace of the Father; not to relieve them from all anxiety and toil, but to furnish them with invincible strength against their enemies, and not to suffer them to be overwhelmed by the heavy burden of contests which they will have to endure. If, therefore, we wish to be *kept* according to the rule which Christ has laid down, we must not desire exemption from evils, or pray to God to convey us immediately into a state of blessed rest, but must rest satisfied with the certain assurance of victory, and, in the meantime, resist courageously all the evils, from which Christ prayed to his Father that we might have a happy issue. In short, God does not *take* his people *out of the world*, because he does not wish them to be effeminate and slothful; but he *delivers them from evil*, that they may not be overwhelmed; for he wishes them to fight, but does not suffer them to be mortally wounded.

16. *They are not of the world.* That the heavenly Father may be more favourably disposed to assist them, he again says that *the whole world* hates them, and, at the same time, states that this hatred does not arise from any fault of theirs, but because the world hates God and Christ.

17. *Sanctify them by thy truth.* This *sanctification* includes the kingdom of God and his righteousness; that is, when God renews us by his Spirit, and confirms in us the grace of renewal, and continues it to the end. He asks, first, therefore, that the Father would sanctify the disciples, or, in other words, that he would consecrate them entirely to himself, and defend them as his sacred inheritance. Next, he points out the means of *sanctification*, and not without reason; for there are fanatics who indulge in much useless prattle about *sanctification*, but who neglect *the truth* of God, by which he conse-

crates us to himself. Again, as there are others who chatter quite as foolishly about *the truth,* and yet disregard *the word,* Christ expressly says that *the truth,* by which God sanctifies his sons, is not to be found any where else than in *the word.*

Thy word is truth; for *the word* here denotes the doctrine of the Gospel, which the apostles had already heard from the mouth of their Master, and which they were afterwards to preach to others. In this sense Paul says that *the Church has been cleansed with the washing of water by the word of life,* (Eph. v. 26.) True, it is God alone who *sanctifies;* but as *the Gospel is the power of God to salvation to every one that believeth,* (Rom. i. 16,) whoever departs from the Gospel as the means must become more and more filthy and polluted.

The truth is here taken, by way of eminence, for the light of heavenly wisdom, in which God manifests himself to us, that he may conform us to his image. The outward preaching of *the word,* it is true, does not of itself accomplish this, for that preaching is wickedly profaned by the reprobate; but let us remember that Christ speaks of the elect, whom the Holy Spirit efficaciously regenerates *by the word.* Now, as the apostles were not altogether destitute of this grace, we ought to infer from Christ's words, that *sanctification* is not instantly completed in us on the first day, but that we make progress in it through the whole course of our life, till at length God, having taken away from us the garment of the flesh, fills us with his righteousness.

18. *As thou hast sent me into the world.* He confirms his prayer by another argument; namely, because the calling of Christ and of the apostles is the same calling, and is common to both. "I now," he says, "appoint them to an office, which I have hitherto held by thy command; and, therefore, it is necessary that they should be furnished with the power of thy Spirit, that they may be able to sustain so weighty a charge."

19. *And for their sakes I sanctify myself.* By these words he explains more clearly from what source that *sanctification* flows, which is completed in us by the doctrine of the Gospel.

It is, because he consecrated himself to the Father, that his holiness might come to us; for as the blessing on the first-fruits is spread over the whole harvest, so the Spirit of God cleanses us by the holiness of Christ, and makes us partakers of it. Nor is this done by imputation only, for in that respect he is said to have been *made to us righteousness;* but he is likewise said to have been *made to us sanctification,* (1 Cor. i. 30,) because he has, so to speak, presented us to his Father in his own person, that we may be renewed to true holiness by his Spirit. Besides, though this sanctification belongs to the whole life of Christ, yet the highest illustration of it was given in the sacrifice of his death; for then he showed himself to be the true High Priest, by consecrating the temple, the altar, all the vessels, and the people, by the power of his Spirit.

20. And I ask not for these only, but for those also who shall believe on me through their word; 21. That all may be one; as thou, Father, art in me, and I in thee, that they also may be one in us that the world may believe that thou hast sent me. 22. And I have given to them the glory which thou gavest to me, that they may be one, as we are one 23. I in them, and thou in me, that they may be perfect in one; and that the world may know that thou hast sent me, and hast loved them,[1] as thou hast loved me.

20. *And I ask not for these only.* He now gives a wider range to his prayer, which hitherto had included the apostles alone; for he extends it to all the disciples of the Gospel, so long as there shall be any of them to the end of the world. This is assuredly a remarkable ground of confidence; for if we believe in Christ through the doctrine of the Gospel, we ought to entertain no doubt that we are already gathered with the apostles into his faithful protection, so that not one of us shall perish. This prayer of Christ is a safe harbour, and whoever retreats into it is safe from all danger of shipwreck; for it is as if Christ had solemnly sworn that he will devote his care and diligence to our salvation.

He began with his apostles, that their salvation, which we know to be certain, might make us more certain of our own salvation; and, therefore, whenever Satan attacks us, let us

---

[1] " Et que tu les aimes ,"—" and that thou lovest them."

learn to meet him with this shield, that it is not to no purpose that the Son of God united us with the apostles, so that the salvation of all was bound up, as it were, in the same bundle. There is nothing, therefore, that ought more powerfully to excite us to embrace the Gospel; for as it is an inestimable blessing that we are presented to God by the hand of Christ, to be preserved from destruction, so we ought justly to love it, and to care for it above all things else. In this respect the madness of the world is monstrous. All desire salvation; Christ instructs us in a way of obtaining it, from which if any one turn aside, there remains for him no good hope; and yet scarcely one person in a hundred deigns to receive what was so graciously offered.

For those who shall believe on me. We must attend to this form of expression. Christ prays *for all who shall believe in him.* By these words he reminds us of what we have sometimes said already, that our faith ought to be directed to him. The clause which immediately follows, *through their word,* expresses admirably the power and nature of faith, and at the same time is a familiar confirmation to us who know that our faith is founded on the Gospel taught by the apostles. Let the world then condemn us a thousand times, this alone ought to satisfy us, that Christ acknowledges us to be his heritage, and pleads with the Father for us.

But woe to the Papists, whose faith is so far removed from this rule, that they are not ashamed to vomit out this horrid blasphemy, that there is nothing in Scripture but what is ambiguous, and may be turned in a variety of ways. The tradition of the Church is therefore their only authoritative guide to what they shall believe. But let us remember that the Son of God, who alone is competent to judge, does not approve of any other faith[1] than that which is drawn from the doctrine of the apostles, and sure information of that doctrine will be found no where else than in their writings.

We must also observe that form of expression, *to believe through the word,* which means that faith springs from hearing, because the outward preaching of men is the instrument by which God draws us to faith. It follows, that God is, strict-

---

[1] " Qui seul en peut et doit prononcer, n'approve point d'autre foy."

ly speaking, the Author of faith, and men are *the ministers by whom we believe,* as Paul teaches, (1 Cor. iii. 5.)

21. *That all may be one.* He again lays down the end of our happiness as consisting in unity, and justly; for the ruin of the human race is, that, having been alienated from God, it is also broken and scattered in itself. The restoration of it, therefore, on the contrary, consists in its being properly united in one body, as Paul declares the perfection of the Church to consist in *believers being joined together in one spirit,* and says that *apostles, prophets, evangelists, and pastors, were given, that they might edify and restore the body of Christ, till it came to the unity of faith;* and therefore he exhorts believers to *grow into Christ, who is the Head, from whom the whole body joined together, and connected by every bond of supply, according to the operation in the measure of every part, maketh increase of it to edification,* (Eph. iv. 3, 11-16.) Wherefore, whenever Christ speaks about unity, let us remember how basely and shockingly, when separated from him, the world is scattered; and, next, let us learn that the commencement of a blessed life is, that we be all governed, and that we all live, by the Spirit of Christ alone.

Again, it ought to be understood, that, in every instance in which Christ declares, in this chapter, that he is *one with the Father,* he does not speak simply of his Divine essence, but that he is called *one,* as regards his mediatorial office, and in so far as he is our Head. Many of the fathers, no doubt, interpreted these words as meaning, absolutely, that Christ is *one* with the Father, because he is the eternal God. But their dispute with the Arians led them to seize on detached passages, and to torture them out of their natural meaning, in order to employ them against their antagonists.[1] Now, Christ's design was widely different from that of raising our minds to a mere speculation about his hidden Divinity; for he reasons from the end, by showing that we ought to be *one,* otherwise the *unity* which he has with the Father would

---

[1] "Et les ont tirees hors de leur simple sens pour s'en servir contre les adversaires."

be fruitless and unavailing. To comprehend aright what was intended by saying, that Christ and the Father are *one*, we must take care not to deprive Christ of his office as Mediator, but must rather view him as he is the Head of the Church, and unite him with his members. Thus will the chain of thought be preserved, that, in order to prevent the *unity* of the Son with the Father from being fruitless and unavailing, the power of that *unity* must be diffused through the whole body of believers. Hence, too, we infer that we are *one* with the Son of God;[1] not because he conveys his substance to us, but because, by the power of his Spirit, he imparts to us his life and all the blessings which he has received from the Father.

That the world may believe. Some explain the word *world* to mean the elect, who, at that time, were still dispersed; but since the word *world*, throughout the whole of this chapter, denotes the reprobate, I am more inclined to adopt a different opinion. It happens that, immediately afterwards, he draws a distinction between all his people and the same *world* which he now mentions.

The verb, *to believe*, has been inaccurately used by the Evangelist for the verb, *to know;* that is, when unbelievers, convinced by their own experience, perceive the heavenly and Divine glory of Christ. The consequence is, that, *believing, they do not believe*, because this conviction does not penetrate into the inward feeling of the heart. And it is a just vengeance of God, that the splendour of Divine glory dazzles the eyes of the reprobate, because they do not deserve to have a clear and pure view of it. He afterwards uses the verb, *to know*, in the same sense.

22. *And I have given to them the glory which thou gavest to me.* Let it be observed here, that, while a pattern of perfect happiness was exhibited in Christ, he had nothing that belonged peculiarly to himself, but rather was rich, in order to enrich those who believed in him. Our happiness lies in having the image of God restored and formed anew in us, which was

---

[1] "Avec le Fils de Dieu"

defaced by sin. Christ is not only the lively image of God, in so far as he is the eternal Word of God, but even on his human nature, which he has in common with us, the likeness of *the glory* of the Father has been engraved, so as to form his members to the resemblance of it. Paul also teaches us this, that *we all, with unveiled face, by beholding* THE GLORY OF GOD, *are changed into the same image,* (2 Cor. iii. 18.) Hence it follows, that no one ought to be reckoned among the disciples of Christ, unless we perceive *the glory of God* impressed on him, as with a seal, by the likeness of Christ. To the same purpose are the words which immediately follow:

23. *I in them, and thou in me;* for he intends to teach that in him dwells all fulness of blessings, and that what was concealed in God is now manifested in him, that he may impart it to his people, as the water, flowing from the fountain by various channels, waters the fields on all sides.

And hast loved them.[1] He means that it is a very striking exhibition, and a very excellent pledge, of the love of God towards believers, which the world is compelled to feel, whether it will or not, when the Holy Spirit dwelling in them sends forth the rays of righteousness and holiness. There are innumerable other ways, indeed, in which God daily testifies his fatherly love towards us, but the mark of adoption is justly preferred to them all. He likewise adds, *and hast loved them,* AS THOU HAST LOVED ME. By these words he intended to point out the cause and origin of the love; for the particle *as,* means *because,* and the words, AS *thou hast loved me,* mean, BECAUSE *thou hast loved me;* for to Christ alone belongs the title of *Well-beloved,* (Matth. iii. 17; xvii. 5.) Besides, that love which the heavenly Father bears towards the Head is extended to all the members, so that he loves none but in Christ.

Yet this gives rise to some appearance of contradiction; for Christ, as we have seen elsewhere,[2] declares that the unspeakable *love of God* towards *the world* was the reason why he gave his only-begotten *Son,* (John iii. 16.) If the cause

---

[1] " *Et que tu les aimes,* ,"—" *And that thou lovest them.*"
[2] Vol. 1. p. 122.

must go before the effect, we infer that God the Father *loved* men apart from Christ; that is, before he was appointed to be the Redeemer. I reply, in that, and similar passages, *love* denotes the mercy with which God was moved towards unworthy persons, and even towards his enemies, before he reconciled them to himself. It is, indeed, a wonderful goodness of God, and inconceivable by the human mind, that, exercising benevolence towards men whom he could not but hate, he removed the cause of the hatred, that there might be no obstruction to his love. And, indeed, Paul informs us that there are two ways in which we are *loved* in Christ; first, because the Father *chose us in him before the creation of the world*, (Eph. i. 4;) and, secondly, because in Christ God *hath reconciled us to himself*, and hath showed that he is gracious to us, (Rom. v. 10.) Thus we are at the same time the enemies and the friends of God, until, atonement having been made for our sins, we are restored to favour with God. But when we are justified by faith, it is then, properly, that we begin to be *loved* by God, as children by a father. That *love* by which Christ was appointed to be the person, in whom we should be freely chosen before we were born, and while we were still ruined in Adam, is hidden in the breast of God, and far exceeds the capacity of the human mind. True, no man will ever feel that God is gracious to him, unless he perceives that God is pacified in Christ. But as all relish for the love of God vanishes when Christ is taken away, so we may safely conclude that, since by faith we are ingrafted into his body, there is no danger of our falling from *the love of God;* for this foundation cannot be overturned, that we are *loved*, because the Father *hath loved* his Son.[1]

24. Father, I will that those whom thou hast given me may also be with me where I am, that they may behold my glory, which thou hast given me; for thou lovedst me before the creation of the world. 25. Righteous Father, the world hath not known thee, but I have known thee, and these have known that thou hast sent me. 26. And I have declared to them thy name, and will declare it; that the love with which thou hast loved me may be in them, and I in them.

---

[1] "Pource que le Pere a aimé son Fils."

24. *Father, I will.* *To will* is put for *to desire;* [1] for it expresses not a command but a prayer. But it may be understood in two ways; either that *he wills* that the disciples may enjoy his eternal presence, or, that God may, at length, receive them into the heavenly kingdom, to which he goes before them.

That they may behold my glory. Some explain *beholding his glory* to mean, partaking of *the glory* which Christ has. Others explain it to be, to know by the experience of faith what Christ is, and how great is his majesty. For my own part, after carefully weighing the whole matter, I think that Christ speaks of the perfect happiness of believers, as if he had said, that his desire will not be satisfied till they have been received into heaven. In the same manner I explain the BEHOLDING of *the glory.* At that time they saw the *glory* of Christ, just as a man shut up in the dark obtains, through small chinks, a feeble and glimmering light. Christ now wishes that they shall make such progress as to enjoy the full brightness of heaven. In short, he asks that the Father will conduct them, by uninterrupted progress, to the full vision of his *glory.*

For thou lovedst me. This also agrees better with the person of the Mediator than with Christ's Divinity alone. It would be harsh to say that the Father loved his Wisdom; and though we were to admit it, the connection of the passage leads us to a different view. Christ, unquestionably, spoke as the Head of the Church, when he formerly prayed that the apostles might be united with him, and might *behold the glory* of his reign. He now says that the love of the Father is the cause of it; and, therefore, it follows that he was *beloved,* in so far as he was appointed to be the Redeemer of the world. With such a love did the Father love him *before the creation of the world,* that he might be the person in whom the Father would love his elect.

25. *Righteous Father.* He compares his disciples to *the*

---

[1] " Quand il dit, *Je veux,* c'est comme s'il disoit, *Je desire,* "—" When he says, *I will,* it is as if he had said, *I desire.*"

world, so as to describe more fully the approbation and favour which they had received from *the Father;* for it is proper that they who alone know God, whom the whole world rejects, should be distinguished above others, and most properly does Christ plead with peculiar warmth for those whom the unbelief of *the world* did not prevent from acknowledging God. By calling him *Righteous Father*, Christ defies *the world* and its malice; as if he had said, "However proudly *the world* may despise or reject God, still it takes nothing from him, and cannot hinder the honour of his righteousness from remaining unimpaired." By these words he declares that the faith of the godly ought to be founded on God, in such a manner that, though *the whole world* should oppose, it would never fail; just as, in the present day, we must charge the Pope with injustice, in order that we may vindicate for God the praise which is due to him.

But I have known thee, and these have known that thou hast sent me. Christ does not merely say that God was *known* by the disciples, but mentions two steps; first, that *he has known the Father;* and, secondly, that the disciples *have known that he was sent by the Father.* But as he adds immediately afterwards, that he has *declared to them the name* of the Father, he praises them, as I have said, for the knowledge of God, which separates them from the rest of the world. Yet we must attend to the order of faith, as it is here described. The Son came out of the bosom of the Father, and, properly speaking, he alone *knows* the Father; and, therefore, all who desire to approach God must betake themselves to Christ meeting them, and must devote themselves to him; and, after having been known by the disciples, he will, at length, raise them to God the Father.

26. *And I have declared to them thy name, and will declare it.* Christ discharged the office of Teacher, but, in order to make known the Father, he employed the secret revelation of the Spirit, and not the sound of his voice alone. He means, therefore, that he taught the apostles efficaciously. Besides, their faith being at that time very weak, he promises greater progress for the future, and thus prepares them to expect

more abundant grace of the Holy Spirit. Though he speaks of the apostles, we ought to draw from this a general exhortation, to study to make constant progress, and not to think that we have run so well that we have not still a long journey before us, so long as we are surrounded by the flesh.

That the love with which thou hast loved me may be in them; that is, that thou mayest love them in me, or, that *the love with which thou hast loved me* may be extended to them; for, strictly speaking, *the love with which God loves* us is no other than that *with which he loved* his Son from the beginning, so as to render us also acceptable to him, and capable of being *loved* in Christ. And, indeed, as was said a little before, so far as relates to us, apart from Christ, we are hated by God, and he only begins to love us, when we are united to the body of his beloved Son. It is an invaluable privilege of faith, that we know that Christ was *loved* by the Father on our account, that we might be made partakers of the same love, and might enjoy it for ever.

And I in them. This clause deserves our attention, for it teaches us that the only way in which we are included in that love which he mentions is, that Christ dwells in us; for, as the Father cannot look upon his Son without having likewise before his eyes the whole body of Christ, so, if we wish to be beheld in him, we must be actually his members.

CHAPTER XVIII.

1. When Jesus had spoken these words, he went out with his disciples over the brook Kedron, where was a garden, into which he entered, and his disciples. 2. And Judas also, who betrayed him, knew the place, for Jesus often resorted thither with his disciples 3 Then Judas, having received a band of soldiers, and officers from the chief priests and Pharisees, came thither with lanterns, and torches, and weapons. 4 Now Jesus, knowing all the things which were coming upon him, went forward and said to them, Whom seek ye? 5. They answered him, Jesus of Nazareth. Jesus saith to them, It is I. And Judas also, who betrayed him, stood with them. 6. As soon therefore as he said to them, It is I, they went backward, and fell to the ground.

1. *When Jesus had spoken these words.* In this narrative

John passes by many things which the other three Evangelists relate, and he does so on purpose, as his intention was to collect many things worthy of being recorded, about which they say nothing; and, therefore, let the reader go to the other Evangelists to find what is wanting here.

Over the brook Kedron. In the Greek original there is an article prefixed to *Kedron,* which would seem to intimate that the *brook* takes its name from the *cedars;*[1] but this is probably an error which has crept into the text; for *the valley* or *brook* KEDRON is often mentioned in Scripture. The place was so called from its being *dark* or *gloomy,* because, being a hollow valley, it was shady.[2] On that point, however, I do not dispute : I only state what is more probable.

The chief thing to be considered is, the intention of the Evangelist in pointing out the place ; for his object was, to show that Christ went to death willingly. He came into a place which, he knew, was well known to *Judas.* Why did he do this but to present himself, of his own accord, to the traitor and to the enemies? Nor was he led astray by inadvertency, for he knew beforehand all that was to happen. John afterwards mentions also that he went forward to meet them. He therefore suffered death, not by constraint, but willingly, that he might be a voluntary sacrifice ; for without obedience atonement would not have been obtained for us.

[1] Is Κέδρων a proper name, or an appellative? CALVIN does not mean that the presence of the article settles this question, but that it depends on the preference which shall be given to one or another of the various readings. If we read τῶν Κέδρων, it will be difficult to resist the conclusion that Κέδρων is the genitive plural of Κέδρος, *a cedar;* but if we read τοῦ Κέδρων, or rather τοῦ Κεδρών, we must treat Κεδρών as an indeclinable Hebrew word, though Josephus chooses sometimes to decline it, as in the phrase, χείμαρρον Κεδρῶνος, *the brook of Kedron,* (Ant. VIII. 1) "Instead of the common reading, τῶν Κέδρων," says Bloomfield, "four of the most ancient MSS. and six ancient Versions, with some Fathers, have τοῦ Κεδρών, which was preferred by Beza, Casaubon, Campbell, Castalio, Drusius, Lightfoot, Bois, Bynæus, Reland, and others of the best Commentators down to Middleton, Kuinoel, and Tittmann, and has been received by Bengel, Griesbach, Knapp, Vater, and Scholz. The common reading, however, is strenuously, but not satisfactorily, defended by Lampe and Matthæi." Our Author proceeds no further than to propose τοῦ instead of τῶν, as a conjectural emendation ; but Bloomfield has given a prodigious list of authorities on the same side.—*Ed.*

[2] The Hebrew name קדרון (*Kidron*) is derived from קדר, (*Kadar,*) *it was black,* and signifies *the black brook* —*Ed.*

Besides, he entered into the garden, not for the purpose of seeking a place of concealment, but that he might have a better opportunity, and greater leisure, for prayer. That he prayed three times to be delivered from death, (Matth. xxvi. 44,) is not inconsistent with that voluntary obedience of which we have spoken;[1] for it was necessary that he should contend with difficulties, that he might be victorious. Now, having subdued the dread of death, he advances to death freely and willingly.

3. *Judas, therefore, having received a band of soldiers.* That *Judas* came accompanied by soldiers and by so large a retinue, is a sign of a bad conscience, which always trembles without any cause. It is certain that the *band of soldiers* was borrowed from the governor, who also sent a captain at the head of a thousand soldiers; for, on account of sudden mutinies, a garrison was stationed in the city, and the governor himself kept a body-guard, wherever he was. The rest were *officers* sent by *the priests;* but John makes separate mention *of the Pharisees,* because they were more enraged than all the rest, as if they had cared more about religion.

4. *Jesus therefore, knowing.* The Evangelist states more clearly with what readiness Christ went forward to death, but, at the same time, describes the great power which he exercised by a single word, in order to inform us that wicked men had no power over him, except so far as he gave permission.

5. *It is I.* He replies mildly that he is the person *whom they seek,* and yet, as if they had been struck down by a violent tempest, or rather by a thunderbolt, he lays them prostrate on the ground. There was no want of power in him, therefore, to restrain their hands, if he had thought proper; but he wished to obey his Father, by whose decree he knew that he was called to die.

[1] On this point the reader will do well to consult our Author's elaborate exposition and argument, *Harmony of the Evangelists,* vol. iii pp. 226-234.

We may infer from this how dreadful and alarming to the wicked the voice of Christ will be, when he shall ascend his throne to judge the world. At that time he stood as a lamb ready to be sacrificed; his majesty, so far as outward appearance was concerned, was utterly gone; and yet when he utters but a single word, his armed and courageous enemies fall down. And what was the word? He thunders no fearful excommunication against them, but only replies, *It is I*. What then will be the result, when he shall come, not to be judged by a man, but to be the Judge of the living and the dead; not in that mean and despicable appearance, but shining in heavenly glory, and accompanied by his angels? He intended, at that time, to give a proof of that efficacy which Isaiah ascribes to his voice. Among other glorious attributes of Christ, the Prophet relates that *he will strike the earth with the rod of his mouth, and will slay the wicked by the breath of his lips*, (Isa. xi. 4.) True, the fulfilment of this prophecy is declared by Paul to be delayed till the end of the world, (2 Thess. ii. 8.) Yet we daily see the wicked, with all their rage and pride, struck down by the voice of Christ; and, when those men fell down who had come to bind Christ, there was exhibited a visible token of that alarm which wicked men feel within themselves, whether they will or not, when Christ speaks by his ministers. Besides, as this was in some measure accidental to the voice of Christ, to whom it peculiarly belongs to raise up men who were lying in a state of death, he will undoubtedly display toward us such power as to raise us even to heaven.

7. He therefore asked them again, Whom seek ye? And they said, Jesus of Nazareth. 8 Jesus answered, I told you that it is I if therefore you seek me, allow these, to go away. 9. That the word which he had spoken might be fulfilled, Of those whom thou gavest to me I have lost none.

7. *He therefore asked them again.* Hence it appears what is the powerful effect of that blindness with which God strikes the minds of wicked men, and how dreadful is their stupidity, when, by a just judgment of God, they have been bewitched by Satan. Oxen and asses, if they fall, are touched with

some kind of feeling; but those men, after having had an open display of the divine power of Christ, proceed as fearlessly as if they had not perceived in him even the shadow of a man; nay, Judas himself remains unmoved. Let us learn, therefore, to fear the judgment of God, by which the reprobate, delivered into the hands of Satan, become more stupid than brute beasts. Nor can it be doubted that Satan hurried them on, with wild fury, to such a desperate hardihood; for there is no insanity that drives a man with such violence as this kind of blindness. Wicked men, after having been *given over to a reprobate mind*, (Rom. i. 28,) care no more about rushing against God than if they had only to do with a fly. They feel his power, indeed, but not so as to be disposed to obey; for sooner will they be broken a hundred times than they will yield. In short, their malice is a veil to hinder them from observing the light of God; their obstinacy renders them harder than stones, so that they never suffer themselves to be subdued.

8. *I have told you that it is I.* Here we see how the Son of God not only submits to death of his own accord, that by his obedience he may blot out our transgressions, but also how he discharges the office of a good Shepherd in protecting his flock. He sees the attack of the wolves, and does not wait till they come to the sheep which have been committed to his care, but immediately goes forward to guard them. Whenever, therefore, either wicked men or devils make an attack upon us, let us not doubt that this good Shepherd is ready[1] to aid us in the same manner. Yet by his example Christ has laid down to shepherds a rule which they ought to follow, if they wish to discharge their office in a right manner.

9. *I have lost none.* This passage appears to be inappropriately quoted, as it relates to their souls rather than to their bodies; for Christ did not keep the apostles safe to the last, but this he accomplished, that, amidst incessant dangers, and even in the midst of death, still their eternal salvation was

---

[1] " Que ce bon Pasteur ne soit prest."

secured. I reply, the Evangelist does not speak merely of their bodily life, but rather means that Christ, sparing them for a time, made provision for their eternal salvation. Let us consider how great their weakness was; what do we think they would have done, if they had been brought to the test? While, therefore, Christ did not choose that they should be tried beyond the strength which he had given to them, he rescued them from eternal destruction. And hence we may draw a general doctrine, that, though he try our faith by many temptations, still he will never allow us to come into extreme danger without supplying us also with strength to overcome. And, indeed, we see how he continually bears with our weakness, when he puts himself forward to repel so many attacks of Satan and wicked men, because he sees that we are not yet able or prepared for them. In short, he never brings his people into the field of battle till they have been fully trained, so that even in perishing they do not perish, because there is gain provided for them both in death and in life.

10 Then Simon Peter, having a sword, drew it, and struck the high priest's servant, and cut off his right ear, and the servant's name was Malchus. 11 Jesus therefore said to Peter, Put up thy sword into the sheath. Shall I not drink the cup which my Father hath given me? 12. Then the band, and the captain, and officers of the Jews, took Jesus, and bound him; 13. And led him away to Annas first; for he was father-in-law to Caiaphas, who was the high priest of that year. 14. And Caiaphas was he who had given counsel to the Jews, that it was expedient that one man should die for the people.

10. *Then Simon Peter, having a sword, drew it.* The Evangelist now describes the foolish zeal of *Peter*, who attempted to defend his Master in an unlawful manner. Boldly and courageously, indeed, he incurs great risk on Christ's account; but as he does not consider what his calling demands, and what God permits, his action is so far from deserving praise, that he is severely blamed by Christ. But let us learn that, in the person of *Peter*, Christ condemns every thing that men dare to attempt out of their own fancy. This doctrine is eminently worthy of attention; for nothing is more common than to defend, under the cloak of zeal, every thing that we do, as if it were of no importance whether God approved, or not, what men suppose to be right, whose prudence is nothing else than mere vanity.

If we saw nothing faulty in the zeal of *Peter*, still we ought to be satisfied on this single ground, that Christ declares that he is displeased with it. But we see that it was not owing to him that Christ did not turn aside from death, and that his name was not exposed to perpetual disgrace; for, in offering violence to the captain and the soldiers, he acts the part of a highwayman, because he resists the power which God has appointed. Christ having already been more than enough hated by the world, this single deed might give plausibility to all the calumnies which his enemies falsely brought against him. Besides, it was exceedingly thoughtless in Peter to attempt to prove his faith by his sword, while he could not do so by his tongue. When he is called to make confession, he denies his Master; and now, without his Master's authority, he raises a tumult.

Warned by so striking an example, let us learn to keep our zeal within proper bounds; and as the wantonness of our flesh is always eager to attempt more than God commands, let us learn that our zeal will succeed ill, whenever we venture to undertake any thing contrary to the word of God. It will sometimes happen that the commencement gives us flattering promises, but we shall at length be punished for our rashness. Let obedience, therefore, be the foundation of all that we undertake. We are also reminded, that those who have resolved to plead the cause of Christ do not always conduct themselves so skilfully as not to commit some fault; and, therefore, we ought the more earnestly to entreat the Lord to guide us in every action by the spirit of prudence.

11. *Put up thy sword into the sheath.* By this command Christ reproves Peter's action. But we must attend to the reason, which is, that a private individual was not permitted to rise in opposition to those who had been invested with public authority; for this may be inferred from the other three Evangelists, who relate Christ's general declaration, *He who strikes with the sword shall perish by the sword,* (Matth. xxvi. 52.) We must also beware of repelling our enemies by

force or violence, even when they unjustly provoke us, except so far as the institutions and laws of the community admit; for whoever goes beyond the limits of his calling, though he should gain the applause of the whole world, will never obtain for his conduct the approbation of God.[1]

Shall I not drink the cup which my Father hath given to me? This appears to be a special reason why Christ ought to be silent, that he might be *led as a lamb to be sacrificed,* (Isa. liii. 7;) but it serves the purpose of an example, for the same patience is demanded from all of us. Scripture compares afflictions to medicinal draughts; for, as the master of a house distributes meat and drink to his children and servants, so God has this authority over us, that he has a right to treat every one as he thinks fit; and whether he cheers us by prosperity, or humbles us by adversity, he is said to administer a sweet or a bitter draught. The draught appointed for Christ was, to suffer the death of the cross for the reconciliation of the world. He says, therefore, that he must *drink the cup which his Father* measured out and delivered to him.

In the same manner we, too, ought to be prepared for enduring the cross. And yet we ought not to listen to fanatics, who tell us that we must not seek remedies for diseases and any other kind of distresses, lest we reject *the cup* which the Heavenly Father[2] presents to us. Knowing that *we must once die,* (Heb. ix. 27,) we ought to be prepared for death; but the time of our death being unknown to us, the Lord permits us to defend our life by those aids which he has himself appointed. We must patiently endure diseases, however grievous they may be to our flesh; and though they do not yet appear to be mortal, we ought to seek alleviation of them; only we must be careful not to attempt any thing but what is permitted by the word of God. In short, provided that this remain always fixed in our hearts, *Let the will of the Lord be done,* (Acts xxi. 14,) when we seek deliverance from the evils which press upon us, we do not fail *to drink the cup* which the Lord has given to us.

[1] The reader will find our Author's views on this subject stated fully in the *Harmony of the Evangelists,* vol. iii. p. 244.
[2] "Le Pere Celeste."

12. *Then the band of soldiers and the captain.* It might be thought strange that Christ, who laid the soldiers prostrate on the ground by a single word, now allows himself to be *taken;* for if he intended at length to surrender to his enemies, what need was there for performing such a miracle? But the demonstration of divine power was advantageous in two respects; for, first, it serves to take away the offence, that we may not think that Christ yielded as if he had been overcome by weakness; and, secondly, it proves that in dying he was altogether voluntary. So far as it was useful, therefore, he asserted his power against his enemies; but when it was necessary to obey the Father, he restrained himself, that he might be offered as a sacrifice. But let us remember that the body of the Son of God was bound, that our souls might be loosed from the cords of sin and of Satan.

13. *And led him away to Annas first.* The other Evangelists omit this circumstance, because it does not greatly affect the substance of the narrative; for nothing was done there that was worthy of being recorded. Perhaps the convenience of the place induced them to imprison Christ in the house of Annas, till the high priest assembled the council.

The high priest of that year. He does not mean that the office of the high priesthood was annual, as many have falsely imagined, but that *Caiaphas was high priest* at that time, which appears plainly from Josephus. By the injunction of the Law, this honour was perpetual, and ended only at the death of him who held it; but ambition and intestine broils gave occasion to the Roman governors to dethrone one high priest and put another in his room, at their own pleasure, either for money or for favour. Thus Vitellius deposed Caiaphas, and appointed Jonathan, the son of Annas, to be his successor.

14. *Who had given counsel to the Jews.* The Evangelist repeats the opinion of Caiaphas, which formerly came under our notice;[1] for God employed the foul mouth of a wicked

[1] Vol. i. p. 453.

and treacherous *high priest* to utter a prediction, (John xi. 50,) just as he guided the tongue of the prophet Balaam, contrary to his wish, so that he was constrained to bless the people, though he desired to curse them, to gain favour with king Balak, (Num. xxiii. 7, 8.)

15. And Simon Peter followed Jesus, and another disciple;[1] and that disciple was known to the high priest; therefore he went in with Jesus into the court of the high priest. 16. But Peter stood without at the door. The other disciple, therefore, who was known to the high priest, went out, and spoke to her that kept the door, and brought in Peter.[2] 17 Then the maid that kept the door said to Peter, Art not thou also one of that man's disciples? He saith, I am not. 18. And the servants and officers, who had kindled a fire of coals, because it was cold, stood there and warmed themselves, and Simon Peter was also standing with them, and warming himself.

15. *And another disciple.* Some have been led astray, by a slight conjecture, to suppose that this *disciple* was the Evangelist[3] John, because he is accustomed to speak of himself without mentioning his name. But what intimacy with a proud *high priest* could John have, who was a mean fisherman? And how was it possible for him, being one of Christ's household, to be in the habit of visiting the house of *the high priest?* It is more probable that he was not one of the twelve, but that he is called a disciple, because he had embraced the doctrine of the Son of God.

John is not very exact in arranging the narrative, being satisfied with drawing up a brief summary; for, after having related that Peter once denied Christ, he intermingles other matters, and afterwards returns to the other two denials. Inattentive readers were led by this circumstance to conclude that the first denial took place in the house of *Annas*. The words, however, convey no such meaning, but rather state clearly that it was the high priest's maid that constrained Peter to deny Christ. We must, therefore, understand that, when Christ was brought before the high priest, admission

---

[1] " Or Simon Pierre, avec un autre disciple, suyvoit Jesus."—" Now Simon Peter, with another disciple, followed Jesus."
[2] " Et parla à la portiere, *laquelle fit entrer* Pierre ;"—" and spoke to her that kept the door, *who brought in* Peter."
[3] " Nostre Evangeliste."

was not granted to any person who chose, but that *the disciple who was known to the high priest* requested, as a personal favour, that Peter might be admitted. There is no reason to doubt that godly zeal was the motive that induced both of them to follow Christ; but since Christ had plainly declared that he spared Peter and the others, he who was so weak would have found it to be far better for him to groan and pray in some dark corner than to go into the presence of men. He now undertakes, with great earnestness, the performance of a duty from which Christ had released him; and when he comes to the confession of faith, in which he ought to have persevered even to death, his courage fails. We ought always to consider what the Lord requires from us, that those who are weak may not undertake what is not necessary.

17. *Then the maid that kept the door said to Peter.* Peter is introduced into the high priest's hall; but it cost him very dear, for, as soon as he sets his foot within it, he is constrained to deny Christ. When he stumbles so shamefully at the first step, the foolishness of his boasting is exposed. He had boasted that he would prove to be a valiant champion, and able to meet death with firmness; and now, at the voice of a single *maid*, and that voice unaccompanied by threatening, he is confounded and throws down his arms. Such is a demonstration of the power of man. Certainly, all the strength that appears to be in men is smoke, which a breath immediately drives away. When we are out of the battle, we are too courageous; but experience shows that our lofty talk is foolish and groundless; and, even when Satan makes no attacks, we contrive for ourselves idle alarms which disturb us before the time. The voice of a feeble woman terrified Peter: and what is the case with us? Do we not continually tremble at the rustling of a falling leaf? A false appearance of danger, which was still distant, made Peter tremble: and are we not every day led away from Christ by childish absurdities? In short, our courage is of such a nature, that, of its own accord, it gives way where there is no enemy; and thus does God revenge the arro-

gance of men by reducing fierce minds to a state of weakness. A man, filled not with fortitude but with wind, promises that he will obtain an easy victory over the whole world; and yet, no sooner does he see the shadow of a thistle, than he immediately trembles. Let us therefore learn not to be brave in any other than the Lord.

I am not. This does not seem, indeed, to be an absolute denial of Christ; but when Peter is afraid to acknowledge that he is *one of Christ's disciples,* it amounts to an assertion that he has nothing to do with him. This ought to be carefully observed, that no one may imagine that he has escaped by acting the part of a sophist, when it is only in an indirect manner that he shrinks from the confession of his faith.

18. *And Simon Peter was standing with them.* When the Evangelist adds that *Peter was standing near the fire, along with the officers and servants,* this serves to connect the various parts of the narrative, as we shall afterwards see. But this shows how great was Peter's stupidity, when, without the least concern, he *warmed himself* along with a multitude of wicked men, after having denied his Master; though it is possible that he may have been restrained by fear lest, in going out of the high priest's house, he should fall into another danger of the same kind.

19. The high priest then asked Jesus concerning his disciples, and concerning his doctrine 20. Jesus answered him, I spoke openly in the world; I always taught in the synagogue and in the temple, where all the Jews assemble, and in secret I have spoken nothing 21. Why askest thou me? Ask those who have heard what I have spoken to them behold, they know what I have said. 22. When he had said these things, one of the officers that stood by struck Jesus with the palm of his hand, saying, Answerest thou the high priest so? 23. Jesus answered him, If I have spoken evil, bear witness of the evil; but if well, why smitest thou me? 24. Now Annas had sent him bound to Caiaphas the high priest.

19. *The high priest then asked Jesus.* The high priest interrogates Christ, as if he had been some seditious person, who had split the Church into parties by collecting *disciples;* and he interrogates him as if he had been a false prophet, who had endeavoured to corrupt the purity of the faith by new

and perverse *doctrines*. Our Lord[1] Jesus Christ, having completely and faithfully discharged the office of teacher, does not enter into a new defence; but, that he may not abandon the cause of truth, he shows that he was prepared to defend all that *he had taught*. Yet he likewise reproves the impudence of the high priest, who inquires about a matter perfectly well known, as if it had been doubtful. Not satisfied with having rejected the Redeemer offered, together with the salvation promised to them, they likewise condemn all the exposition of the Law.

20. *I spoke openly in the world.* It is a childish error into which some have fallen, who think that this reply of Christ condemns those who expound the word of God in private apartments, when the tyranny of wicked men does not allow them to expound it publicly; for Christ does not argue as to what is lawful and what is not lawful, but his intention was to put down the insolent malice of Caiaphas.

This passage, however, appears to be inconsistent with another saying of Christ, where he enjoins the apostles to *proclaim on the house-tops what he had whispered in their ear,* (Matth. x. 27;) and again, when he declares that *it is not given to all to know the mysteries of the kingdom of heaven,* (Matth. xiii. 11,) and that he therefore confers this favour on none but the twelve apostles. I answer, when he says in the passage now under review, that *he spoke nothing in secret,* this refers to the substance of the doctrine, which was always the same, though the form of teaching it was various; for he did not speak differently among the disciples, so as to instruct them in something different; nor did he act cunningly, as if he purposely intended to conceal from the people what he spoke to a small number of persons in the house. He could, therefore, testify with a good conscience that he had openly declared and honestly proclaimed the substance of his doctrine.

22. *When he had said these things.* This is added, in order to inform us, first, how great was the rage of the enemies of

[1] "Nostre Seigneur."

Christ, and how tyrannical their government was; and, secondly, what sort of discipline existed among those priests. They sit like judges, but they are as cruel as ferocious beasts. A council is assembled, in which the utmost gravity ought to have prevailed; and yet a single *officer* is so daring and presumptuous, that, in the midst of the judicial proceedings, and in the presence of the judges, he strikes the person accused, who was not found to be in any respect guilty. We need not wonder, therefore, that the doctrine of Christ is condemned by so barbarous an assembly, from which not only all justice, but likewise all humanity and modesty, are banished.

23. *If I have spoken evil.* That is, "If I have sinned, accuse me, that, when the cause has been tried, I may be punished according to the offence; for this is not a lawful mode of procedure, but very different order and very different modesty ought to be maintained in judicial courts." Christ complains, therefore, that a grievous injury has been done to him, if he has committed no offence, and that, even if he has committed an offence, still they ought to proceed in a lawful manner, and not with rage and violence.

But Christ appears not to observe, in the present instance, the rule which he elsewhere lays down to his followers; for he does not *hold out the right cheek to him who had struck him on the left,* (Matth. v. 39.) I answer, in Christian patience it is not always the duty of him who has been struck to brook the injury done him, without saying a word, but, first, to endure it with patience, and, secondly, to give up all thoughts of revenge, and to endeavour to *overcome evil by good,* (Rom. xii. 21.) Wicked men are already too powerfully impelled by the spirit of Satan to do injury to others, in order that nobody may provoke them. It is a foolish exposition of Christ's words, therefore, that is given by those who view them in such a light as if we were commanded to hold out fresh inducements to those who already are too much disposed to do mischief; for he means nothing else than that each of us should be more ready to bear a second injury than to take revenge for the first; so that there is nothing to prevent a

Christian man from expostulating, when he has been unjustly treated, provided that his mind be free from rancour, and his hand from revenge.

24. *Now Annas had sent him bound.* This sentence must be read by way of parenthesis; for, having said that Christ was taken to the house of Annas, and having continued his narrative, as if the assembly of the priests had been held there, the Evangelist now reminds the reader that Christ was taken from the house of Annas to the high priest's house. But as the tense of the Greek verb (ἀπέστειλε) has led many people into a mistake, I have preferred translating it by the pluperfect tense, *Had sent.*[1]

25. And Simon Peter was standing there and warming himself. They said therefore to him, Art not thou also one of his disciples? He denied it,[2] and said, I am not. 26. One of the servants of the high priest, who was a kinsman of him whose ear Peter had cut off, said, Did not I see thee in the garden with him? 27. Then Peter denied it again;[3] and immediately the cock crew.

25. *He denied it.* How shocking the stupidity of Peter, who, after having denied his Master, not only has no feeling of repentance, but hardens himself by the very indulgence he takes in sinning! If each of them in his turn had asked him, he would not have hesitated to deny his Master a thousand times. Such is the manner in which Satan hurries along wretched men, after having degraded them. We must also attend to the circumstance which is related by the other Evangelists, (Matth. xxvi. 74; Mark xiv. 71,) that *he began to curse and to swear, saying, that he did not know Christ.* Thus it happens to many persons every day. At first, the fault will not be very great; next, it becomes habitual, and at length, after that conscience has been laid asleep, he who has accustomed himself to despise God will think nothing unlawful for him, but will dare to commit the greatest wickedness. There is nothing better for us, therefore, than to be early on

---

[1] "J'ay mieux aimé tourner en ceste sorte, Avoit envoyé; que, Il a envoyé;"—" I have chosen to render it in this way, *Annas* HAD SENT, rather than, *Annas* SENT."
[2] " Il le nia."   [3] " Le nia derechef."

our guard, that he who is tempted by Satan, while he is yet uncorrupted, may not allow himself the smallest indulgence.

27. *Immediately the cock crew.* The Evangelist mentions *the crowing of the cock*, in order to inform us, that Peter was warned by God at the very time; and for this reason the other Evangelists tell us, that *he then remembered the words of the Lord*, (Matth. xxvi. 75; Mark xiv. 72,) though Luke relates that the mere *crowing of the cock* did not produce any effect on Peter, till Christ *looked at him*, (Luke xxii. 61.) Thus, when any person has once begun to fall through the suggestions of Satan, no voice, no sign, no warning, will bring him back, until the Lord himself cast his eyes upon him.

28. Then they lead Jesus from Caiaphas into the hall of the governor;[1] and it was early in the morning, and they themselves did not enter into the hall, that they might not be defiled, but might eat the passover.[2] 29. Pilate therefore went out to them, and said, What accusation do you bring against this man? 30 They answered and said to him, If he were not a malefactor, we would not have delivered him to thee. 31. Pilate therefore said to them, Take you him, and judge him according to your law. The Jews therefore said to him, We are not allowed to put any man to death 32. That the word of Jesus might be fulfilled, which he had spoken, signifying by what death he should die.

28. *Then they lead Jesus.* That trial, which the Evangelist mentions, took place before daybreak; and yet there can be no doubt, that they had their bellows at work throughout the whole of the city to inflame the people. Thus the rage of the people was suddenly kindled, as if all, with one consent, demanded that Christ should be put to death. Now, the trial was conducted by the priests, not that they had it in their power to pronounce a sentence, but that, after having excited a prejudice against him by their previous decision, they might deliver him to the governor, as if he had already been fully tried.[3] The Romans gave the name *Prætorium* both to

[1] " In Prætorium ;"—" au Pretoire ,"—" into the Pretorium."
[2] " L'agneau de pasque ;"—" the paschal lamb."
[3] " Mais à fin de le livrer au juge, etant desja chargé, et comme suffisament conveincu par leur premiere cognoissance et les interrogatoires qu'ils luy avoient faites;"—" but to deliver him to the judge as a person already accused, and as having been sufficiently convicted by their previous trial, and by the questions which they had put to him."

the governor's house or palace,[1] and to the judgment-seat, where he was wont to decide causes.

That they might not be defiled. In abstaining from all *defilement,* that, being purified according to the injunction of the Law, *they may eat* the Lord's *Passover,* their religion, in this respect, deserves commendation. But there are two faults, and both of them are very heinous. The first is,[2] they do not consider that they carry more pollution within their hearts, than they can contract by entering any place however profane; and the second is, they carry to excess their care about smaller matters, and neglect what is of the highest importance. *To the defiled and to unbelievers,* says Paul, *nothing is pure; because their minds are polluted,* (Titus i. 15.) But these hypocrites, though they are so full of malice, ambition, fraud, cruelty, and avarice, that they almost infect heaven and earth with their abominable smell, are only afraid of external pollutions. So then it is an intolerable mockery, that they expect to please God, provided that they do not contract defilement by touching some unclean thing, though they have disregarded true purity.

Another fault connected with hypocrisy is, that, while it is careful in performing ceremonies, it makes no scruple of neglecting matters of the highest importance; for God enjoined on the Jews those ceremonies which are contained in the Law, for no other reason, than that they might be habituated to the love and practice of true holiness. Besides, no part of the Law forbade them to enter into the house of a Gentile, but it was a precaution derived from the traditions of the fathers, that no person might, through oversight, contract any pollution from an unclean house. But those venerable expounders of the Law, while they carefully *strain at a gnat, swallow the camel*[3] without any hesitation, (Matth. xxiii. 24;) and it is usual with hypocrites to reckon it a greater crime to kill a flea than to kill a man. This fault is closely allied to the other, of greatly preferring the traditions of men to the holy commandments of God. In order *that they may*

---

[1] "La maison ou palais du gouverneur."
[2] "La premiere faute est."
[3] See *Harmony of the Evangelists,* vol. iii. p 93.

eat the passover in a proper manner, they wish to keep themselves pure; but they suppose uncleanness to be confined within the walls of the governor's house, and yet they do not hesitate, while heaven and earth are witnesses, to pursue an innocent person to death. In short, they observe the shadow of *the passover* with a false and pretended reverence, and yet not only do they violate the true *passover* by sacrilegious hands, but endeavour, as far as lies in their power, to bury it in eternal oblivion.[1]

29. *Pilate therefore went out to them.* This heathen is not unwilling to encourage a superstition, which he ridicules and despises; but in the main point of the cause, he performs the duty of a good judge, when he orders them, if they have any accusation, to bring it forward. The priests, on the other hand, not having sufficient authority to condemn him whom they pronounce to be guilty, make no other reply, than that he ought to abide by their previous decision.

30. *If he were not a malefactor, we would not have delivered him to thee.* They indirectly complain of Pilate, that he has not a proper reliance on their integrity. "Why do you not, without further concern," say they, "hold it to be certain, that the person whom we prosecute deserves to die?" Such is the manner in which wicked men, whom God has raised to a high degree of honour, blinded as it were by their own greatness, allow themselves to do whatever they choose. Such, too, is the intoxicating nature of pride.[2] They wish that Christ should be reckoned a malefactor, and for no other reason[3] but because they accuse him. But if we come to the truth of the matter, what deeds of *a malefactor* shall we find in him, except that he has cured every kind of diseases, has driven the devils out of men, has made the paralytics and the lame to walk, has restored sight to the blind, hearing to the deaf, and life to the dead? Such were the real facts, and

[1] "De la ruiner et en abolir la memoire à jamais."
[2] "Voyla aussi comme orgueil remplit les gens d'une yvrognerie, et les met hors du sens"—"See, too, how pride fills people with a sort of drunkenness, and puts them out of their senses."
[3] "Et non pour autre raison."

those men knew them well; but, as I said a little ago, when men are intoxicated with pride, nothing is more difficult than to arouse them to form a sound and correct judgment.

31. *According to your law.* Pilate, offended by their barbarous and violent proceedings, undoubtedly reproaches them by stating that this form of condemnation, which they were eager to carry into effect, was at variance with the common law of all nations and with the feelings of mankind; and, at the same time, he censures them for boasting that they had a *law* given to them by God.

Take you him. He says this ironically; for he would not have allowed them to pronounce on a man a sentence of capital punishment; but it is as if he had said, "Were he in your power, he would instantly be executed, without being heard in his own defence; and, is this the equity of your Law, to condemn a man without any crime?" Thus do wicked men, falsely assuming the name of God as an excuse for their conduct, expose his holy doctrine to the reproaches of enemies, and the world eagerly seizes on it as an occasion of slander.

We are not allowed. Those who think that the Jews refuse an offer, which Pilate had made to them, are mistaken; but rather, knowing that he had said to them in mockery, *Take you him,* they reply, "You would not allow it; and since you are the judge, execute your office."

32. *That the word of Jesus might be fulfilled.* Finally, the Evangelist adds, that it was necessary that this should be done, in order that the prediction which Christ had uttered might be fulfilled, *The Son of man shall be delivered into the hands of the Gentiles,* (Matth. xx. 19.) And, indeed, if we wish to read with advantage the history of Christ's death, the chief point is, to consider the eternal purpose of God. The Son of God is placed before the tribunal of a mortal man. If we suppose that this is done by the caprice of men, and do not raise our eyes to God, our faith must necessarily be confounded and put to shame. But when we perceive that, by the condemnation of Christ, our condemnation before God is blotted out, because it pleased the Heavenly Father to take

this method of reconciling mankind to himself, raised on high by this single consideration, we boldly, and without shame, glory even in Christ's ignominy. Let us therefore learn, in each part of this narrative, to turn our eyes to God as the Author of our redemption.

33. Then Pilate went again into the hall, and called Jesus, and said to him, Art thou the King of the Jews? 34. Jesus answered him, Sayest thou this from thyself, or did others tell it thee of me? 35. Pilate answered, Am I a Jew? Thine own nation and the priests have delivered thee to me what hast thou done? 36. Jesus answered, My kingdom is not of this world: if my kingdom were of this world, my servants would have striven that I should not be delivered to the Jews. But now my kingdom is not from hence.

33. *Then Pilate went again into the hall.* It is probable that many things were said on both sides, which the Evangelist passes over; and this conclusion might be readily drawn from the other Evangelists. But John dwells chiefly on a single point, that Pilate made a laborious inquiry whether Christ was justly or unjustly accused. In the presence of the people, who were inflamed with sedition, nothing could be done but in a riotous manner. He therefore *goes again into the hall;* and, indeed, his intention is to acquit Christ, but Christ himself, in order that he may obey his Father, presents himself to be condemned; and this is the reason why he is so sparing in his replies. Having a judge who was favourable, and who would willingly have lent an ear to him, it was not difficult for him to plead his cause; but he considers for what purpose he came down into the world, and to what he is now called by the Father. Of his own accord, therefore, he refrains from speaking, that he may not escape from death.

Art thou the King of the Jews? It would never have struck Pilate's mind to put this question about *the kingdom,* if this charge had not been brought against Christ by the Jews. Now, Pilate takes up what was more offensive than all the rest, that, having disposed of it, he may acquit the prisoner. The tendency of Christ's answer is to show that there is no ground for that accusation; and thus it contains an indirect refutation; as if he had said, "It is absurd to bring that charge against me, for not even the slightest suspicion of it can fall upon me."

Pilate appears to have taken amiss that Christ asked him why he suspected him of such a crime;[1] and, therefore, he angrily reproaches him, that all the evil comes from *his own nation.* "I sit here as a judge," says he; "it is not foreigners, but your own countrymen, who accuse you. There is no reason, therefore, why you should involve me in your quarrels. You would be allowed by me and by the Romans to live at peace; but you raise disturbances among yourselves, and I am reluctantly compelled to bear a part in them."

36. *My kingdom is not of this world.* By these words he acknowledges that he is *a king,* but, so far as was necessary to prove his innocence, he clears himself of the calumny; for he declares, that there is no disagreement between his kingdom and political government or order;[2] as if he had said, "I am falsely accused, as if I had attempted to produce a disturbance, or to make a revolution in public affairs. I have preached about *the kingdom of God;* but that is spiritual, and, therefore, you have no right to suspect me of aspiring to kingly power." This defence was made by Christ before Pilate, but the same doctrine is useful to believers to the end of the world; for if the kingdom of Christ were earthly, it would be frail and changeable, because *the fashion of this world passeth away,* (1 Cor. vii. 31;) but now, since it is pronounced to be heavenly, this assures us of its perpetuity. Thus, should it happen, that the whole world were overturned, provided that our consciences are always directed to *the kingdom* of Christ, they will, nevertheless, remain firm, not only amidst shakings and convulsions, but even amidst dreadful ruin and destruction. If we are cruelly treated by wicked men, still our salvation is secured by *the kingdom* of Christ, which is not subject to the caprice of men. In short, though there are innumerable storms by which *the world* is continually agitated, *the kingdom* of Christ, in which we ought to seek tranquillity, is separated from *the world.*

[1] "De tel crime."
[2] "Et le gouvernement ou ordre politique."

We are taught, also, what is the nature of this *kingdom;* for if it made us happy according to the flesh, and brought us riches, luxuries, and all that is desirable for the use of the present life, it would smell of the earth and of the world; but now, though our condition be apparently wretched, still our true happiness remains unimpaired. We learn from it, also, who they are that belong to this *kingdom;* those who, having been renewed by the Spirit of God, contemplate the heavenly life in holiness and righteousness. Yet it deserves our attention, likewise, that it is not said, that *the kingdom* of Christ is not *in* this *world;* for we know that it has its seat in our hearts, as also Christ says elsewhere, *The kingdom of God is within you,* (Luke xvii. 21.) But, strictly speaking, *the kingdom of God,* while it dwells in us, is a stranger to the world, because its condition is totally different.

My servants would strive. He proves that he did not aim at an earthly kingdom, because no one moves, no one takes arms in his support; for if a private individual lay claim to royal authority, he must gain power by means of seditious men. Nothing of this kind is seen in Christ; and, therefore, it follows that he is not an earthly *king.*

But here a question arises, Is it not lawful to defend the *kingdom* of Christ by arms? For when *Kings* and *Princes*[1] are commanded to *kiss the Son of God,* (Ps. ii. 10-12,) not only are they enjoined to submit to his authority in their private capacity, but also to employ all the power that they possess, in defending the Church and maintaining godliness. I answer, first, they who draw this conclusion, that the doctrine of the Gospel and the pure worship of God ought not to be defended by arms, are unskilful and ignorant reasoners; for Christ argues only from the facts of the case in hand, how frivolous were the calumnies which the Jews had brought against him. Secondly, though godly kings defend *the kingdom* of Christ by the sword, still it is done in a different manner from that in which worldly kingdoms are wont to be defended; for the kingdom of Christ, being spiritual, must be founded on the doctrine and power of the

---

[1] "Quand il est commandé aux Rois et Princes."

Spirit. In the same manner, too, its edification is promoted; for neither the laws and edicts of men, nor the punishments inflicted by them, enter into the consciences. Yet this does not hinder princes from accidentally defending the kingdom of Christ; partly, by appointing external discipline, and partly, by lending their protection to the Church against wicked men. It results, however, from the depravity of *the world*, that the *kingdom* of Christ is strengthened more by the blood of the martyrs than by the aid of arms.

37. Pilate therefore said to him, Art thou then a king? Jesus answered, Thou sayest that I am a king. For this cause was I born, and for this cause came I into the world, that I may bear testimony to the truth: every one that is of the truth heareth my voice. 38. Pilate saith to him, What is truth? And when he had said this, he went out again to the Jews, and said to them, I find no guilt in him. 39. But you have a custom, that I should release to you some one at the passover, do you wish then that I should release to you the King of the Jews? 40. Then they all cried out again, saying, Not this man, but Barabbas. Now Barabbas was a robber.

37. *Thou sayest that I am a king.* Although Pilate had already learned, from the former answer, that Christ claims for himself some sort of kingdom, yet now Christ asserts the same thing more firmly; and, not satisfied with this, he makes an additional statement, which serves for a seal, as it were, to ratify what he had said. Hence we infer, that the doctrine concerning Christ's *kingdom* is of no ordinary importance, since he has deemed it worthy of so solemn an affirmation.

For this cause was I born, that I may bear witness to the truth. This is, no doubt, a general sentiment; but it must be viewed in relation to the place which it holds in the present passage. The words mean, that it is natural for Christ to speak *the truth;* and, next, that he was sent *for this purpose* by the Father; and, consequently, that this is his peculiar office. There is no danger, therefore, that we shall be deceived by trusting him, since it is impossible that he who has been commissioned by God, and whose natural disposition leads him to maintain *the truth,* shall teach any thing that is not *true.*

Every one that is of the truth. Christ added this, not so much for the purpose of exhorting Pilate, (for he knew that he would gain nothing by doing so,) as of defending his doctrine against the base reproaches which had been cast on it; as if he had said, "It is imputed to me as a crime that I have asserted that *I am a king;* and yet this is an unquestionable truth, which is received with reverence and without hesitation by all who have a correct judgment and a sound understanding." When he says, that they are *of the truth,* he does not mean that they naturally know the truth, but that they are directed by the Spirit of God.

38. *What is truth?* Some think that Pilate puts this question through curiosity, as irreligious men are sometimes accustomed to be eagerly desirous of learning something that is new to them, and yet do not know why they wish it; for they intend nothing more than to gratify their ears. For my own part, I rather think that it is an expression of disdain; for Pilate thought himself highly insulted when Christ represented him as destitute of all knowledge of *the truth.* Here we see in Pilate a disease which is customary among men. Though we are all aware of our ignorance, yet there are few who are willing to confess it; and the consequence is, that the greater part of men reject the true doctrine. Afterwards, the Lord, who is the Teacher of the humble, blinds the proud, and thus inflicts on them the punishment which they deserve. From the same pride arises such disdain, that they do not choose to submit to learn, because all lay claim to sagacity and acuteness of mind. *Truth* is believed to be a common thing; but God declares, on the contrary, that it far exceeds the capacity of the human understanding.

The same thing happens in other matters. The principal articles of theology are, the curse pronounced on the human race, the corruption of nature, the mortification of the flesh, the renewal of the life, the reconciliation effected by free grace through the only sacrifice, the imputation of righteousness, by means of which a sinner is accepted by God, and the illumination of the Holy Spirit. These, being paradoxes, are disdainfully rejected by the ordinary understanding of men. Few, therefore, make progress in the school of God, because we scarcely find one person in ten who attends to the first and elementary instructions; and why is this, but because they measure the secret wisdom of God by their own understanding?

That Pilate spoke in mockery is evident from this circumstance, that he immediately goes out. In short, he is angry with Christ for boasting that he brings forward *the truth*, which formerly lay hidden in darkness. Yet this indignation of Pilate shows that wicked men never reject the doctrine of the Gospel so spitefully as not to be somewhat moved by its efficacy; for, though Pilate did not proceed so far as to become humble and teachable, yet he is constrained to feel some inward compunction.

39. *But you have a custom.* Pilate was all along pondering in what way he might save Christ's life; but, the people being so fiercely enraged, he attempted to keep a middle path, in order to allay their fury; for he thought that it would be enough if Christ, being dismissed as *a malefactor*, were marked with perpetual ignominy. He therefore selects *Barabbas* above all others, in order that, by a comparison with that man, the hatred which they bore to Christ might be softened down; for Barabbas was universally and strongly detested on account of his atrocious crimes. And, indeed, is there any thing more detestable than *a robber?* But Luke (xxiii. 19) relates that, in addition to this, he was guilty of other crimes.

That the Jews preferred him to Christ, did not happen without a singular interposition of the providence of God; for it would have been highly unbecoming, that the Son of God should be rescued from death by so dishonourable a price. Yet, by his death, he was thrown into the deepest ignominy, so that, in consequence of the release of *Barabbas*, he was crucified between two robbers; for he had taken upon himself the sins of all, which could not be expiated in any other way; and the glory of his resurrection, by which it was speedily followed, caused his death itself to be a splendid triumph.

This *custom*, by which the Roman governor delivered up to the Jews, every year, at the passover, some criminal, involved a base and heinous crime. It was done, no doubt, in order to honour the sacredness of the day, but was, in reality, nothing else than a shameful profanation of it; for Scripture declares, that *he who acquitteth the guilty is abomination in the sight of God,* (Prov. xvii. 15;) and therefore he is far from taking delight in that improper kind of forgiveness. Let us learn by this example, that nothing is more ridiculous, than to attempt to serve God by our inventions; for, as soon as men begin to follow their own imaginations, there will be no end till, by falling into some of the most absurd fooleries, they openly insult God. The rule for the worship of God, therefore, ought to be taken from nothing else than from his own appointment.

CHAPTER XIX.

1. Then Pilate therefore took Jesus, and scourged him. 2. And the soldiers, platting a crown of thorns, put it on his head, and put on him a purple robe, 3. And said, Hail, King of the Jews! and struck him with the palms of their hands. 4. Pilate therefore went out again, and said to them, Behold, I bring him out to you, that you may know that I find no guilt in him. 5 Jesus then went out, wearing the crown of thorns and the purple robe. Then he said to them,[1] Behold the man! 6 When therefore the chief priests and officers saw him, they cried out, saying, Crucify him, crucify him. Pilate saith to them, Take you him, and crucify him; for I find no guilt in him.

1. *Then Pilate therefore took Jesus.* Pilate adheres to his original intention; but to the former ignominy he adds a second, hoping that, when Christ shall have been scourged, the Jews will be satisfied with this light chastisement. When he labours so earnestly, and without any success, we ought to recognise in this the decree of Heaven, by which Christ was appointed to death. Yet his innocence is frequently attested by the testimony of the judge, in order to assure us that he was free from all sin, and that he was substituted as a guilty person in the room of others, and bore the punishment due to the sins of others. We see also in Pilate a remarkable example of a trembling conscience. He acquits Christ with his mouth, and acknowledges that

[1] " Et Pilate leur dit."—" And Pilate said to them."

there is no guilt in him, and yet inflicts punishment on him, as if he were guilty. Thus, they who have not so much courage as to defend, with unshaken constancy, what is right, must be driven hither and thither, and led to adopt opposite and conflicting opinions.

We all condemn *Pilate;* and yet, it is shameful to relate that there are so many *Pilates* [1] in the world, who *scourge Christ,* not only in his members, but also in his doctrine. There are many who, for the purpose of saving the life of those who are persecuted for the sake of the Gospel, constrain them wickedly to deny Christ. What is this, but to expose Christ to ridicule, that he may lead a dishonourable life? Others select and approve of certain parts of the Gospel, and yet tear the whole Gospel to pieces. They think that they have done exceedingly well, if they have corrected a few gross abuses. It would be better that the doctrine should be buried for a time, than that it should be *scourged* in this manner, for it would spring up again in spite of the devil and of tyrants; but nothing is more difficult than to restore it to its purity after having been once corrupted.

2. *And the soldiers, platting a crown of thorns.* This was unquestionably done by the authority of Pilate, in order to affix a mark of infamy on the Son of God, for having *made himself a king;* and that in order to satisfy the rage of the Jews, as if he had been convinced that the accusations which they brought against Christ were well founded. Yet the wickedness and insolence of the soldiers is indulged more freely than had been ordered by the judge; as ungodly men eagerly seize on the opportunity of doing evil whenever it is offered to them. But we see here the amazing cruelty of the Jewish nation,[2] whose minds are not moved to compassion by so piteous a spectacle; but all this is directed by God, in order to reconcile the world to himself by the death of his Son.

6. *Take you him.* He did not wish to deliver Christ into their hands, or to abandon him to their fury; only he declares

---

[1] " Tant de Pilates."
[2] " Cependant on voit icy une cruanté merveilleuse en ce peuple des Juifs."

that he will not be their executioner. This is evident from
the reason immediately added, when he says that *he finds no
guilt in him;* as if he had said, that he will never be persuaded to shed innocent blood for their gratification. That
it is only the priests and officers who demand that he shall
be crucified, is evident from the circumstance that the madness of the people was not so great, except so far as those
bellows contributed afterwards to kindle it.

7. The Jews answered him, We have a law, and according to our law
he ought to die, because he made himself the Son of God. 8. When
therefore Pilate heard this saying, he was the more afraid; 9 And went
again into the hall, and said to Jesus, Whence art thou? And Jesus
gave him no answer. 10 Then Pilate said to him, Speakest thou not to
me? Knowest thou not that I have power to crucify thee, and have power
to release thee? 11 Jesus answered, Thou wouldest have no power against
me, unless it were given to thee from above, therefore he who hath
delivered me to thee hath the greater sin.

7. *We have a law.* They mean that, in proceeding against
Christ, they do what is right, and are not actuated by hatred
or sinful passion; for they perceived that Pilate had indirectly reproved them. Now, they speak as in the presence
of a man who was ignorant of *the law;* as if they had said,
" We are permitted to live after our own manner, and our
religion does not suffer any man to boast of being *the Son of
God.*" Besides, this accusation was not altogether void of
plausibility, but they erred grievously in the application of
it. The general doctrine was undoubtedly true, that it was
not lawful for men to assume any honour which is due to
God, and that they who claimed for themselves what is peculiar to God alone *deserved to be put to death.* But the source
of their error related to the person of Christ, because they
did not consider what are the titles given by Scripture to the
Messiah, from which they might easily have learned that he
was *the Son of God,* and did not even deign to inquire
whether or not Jesus was the Messiah whom God had
formerly promised.

We see, then, how they drew a false conclusion from
a true principle, for they reason badly. This example warns
us to distinguish carefully between a general doctrine and
the application of it;[1] for there are many ignorant and

---

[1] " Entre la doctrine generale et l'application d'icelle."

unsteady persons who reject the very principles of Scripture, if they have once been deceived by the semblance of truth; and such licentiousness makes too great progress in the world every day. Let us, therefore, remember that we ought to guard against imposition, so that principles which are true may remain in all their force, and that the authority of Scripture may not be diminished.

On the other hand, we may easily find a reply to wicked men, who falsely and improperly allege the testimony of Scripture, and the principles which they draw from it, to support their bad designs; just as the Papists, when they extol in lofty terms the authority of the Church, bring forward nothing about which all the children of God are not agreed. They maintain that the Church is the mother of believers, that she is the pillar of truth, that she ought to be heard, that she is guided by the Holy Spirit.[1] All this we ought to admit, but when they wish to appropriate to themselves all the authority that is due to the Church, they wickedly, and with sacrilegious presumption, seize what does not at all belong to them. For we must inquire into the grounds of what they assume as true, that they deserve the title of The Church; and here they utterly fail. In like manner, when

[1] These statements regarding "*The Church*" our Author considers to be what logicians call the major proposition of the syllogism; and by the Latin word "*hypothesis*," rendered in French "*l'application*," he evidently means the minor proposition, which he declares not only to be unsupported by proof, but to be utterly false. His own early training and habits, as a lawyer, naturally led him to throw the argument into this form, especially when it related to a criminal prosecution, for even in our own times indictments invariably take the form of a syllogism. He appears to have conceived the accusation against Christ to run thus: "Any mere man, declaring himself to be *the Son of God*, is guilty of blasphemy, and deserves to die. But Jesus of Nazareth, who is a mere man, *hath made himself to be the Son of God*. Therefore, *according to our law*, Jesus *ought to die*." The major proposition cannot be questioned, being manifestly taken from the law of Moses. The minor proposition consists of two parts 1. Jesus is a mere man. 2 Jesus *hath made himself to be the Son of God*. The second part is true, but the first is false; and, consequently, the whole argument, plausible as it had seemed, falls to the ground. It ought to have been known and acknowledged by the Jews, that the honourable rank of *the Son of God*, though it could not without blasphemy be claimed by a mere child of Adam, belonged of right to Jesus of Nazareth, of whom, even before his birth, the angel said to the Virgin Mary, *That holy thing which shall be born of thee shall be called the Son of God*, (Luke i. 35.)—*Ed.*

they exercise furious cruelty against all the godly, they do so on this pretence, that they have been ordained to defend the faith and peace of the Church. But when we examine the matter more closely, we plainly see that there is nothing which they have less at heart than the defence of true doctrine, that nothing affects them less than a care about peace and harmony, but that they only fight to uphold their own tyranny. They who are satisfied with general principles, and do not attend to the circumstances, imagine that the Papists do right in attacking us; but the investigation of the matter quickly dissipates that smoke by which they deceive the simple.[1]

8. *He was the more afraid.* These words may be explained in two ways. The first is, that Pilate dreaded lest some blame should be imputed to him, if a tumult arose, because he had not condemned Christ. The second is, that, after having heard the name of *the Son of God,* his mind was moved by religion. This second view is confirmed by what immediately follows:

9. *And he entered again into the hall, and said to Jesus,* WHENCE ART THOU? For it is evident from this that he was in a state of perplexity and anguish, because *he was afraid* that he would be punished for sacrilege, if he laid his hand on *the Son of God.* It ought to be observed that, when he asks *whence Christ is,* he does not inquire about his country, but the meaning is, as if he had said, " Art thou a man born on the earth, or art thou some god?" The interpretation which I give to this passage, therefore, is, that Pilate, struck with the fear of God, was in perplexity and doubt as to what he ought to do;[2] for he saw, on the one hand, the excitement

---

[1] " Ces fumees, par lesquelles ils abusent les simples."
[2] " Il estoit en perplexité et doute de ce qu'il devoit faire."—The Latin phraseology is highly idiomatic, being formed on a noted passage of *Plautus*:—" Quod inter sacrum, ut aiunt, et saxum hæserit."—" That he stuck fast, as they say, between the victim and the sacrificial knife." A close resemblance to this may be observed in a French idiom—" *Etre entre le marteau et l'enclume;*"—*To be between the hammer and the anvil.* —*Ed.*

of a mutiny, and, on the other hand, conscience held him bound not to offend God for the sake of avoiding danger.

This example is highly worthy of observation. Though the countenance of Christ was so disfigured, yet, as soon as Pilate hears the name of God, he is seized with the *fear* of violating the majesty of God in a man who was utterly mean and despicable. If reverence for God had so much influence on an irreligious man, must not they be worse than reprobate, who now judge of divine things in sport and jest, carelessly, and without any *fear?* for, indeed, Pilate is a proof that men have naturally a sentiment of religion, which does not suffer them to rush fearlessly in any direction they choose, when the question relates to divine things. This is the reason why I said that those who, in handling the doctrine of Scripture, are not more impressed with the majesty of God, than if they had been disputing about the shadow of an ass, *are given up to a reprobate mind,* (Rom. i. 28.) Yet they will one day feel to their destruction, what veneration is due to the name of God, which they now treat with such disdainful and outrageous mockery. It is shocking to relate how haughtily the Papists condemn the plain and ascertained truth of God, and with what cruelty they shed innocent blood. Whence, I beseech you, comes that drunken stupidity, but because they do not recollect that they have anything to do with God?

And Jesus gave him no answer. We ought not to think it strange that Jesus makes no reply; at least, if we keep in mind what I have formerly mentioned, that he did not stand before Pilate to plead his own cause,—as is customary with persons accused who are desirous to be acquitted,—but rather to suffer condemnation; for it was proper that he should be condemned, when he appeared in our room. This is the reason why he makes no defence; and yet Christ's silence is not inconsistent with what Paul says, *Remember that Christ, before Pilate, made a good confession,* (1 Tim. vi. 13;) for there he maintained the faith of the Gospel, as far as was necessary, and his death was nothing else than the sealing of the doctrine delivered by him. Christ left nothing undone of what was necessary to make a lawful confession, but he kept silence as to asking an acquittal. Besides, there was some danger that Pilate would acquit Christ as one of the pretended gods, as Tiberius wished to rank him among the gods of the Romans. Justly, therefore, does Christ, by his silence, frown on this foolish superstition.

10. *Knowest thou not that I have power to crucify thee?* This shows that the dread with which Pilate had been suddenly seized was transitory, and had no solid root; for now, forgetting all fear, he breaks out into haughty and monstrous contempt of God. He threatens Christ, as if there had not been a Judge in heaven; but this must always happen with irreligious men, that, shaking off the fear of God, they quickly return to their natural disposition. Hence also we infer, that it is not without good reason that *the heart of man* is called *deceitful,* (Jer. xvii. 9;) for, though some fear of God dwells in it, there likewise comes from it mere impiety. Whoever, then, is not regenerated by the Spirit of God, though he pretend for a time to reverence the majesty of God, will quickly show, by opposite facts, that this fear was hypocritical.

Again, we see in Pilate an image of a proud man, who is driven to madness by his ambition; for, when he wishes to exalt his power, he deprives himself of all praise and reputation for justice. He acknowledges that Christ is innocent, and therefore he makes himself no better than a robber, when he boasts that he has power to cut his throat! Thus, wicked consciences, in which faith and the true knowledge of God do not reign, must necessarily be agitated, and there must be within them various feelings of the flesh, which contend with each other; and in this manner God takes signal vengeance on the pride of men, when they go beyond their limits, so as to claim for themselves infinite power. By condemning themselves for injustice, they stamp on themselves the greatest reproach and disgrace. No blindness, therefore, is greater than that of pride; and we need not wonder, since pride feels the hand of God, against which it strikes, to be armed with vengeance. Let us therefore remember, that we ought not rashly to indulge in foolish boastings, lest we expose ourselves to ridicule; and especially that those who occupy a high rank ought to conduct themselves modestly, and not to be ashamed of being subject to God and to his laws.

11. *Thou wouldest have no power.* Some explain this in a general sense, that nothing is done in the world but by the permission of God; as if Christ had said, that Pilate, though he thinks that he can do all things, will do nothing more than God permits. The statement is, no doubt, true, that this world is regulated by the disposal of God, and that, whatever may be the efforts of wicked men, still they cannot even move a finger but as the secret power of God directs. But I prefer the opinion of those who confine this passage to the office of the magistrate; for by these words Christ rebukes the foolish boasting of Pilate, in extolling himself, as if his power had not been from God; as if he had said, Thou claimest every thing for thyself, as if thou hadst not to render an account one day to God; but it was not without His providence that thou wast made a judge. Consider, then, that His heavenly throne is far higher than thy tribunal. It is impossible to find any admonition better fitted to repress the insolence of those who rule over others, that they may not abuse their authority. The father imagines that he may do what he pleases towards his children, the husband towards his wife, the master towards his servants, the prince towards his people, unless when they look to God, who hath determined that their authority shall be limited by a fixed rule.

Therefore he who delivered me to thee. Some think that this declares the Jews to be more guilty than Pilate, because, with wicked hatred and malicious treachery, they are enraged against an innocent man, that is, those of them who were private individuals, and not clothed with lawful authority. But I think that this circumstance renders their guilt more heinous and less excusable on another ground, that they constrain a divinely appointed government to comply with their lawless desires; for it is a monstrous sacrilege to pervert a holy ordinance of God for promoting any wickedness. The robber, who, with his own hand, cuts the throat of a wretched passenger, is justly held in abhorrence; but he who, under the forms of a judicial trial, puts to death an innocent man, is much more wicked. Yet Christ does not aggravate their guilt, for the purpose of extenuating that of Pilate; for he does not institute a comparison between him and them, but rather includes them all in the same condemnation, because they equally pollute a holy power. There is only this difference, that he makes a direct attack on the Jews, but indirectly censures Pilate, who complies with their wicked desire.

12. From that time Pilate sought to release him; but the Jews cried out, saying, If thou release this man, thou art not Cesar's friend whoever maketh himself a king speaketh against Cesar. 13. When Pilate, therefore, had heard this saying, he brought Jesus out, and sat down on the judgment-seat, in a place which is called the Stone-pavement, and in Hebrew, Gabbatha. 14 And it was the preparation of the passover, about the sixth hour; and he saith to the Jews, Behold your King! [1] 15. But they cried out, Away with him, away with him, crucify him. Pilate saith to them, Shall I crucify your King? The chief priests answered, We have no king but Cesar. 16 Then, therefore, he delivered him to them to be crucified; and they took Jesus, and led him away.

12. *From that time Pilate sought to release him.* Though *Pilate* does not conduct himself conscientiously, and is actuated more by ambition than by a regard to justice, and, on that account, is wretchedly irresolute, yet his modesty is commendable on this ground, that, when he is severely reproved by Christ, he does not fly into a passion, but, on the contrary, is still more disposed to release him. He is a judge, and yet he meekly permits the accused person to be his reprover; and, indeed, scarcely one person in a hundred will be found, who so mildly suffers a reproof, even from one who is his equal.

Thou art not Cesar's friend. By threats they prevail on Pilate to condemn Christ; for they could do nothing that was more hateful, or more fitted to produce terror, than to hold him suspected of disloyalty to Cesar. "Thou showest," say they, "that thou dost not care about Cesar's authority,

[1] *Judge of the falsehood of your accusation, by the description of the man who, you say, has aspired to Royalty! What do you find in so mean a person that breathes of tyranny or usurpation? Has he soldiers, or money, or birth? And what can you gain by putting to death a man who is incapable of doing the smallest injury?*—Theophylact on the passage.

if thou acquit him who has endeavoured to throw every thing into confusion." This wickedness at length broke down the resolution of Pilate, who, till now, had only been shaken by their furious clamours. Nor is it without a good reason that the Evangelist so laboriously examines and details those circumstances; for it is of great importance to us to know, that Pilate did not condemn Christ, before he had several times acquitted him with his own mouth, in order that we may learn from it, that it was for our sins that he was condemned, and not on his own account. We may also learn from it, how voluntarily he offered himself to die, when he disdained to avail himself of the favourable disposition of the judge towards him; and, indeed, it was this obedience that caused his death to be *a sacrifice of sweet savour*, (Eph. v. 2,) for blotting out all sins.

13. *And sat down on the judgment-seat.* Hence we see what conflicting opinions passed through the mind of Pilate, as if he had been a stage-player who was acting two characters. He ascends *the judgment-seat*, in order to pronounce sentence of death on Christ solemnly, and in the customary form;[1] and yet he declares openly, that he does so reluctantly and against his conscience. When he calls Christ *king*, he speaks ironically, meaning that it was a trivial charge which the Jews brought against him; or rather, for the purpose of allaying their fury, he warns them, that it would bring disgrace on the whole nation, if a report were spread abroad, that a person of that nation had been condemned to die for aspiring to kingly power.

In the place which is called the Stone-pavement, but in the Hebrew, Gabbatha. When the Evangelist says, that גבתא (*Gabbatha*) was the name of the place *in* HEBREW, he means the Chaldaic or Syriac language, which was then in common use; for in *Hebrew*, גבה (*Gabach*) means *to be lofty*. It was proper, therefore, that Christ should be condemned from *a lofty place*, that he, coming from heaven as the supreme Judge, may acquit us at the last day.

[1] "Solennellement à la façon accoustumee."

14. *About the sixth hour.* The Evangelists appear to differ, and even to contradict each other, in the computation of time. The other three Evangelists say that *the darkness* came on *about the sixth hour,* while Christ was hanging on the cross, (Matth. xxvii. 45; Mark xv. 33; Luke xxiii. 44.) Mark, too, says expressly that it was *the third hour* when the sentence was pronounced on him, (Mark xv. 25.) But this may be easily explained. It is plain enough from other passages that the day was at that time divided into four parts, as the night also contained four watches; in consequence of which, the Evangelists sometimes allot not more than four hours to each day, and extend each hour to three, and, at the same time, reckon the space of an hour, which was drawing to a close, as belonging to the next part. According to this calculation, John relates that Christ was condemned *about the sixth hour,* because the time of the day was drawing towards *the sixth hour,* or towards the second part of the day. Hence we infer that Christ was crucified at or about *the sixth hour;* for, as the Evangelist afterwards mentions, (ver. 20,) *the place was near to the city.* The darkness began between the sixth and ninth hour, and lasted till the ninth hour, at which time Christ died.

15. *We have no king but Cesar.* This is a display of shocking madness, that the priests, who ought to have been well acquainted with the Law, reject Christ, in whom the salvation of the people was wholly contained, on whom all the promises depended, and on whom the whole of their religion was founded; and, indeed, by rejecting Christ, they deprive themselves of the grace of God and of every blessing. We see, then, what insanity had seized them. Let us suppose that Jesus Christ was not the Christ;[1] still they have no excuse for acknowledging *no other king but Cesar.* For, first, they revolt from the spiritual kingdom of God; and, secondly, they prefer the tyranny of the Roman Empire, which they greatly abhorred, to a just government, such as God had promised to them. Thus wicked men, in order to fly from

---

[1] " Que Jesus Christ ne fust point le Christ."

Christ, not only deprive themselves of eternal life, but draw down on their heads every kind of miseries. On the other hand, the sole happiness of the godly is, to be subject to the royal authority of Christ, whether, according to the flesh, they are placed under a just and lawful government, or under the oppression of tyrants.

16. *Then, therefore, he delivered him to them to be crucified.* Pilate was, no doubt, constrained by their importunity to *deliver* Christ; and yet this was not done in a tumultuous manner, but he was solemnly condemned in the ordinary form, because there were also two robbers who, after having been tried, were at the same time condemned to be crucified. But John employs this expression, in order to make it more fully evident that Christ, though he had not been convicted of any crime, was given up to the insatiable cruelty of the people.

17. And he, bearing his cross, went forth to a place which is called (the place) of a Skull, and, in Hebrew, Golgotha;[1] 18. Where they crucified him, and two others with him, on either side one, and Jesus in the midst 19. And Pilate wrote also a title, and put it on the cross; and it was written, JESUS OF NAZARETH, THE KING OF THE JEWS. 20. This title then many of the Jews read, because the place where Jesus was crucified was near to the city; and it was written in Hebrew, and Greek, and Latin. 21. The chief priests of the Jews, therefore, said to Pilate, Write not, The King of the Jews; but that he said, I am King of the Jews. 22. Pilate answered, What I have written I have written.

17. *He went forth to a place.* The circumstances which are here related contribute greatly, not only to show the truth of the narrative, but likewise to build up our faith. We must look for righteousness through the satisfaction made by Christ. To prove that he is the sacrifice for our sins, he wished both to be led out of the city, and to be hanged on a tree; for the custom was, in compliance with the injunction of the Law, that the sacrifices, the blood of which was shed for sin, were carried out of the camp, (Lev. vi. 30; xvi. 27;) and the same Law declares that *he who hangeth on a tree is accursed*, (Deut. xxi. 23.) Both were

---

[1] " *Ou, Calvaire,*"—" *or, Calvary.*"

fulfilled in Christ, that we might be fully convinced that atonement has been made for our sins by the sacrifice of his death; that *he was made subject to the curse, in order that he might redeem us from the curse of the law,* (Gal. iii. 13;) that *he was made sin, in order that we might be the righteousness of God in him,* (2 Cor. v. 21;) that he was led out of the city, in order that he might carry with him, and take away, our defilements which were laid on him, (Heb. xiii. 12.) To the same purpose is the statement about the robbers, which immediately follows:—

18. *And two others with him, on either side one, and Jesus in the midst.* As if the severity of the punishment had not been sufficient of itself, he is hanged *in the midst* between two robbers, as if he not only had deserved to be classed with other robbers, but had been the most wicked and the most detestable of them all. We ought always to remember, that the wicked executioners of Christ did nothing but what had been determined by the hand and purpose of God;[1] for God did not surrender his Son to their lawless passions, but determined that, according to his own will and good pleasure, he should be offered as a sacrifice. And if there were the best reasons for the purpose of God in all those things which he determined that his Son should suffer, we ought to consider, on the one hand, the dreadful weight of his wrath against sin, and, on the other hand, his infinite goodness towards us. In no other way could our guilt be removed than by the Son of God becoming a curse for us. We see him driven out into an accursed place, as if he had been polluted by a mass of all sorts of crimes, that there he might appear to be accursed before God and men. Assuredly we are prodigiously stupid, if we do not plainly see in this mirror with what abhorrence God regards sin; and we are harder than stones, if we do not tremble at such a judgment as this.

When, on the other hand, God declares that our salvation was so dear to him, that he did not spare his only-begotten

---

[1] "N'ont rien fait qui n'eust este decreté et ordonné par le conseil de Dieu,"—" did nothing which had not been decreed and appointed by the purpose of God"

Son, what abundant goodness and what astonishing grace do we here behold! Whoever, then, takes a just view of the causes of the death of Christ, together with the advantage which it yields to us, will not, like *the Greeks,* regard the doctrine of *the cross as foolishness,* nor, like the Jews, will he regard it as *an offence,* (1 Cor. i. 23,) but rather as an invaluable token and pledge of the power, and wisdom, and righteousness, and goodness of God.

When John says, that the name of the place was *Golgotha,* he means that, in the Chaldaic or Syriac language, it was called גלגלתא, *(Gulgaltha.)* The name is derived from גלגל, *(Gilgel,*[1]*)* which signifies, *to roll;* because *a skull* is round like a ball or globe.[2]

19. *And Pilate wrote also a title.* The Evangelist relates a memorable action of Pilate, after having pronounced the sentence. It is perhaps true that it was customary to affix *titles,* when malefactors were executed, that the cause of the punishment might be known to all, and might serve the purpose of an example. But in Christ there is this extraordinary circumstance, that the *title* which is affixed to him implies no disgrace; for Pilate's intention was, to avenge himself indirectly on the Jews, (who, by their obstinacy, had extorted from him an unjust sentence of death on an innocent man,) and, in the person of Christ, to throw blame on the whole nation. Thus he does not brand Christ with the commission of any crime.

But the providence of God, which guided the pen of Pilate, had a higher object in view. It did not, indeed, occur to Pilate to celebrate Christ as the Author of salvation, and the Nazarene of God, and the King of a chosen people; but God dictated to him this commendation of the Gospel, though he knew not the meaning of what he wrote. It was the same secret guidance of the Spirit that caused *the title* to be pub-

---

[1] The Pihel of גלל, *(Galal)*—*Ed*

[2] "The place where Christ was crucified appears to have received this name, not—as some have imagined—because the shape of the mountain resembled a human head, but because it was filled with the skulls of malefactors who had been put to death there."—Schleusner on the word Γολγοθᾶ.

lished in three languages; for it is not probable that this was an ordinary practice, but the Lord showed, by this preparatory arrangement, that the time was now at hand, when the name of his Son should be made known throughout the whole earth.

21. *The chief priests of the Jews said therefore to Pilate.* They feel that they are sharply rebuked; and, therefore, they would wish that *the title* were changed, so as not to involve the nation in disgrace, but to throw the whole blame on Christ. But yet they do not conceal their deep hatred of the truth, since the smallest spark of it is more than they are able to endure. Thus Satan always prompts his servants to endeavour to extinguish, or, at least, to choke, by their own darkness, the light of God, as soon as the feeblest ray of it appears.

22. *What I have written I have written.* Pilate's firmness must be ascribed to the providence of God; for there can be no doubt that they attempted, in various ways, to change his resolution. Let us know, therefore, that he was held by a Divine hand, so that he remained unmoved. Pilate did not yield to the prayers of the priests, and did not allow himself to be corrupted by them; but God testified, by his mouth, the firmness and stability of the kingdom of his Son. And if, in the writing of Pilate, the kingdom of Christ was shown to be so firm that it could not be shaken by all the attacks of its enemies, what value ought we to attach to the testimonies of the Prophets, whose tongues and hands God consecrated to his service?

The example of *Pilate* reminds us, also, that it is our duty to remain steady in defending the truth. A heathen refuses to retract what he has justly and properly written concerning Christ, though he did not understand or consider what he was doing. How great, then, will be our dishonour, if, terrified by threatenings or dangers, we withdraw from the profession of his doctrine, which God hath sealed on our hearts by his Spirit! Besides, it ought to be observed how detestable is the tyranny of the Papists, which prohibits the reading of the Gospel, and of the whole of the Scripture, by the common people. Pilate, though he was a reprobate man, and, in other respects, an instrument of Satan, was nevertheless, by a secret guidance, appointed to be a herald of the Gospel, that he might publish a short summary of it in three languages. What rank, therefore, shall we assign to those who do all that they can to suppress the knowledge of it, since they show that they are worse than Pilate?

23. Then the soldiers, when they had crucified Jesus, took his garments, and made four parts, to each soldier a part. They took also his coat.[1] But the coat was without seam, woven from the top throughout. 24. They said therefore among themselves, Let us not rend it, but cast lots for it, whose it shall be; that the Scripture might be fulfilled, which saith, They divided my garments among them, and cast lots on my vesture. these things therefore the soldiers did.

23. *Then the soldiers.* The other Evangelists also mention the *parting* of Christ's *garments among the soldiers,* (Matth. xxvii. 35; Mark xv. 24; Luke xxiii. 34.) There were *four* soldiers who *parted* among themselves all his *garments,* except *the coat,* which, being *without seam,* could not be divided, and therefore *they cast lots* on it. To fix our minds on the contemplation of the purpose of God, the Evangelists remind us that, in this occurrence also, there was a fulfilment of Scripture. It may be thought, however, that the passage, which they quote from Psalm xxii. 19, is inappropriately applied to the subject in hand; for, though David complains in it that he was exposed as a prey to his enemies, he makes use of the word *garments* to denote metaphorically all his property; as if he had said, in a single word, that "he had been stripped naked and bare by wicked men;" and, when the Evangelists disregard the figure, they depart from the natural meaning of the passage. But we ought to remember, in the first place, that the psalm ought not to be restricted to David, as is evident from many parts of it, and especially from a clause in which it is written, *I will proclaim thy name among the Gentiles,* (Ps. xxii. 22,) which must be explained as referring to Christ. We need not wonder, therefore, if that which was faintly

---

[1] ("Ils preinrent) aussi le saye."

shadowed out in David is beheld in Christ with all that superior clearness which the truth ought to have, as compared with the figurative representation of it.

Let us also learn that Christ was stripped of his *garments*, that he might clothe us with righteousness; that his naked body was exposed to the insults of men, that we may appear in glory before the judgment-seat of God. As to the allegorical meaning to which some men have tortured this passage, by making it mean, that heretics tear Scripture in pieces, it is too far-fetched; though I would not object to such a comparison as this,—that, as the *garments* of Christ were once divided by ungodly *soldiers*, so, in the present day, there are perverse men who, by foreign inventions, tear the whole of the Scripture, with which Christ is clothed, in order that he may be manifested to us. But the wickedness of the Papists, accompanied by shocking blasphemy against God, is intolerable. They tell us, that Scripture is torn in pieces by heretics, but that *the coat*—that is, the Church—remains entire; and thus they endeavour to prove that, without paying any attention to the authority of Scripture, the unity of faith consists in the mere title of the Church; as if the unity of the Church were itself founded on any thing else than the authority of Scripture. When, therefore, they separate faith from Scripture, so that it may continue to be attached to the Church alone, by such a divorce they not only strip Christ of his *garments*, but tear in pieces his body by shocking sacrilege. And though we should admit what they maintain, that *the coat without seam* is a figure of the Church, they will be very far from gaining their point: for it will still remain to be proved, that the Church is placed under their authority, of which they show no sign whatever.

25. Now there stood by the cross of Jesus his mother, and his mother's sister, Mary of Cleophas, and Mary Magdalene 26. Jesus, therefore, seeing his mother, and the disciple whom he loved standing by her, saith to his mother, Woman, behold thy son! 27. Then he saith to the disciple, Behold thy mother! And from that hour, the disciple took her to his own home.

25. *Now there stood by the cross of Jesus.* The Evangelist here mentions incidentally, that while Christ obeyed God

the Father, he did not fail to perform the duty which he owed, as a son, towards *his mother.* True, he forgot himself, and he forgot every thing, so far as was necessary for the discharge of obedience to his Father, but, after having performed that duty, he did not neglect what he owed to *his mother.* Hence we learn in what manner we ought to discharge our duty towards God and towards men. It often happens that, when God calls us to the performance of any thing, our parents, or wife, or children, draw us in a contrary direction, so that we cannot give equal satisfaction to all. If we place men in the same rank with God, we judge amiss. We must, therefore, give the preference to the command, the worship, and the service of God; after which, as far as we are able, we must give to men what is their due.

And yet the commands of the first and second table of the Law never jar with each other, though at first sight they appear to do so; but we must begin with the worship of God, and afterwards assign to men an inferior place. Such is the import of the following statements: *He who loveth father or mother more than me, is not worthy of me,* (Matth. x. 41;) and, *If any one hate not his father, and mother, and wife, and children, and brethren, and sisters, he cannot be my disciple,* (Luke xiv. 26.) We ought, therefore, to devote ourselves to the interests of men, so as not in any degree to interfere with the worship and obedience which we owe to God. When we have obeyed God, it will then be the proper time to think about parents, and wife, and children; as Christ attends to *his mother,* but it is after that he is on the cross, to which he has been called by his Father's decree.

Yet, if we attend to the time and place when these things happened, Christ's affection for *his mother* was worthy of admiration. I say nothing about the severe tortures of his body; I say nothing about the reproaches which he suffered; but, though horrible blasphemies against God filled his mind with inconceivable grief, and though he sustained a dreadful contest with eternal death and with the devil, still, none of these things prevent him from being anxious about *his mother.* We may also learn from this passage, what is the honour which God, by the Law, commands us to render to parents, (Exod. xx. 12.) Christ appoints *the disciple* to be his substitute, and charges him to support and take care of *his mother;* and hence it follows, that the honour which is due to parents consists, not in cold ceremony,[1] but in the discharge of all necessary duties.

On the other hand, we ought to consider the faith of those holy women.[2] It is true that, in following Christ to the cross, they displayed more than ordinary affection; but, if they had not been supported by faith, they could never have been present at this exhibition. As to John himself, we infer that, though his faith was choked for a short time, it was not wholly extinguished. How shameful will it be, if the dread of the cross deters us from following Christ, when the glory of his resurrection is placed before our eyes, whereas the women beheld in it nothing but disgrace and cursing!

Mary of Cleophas, and Mary Magdalene. He calls her either the wife or the daughter *of Cleophas;* but I prefer the latter interpretation.[3] He says, that she was *the sister of the mother of Jesus,* and, in saying so, he adopts the phraseology of the Hebrew language, which includes cousins, and other relatives,[4] under the term *brothers.* We see that it was not in vain that *Mary Magdalene* was delivered from *seven devils,* (Mark xvi. 9; Luke viii. 2;) since she showed herself, to the last, to be so faithful a disciple to Christ.

26. *Woman, behold thy son!*[5] As if he had said, "Henceforth I shall not be an inhabitant of the earth, so as to have it in my power to discharge to thee the duties of a *son;* and, therefore, I put this man in my room, that he may perform my office." The same thing is meant, when he says to John,

---

[1] "En froide ceremonie."
[2] "De ces sainctes femmes"
[3] "Il y en a aucuns qui pensent que c'estoit la femme de Cleopas. mon opinion est que c'estoit plustost sa fille"—"There are some who think that she was the wife of Cleophas my opinion is, that she was rather his daughter."
[4] "Les cousins et autres parens."
[5] "One who will take as much care of you as if he had been your son."
—*Beausobre.*

Behold thy mother! For by these words he charges him to treat her as a *mother*, and to take as much care of her as if she had been his own *mother*.

In refraining from mentioning his *mother's* name, and in simply calling her *Woman!* some think that he did so, in order not to pierce her heart with a deeper wound. I do not object to this view; but there is another conjecture which is equally probable, that Christ intended to show that, after having completed the course of human life, he lays down the condition in which he had lived, and enters into the heavenly kingdom, where he will exercise dominion over angels and men; for we know that Christ was always accustomed to guard believers against looking at the flesh, and it was especially necessary that this should be done at his death.

27. *The disciple took her to his own home.* It is a token of the reverence due by a *disciple* to his master, that John so readily obeys the command of Christ. Hence also it is evident, that the Apostles had their families; for John could not have exercised hospitality towards the mother of Christ, or have *taken her to his own home,* if he had not had a house and a regular way of living. Those men, therefore, are fools, who think that the Apostles relinquished their property, and came to Christ naked and empty; but they are worse than fools, who make perfection to consist in beggary.

28. After this, Jesus, knowing that all things were now accomplished, that the Scripture might be fulfilled, saith, I thirst. 29. And a vessel full of vinegar was placed there, and, filling a sponge with vinegar, they fixed it on hyssop, and put it to his mouth. 30. When, therefore, Jesus had received the vinegar, he said, It is finished; and, bowing his head, he yielded up his breath.

28. *Jesus, knowing that all things were now accomplished.* John purposely passes by many things which are related by the other three Evangelists. He now describes the last act, which was an event of the greatest importance.

When John says that *a vessel was placed there,* he speaks of it as a thing that was customary. There has been much controversy on this subject; but I agree with those who think (and, indeed, the custom is proved by histories) that it was a kind of beverage usually administered for the purpose of accelerating the death of wretched malefactors, when they had undergone sufficient torture.[1] Now, it ought to be remarked, that Christ does not ask any thing to *drink* till *all things have been accomplished;* and thus he testified his infinite love towards us, and the inconceivable earnestness of his desire to promote our salvation. No words can fully express the bitterness of the sorrows which he endured; and yet he does not desire to be freed from them, till the justice of God has been satisfied, and till he has made a perfect atonement.[2]

But how does he say, that all things were accomplished, while the most important part still remained to be performed, that is, his death? Besides, does not his resurrection contribute to the *accomplishment* of our salvation? I answer, John includes those things which were immediately to follow. Christ had not yet died, and had not yet risen again; but he saw that nothing now remained to hinder him from going forward to death and resurrection. In this manner he instructs us, by his own example, to render perfect obedience, that we may not think it hard to live according to his good pleasure, even though we must languish in the midst of the most excruciating pains.

That the Scripture might be fulfilled. From what is stated by the other Evangelists, (Matth. xxvii. 48 ; Mark xv. 23, 36 ; Luke xxiii. 36,) it may readily be concluded that the passage referred to is Ps. lxix. 22, *They gave me gall for my food, and in my thirst they gave me vinegar to drink.* It is, undoubtedly, a metaphorical expression, and David means by it, not only that they refused to him the assistance which he needed, but that they cruelly aggravated his distresses. But

---

[1] " On dispute diversement de ceci ; mais je m'accorde à l'opinion de ceux qui disent (comme aussi l'usage en est approuvee par les histoires) que c'estoit une sorte de bruvage, duquel coustumierement on usoit pour avancer la mort des poures malfaiteurs, apres qu'ils avoyent este assez tormentez."

[2] The French copy gives an additional clause to this sentence — " Comme s'il s'estoit oublié jusqu'à ce qu'ayant satisfait au payement de nos offenses, il declare qu'il n'est pas insensible, mais que l'amour qu'il nous portoit a surmonté toutes les angoisses ,"—" As if he had forgotten his own concerns till he had given full satisfaction for our sins, he declares that he is not incapable of feeling, but that the love which he bore to us rose superior to all the pains which he endured."

there is no inconsistency in saying that what had been dimly shadowed out in David was more clearly exhibited in Christ: for thus we are enabled more fully to perceive the difference between truth and figures, when those things which David suffered, only in a figurative manner, are distinctly and perfectly manifested in Christ. To show that he was the person whom David represented, Christ chose to drink *vinegar;* and he did so for the purpose of strengthening our faith.

I thirst. Those who contrive a metaphorical meaning for the word *thirst,* as if he meant that, instead of a pleasant and agreeable beverage, they gave him bitterness, as if they intended to flay his throat,[1] are more desirous to be thought ingenious than to promote true edification; and, indeed, they are expressly refuted by the Evangelist, who says that Christ asked for vinegar when he was near death; from which it is evident that he did not desire any luxuries.[2]

29. *And, having filled a sponge with vinegar, they fixed it on hyssop.* When he says that they *fixed the sponge on hyssop,* the meaning is, that they fastened it to the end of a bunch of *hyssop,* that it might be raised to Christ's mouth; for, in that country, *hyssops* grow as large as small shrubs.[3]

30. *It is finished.* He repeats the same word which he had lately employed.[4] Now this word, which Christ employs, well deserves our attention; for it shows that the whole accomplishment of our salvation, and all the parts of it, are contained in his death. We have already stated that his resurrection is not separated from his death, but Christ only intends to keep our faith fixed on himself alone, and not to allow it to turn aside in any direction whatever. The

---

[1] " Comme s'il vouloit dire qu'au lieu de bruvage doux et aimable, on luy a donné de l'amertume, comme pour luy escorcher le gosier."
[2] " En quoy il appert qu'il n'estoit question de nulles delices."
[3] " Car là les hyssopes sont grans comme petits arbrisseaux."
[4] The repetition of the word is concealed by the circumstance, that it is rendered, in the 28th verse, by *impleta,* ACCOMPLISHED, and, in the 30th verse, by *consummatum,* FINISHED. Ὅτι πάντα ἤδη τετέλεσται, (verse 28,) *that all things were now* ACCOMPLISHED Τετέλεσται, (verse 30,) *It is* FINISHED, or, *it is* ACCOMPLISHED.—*Ed*

meaning, therefore, is, that every thing which contributes to the salvation of men is to be found in Christ, and ought not to be sought anywhere else; or—which amounts to the same thing—that the perfection of salvation is contained in him.

There is also an implied contrast; for Christ contrasts his death with the ancient sacrifices and with all the figures; as if he had said, " Of all that was practised under the Law, there was nothing that had any power in itself to make atonement for sins, to appease the wrath of God, and to obtain justification; but now the true salvation is exhibited and manifested to the world." On this doctrine depends the abolition of all the ceremonies of the Law; for it would be absurd to follow shadows, since we have the body in Christ.

If we give our assent to this word which Christ pronounced, we ought to be satisfied with his death alone for salvation, and we are not at liberty to apply for assistance in any other quarter; for he who was sent by the Heavenly Father to obtain for us a full acquittal, and to accomplish our redemption, knew well what belonged to his office, and did not fail in what he knew to be demanded of him. It was chiefly for the purpose of giving peace and tranquillity to our consciences that he pronounced this word, *It is finished.* Let us stop here, therefore, if we do not choose to be deprived of the salvation which he has procured for us.[1]

But the whole religion of Popery tends to lead men to contrive for themselves innumerable methods of seeking salvation; and hence we infer, that it is full to overflowing with abominable sacrileges. More especially, this word of Christ condemns the abomination of the Mass. All the sacrifices of the Law must have ceased, for the salvation of men has been completed by the one sacrifice of the death of Christ. What right, then, have the Papists, or what plausible

---

[1] The last few sentences—commencing with "for he who was sent by the Heavenly Father"—are not contained in the Latin original, but have been taken from the Author's French Version. " Car celuy qui estoit envoyé du Pere celeste pour nous acquitter pleinement, et achever nostre redemption, scavoit bien son office, et n'est pas espargné en ce qu'il scavoit estre requis. Or notamment pour appaiser nos consciences, et nous faire contenter, il a prononcé ce mot, *Que c'estoit fait.* Arrestons-nous-y donc, si nous ne voulons estre frustrez du salut qu'il nous a acquis."

excuse can they assign for saying, that they are authorised to prepare a new sacrifice, to reconcile God to men? They reply that it is not a new sacrifice, but the very sacrifice which Christ offered. But this is easily refuted; for, in the first place, they have no command to offer it; and, secondly, Christ, having once accomplished, by a single oblation, all that was necessary to be done, declares, from the cross, that all *is finished.* They are worse than forgers, therefore, for they wickedly corrupt and falsify the testament sealed by the precious blood of the Son of God.

He yielded up his breath. All the Evangelists take great care to mention the death of Christ, and most properly; for we obtain from it our confident hope of life, and we likewise obtain from it a fearless triumph over death, because the Son of God has endured it in our room, and, in his contest with it, has been victorious. But we must attend to the phraseology which John employs, and which teaches us, that all believers, who die with Christ, peacefully commit their souls to the guardianship of God, who is faithful, and will not suffer to perish what he hath undertaken to preserve. The children of God, as well as the reprobate, die; but there is this difference between them, that the reprobate give up the soul, without knowing where it goes, or what becomes of it;[1] while the children of God commit it, as a precious trust, to the protection of God, who will faithfully guard it till the day of the resurrection. The word *breath* is manifestly used here to denote the immortal soul.

31. The Jews, therefore, that the bodies might not remain upon the cross on the Sabbath-day, (for it was the preparation, and it was the great day of that Sabbath,) besought Pilate that their legs might be broken, and that they might be taken away. 32. Then the soldiers came, and broke the legs of the first, and of the other who was crucified with him. 33. But when they came to Jesus, and saw that he was already dead, they broke not his legs; 34. But one of the soldiers pierced his side with a spear, and immediately there came out of it blood and water. 35. And he who saw it hath borne testimony of it, and his testimony is true, and he knoweth that he saith true, that you may believe. 36. And these things were done,[2] that the Scripture might be fulfilled, A bone of him shall not be broken 37. And again, another Scripture saith, They shall look on him whom they pierced.

[1] " Ne sçachant ou il va, ne qu'il devient."
[2] " Car ces choses ont este faites;"—" *For* these things were done."

31. *For it was the preparation.* This narrative also tends to the edification of our faith; first, because it shows that what had been foretold in the Scriptures is fulfilled in the person of Christ; and, secondly, because it contains a mystery of no ordinary value. The Evangelist says, that *the Jews besought* that the bodies *might be taken down* from the crosses. This had undoubtedly been enjoined by the Law of God; but the Jews, as is usually the case with hypocrites, direct their whole attention to small matters, and yet pass by the greatest crimes without any hesitation; for, in order to a strict observance of their Sabbath, they are careful to avoid outward pollution; and yet they do not consider how shocking a crime it is to take away the life of an innocent man. Thus we saw a little before, that *they did not enter into the governor's hall, that they might not be defiled,* (John xviii. 28,) while the whole country was polluted by their wickedness. Yet, by their agency, the Lord carries into effect what was of the greatest importance for our salvation, that, by a wonderful arrangement, the body of Christ remains uninjured, and *blood and water flow out of his side.*

And it was the great day of that Sabbath.[1] Another reading more generally approved is, *and that Sabbath-day was great;* but the reading which I have adopted is supported by many manuscripts that are ancient and of great authority. Let the reader choose for himself. If we read ἐκείνου in the genitive case, (ἐκείνου τοῦ σαββάτου, *of that Sabbath,*) the word *Sabbath* must be understood to denote *the week;* as if the Evangelist had said, that the festival of that week was very solemn, on account of the Passover. Now, the Evangelist speaks of the following day, which began at sunset. But, if we choose rather to read ἐκείνη in the nominative case, ἦν γὰρ μεγάλη ἡ ἡμέρα ἐκείνη τοῦ σαββάτου, *and* THAT *was the great day of the Sabbath,* the meaning will be nearly the same in substance; only there would be this difference in the words, that the

---

[1] ἦν γὰρ μεγάλη ἡ ἡμέρα ἐκείνη τοῦ σαββάτου. "*A very solemn festival*, namely, as being not only an ordinary Sabbath, but the extraordinary one on the 15th of Nisan. For ἐκείνη, very many MSS., Versions, and early Editions, have ἐκείνου, which is received by most Editors from Wetstein to Scholz, with the approbation of Bishop Middleton."—*Bloomfield.*

Passover, which was to take place on the following day, would render that Sabbath more solemn.

33. *But when they came to Jesus, and saw that he was already dead.* That they *break the legs* of the two robbers, and after having done so, find that Christ is already dead, and therefore do not touch his body, appears to be a very extraordinary work of the providence of God. Ungodly men will, no doubt, say that it happens naturally that one man dies sooner than another; but, if we examine carefully the whole course of the narrative, we shall be constrained to ascribe it to the secret purpose of God, that the death of Christ was brought on much more rapidly than men could have at all expected, and that this prevented *his legs from being broken.*

34. *But one of the soldiers pierced his side with a spear.* When *the soldier pierced Christ's side with his spear,* he did so for the purpose of ascertaining if he was dead; but God had a higher object in view, as we shall immediately see. It was a childish contrivance of the Papists, when, out of the Greek word λόγχη, which means *a spear,*[1] they manufactured the proper name of a man, and called this soldier *Longinus,* and, to give an air of plausibility to their story, foolishly alleged that he had been formerly blind, and that, after having received his sight, he was converted to the faith. Thus they have placed him in the catalogue of the saints.[2] Since their

[1] "Du mot Grec *lonchi,* qui signifie une lance."
[2] Dr Bloomfield subjoins the following note to this verse :—" The epitaph of this soldier, (if genuine,) said to be found in the Church of St Mary, at Lyons, is as follows :—' *Qui Salvatoris latus Cruce Cuspide fixit,* LONGINUS *hic jacet.*'—' *Here lies* LONGINUS, *who pierced the Saviour's side on the Cross with a spear.*'" As the learned annotator has thus summarily adverted to this legendary tale, it is right that the reader should be briefly put in possession of the whole of it, as it has been collected by Moreri from Tillemont and other ecclesiastical writers, in his " *Dictionary,*" under the head, *St Longin*—(St Longinus.) This *St Longinus* is twofold " some saying, that he was *the soldier* that pierced our Lord's side with a spear; and some, that he was *the centurion* who commanded the guard at the cross. The legends report both these persons to have been converted to the Christian faith, to have suffered martyrdom, and to have been canonized." Moreri, however, though an ecclesiastic of the Romish Church, was constrained to add, " *The acts of both Longinuses are manifestly false; and the circumstances they allege mutually refute each other.*"

prayers, whenever they call on God, rest on such intercessors, what, I ask, will they ever be able to obtain? But they who despise Christ, and seek the intercessions of the dead, deserve that the devil should drive them to ghosts and phantoms.

And immediately there came out blood and water. Some men have deceived themselves by imagining that this was a miracle; for it is natural that the *blood*, when it is congealed, should lose its red colour, and come to resemble *water*. It is well known also that water is contained in the membrane which immediately adjoins the intestines. What has led them astray is, that the Evangelist takes so much pains to explain that *blood* flowed along with the *water*, as if he were relating something unusual and contrary to the order of nature. But he had quite a different intention; namely, to accommodate his narrative to the passages of Scripture which he immediately subjoins, and more especially that believers might infer from it what he states elsewhere, that Christ *came with water and blood*, (1 John v. 6.) By these words he means that Christ brought the true atonement and the true washing; for, on the one hand, forgiveness of sins and justification, and, on the other hand, the sanctification of the soul, were prefigured in the Law by those two symbols, *sacrifices* and *washings*. In *sacrifices*, blood atoned for sins, and was the ransom for appeasing the wrath of God. *Washings* were the tokens of true holiness, and the remedies for taking away uncleanness and removing the pollutions of the flesh.

That faith may no longer rest on these elements, John declares that the fulfilment of both of these graces is in Christ; and here he presents to us a visible token of the same fact.

It would appear that the name *Longinus* has been formed from the Greek λόγχη, spear. *longinus* being the Latin form of λόγχιμος—*spear-man*. Thus, *St Longinus* is found to be a similar saint to the *Sancta Veronica*, reported by Brydone. "The Greeks," continues Moreri, "celebrate the martyrdom of Longinus, *the centurion*, on the 16th of October, the Latins on the 15th of March, and the Copts on the 1st of November. The martyrdom of Longinus, *the soldier*, is not acknowledged by the Greeks; but the Latins commemorate it on different days; some on the 15th of March, some on the 1st of September, others on the 22d of November, or 11th of December." We thus see how little this offspring of credulity and superstition merits the attention of the readers of the Gospel.—*Granville Penn's Annotations.*

The sacraments which Christ has left to his Church have the same design; for the purification and sanctification of the soul, which consists in *newness of life*, (Rom. vi. 4,) is pointed out to us in Baptism, and the Lord's Supper is the pledge of a perfect atonement. But they differ widely from the ancient figures of the Law; for they exhibit Christ as being present, whereas the figures of the Law pointed out that he was still at a distance. For this reason I do not object to what Augustine says, that our sacraments have flowed from Christ's side; for, when Baptism and the Lord's Supper lead us to Christ's side, that by faith we may draw from it, as from a fountain, what they represent, then are we truly washed from our pollutions, and renewed to a holy life, and then do we truly live before God, redeemed from death, and delivered from condemnation.

36. *A bone of him shall not be broken.* This citation is made from Exod. xii. 46, and Numb. ix. 12, where Moses treats of the paschal lamb. Now, Moses takes for granted that that lamb was a figure of the true and only sacrifice, by which the Church was to be redeemed. Nor is this inconsistent with the fact, that it was sacrificed as the memorial of a redemption which had been already made; for, while God intended that it should celebrate the former favour, he also intended that it should exhibit the spiritual deliverance of the Church, which was still future. On that account Paul, without any hesitation, applies to Christ the rule which Moses lays down about eating the lamb: *for even Christ, our Passover, is sacrificed for us. Therefore let us keep the feast, not with old leaven, neither with the leaven of malice and wickedness, but with the unleavened bread of sincerity and truth,* (1 Cor. v. 7, 8.) From this analogy, or resemblance, faith derives no ordinary advantage, for, in all the ceremonies of the Law, it beholds the salvation which has been manifested in Christ. Such is also the design of the Evangelist John, when he says that Christ was not only the pledge of our redemption, but also the price of it, because in him we see accomplished what was formerly exhibited to the ancient people under the figure of the passover. Thus also the Jews are reminded

that they ought to seek in Christ the substance of all those things which the Law prefigured, but did not actually accomplish.

37. *They shall look on him whom they pierced.* This passage is violently tortured by those who endeavour to explain it literally as referring to Christ. Nor is this the purpose for which the Evangelist quotes it, but rather to show that Christ is that God who formerly complained, by Zechariah, that the Jews had *pierced* his heart, (Zech. xii. 10) Now, God speaks there after the manner of men, declaring that He is wounded by the sins of his people, and especially by their obstinate contempt of his word, in the same manner as a mortal man receives a deadly wound, when his heart is *pierced;* as he says, elsewhere, that *his Spirit was deeply grieved.*[1] Now, as Christ is *God manifested in the flesh,* (1 Tim. iii. 16,) John says that in his visible flesh was plainly accomplished what his Divine Majesty had endured from the Jews, so far as it was capable of enduring; not that God can be at all affected by the outrages of men, or that the reproaches which are cast at him from the earth ever reach him, but because by this mode of expression he intended to declare with what enormous sacrilege the wickedness of men is chargeable, when it rises in rebellion against heaven. What was done by the hand of a Roman soldier the Evangelist John justly imputes to the Jews; as they are elsewhere said *to have crucified the Son of God,* (Acts ii. 36,) though they did not lay a finger on his body.

A question now arises as to this passage taken from the prophet,[2] Does God promise to the Jews repentance to salvation, or, does he threaten that he will come as an avenger? For my own part, when I closely examine the passage, I think that it includes both; namely, that out of a worthless and unprincipled nation God will gather a remnant for salvation, and that, by his dreadful vengeance, he will show to

---

[1] Here CALVIN'S Latin Copy refers to the words of our blessed Lord in Matth. xxvi. 38, *My soul is sorrowful, even to death*, but the French Copy refers to Isa lxiii. 10, *But they rebelled, and* GRIEVED HIS HOLY SPIRIT —*Ed.*

[2] " On fait une question sur ce passage du prophete."

despisers who it is with whom they have to do; for we know that they were wont to treat the prophets as insolently as if the prophets had told nothing but fables, and had received no commission from God. God declares that they will not pass unpunished, for he will at length maintain his cause.

38. After these things, Joseph of Arimathea (who was a disciple of Jesus, but secretly, through fear of the Jews) besought Pilate that he might take away the body of Jesus, and Pilate gave him leave He came, then, and took the body of Jesus. 39. And Nicodemus, also, (who at first came to Jesus by night,) came bearing a mixture of myrrh and aloes, about a hundred pounds weight. 40 Then they took the body of Jesus, and wound it in linen clothes with spices, as the custom of the Jews is to bury. 41. And in the place where he was crucified there was a garden; and in the garden there was a new sepulchre, in which no person had yet been laid. 42. There they laid Jesus, therefore, on account of the preparation of the Jews; for the sepulchre was near at hand.

38. *Joseph of Arimathea besought Pilate.* John now relates by whom, and in what place, and with what magnificence, Christ was buried. He mentions two persons who buried Christ; namely, *Joseph* and *Nicodemus*, the former of whom requested Pilate to give him the dead body, which otherwise would have been exposed to the lawless violence of the soldiers. Matthew (xxvii. 57) says, that he was *a rich man*, and Luke (xxiii. 50) says, that he was *a counsellor;* that is, he held the rank of a senator. As to *Nicodemus*, we have seen, in the Third Chapter of this Gospel, that he held an honourable rank among his own countrymen; and that he was also *rich*, may be easily inferred from the great expense which he laid out in procuring this *mixture.*

Till now, therefore, *riches* had prevented them from professing to be the disciples of Christ, and might afterwards have no less influence in keeping them from making a profession so much hated and abhorred. The Evangelist expressly says, that *Joseph* has formerly been kept back by this *fear* from venturing to declare openly that he was *a disciple* of Christ; and as to *Nicodemus*, he repeats what we have already seen, that he came to Jesus secretly, and *by night*, (John iii. 2, and vii. 50.) Whence, therefore, do they derive such heroic magnanimity that, when affairs are at the lowest ebb, they fearlessly come forth to public view? I say nothing of the great and evident danger which they must have incurred; but the most important point is, that they did not scruple to place themselves in a state of perpetual warfare with their own nation. It is therefore certain that this was effected by a heavenly impulse, so that they who, *through fear*, did not render the honour due to him while he was alive, now run to his dead body, as if they had become new men.

They bring their spices to embalm the body of Christ; but they would never have done so, if they had been perfumed with the sweet savour of his death. This shows the truth of what Christ had said, *Unless a grain of corn die, it remaineth alone; but when it is dead, it bringeth forth much fruit*, (John xii. 24.) For here we have a striking proof that his death was more quickening than his life; and so great was the efficacy of that sweet savour which the death of Christ conveyed to the minds of those two men, that it quickly extinguished all the passions belonging to the flesh. So long as ambition and the love of money reigned in them, the grace of Christ had no charms for them; but now they begin to disrelish the whole world.

Besides, let us learn that their example points out to us what we owe to Christ. Those two men, as a testimony of their faith, not only took down Christ from the cross with great hazard, but boldly carried him to the grave. Our slothfulness will be base and shameful if, now that he reigns in the heavenly glory, we withhold from him the confession of our faith. So much the less excusable is the wickedness of those who, though they now deny Christ by base hypocrisy, plead in his behalf the example of Nicodemus. In one thing, I admit, they resemble him, that they endeavour, as far as lies in their power, to bury Christ; but the time for burying is past, since he hath ascended to the right hand of the Father, that he may reign gloriously over angels and men, and that every tongue may proclaim his dominion, (Philip. ii. 9, 10.)

Secretly, through fear of the Jews. As this fear is contrasted with the holy boldness which the Spirit of the Lord wrought in the heart of *Joseph*, there is reason to believe that it was not free from blame. Not that all fear, by which believers guard against tyrants and enemies of the Church, is faulty, but because the weakness of faith is manifested, whenever the confession of faith is withheld *through fear*. We ought always to consider what the Lord commands, and how far he bids us advance. He who stops in the middle of the course shows that he does not trust in God, and he who sets a higher value on his own life than on the command of God is without excuse.

Who was a disciple of Jesus. When we perceive that the Evangelist bestows on *Joseph* the honourable designation of *a disciple*, at a time when he was excessively timid, and did not venture to profess his faith before the world, we learn from it how graciously God acts towards his people, and with what fatherly kindness he forgives their offences. And yet the false *Nicodemites* have no right to flatter themselves, who not only keep their faith concealed within their own breast, but, by pretending to give their consent to wicked superstitions, do all that is in their power to deny that they are *disciples* of Christ.

40. *As the custom of the Jews is to bury.* When Christ had endured extreme ignominy on the cross, God determined that his burial should be honourable, that it might serve as a preparation for the glory of his resurrection. The money expended on it by *Nicodemus* and *Joseph* is very great, and may be thought by some to be superfluous; but we ought to consider the design of God, who even led them, by his Spirit, to render this honour to his own Son, that, by the sweet savour of his grave, he might take away our dread of the cross. But those things which are out of the ordinary course ought not to be regarded as an example.

Besides, the Evangelist expressly states that he was buried according to *the custom of the Jews.* By these words he informs us that this was one of the ceremonies of the Law; for the ancient people, who did not receive so clear a statement of the resurrection, and who had not such a demonstration and pledge of it as we have in Christ, needed such aids to support them, that they might firmly believe and expect the coming of the Mediator.¹ We ought, therefore, to attend to the distinction between us, who have been enlightened by the brightness of the Gospel, and the Fathers, to whom the figures supplied the absence of Christ. This is the reason why allowance could then be made for a greater pomp of ceremonies, which, at the present day, would not be free from blame; for those who now bury the dead at so great an expense do not, strictly speaking, bury dead men, but rather, as far as lies in their power, draw down from heaven Christ himself, the King of life, and lay him in the tomb, for his glorious resurrection² abolished those ancient ceremonies.

Among the heathen, too, there was great anxiety and ceremony in burying the dead, which unquestionably derived its origin from the ancient Fathers of the Jews,³ in the same manner as sacrifices; but, as no hope of the resurrection existed among them, they were not imitators of the Fathers, but apes of them; for the promise and word of God is, as it were, the soul, which gives life to ceremonies. Take away the word, and all the ceremonies which men observe, though outwardly they may resemble the worship of godly persons, is nothing else than foolish or mad superstition. For our part, as we have said, we ought now to maintain sobriety and moderation in this matter, for immoderate expense quenches the sweet savour of Christ's resurrection.

41. *Now, in the place where he was crucified there was a garden.* This is the *third* point, as I have said, which ought to be observed in the history of the burial. It is related by the Evangelist for various reasons. In the first place, it did not happen by accident, but by an undoubted providence of God, that the body of Christ was buried *in a new sepulchre;* for although he died as all other men die, still, as he was to be *the first-born from the dead,* (Col. i. 18,) and *the first-fruits of them that rise,* (1 Cor. xv. 20,) he had *a new sepulchre, in which no person had ever been laid.* True,

---

¹ " La venue du Messias;"—" the coming of the Messiah."
² " Sa resurrection glorieuse "
³ " Des Peres anciens des Juifs."

Nicodemus and *Joseph* had a different object in view; for, in consequence of the short time that now remained till sunset, which was the commencement of the Sabbath, they looked to the convenience of the place, but, contrary to their intention, God provided for his own Son *a sepulchre* which had not yet been used. The good men are merely gratified by *the place being near at hand*, that they might not violate the Sabbath; but God offers them what they did not seek, that the burial of his Son might have some token to distinguish him from the rank of other men. The local situation served also to prove the truth of his resurrection, and to throw no small light on the narrative which is contained in the following chapter.

CHAPTER XX.

1. Now, on the first day of the week,[1] Mary Magdalene goeth early to the sepulchre, while it was yet dark, and seeth the stone rolled away from the sepulchre. 2. Then she runneth, and cometh to Simon Peter, and to the other disciple whom Jesus loved, and saith to them, They have taken away the Lord out of the sepulchre, and we know not where they have laid him. 3. Peter therefore went forth, and the other disciple, and came to the sepulchre. 4 And they both ran together, and the other disciple outran Peter, and came first to the sepulchre. 5. And, stooping down, he saw the linen clothes lying; yet he went not in 6. Then Simon Peter came following him, and entered into the sepulchre, and saw the linen clothes lying, 7 And the napkin that was about his head, not lying with the linen clothes, but wrapped together in a place by itself. 8. Then the other disciple, who came first to the sepulchre, went in also, and he saw and believed 9. For as yet they knew not the scripture, that he must rise from the dead.

1. *Now, on the first day of the week.* As the resurrection of Christ is the most important article of our faith, and without it the hope of eternal life is extinguished, for this reason the Evangelists are the more careful to prove it, as John here collects many proofs, in order to assure us that Christ is risen from the dead. It may be thought strange, however, that he does not produce more competent witnesses; for he begins with a woman; but thus the saying is fulfilled, that *God*

---

[1] "Or le premier (des jours) du Sabbath, *ou, le premier jour de la semaine;*"—"Now, the first (of the days) of the Sabbath, *or, the first day of the week.*"

chooseth what is weak, and foolish, and contemptible in the world, that he may bring to nought the wisdom, and excellence, and glory, of the flesh, (1 Cor. i. 27.) There certainly was nothing more of earthly grandeur in the disciples than in the women who followed Christ; but as Christ was pleased to reckon them the principal witnesses of his resurrection, on this single ground their testimony is entitled to the greatest deference, and is not liable to any objection. As to the priests and scribes, and the whole people, and even Pilate, nothing but gross and wilful blindness prevented them from firmly believing that Christ was risen. All of them, therefore, deserved that *seeing they should not see;* yet Christ revealed himself to the little flock.

Before proceeding farther, however, it is necessary to show how the Evangelists agree with each other; for, at first sight, there appears to be some contradiction in their words. John mentions but one woman, *Mary Magdalene;* Matthew (xxviii. 1) mentions two, *Mary Magdalene, and the other Mary;* Mark (xvi. 1) mentions three, *Mary Magdalene, and Mary* (the mother) *of James, and Salome;* Luke (xxiv. 10, 22) does not fix the number, but only relates that *women came,* who had followed Christ from Galilee. But the difficulty is easily solved in this manner. As Matthew inserts the names of two women who were best known, and had the highest reputation among the disciples, so John satisfies himself with mentioning the name of *Mary Magdalene* alone, but yet does not exclude the others; and, indeed, it is evident, from viewing his words in their connection, that she was not alone, for, shortly afterwards, *Mary Magdalene* says, in the plural number, WE *know not where they have laid him.* Although, therefore, John says nothing about her companions, yet the other Evangelists, who relate that there were many along with her, say nothing that is contradicted by John's narrative.

The discrepancy as to the *time* may be easily solved. When John says that they came before daybreak, we must understand, that they had set out on their journey during the darkness of the night; that, before they came to the sepulchre, the day had dawned; and that in the evening, after sunset, when the Sabbath was ended, they had bought the spices;

and thus the narrative of the other Evangelists must be reconciled.

It may be thought that there is another appearance of contradiction in its being stated by John, that *Mary* spoke to none but himself and *Peter*, while Luke (xxiv. 10, 11) relates, that she came to the eleven Apostles, and that *her words appeared to them to be idle tales.* But this is easily explained, for John intentionally passed by the rest of the Apostles, because it was only himself and *Peter* that came to the sepulchre. As to Luke mentioning Peter alone, it is for the same reason as we have just now assigned in reference to *Mary Magdalene* and the rest of the women. It is also probable, that the other nine disciples were restrained by fear, lest they should be too easily observed if they went in a body. Nor is this inconsistent with what Luke appears to suggest, that they despised Mary's words; for immediately afterwards he adds, that *Peter ran*, (Luke xxiv. 12.) He therefore means simply that, when they first heard it, they appeared to be astonished, but that at length *Peter* took courage, and followed her for the purpose of seeing.

When Luke relates that Christ appeared to Mary before that she had informed the disciples that the grave was empty, the order of the narrative is inverted. This is evident from the context, for he adds what, John tells us, happened before she saw Jesus; nor is there any thing strange in this, for the Hebrew writers frequently relate first what is later in the order of time.

On the first day of the week; or, literally, *on the first day of the Sabbaths.* The Evangelists do not relate when or how Christ rose; for it was enough for them to explain at what time, and to what persons, his resurrection was made known. John therefore says, that Mary came *on the first day of the Sabbaths*. Literally, the words may be rendered, *on* ONE ($\mu\iota\tilde{q}$) *day of the Sabbaths;* but it is customary with the Hebrews to use the word אֶחָד *(ehad) one*, instead of *first*, because in reckoning we begin with *one*. Now, as every seventh day was dedicated to *rest*, they called the whole week a *Sabbath*, conferring this honour on the sacredness of the day, that the rest of the time was named from it. The women, therefore, came to the sepulchre on the day after the Sabbath, having on the same day (but after sunset) *bought spices;* and afterwards went out of the city secretly, and during the darkness of the night, as people are wont to do when they are afraid. Now, it was *the first day of the Sabbaths,* with respect to the following *Sabbath,* because it was the commencement of the week, of which *the Sabbath* was the close.

3. *Peter therefore went forth.* There being so little faith, or rather almost no faith, both in the disciples and in the women, it is astonishing that they had so great zeal; and, indeed, it is not possible that religious feelings led them to seek Christ. Some seed of faith, therefore, remained in their hearts, but quenched for a time, so that they were not aware of having what they had. Thus the Spirit of God often works in the elect in a secret manner. In short, we must believe that there was some concealed root, from which we see fruit produced. Though this feeling of piety, which they possessed, was confused, and was accompanied by much superstition, still I give to it—though inaccurately—the name of *faith,* because it was only by the doctrine of the Gospel that it was produced, and it had no tendency but towards Christ. From this seed there at length sprang a true and sincere *faith,* which, leaving the sepulchre, ascended to the heavenly glory of Christ.

When Scripture speaks of the feeble beginnings of faith, it says that Christ is born in us, and that we, on the other hand, are born in him; but the disciples must be placed almost below infancy, for they are ignorant of the resurrection of Christ, but yet the Lord nourishes them as a mother nourishes the child that is contained in her womb. Formerly they resembled children, and had made a little progress, but the death of Christ had rendered them so weak, that they must be again begotten and *formed,* as Paul says of the Galatians, *My little children, of whom* I TRAVAIL IN BIRTH *again until* CHRIST BE FORMED *in you,* (Gal. iv. 19.)

When we find that Peter, though he made less haste, is the first to enter into the sepulchre, let us learn from it that many persons have more given to them in the end than appears at the beginning. And, indeed, we sometimes see many, who were full of fervour at the commencement, give way when they come to the conflict; while others, who appeared to be slow and indolent, assume new courage when danger is at hand.

5. *And seeth the linen clothes lying.* The linen clothes might be regarded as the spoils, intended to lead to the belief of Christ's resurrection; for it was not probable that his body had been stripped naked, in order that it might be removed to another place. This would not have been done by a friend, nor even by an enemy.

7. *And the napkin which was about his head.* When the Evangelist says, that *a napkin* was wrapped *about his head*, this refutes the falsehood of the Papists, who pretend that the whole body was sewed up in one linen garment, which they hold out to the wretched populace, calling it "the holy winding-sheet."[1] I say nothing about their gross ignorance of the Latin language, which led them to suppose that the word *napkin*—denoting what was used for wiping the sweat from the face, such as *a handkerchief*[2]—signified a covering for the whole body; nor do I say any thing about their impudence in boasting that they have this very *napkin* in five or six different places. But this gross falsehood is intolerable, because it openly contradicts the evangelical history. To this is added a fabulous miracle, which they have contrived, to this effect, that the likeness of Christ's body continued to be visible in the linen cloth. I appeal to you, if such a miracle had been wrought, would nothing have been said about it by the Evangelist, who is so careful to relate events which were not of so great importance? Let us be satisfied with this simple view of the matter, that Christ, by laying aside the tokens of death, intended to testify that he had clothed himself with a blessed and immortal life.

8. *And he saw and believed.* It is a poor exposition which

[1] "L'appelant le sainct suaire."
[2] "Comme pourroit estre un couvre-chef."

some give of these words, that John *believed* what he had heard Mary say, namely, that Christ's body had been carried away; for there is no passage in which the word *believe* bears this meaning, especially when it is used simply and without any addition. Nor is this inconsistent with the fact, that *Peter and John* return home, while they are still in doubt and perplexity; for in some passages John had employed this phraseology, when he intended to describe the increase of faith. Besides, Luke (xxiv. 12) relates that *Peter wondered* at seeing the sepulchre in such good order; meaning by this, that Peter thought of something greater and loftier than what Mary had told him.

9. *For as yet they knew not the Scripture, that he must rise again from the dead.* They had often heard from the mouth of Christ what they now saw with their eyes, but this flowed from their hearts. Being now warned by the sight of a strange spectacle, they begin to think of Christ as having something Divine, though they are still far from having a clear and accurate knowledge of him. John, therefore, accuses himself, when he acknowledges that the first time that he *believed* was, when he beheld the proofs of Christ's resurrection.

Besides, he represents more strongly his own guilt and that of his brethren, by adding, that they not only had forgotten the words of Christ, but that they did not believe *the Scriptures;* for to this ignorance he ascribes the deficiency of their faith. Hence, too, we may draw a useful instruction, that we ought to ascribe it to our carelessness, when we are ignorant of what we ought to know about Christ, because we have not profited as we ought to have done by *the Scriptures*, which clearly reveal the excellence of Christ.

Not to go farther for an instance of this, it may be thought that the resurrection of Christ is taught in them obscurely, and only under figures; but the attentive reader will find abundantly clear testimonies. Paul proves (Acts xiii. 34) that Christ must have risen from the dead, because God declares by the prophet Isaiah, (lv. 3,) that, under his reign, *the mercy promised to David would be sure.* An unskilful person might imagine that what Paul quotes is not at all to the purpose; but they who believe the principles of faith, and are well acquainted with *the Scriptures*, have no difficulty in perceiving the force of this argument; for, in order that Christ may secure to us for ever the grace of God, Christ himself must live for ever.

There are many passages of the same kind, which it is not now necessary to collect. Let us therefore rest satisfied with the three following. It is written, *Thou wilt not permit thy Holy One to see corruption*, (Ps. xvi. 10.) Peter and Paul explain this prediction as referring to Christ, (Acts ii. 27, and xiii. 35,) and justly; for there is not one of all the sons of Adam who is not of himself liable to corruption. Consequently, the immortality of Christ is there declared. It is likewise beyond all doubt that the following passage refers to Christ, *The Lord said to my Lord, Sit thou at my right hand, until I make thy enemies thy footstool*, (Ps. cx. 1.) Now, death will not be destroyed till the last day. The kingdom is then given to Christ till the end of the world, and this kingdom cannot exist without his life. But Isaiah speaks more clearly than all the rest, when, after having foretold the death of Christ, he immediately adds, that *it is impossible to declare his age*, (Isa. liii. 8.) In short, we ought to believe that the doctrine of Scripture is so full and complete in every respect, that whatever is defective in our faith ought justly to be attributed to ignorance of *the Scriptures*.

10. Then the disciples went away again to their own homes. 11. But Mary stood without at the sepulchre, weeping, and as she wept, she stooped down to the sepulchre, 12 And seeth two angels in white garments sitting, one at the head, and the other at the feet, where the body of Jesus had lain. 13. And they say to her, Woman, why weepest thou? She saith to them, Because they have taken away my Lord, and I know not where they have laid him 14 Having said this, she turned back, and seeth Jesus standing, and knew not that it was Jesus. 15. Jesus saith to her, Woman, why weepest thou? She, thinking that he was the gardener, saith to him, Sir, if thou hast carried him hence, tell me where thou hast laid him, and I will take him away.

10. *Then the disciples went away again to their own homes.* It is possible that their minds were still in a state of doubt and uncertainty, when they returned home; for, though John

says that *they believed,* yet their faith was not strong, but was only some confused remembrance of the miracle and resembled a trance, until it was more fully confirmed; and, indeed, a strong faith could not be produced merely by the sight which they had beheld. Besides, Christ did not present himself to their view, until they had been more fully awakened from their carnal stupidity. They had indeed given a praiseworthy demonstration of their zeal, in hastening to the sepulchre; yet Christ hid himself from them, because they sought him with too great superstition.

11. *But Mary stood at the sepulchre without.* The Evangelist now begins to describe the manner in which Christ appeared both to the women and to the disciples, to testify his resurrection. Though he mentions but one woman, *Mary,* yet I think it is probable that the other women were also along with her; for it is not reasonable to suppose, as some have done, that the women fainted through fear. Those writers wish to avoid a contradiction, but I have already shown that no such contradiction exists.

As to the women remaining *at the sepulchre,* while the disciples return to the city, they are not entitled to great accommodation on this account; for the disciples carry with them consolation and joy, but the women torment themselves by idle and useless *weeping.* In short, it is superstition alone, accompanied by carnal feelings, that keeps them *near the sepulchre.*

12. *And seeth two angels.* What an amazing forbearance displayed by our Lord, in bearing with so many faults in Mary and her companions! For it is no small honour which he confers on them by sending his *angels,* and, at length, making himself known to them, which he had not done to the apostles. Though the apostles and the women were afflicted with the same disease, yet the stupidity of the apostles was less excusable, because they had profited so little by the valuable and careful instruction which they had received. One purpose, certainly, which Christ had in view in selecting

the women, to make the first manifestation of himself to them, was, to fill the apostles with shame.

In white garments. Whether *Mary* knew them to be *angels*, or thought that they were men, is uncertain. We know that *white garments* were an emblem of the heavenly glory; as we find that Christ was clothed in *white garments*, when he was transfigured on the mountain, and showed his glorious majesty to his three apostles,[1] (Matth. xvii. 2.) Luke relates that the angel who appeared to Cornelius *stood before him* IN BRIGHT CLOTHING, (Acts x. 30.) Nor do I deny that linen garments were commonly used by the inhabitants of Eastern countries; but by the dress of the *angels* God pointed out something remarkable and uncommon, and put marks on them, as it were, that they might be distinguished from men. Besides, Matthew (xxviii. 3) compares the countenance of the angel, who conversed with the women, to *lightning.* And yet it is possible that their fear arose solely from their minds being struck with admiration, for it appears that they stood astonished.

Again, whenever we read that the *angels* appeared in the visible form of men and clothed with *garments*, this was done on account of the ignorance of men. For my part, I have no doubt that they sometimes were clothed with real bodies; but whether or not those *two angels* had merely the appearance of bodies, would be a useles inquiry, and I shall therefore leave it undetermined. To me it is enough that the Lord gave them a human shape, that the women might see and hear them, while the magnificent and uncommon dress which they wore distinguished them from the ordinary rank of men, and pointed out something divine and heavenly.

One at the head, and the other at the feet. One angel only is mentioned by Matthew, (xxviii. 2.) This, however, does not contradict John's narrative; for both angels did not address Mary at the same time, but only one of them who had a commission to speak. There is no good ground for Augustine's allegory, that the position of the angels—*one at the head, and the other at the feet*—pointed out that the Gospel

---

[1] " Quand il se transfigura en la montagne, et monstra sa majesté glorieuse à ses trois apostres.'

would be preached from the East to the West. It is more worthy of observation, that Christ, by preparatory arrangements of this nature, made a commencement of the glory of his kingdom; for, by the honour which the angels render to the sepulchre, not only is the ignominy of the cross taken away, but the heavenly majesty of Christ shines.

13. *Woman, why weepest thou?* From the statements of the Evangelists, it may be readily concluded, that the angel held a long conversation; but John gives a brief summary of what was spoken, because this was sufficient for proving the resurrection of Christ. The conversation consists of reproof mingled with comfort. The angel reproves Mary for her excessive *weeping*, but, at the same time, mingles joy, when he says that there is no reason to weep, since Christ has risen.

14. *And seeth Jesus standing.* It may be asked, Whence arose this mistake, that Mary does not recognize Jesus, with whom she must have been intimately acquainted? Some think that he appeared in a different form, but I think that the fault lay rather in the eyes of the women, as Luke (xxiv. 16) says of the two disciples, *their eyes were withheld from knowing him.* We will not say, therefore, that Christ was continually assuming new shapes, like *Proteus*,[1] but that it is in the power of God, who gave eyes to men, to lessen

---

[1] *Proteus*, (Πρωτεύς,) a king of Egypt, is mentioned by Herodotus, who relates that at Memphis, his native place, a magnificent temple was erected for him. The historian quotes as his authorities, the Egyptian priests with whom he had conversed, and who detailed to him the most memorable transactions of that reign, connected with the carrying of Helena into Egypt, and he produces passages from the Iliad and the Odyssey, to prove that Homer was well acquainted with the leading facts, though he chose to disguise or palliate them, so as to make a better figure in his story, (Herodotus, Book II. 112-116.) The key to the present allusion, however, must be found in the fabulous accounts of *Proteus*, as a sea deity, whom Ovid describes as PROTEA AMBIGUUM, *the shape-changing Proteus*, (Metamorphoses, Book II. Fable I. v 9,) and whose alleged habit of frequently changing his shape passed into a proverb. "He had (says Lempriere) received the gift of prophecy from Neptune, and from his knowledge of futurity mankind received the greatest services. He was difficult of access, and, when consulted, he refused to give answers, by immediately *assuming different shapes*, and eluding the grasp, if not properly secured by fetters." Proverbial references to this fable occur frequently in the ancient writers.—Ed.

their sharpness of vision whenever he thinks proper, that *seeing they may not see.*

In Mary we have an example of the mistakes into which the human mind frequently falls. Though Christ presents himself to our view, yet we imagine that he assumes various shapes, so that our senses conceive of any thing rather than of the true Christ; for not only are our powers of understanding liable to be deceived, but they are also bewitched by the world and by Satan, that they may have no perception of the truth.

15. *Lord, if thou hast carried him hence.* She calls him *Lord,* according to the custom of her nation; for the same appellation, *Lord,* (Κύριε,[1]) is employed by the Hebrews in addressing labourers and other persons of low condition. We see that Mary has no view of this matter but what is earthly. She desires only to obtain the dead body of Christ, that she may keep it hidden in the sepulchre; but she leaves out the most important matter, the elevation of her mind to the divine power of his resurrection. We need not wonder, therefore, if such grovelling views place a veil before her eyes.

16. Jesus saith to her, Mary! She turned herself, and said to him, Rabboni! which means, Master! 17. Jesus saith to her, Touch me not; for I am not yet ascended to my Father; but go to my brethren, and say to them, I ascend to my Father and your Father, and to my God and your God. 18. Mary Magdalene went and told the disciples that she had seen the Lord, and that he had said these things to her.

16. *Jesus saith to her, Mary!* That Christ allowed Mary, a short time, to fall into a mistake, was useful for confirming her faith; but now, by a single word, he corrects her mistake. He had formerly addressed her, but his discourse seemed to be that of an unknown person; he now assumes the character of the Master, and addresses his disciple by name, as we have formerly seen that *the good shepherd calleth to him by name every sheep of his flock,* (John x. 3.) That *voice of the shepherd,* therefore, enters into Mary's heart, opens her eyes,

---

[1] The salutation, Κύριε, was addressed to persons of various ranks, and answers to the modern term, *Sir.—Ed.*

arouses all her senses, and affects her in such a manner, that she immediately surrenders herself to Christ.

Thus in *Mary* we have a lively image of our calling; for the only way in which we are admitted to the true knowledge of Christ is, when he first knows us, and then familiarly invites us to himself, not by that ordinary voice which sounds indiscriminately in the ears of all, but by that voice with which he especially calls the sheep which the Father hath given to him. Thus Paul says, *After that you have known God, or rather, after that you have been known by him,* (Gal. iv. 9.)

And said to him, Rabboni! The efficacy of the address is evident from this circumstance, that Mary immediately renders to Christ the honour which is due to him; for the word *Rabboni* is not only respectful, but involves a profession of obedience. Mary therefore declares, that she is a disciple of Christ, and submits to him as her *Master.* This is a secret and wonderful change effected on the human understanding, when God, enlightening her by his Spirit, renders her clear-sighted, who formerly was slow of apprehension, and, indeed, altogether blind. Besides, the example of Mary ought to serve the purpose of exhortation, that all whom Christ invites to himself may reply to him without delay.

The word *Rabboni* is Chaldee, though the Chaldeans pronounce it *Ribboni;* but it is customary to make a change on words, when they are transferred to a foreign tongue. The meaning is the same as if we were to say, *My Lord!* or, *My Master!* But in the time of Christ this mode of expression had gained currency, of using *Rabbi* and *Rabboni* instead of *Master.*

17. *Touch me not.* This appears not to agree with the narrative of Matthew; for he expressly says, that the women *held him* BY THE FEET, *and worshipped him,* (Matth. xxviii. 9.) Now, since he allowed himself to be *touched* by his disciples, what reason was there for forbidding Mary to *touch* him? The answer is easy, provided that we remember that the women were not repelled from *touching* Christ, till their eagerness to *touch* him had been carried to excess; for, so far

as it was necessary for removing doubt, he unquestionably did not forbid them to *touch* him, but, perceiving that their attention was too much occupied with embracing *his feet*, he restrained and corrected that immoderate zeal. They fixed their attention on his bodily presence, and did not understand any other way of enjoying his society than by conversing with him on the earth. We ought, therefore, to conclude, that they were not forbidden to *touch* him, until Christ saw that, by their foolish and unreasonable desire, they wished to keep him in the world.

For I am not yet ascended to my Father. We ought to attend to this reason which he adds; for by these words he enjoins the women to restrain their feelings, until he be received into the heavenly glory. In short, he pointed out the design of his resurrection; not such as they had imagined it to be, that, after having returned to life, he should triumph in the world, but rather that, by his *ascension* to heaven, he should enter into the possession of the kingdom which had been promised to him, and, seated at the right hand *of the Father*, should govern the Church by the power of his Spirit. The meaning of the words therefore is, that his state of resurrection would not be full and complete, until he should sit down in heaven at the right hand of the Father; and, therefore, that the women did wrong in satisfying themselves with having nothing more than the half of his resurrection, and desiring to enjoy his presence in the world. This doctrine yields two advantages. The first is, that those who are desirous to succeed in seeking Christ must raise their minds upwards; and the second is, that all who endeavour to go to him must rid themselves of the earthly affections of the flesh, as Paul exhorts, *If ye then be risen with Christ, seek those things which are above, where Christ sitteth at the right hand of God,* (Col. iii. 1.)

But go to my brethren. Some limit the word *brethren* to the cousins and relatives[1] of Christ, but, in my opinion, improperly; for why should he have sent to them rather than to the disciples? They reply, Because John elsewhere testi-

---

[1] "Aux cousins et parens de Christ."

fies, that HIS BRETHREN *did not believe in him,* (John vii. 5.) But I do not think it probable that Christ conferred so great an honour on those who are there mentioned. It must also be admitted, that Mary Magdalene[1] fully obeyed the injunctions of Christ. Now, it immediately follows, that she went *to the disciples;* from which we conclude, that Christ had spoken of them.[2]

Besides, Christ knew that *the disciples,* whom those men, by their opinion, treat as separated, were assembled in one place; and it would have been exceedingly absurd that he should pay attention to I know not what sort of persons, and disregard *the disciples,* who, having been collected into one place, were subjected to a violent conflict between hope and fear. To this it may be added, that Christ appears to have borrowed this expression from Psalm xxii. 22, where we find these words: *I will declare thy name to my brethren;* for it is beyond all controversy, that this passage contains the fulfilment of that prediction.

I conclude, therefore, that Mary was sent to the disciples in general; and I consider that this was done by way of reproach, because they had been so tardy and sluggish to believe. And, indeed, they deserve not only to have *women* for their teachers, but even oxen and asses; since the Son of God had been so long and laboriously employed in teaching, and yet they had made so little, or hardly any progress. Yet this is a mild and gentle chastisement, when Christ thus sends his disciples to the school of the women, that, by their agency, he may bring them back to himself. Here we behold also the inconceivable kindness of Christ, in choosing and appointing *women* to be the witnesses of his resurrection to the Apostles; for the commission which is given to them is the only foundation of our salvation, and contains the chief point of heavenly wisdom.

It ought likewise to be observed, however, that this occurrence was extraordinary, and—we might almost say—accidental. They are commanded to make known to the Apostles

---

[1] " Marie Magdalene."
[2] " Que Christ avoit parlé de ses disciples et Apostres,"—" that Christ had spoken of his disciples and Apostles."

what they afterwards, in the exercise of the office committed to them, proclaimed to the whole world. But, in executing this injunction, they do not act as if they had been Apostles; and, therefore, it is wrong to frame a law out of this injunction of Christ, and to allow women to perform the office of baptizing. Let us be satisfied with knowing that Christ displayed in them the boundless treasures of his grace, when he once appointed them to be the teachers of the Apostles, and yet did not intend that what was done by a singular privilege should be viewed as an example. This is peculiarly apparent in *Mary Magdalene, who had formerly been possessed by seven devils,* (Mark xvi. 9; Luke viii. 2;) for it amounted to this, that Christ had brought her out of the lowest hell, that he might raise her above heaven.

If it be objected, that there was no reason why Christ should prefer the women to the Apostles, since they were not less carnal and stupid, I reply, it does not belong to us, but to the Judge, to estimate the difference between the Apostles and the women. But I go farther, and say, that the Apostles deserved to be more severely censured, because they not only had been better instructed than all others, but, after having been appointed to be the teachers of the whole world, and after having been called *the light of the world,* (Matth. v. 14,) and *the salt of the earth,* (Matth. v. 13,) they so basely apostatized. Yet it pleased the Lord, by means of those weak and contemptible vessels, to give a display of his power.

I ascend to my Father. By using the word *ascend* he confirms the doctrine which I have lately explained; that he rose from the dead, not for the purpose of remaining any longer on the earth, but that he might enter into the heavenly life, and might thus draw believers to heaven along with him. In short, by this term he forbids the Apostles to fix their whole attention on his resurrection viewed simply in itself, but exhorts them to proceed farther, until they come to the spiritual kingdom, to the heavenly glory, to God himself. There is great emphasis, therefore, in this word *ascend;* for Christ stretches out his hand to his disciples that they may not seek their happiness anywhere else than in heaven; *for where our treasure is, there also must our heart be,* (Matth. vi. 21.) Now, Christ declares, that he *ascends* on high; and, therefore, we must *ascend,* if we do not wish to be separated from him.

When he adds, that he *ascends* TO GOD, he quickly dispels the grief and anxiety which the Apostles might feel on account of his departure; for his meaning is, that he will always be present with his disciples by Divine power. True, the word *ascend* denotes the distance of places; but though Christ be absent in body, yet, as he is with God, his power, which is everywhere felt, plainly shows his spiritual presence; for why did he ascend to God, but in order that, being seated at God's right hand,[1] he might reign both in heaven and in earth? In short, by this expression he intended to impress on the minds of his disciples the Divine power of his kingdom, that they might not be grieved on account of his bodily absence.

To my Father and your Father, and to my God and your God. The benefit and efficacy of that brotherly union, which has been lately mentioned, is expressed, when Christ declares that we have this in common with himself, that he who is *his God and his Father* is also *our God and our Father. I ascend,* says he, *to my Father, who is also your Father.* In other passages we learn that we are made partakers of all the blessings of Christ; but this is the foundation of the privilege, that he imparts to us the very fountain of blessings. It is, unquestionably, an invaluable blessing, that believers can safely and firmly believe, that He who is the God of Christ is *their God,* and that He who is the Father of Christ is *their Father.* Nor have we any reason to fear that this confidence will be charged with rashness, since it is founded on Christ, or that it will be proud boasting, since Christ himself has dictated it to us with his own mouth.

Christ calls Him *his God,* in so far as, by *taking upon him the form of a servant, he humbled himself,* (Philip. ii. 7.) This is, therefore, peculiar to his human nature, but is applied to his whole person, on account of the unity, because he is

---

[1] "A sa dextre glorieuse,"—"at his glorious right hand."

both God and Man. As to the second clause, in which he says that he *ascends to his Father and our Father*,[1] there is also a diversity between him and us; for he is the Son of God by nature, while we are the sons of God only by adoption; but the grace which we obtain through him is so firmly established, that it cannot be shaken by any efforts of the devil, so as to hinder us from always calling him our Father, who hath adopted us through his Only-begotten Son.

19. When, therefore, it was evening on that day, which was the first day of the Sabbath,[2] and while the doors were shut, where the disciples were assembled through fear of the Jews, Jesus came, and stood in the midst, and saith to them, Peace be to you. 20. And when he had said this, he showed them his hands and his side. Then the disciples rejoiced when they saw the Lord. 21. Then said Jesus to them again, Peace be to you, as the Father hath sent me, I also send you. 22. When he had said this, he breathed on them, and said to them, Receive the Holy Spirit. 23. To those whose sins you remit they shall be remitted, and to those whose sins you retain they shall be retained.

19. *When, therefore, it was evening.* The Evangelist now relates that the resurrection of Christ was proved to the disciples by his presence. It did not happen without the providence of God, that all were assembled in one place, that the event might be more certain and more manifest. It is worthy of notice how gently Christ acted towards them, in not keeping them in suspense any longer than till the evening. Besides, he enlightened them, bringing the pledge of a new life, while darkness was overspreading the world.

Where the disciples were assembled. As to their having *assembled*, it was an indication of faith, or, at least, of religious feelings. As to the circumstance of their keeping themselves concealed by *shut doors*, we perceive in it some proof of their weakness; for, though the strongest and boldest minds are sometimes seized with fear, yet it may easily be inferred that the apostles, at that time, trembled in such a manner as to manifest the deficiency of their faith. This example is worthy of notice; for, though they are less courageous than they ought to have

---

[1] " Ou il dit qu'il monte a son Pere et nostre Pere "
[2] " Qui estoit le premier jour des Sabbaths, *ou, le premier de la septmaine ;*"—" which was the first day of the Sabbaths, *or the first* (day) *of the week.*"

been, still they do not give way to their weakness. True, they seek concealment for the sake of avoiding danger, but they gather courage so far as to remain together; otherwise they would have been scattered hither and thither, and no man would have ventured to look at his neighbour. In this manner we ought to struggle against the weakness of our flesh, and not to indulge fear, which tempts us to apostacy. Christ also blesses their zeal, when he appears to them while they are assembled; and Thomas is justly deprived of the favour bestowed on all his brethren, because, like a wandering soldier, he had withdrawn from the standard of union. Here, then, is a lesson for those who are excessively timid, to sharpen and encourage themselves to correct their carnal fear; and particularly they ought to beware lest fear should cause them to scatter.

And while the doors were shut. This circumstance was expressly added, because it contains a manifest proof of the Divine power of Christ; but this is utterly at variance with the meaning of the Evangelist. We ought, therefore, to believe that Christ did not enter without a miracle, in order to give a demonstration of his Divinity, by which he might stimulate the attention of his disciples; and yet I am far from admitting the truth of what the Papists assert, that the body of Christ passed through *the shut doors.* Their reason for maintaining this is, for the purpose of proving not only that the glorious body of Christ resembled a spirit, but that it was infinite, and could not be confined to any one place. But the words convey no such meaning; for the Evangelist does not say that he entered through *the shut doors,* but that he suddenly *stood in the midst* of his disciples, though *the doors* had been *shut,* and had not been opened to him by the hand of man. We know that Peter (Acts x. 10) went out of a prison which was locked; and must we, therefore, say that he passed through the midst of the iron and of the planks? Away, then, with that childish trifling, which contains nothing solid, and brings along with it many absurdities! Let us be satisfied with knowing that Christ intended, by a remarkable miracle, to confirm his disciples in their belief of his resurrection.

Peace be to you! This is the ordinary form of salutation among the Hebrews; and by the word *peace* they denote all that cheerfulness and prosperity which is usually desired for a happy life. The phrase, therefore, means, "May you be well and prosperous!" I mention this, because there are some who, in explaining these words, enter into unnecessary discussions about *peace* and harmony, though Christ intended nothing else than to desire that his disciples might be happy and prosperous.

20. *He showed them his hands and his side.* It was necessary to add this confirmation, that by all these methods they might be fully assured that Christ was risen. If any person think it strange and inconsistent with the glory of Christ, that he should bear the marks of his wounds even after his resurrection, let him consider, first, that Christ rose not so much for himself as for us; and, secondly, that whatever contributes to our salvation is glorious to Christ; for, when he humbled himself for a time, this took nothing away from his majesty, and now, since those *wounds*, of which we are speaking, serve to confirm the belief of his resurrection, they do not diminish his glory. But if any person should infer from this, that Christ has still the wounded *side* and the pierced *hands*, that would be absurd; for it is certain that the use of the *wounds* was temporary, until the Apostles were fully convinced that he was risen from the dead.

Then were the disciples glad when they saw the Lord. This means, that all the grief which had been occasioned to them by the death of Christ was dispelled by his new life.

21. *Jesus saith to them again, Peace be to you.* This second salutation appears to me to have no other object than that the Lord should receive such a degree of attention as was due to the greatness and importance of the subjects on which he was about to speak.

As the Father hath sent me. By these words, Christ, as it were, instals them in the office to which he had previously appointed them. True, they had been already sent throughout Judea, but only as heralds, to issue a command that the supreme Teacher should be heard, and not as Apostles, to execute a perpetual office of teaching. But now the Lord ordains them to be his ambassadors, to establish his kingdom in the world. Let it therefore be held by us as an ascertained truth, that the Apostles were now, for the first time, appointed to be ordinary ministers of the Gospel.

His words amount to a declaration, that hitherto he has discharged the office of a Teacher, and that, having finished his course, he now confers on them the same office; for he means that the Father appointed him to be a Teacher on this condition, that he should be employed, for a time, in pointing out the way to others, and should, afterwards, put those persons in his room to supply his absence. For this reason Paul says that *he gave some, apostles; some, evangelists; some, pastors,* to govern the Church till the end of the world, (Eph. iv. 11.) Christ therefore testifies, first, that, though he held a temporary office of teaching, still the preaching of the Gospel is not for a short time, but will be perpetual. Again, that his doctrine may not have less authority in the mouth of the Apostles, he bids them succeed to that office which he has received *from his Father,* places them in his room, and bestows on them the same authority; and it was proper that their ministry should be ratified in this manner, for they were unknown persons and of mean condition. Moreover, though they had the highest splendour and dignity, yet we know that all that belongs to men does not approach to the excellence of faith.

It is not without reason, therefore, that Christ communicates to his Apostles the authority which he received *from the Father,* that thus he may declare that the preaching of the Gospel was committed to him, not by human authority, but by the command of God. But he does not substitute them in his room, in such a manner as to resign to them the highest authority as a teacher, which the Father intended to be vested in him alone. He therefore continues, and will eternally continue to be, the only Teacher of the Church; but there is only this difference, that he spoke with his mouth so long as he dwelt on earth, but now speaks by the Apostles.

The succession or substitution,[1] therefore, is of such a nature that it takes nothing from Christ, but his authority remains full and entire, and his honour unimpaired; for that decree by which we are enjoined to hear him, and not others, cannot be set aside: *This is my beloved Son, in whom I am well pleased; hear ye him,* (Matth. xvii. 5.) In short, Christ intended here to adorn the doctrine of the Gospel and not men.

It ought likewise to be observed, that the only subject which is handled in this passage is the preaching of the Gospel; for Christ does not send his Apostles to atone for sins, and to procure justification, *as he was sent by the Father.* Accordingly, he makes no allusion in this passage to anything which is peculiar to himself, but only appoints ministers and pastors to govern the Church; and on this condition, that he alone keeps possession of the whole power, while they claim nothing for themselves but the ministry.

22. *He breathed on them.* Not one of the sons of men is qualified for discharging so difficult an office, and, therefore, Christ prepares the Apostles for it by the grace of his Spirit. And, indeed, to govern the Church of God, to carry the embassy of eternal salvation, to erect the kingdom of God on earth, and to raise men to heaven, is a task far beyond human capacity. We need not be astonished, therefore, that no man is found qualified unless he be inspired by the Holy Spirit; for no man can speak a word concerning Christ unless the Spirit guide his tongue, (1 Cor. xii. 3;) so far is it from being true that there is any man who is competent to discharge faithfully and honestly all the duties of so excellent an office. Again, it is the glory of Christ alone to form those whom he appoints to be teachers of his Church; for the reason why the fulness of the Spirit has been poured out upon him is, that he may bestow it upon each person according to a certain measure.

Receive ye the Holy Spirit. Though he continues to be the only Shepherd of his Church, he must necessarily display the power of his Spirit in the ministers whose agency

---

[1] " La succession ou subrogation."

he employs; and this also he testified by the outward symbol, when *he breathed on* the Apostles; for this would not be applicable, if the Spirit did not proceed from him. So much the more detestable is the sacrilege of the Papists, who seize and claim for themselves the honour which belongs to the Son of God; for their mitred bishops, when they make priests, have the effrontery to boast of breathing the Holy Spirit on them. But the fact plainly shows how different their stinking breath is from the Divine *breathing* of Christ; for what else is it that they do than to change horses into asses? Besides, not only does Christ communicate to his disciples *the Spirit* which he has received, but he bestows it as his own, as the Spirit which he has in common with the Father. Consequently, all those who boast of giving *the Spirit* by *breathing* lay claim to the glory of Divinity.

It ought to be observed, that those whom Christ calls to the pastoral office he likewise adorns with the necessary gifts, that they may be qualified for discharging the office, or, at least, may not come to it empty and unprovided. And if this be true, there is no difficulty in refuting the foolish boasting of the Papists, who, while they employ lofty terms of commendation in extolling their hierarchy, cannot show a single spark of the Holy Spirit in their bishops. They wish us to believe that they are the lawful pastors of the Church, and, in like manner, that they are the apostles and vicars of Christ, while it is evident that they are utterly destitute of the grace of the Holy Spirit. A sure criterion is here laid down for judging of the calling of those who govern the Church of God; and that criterion is, if we see that they have *received the Holy Spirit.*

What Christ chiefly, however, intended by it was, to uphold the dignity of the rank of the Apostles; for it was reasonable that those, who had been chosen to be the earliest and most distinguished preachers of the Gospel, should possess uncommon authority. But if Christ, at that time, bestowed the Spirit on the Apostles by *breathing,* it may be thought that it was superfluous to send the Holy Spirit afterwards. I reply, the Spirit was given to the Apostles on this occasion in such a manner, that they were only sprinkled by his grace, but were not filled with full power; for, when the Spirit appeared on them in *tongues of fire*, (Acts ii. 3,) they were entirely renewed. And, indeed, he did not appoint them to be heralds of his Gospel, so as to send them forth immediately to the work, but ordered them to take repose, as we read elsewhere, *Remain ye in the city of Jerusalem till ye are endued with power from on high*, (Luke xxiv. 49.) And if we take all things properly into consideration, we shall conclude, not that he furnishes them with necessary gifts for present use, but that he appoints them to be the organs of his Spirit for the future; and, therefore, this *breathing* ought to be understood as referring chiefly to that magnificent act of sending the Spirit which he had so often promised.

Although Christ might have bestowed grace on his Apostles by a secret inspiration, he chose to add a visible *breathing* in order to confirm them more fully. Christ took this outward emblem from the ordinary manner of speaking in the Scriptures, which very frequently compare the Spirit to *wind;* a comparison which we briefly accounted for in the exposition of the Third Chapter of this Gospel.[1] But let the reader observe, that with the visible and outward sign the word is also joined; for this is the source from which the sacraments derive their efficacy; not that the efficacy of the Holy Spirit is contained in the word which sounds in our ears, but because the effect of all those things which believers receive from the sacraments depends on the testimony of the word. Christ *breathes on* the Apostles: they receive not only the *breathing*, but also *the Spirit.* And why, but because Christ promises to them?

In like manner, in baptism we *put on Christ*, (Gal. iii. 27,) we are *washed by his blood*, (Rev. i. 5,) *our old man is crucified*, (Rom. vi. 6,) in order that the righteousness of God may reign in us. In the Holy Supper we are spiritually fed with the flesh and blood of Christ. Whence do they derive so great efficacy but from the promise of Christ, who does and accomplishes by his Holy Spirit what he declares by his word? Let us therefore learn, that all the sacraments which

---

[1] See Vol. I. p. 114.

men have contrived are nothing else than absolute mockeries or frivolous amusements, because the signs can have no truth unless they be accompanied by the word of the Lord. Now, since we never sport in this manner with sacred things, without wickedly pouring contempt on God and ruining souls, we ought to be most carefully on our guard against those stratagems of Satan.

If it be objected, that we ought not to blame the Popish bishops, when by *breathing* they consecrate their priests, because in those cases the word of Christ accompanies the sign, the answer is obvious. In the first place, Christ did not speak to the Apostles so as to appoint a perpetual sacrament in the Church, but intended to declare once what we said a little ago, that *the Spirit* proceeds from no other than from himself alone. Secondly, he never appoints men to an office without at the same time communicating strength to his ministers, and furnishing them with ability. I do not mention that in Popery the priests are ordained for a totally different, or rather a contrary purpose; namely, to murder Christ daily, while the disciples were made Apostles in order to slay men by the sword of the Gospel. Yet we ought also to believe that it is Christ alone who gives all the blessings which he represents and promises by outward signs; for he does not bid the Apostles *receive the Holy Spirit* from the outward *breathing*, but from himself.

23. *To all whose sins you shall remit.* Here, unquestionably, our Lord has embraced, in a few words, the sum of the Gospel; for we must not separate this power of forgiving sins from the office of teaching, with which it is closely connected in this passage. Christ had said a little before, *As the living Father hath sent me, so I also send you.*[1] He now makes a declaration of what is intended and what is meant by this embassy, only he interwove with that declaration what was necessary, that he gave to them his Holy Spirit, in order that they might have nothing from themselves.

---

[1] Our Author appears here to mingle two passages, John vi. 57, *As the* LIVING *Father hath sent me, and I live by the Father*, and John xx. 21, *As the Father hath sent me, so I also send you.—Ed.*

The principal design of preaching the Gospel is, that men may be reconciled to God, and this is accomplished by the unconditional pardon of sins; as Paul also informs us, when he calls the Gospel, on this account, *the ministry of reconciliation,* (2 Cor. v. 18.) Many other things, undoubtedly, are contained in the Gospel, but the principal object which God intends to accomplish by it is, to receive men into favour by not imputing their sins. If, therefore, we wish to show that we are faithful ministers of the Gospel, we must give our most earnest attention to this subject; for the chief point of difference between the Gospel and heathen philosophy lies in this, that the Gospel makes the salvation of men to consist in the forgiveness of sins through free grace. This is the source of the other blessings which God bestows, such as, that God enlightens and regenerates us by his Spirit, that he forms us anew to his image, that he arms us with unshaken firmness against the world and Satan. Thus the whole doctrine of godliness, and the spiritual building of the Church, rests on this foundation, that God, having acquitted us from all sins, adopts us to be his children by free grace.

While Christ enjoins the Apostles to *forgive sins,* he does not convey to them what is peculiar to himself. It belongs to him to *forgive sins.* This honour, so far as it belongs peculiarly to himself, he does not surrender to the Apostles, but enjoins them, in his name, to proclaim *the forgiveness of sins,* that through their agency he may reconcile men to God. In short, properly speaking, it is he alone who *forgives sins* through his apostles and ministers.[1]

But it may be asked, Since he appoints them to be only the witnesses or heralds of this blessing, and not the authors of it, why does he extol their power in such lofty terms? I reply, he did so in order to confirm their faith. Nothing is of more importance to us, than to be able to believe firmly, that our sins do not come into remembrance before God. Zacharias, in his song, calls it *the knowledge of salvation,* (Luke i. 77;) and, since God employs the testimony of men to prove it, consciences will never yield to it, unless they perceive God

---

[1] "Par ses apostres et ministres."

himself speaking in their person. Paul accordingly says, *We exhort you to be reconciled to God, as if Christ besought you by us,* (2 Cor. v. 20.)

We now see the reason why Christ employs such magnificent terms, to commend and adorn that ministry which he bestows and enjoins on the Apostles. It is, that believers may be fully convinced, that what they hear concerning the forgiveness of sins is ratified, and may not less highly value the reconciliation which is offered by the voice of men, than if God himself stretched out his hand from heaven. And the Church daily receives the most abundant benefit from this doctrine, when it perceives that her pastors are divinely ordained to be sureties for eternal salvation, and that it must not go to a distance to seek the forgiveness of sins, which is committed to their trust.

Nor ought we to esteem less highly this invaluable treasure, because it is exhibited in earthen vessels; but we have ground of thanksgiving to God, who hath conferred on men so high an honour, as to make them the ambassadors and deputies of God, and of his Son, in declaring the forgiveness of sins. There are fanatics who despise this embassy; but let us know, that, by doing so, they trample under foot the blood of Christ.

Most absurdly do the Papists, on the other hand, torture this passage, to support their magical absolutions. If any person do not confess his sins in the ear of the priest, he has no right, in their opinion, to expect forgiveness; for Christ intended that sins should be forgiven through the Apostles, and they cannot absolve without having examined the matter; therefore, confession is necessary. Such is their beautiful argument.[1] But they fall into a strange blunder, when they pass by the most important point of the matter; namely, that this right was granted to the Apostles, in order to maintain the credit of the Gospel, which they had been commissioned to preach. For Christ does not here appoint confessors, to inquire minutely into each sin by means of low mutterings, but preachers of his Gospel, who shall cause their voice to be

---

[1] "Voila leur bel argument."

heard, and who shall seal on the hearts of believers the grace of the atonement obtained through Christ. We ought, therefore, to keep by the manner of *forgiving sins,* so as to know what is that power which has been granted to the apostles.

And to those whose sins you retain. Christ adds this second clause, in order to terrify the despisers of his Gospel, that they may know that they will not escape punishment for this pride. As the embassy of salvation and of eternal life has been committed to the apostles, so, on the other hand, they have been armed with *vengeance* against all the ungodly, who reject the salvation offered to them, as Paul teaches, (2 Cor. x. 6.) But this is placed last in order, because it was proper that the true and real design of preaching the Gospel should be first exhibited. That we are reconciled to God belongs to the nature of the Gospel; that believers are adjudged to eternal life may be said to be accidentally connected with it.[1] For this reason, Paul, in the passage which I lately quoted, when he threatens vengeance against unbelievers, immediately adds, *after that your obedience shall have been fulfilled,* (2 Cor. x. 6;) for he means, that it belongs peculiarly to the Gospel to invite all to salvation, but that it is accidental to it that it brings destruction to any.

It ought to be observed, however, that every one who hears the voice of the Gospel, if he do not embrace the forgiveness of sins which is there promised to him, is liable to eternal damnation; for, as it is a *life-giving savour* to the children of God, so to those who perish *it is the savour of death to death,* (2 Cor. ii. 16.) Not that the preaching of the Gospel is necessary for condemning the reprobate, for by nature we are all lost, and, in addition to the hereditary curse, every one draws down on himself additional causes of death, but because the obstinacy of those who knowingly and willingly despise the Son of God deserves much severer punishment.

24. But Thomas, one of the twelve, who was called Didymus,[2] was not with them when Jesus came. 25. The other disciples, therefore, said to him, We have seen the Lord. But he said to them, If I do not see in

---

[1] "Cela luy est comme un accident."
[2] "Qui est appelé Gemeau;"—"who is called Twin."

his hands the print [1] of the nails, and put my finger into the print of the nails,[2] and put my hand into his side, I will not believe 26 And after eight days, his disciples were again within, and Thomas with them. Then Jesus came, while the doors were shut, and stood in the midst, and said, Peace be to you 27 Then he saith to Thomas, Reach hither thy finger, and behold my hands, and reach thy hand, and put it into my side; and be not faithless, but believing. 28. Thomas answered, and said to him, My Lord and my God ! 29. Jesus saith to him, Because thou hast seen me, Thomas, thou hast believed; blessed are they who have not seen, and have believed.

24. *But Thomas, one of the twelve.* The unbelief of *Thomas* is here related, that by means of it the faith of the godly may be more fully confirmed. He was not only slow and reluctant to believe, but even obstinate. His dulness of apprehension was the reason why Christ again permitted them both to see and to feel him, in the same manner as before. In this manner, a new addition to the proof of Christ's resurrection was given, not only to *Thomas*, but also to us. Besides, the obstinacy of Thomas is an example to show, that this wickedness is almost natural to all men, to retard themselves of their own accord, when the entrance to faith is opened to them.

25. *Unless I see in his hands the print of the nails.* This points out the source of the vice to be, that every one wishes to be wise from his own understanding, and flatters himself beyond measure. *If I do not see,* says he, "and if I do not touch, *I will not believe.*"[3] These words have no approach to faith, but it is what may be called a sensual judgment, by which I mean, a judgment which is founded on the perception of the senses.[4] The same thing happens to all who are so devoted to themselves,[5] that they leave no room for the word of God. It is of no consequence, whether you read *the place*, or *the shape*, or THE PRINT *of the nails;* for transcribers may have exchanged τύπον (*print*) for τόπον, (*place*,) or τόπον (*place*) for τύπον, (*print;*) but the meaning is not altered on that ac-

---

[1] " *Ou, le lieu, ou, les enseignes,*"—" *or, the place, or, the marks.*"
[2] " *Et si je ne mets mon doigt ou estoyent les cloux,*"—" *and if I do not put my finger where the nails were.*"
[3] " *Si je ne voy point, dit il, et si je ne touche, je ne croirai point.*"
[4] " *C'est à dire, qui est fondé sur l'apprehension des sens.*"
[5] " *Qui sont tellement adonnez à leur propre sens*"

count. Let the reader, therefore, choose which of them he shall prefer.[1]

26. *Reach hither thy finger.* We have already spoken once about Christ's entrance, and the form of salutation which he employed. When Christ so readily yields to the improper request of *Thomas*,[2] and, of his own accord, invites him to *feel his hands, and touch the wound of his side,* we learn from this how earnestly desirous he was to promote our faith and that of *Thomas;* for it was not to *Thomas* only, but to us also, that he looked, that nothing might be wanting which was necessary for confirming our faith.

The stupidity of Thomas was astonishing and monstrous; for he was not satisfied with merely beholding Christ out wished to have his hands also as witnesses of Christ's resurrection. Thus he was not only obstinate, but also proud and contemptuous in his treatment of Christ. Now, at least, when he saw Christ, he ought to have been overwhelmed with shame and amazement; but, on the contrary, he boldly and fearlessly stretches forth his hand, as if he were not conscious of any guilt; for it may be readily inferred from the words of the Evangelist, that he did not repent before that he had convinced himself by touching. Thus it happens that, when we render to the word of God less honour than is due to it, there steals upon us, without our knowledge, a growing obstinacy, which brings along with it a contempt of the word of God, and makes us lose all reverence for it. So much the more earnestly should we labour to restrain the wantonness of our mind, that none of us, by improperly indulging in contradiction, and extinguishing, as it were, the feeling of piety, may block up against ourselves the gate of faith.

My Lord and my God! Thomas awakes at length, though late, and as persons who have been mentally deranged

---

[1] " Car les deux mots Grecs ne sont point differens qu'en une lettre, et il est aise de prendre l'un pour l'autre,"—" for the two Greek words differ only in a single letter, and one of them might easily be taken for the other."

[2] " Ce qu'il avoit demandé par l'obstination et l'opiniastreté;"—"what he had asked through obstinacy and stubbornness"

commonly do when they come to themselves, exclaims, in astonishment, *My Lord and my God!* For the abruptness of the language has great vehemence; nor can it be doubted that shame compelled him to break out into this expression, in order to condemn his own stupidity. Besides, so sudden an exclamation shows that faith was not wholly extinguished in him, though it had been choked; for in the side or hands of Christ he does not handle Christ's Divinity, but from those signs he infers much more than they exhibited. Whence comes this, but because, after forgetfulness and deep sleep, he suddenly comes to himself? This shows, therefore, the truth of what I said a little ago, that the faith which appeared to be destroyed was, as it were, concealed and buried in his heart.

The same thing happens sometimes with many persons; for they grow wanton for a time, as if they had cast off all fear of God, so that there appears to be no longer any faith in them; but as soon as God has chastised them with a rod, the rebellion of their flesh is subdued, and they return to their right senses. It is certain that disease would not, of itself, be sufficient to teach piety; and hence we infer, that, when the obstructions have been removed, the good seed, which had been concealed and crushed, springs up. We have a striking instance of this in David; for, so long as he is permitted to gratify his lust, we see how he indulges without restraint. Every person would have thought that, at that time, faith had been altogether banished from his mind; and yet, by a short exhortation of the Prophet, he is so suddenly recalled to life, that it may easily be inferred, that some spark, though it had been choked, still remained in his mind, and speedily burst into a flame. So far as relates to the men themselves, they are as guilty as if they had renounced faith and all the grace of the Holy Spirit; but the infinite goodness of God prevents the elect from falling so low as to be entirely alienated from God. We ought, therefore, to be most zealously on our guard not to fall from faith; and yet we ought to believe that God restrains his elect by a secret bridle, that they may not fall to their destruction, and that He always cherishes miraculously in their hearts some sparks of faith, which he afterwards, at the proper time, kindles anew by the breath of his Spirit.

There are two clauses in this confession. *Thomas* acknowledges that Christ is *his Lord*, and then, in the second clause,[1] he ascends higher, and calls him also *his God*. We know in what sense Scripture gives to Christ the name of *Lord*. It is, because the Father hath appointed him to be the highest governor, that he may hold all things under his dominion, *that every knee may bow before him*, (Philip. ii. 10,) and, in short, that he may be the Father's vicegerent in governing the world. Thus the name *Lord* properly belongs to him, so far as he is the Mediator manifested in the flesh, and the Head of the Church. But *Thomas*, having acknowledged him to be *Lord*, is immediately carried upwards to his eternal Divinity, and justly; for the reason why Christ descended to us, and first was humbled, and afterwards was placed at the Father's right hand, and obtained dominion over heaven and earth, was, that he might exalt us to his own Divine glory, and to the glory of the Father. That our faith may arrive at the eternal Divinity of Christ, we must begin with that knowledge which is nearer and more easily acquired. Thus it has been justly said by some, that by Christ Man we are conducted to Christ God, because our faith makes such gradual progress that, perceiving Christ on earth, born in a stable, and hanging on a cross, it rises to the glory of his resurrection, and, proceeding onwards, comes at length to his eternal life and power, in which his Divine Majesty is gloriously displayed.

Yet we ought to believe, that we cannot know Christ as *our Lord*, in a proper manner, without immediately obtaining also a knowledge of his Divinity. Nor is there any room to doubt that this ought to be a confession common to all believers, when we perceive that it is approved by Christ. He certainly would never have endured that the Father should be robbed of the honour due to him, and that this honour should be falsely and groundlessly conveyed to himself. But he plainly ratifies what Thomas said; and, therefore, this

---

[1] " Au second membre."

passage is abundantly sufficient for refuting the madness of Arius; for it is not lawful to imagine two Gods. Here also is declared the unity of person in Christ; for the same Jesus Christ[1] is called both *God* and *Lord*. Emphatically, too, he twice calls him *his own*, MY *Lord and* MY *God!* declaring, that he speaks in earnest, and with a lively sentiment of faith.

29. *Because thou hast seen me, Thomas.* Christ blames nothing in Thomas, but that he was so slow to believe, that he needed to be violently drawn to faith by the experience of the senses; which is altogether at variance with the nature of faith. If it be objected, that nothing is more unsuitable than to say that *faith* is a conviction obtained from *touching* and *seeing*, the answer may be easily obtained from what I have already said; for it was not by mere *touching* or *seeing* that Thomas was brought to believe that Christ is God, but, being awakened from sleep, he recalled to remembrance the doctrine which formerly he had almost forgotten. Faith cannot flow from a merely experimental knowledge of events, but must draw its origin from the word of God. Christ, therefore, blames Thomas for rendering less honour to the word of God than he ought to have done, and for having regarded faith—which springs from hearing, and ought to be wholly fixed on the word—as bound to the other senses.

Blessed are they who have not seen, and have believed. Here Christ commends faith on this ground, that it acquiesces in the bare word, and does not depend on carnal views or human reason.[2] He therefore includes, in a short definition, the power and nature of faith; namely, that it does not rest satisfied with the immediate exercise of sight, but penetrates even to heaven, so as to believe those things which are hidden from the human senses. And, indeed, we ought to give to God this honour, that we should view His truth as ($αὐτό-πιστος$[3]) beyond all doubt without any other proof.[4] Faith

---

[1] "Un mesme Jesus Christ."
[2] "Du sens charnel, ne de la raison humaine"
[3] $αὐτόπιστος$, *that which is worthy of being believed on its account.*
[4] "Que sa verité nous soit indubitable sans autre probation."

has, indeed, its own *sight*, but one which does not confine its view to the world, and to earthly objects. For this reason it is called *a demonstration of things invisible or not seen*, (Heb. xi. 1;) and Paul contrasts it with *sight*, (2 Cor. v. 7,) meaning, that it does not rest satisfied with looking at the condition of present objects, and does not cast its eye in all directions to *those things which are visible* in the world, but depends on the mouth of God, and, relying on His word, rises above the whole world, so as to fix its anchor in heaven. It amounts to this, that faith is not of a right kind, unless it be founded on the word of God, and rise to the invisible kingdom of God, so as to go beyond all human capacity.

If it be objected, that this saying of Christ is inconsistent with another of his sayings, in which he declares that *the eyes which behold him present are blessed*, (Matth. xiii. 16,) I answer, Christ does not there speak merely of bodily sight, as he does in this passage, but of revelation, which is common to all believers, since he appeared to the world as a Redeemer. He draws a comparison between the Apostles and *the holy kings and prophets*, (Matth. xiii. 17,) who had been kept under the dark shadows of the Mosaic Law. He says, that now the condition of believers is much more desirable, because a brighter light shines around them, or rather, because the substance and truth of the figures was made known to them. There were many unbelievers who, at that time, *beheld* Christ with *the eyes* of flesh, and yet were not *more blessed* on that account; but we, who have never beheld Christ with the eyes, enjoy that *blessedness* of which Christ speaks with commendation. Hence it follows, that he calls those eyes *blessed* which spiritually behold in him what is heavenly and divine; for we now behold Christ in the Gospel in the same manner as if he visibly stood before us. In this sense Paul says to the Galatians, (iii. 1,) that *Christ was crucified before their eyes;* and, therefore, if we desire to see in Christ what may render us *happy* and *blessed*, let us learn to *believe*, when we *do not see*. To these words of Christ corresponds what is stated in another passage, in which the Apostle commends believers, who *love Christ whom they have not seen, and rejoice with unspeakable joy, though they do not behold him,* (1 Pet. i. 8.)

The manner in which the Papists torture these words, to prove their doctrine of transubstantiation, is exceedingly absurd. That we may be *blessed,* they bid us believe that Christ is present under the appearance of bread. But we know that nothing was farther from Christ's intention than to subject faith to the inventions of men; and as soon as it passes, in the smallest degree, beyond the limits of the word, it ceases to be faith. If we must believe without reserve all that we do not see, then every monster which men may be pleased to form, every fable which they may contrive, will hold our faith in bondage. That this saying of Christ may apply to the case in hand, we must first prove from the word of God the very point in question. They bring forward the word of God, indeed, in support of their doctrine of transubstantiation; but when the word is properly expounded, it gives no countenance to their foolish notion.

30. Many other signs also Jesus did in the presence of the disciples, which are not written in this book 31. But these are written, that you may believe that Jesus is the Christ, the Son of God, and that, believing, you may have life through his name.

30. *Many other signs also Jesus did.* If the Evangelist had not cautioned his readers by this observation, they might have supposed that he had left out none of the miracles which Christ had performed, and had given a full and complete account of all that happened. John, therefore, testifies, first, that he has only related some things out of a large number; not that the others were unworthy of being recorded, but because these were sufficient to edify faith. And yet it does not follow that they were performed in vain, for they profited that age. Secondly, though at the present day we have not a minute knowledge of them, still we must not suppose it to be of little importance for us to know that the Gospel was sealed by a vast number of miracles.

31. *But these are written, that you may believe.* By these words he means, that he committed to writing what ought

to satisfy us, because it is abundantly sufficient for confirming our faith; for he intended to reply to the vain curiosity of men, which is insatiable, and allows itself excessive indulgence. Besides, John was well aware of what the other Evangelists had written; and, as nothing was farther from his intention than to set aside their writings, he unquestionably does not separate their narrative from his own.

It may be thought strange, however, that faith is founded on miracles, while it ought to rest exclusively on the promises and word of God. I reply, no other use is here assigned to miracles than to be the aids and supports of faith; for they serve to prepare the minds of men, that they may cherish greater reverence for the word of God, and we know how cold and sluggish our attention is, if we be not excited by something else. Besides, it adds no small authority to the doctrine already received, when, for the purpose of supporting it, he stretches out his mighty hand from heaven; as Mark says that the Apostles taught, *the Lord working with them, and confirming the word by accompanying signs,* (Mark xvi. 20.) Although, therefore, strictly speaking, faith rests on the word of God, and looks to the word as its only end, still the addition of miracles is not superfluous, provided that they be also viewed as relating to the word, and direct faith towards it. Why miracles are called *signs* we have already explained. It is because, by means of them, the Lord arouses men to contemplate his power, when he exhibits any thing strange and unusual.

That Jesus is the Christ. He means *the Christ*, such as he had been promised in the Law and the Prophets, as the Mediator between God and men, the Father's highest Ambassador, the only Restorer of the world, and the Author of perfect happiness. For John did not seize upon an empty and unmeaning title to adorn the Son of God, but included, under the name *Christ*, all the offices which the Prophets ascribe to him. We ought, therefore, to contemplate him such as he is there described. This shows more fully what was said a little ago, that faith does not confine its view to miracles, but carries us direct to the word; for it is as if John had said, that what the Prophets formerly taught by the word has been proved by miracles. And, indeed, we see that the Evangelists themselves do not occupy their whole attention in relating miracles, but dwell more largely on doctrine, because miracles by themselves would produce nothing but a confused admiration. The meaning of the words therefore is, that *these things have been written, that we may believe*, so far as faith can be aided by *signs*.

The Son of God. The Evangelist adds this, because not one of the ordinary rank of men could have been found, who was competent to perform so great undertakings; that is, to reconcile the Father to us, to atone for the sins of the world, to abolish death, to destroy the kingdom of Satan, to bring to us true righteousness and salvation. Besides, as the name, *Son of God*, belongs only to Christ, it follows that he is a *Son*, not by adoption, but by nature; and, therefore, under this name is comprehended the eternal Divinity of Christ. And, indeed, he who, after having received those striking proofs, which are to be found in the Gospel, does not perceive Christ to be God, does not deserve to look even at the sun and the earth, for he is blind amidst the brightness of noonday.

That, believing, you may have life. This effect of faith was also added, to restrain the foolish longings of men, that they may not desire to know more than what is sufficient for obtaining *life*. For what obstinacy was it, not to be satisfied with eternal salvation, and to wish to go beyond the limits of the heavenly kingdom? Here John repeats the most important point of his doctrine, that we obtain eternal *life* by *faith*, because, while we are out of Christ, we are dead, and we are restored to life by his grace alone. On this subject we have spoken largely enough in our exposition of the Third and Fifth Chapters of this Gospel.

Through his name. As to his saying, *through the name* of Christ, rather than *through Christ*, the reason of this form of expression has been assigned by us in our exposition of the twelfth verse of the First Chapter of this Gospel. The reader may consult that passage, if he think proper, that I may not be troubled with repeating the same things frequently.[1]

[1] See Vol I. p. 42

CHAPTER XXI.

1. After these things Jesus manifested himself again to the disciples at the sea of Tiberias ; and he manifested himself thus. 2. Simon Peter, and Thomas, who is called Didymus,[1] and Nathanael, who was of Cana of Galilee, and the sons of Zebedee, and two others of his disciples, were together. 3. Simon Peter saith to them, I am going to fish ; they say to him, We also go with thee. They went forth, and entered into a ship immediately, and that night they caught nothing. 4. And when it was morning, Jesus stood on the shore ; and the disciples knew not that it was Jesus 5 Jesus saith to them, Children, have you any thing to eat ?[2] They answered him, No. 6. But he said to them, Cast the net on the right side of the ship, and you will find. They cast it, therefore ; and now they were not able to draw it for the multitude of fishes. 7. Therefore the disciple whom Jesus loved saith to Peter, It is the Lord. When, therefore, Simon Peter heard that it was the Lord, he girded his coat about him, (for he was naked,) and threw himself into the sea. 8. And the other disciples came in the boat, (for they were not far from land, but about two hundred cubits,) dragging the net with fishes 9 As soon, then, as they came to land, they saw a fire burning, and fish laid on it, and bread. 10. Jesus saith to them, Bring some of the fish which you have now caught. 11 Simon Peter, therefore, went up, and drew the net to land, full of great fishes, a hundred and fifty-three ; and although they were so many, the net was not broken. 12. Jesus saith to them, Come and dine. And not one of the disciples dared to ask him, Who art thou ? knowing that he was the Lord 13. Jesus therefore cometh, and taketh the bread, and giveth it to them, and fish likewise. 14. This is now the third time that Jesus manifested himself to his disciples, after that he was risen from the dead.

1. *After these things Jesus manifested himself again.* The Evangelist still labours to prove the resurrection of Christ, and relates, that he appeared to seven disciples, among whom he mentions *Thomas,* not out of respect to him, so much as because his testimony ought to be the more readily believed in proportion to the obstinacy of his unbelief. The Evangelist enters sufficiently into detail ; for he carefully collects all the circumstances which contribute to prove the truth of the history. We have formerly mentioned that *the Lake of Tiberias,* according to the Hebrew custom, is called *the Sea of Tiberias.*

---

[1] " Qui est dit Gemeau ; "—" who is called *Twin.*"
[2] " Avez-vous quelque petit poisson à manger ? "—" Have you any little fish to eat ? "

3. *I am going to fish.* That Peter gave his attention to *fishing,* ought not to be regarded as inconsistent with his office. By *breathing on* him, Jesus had ordained him to be an Apostle, as we saw a little before; but he abstained from the exercise of the apostleship for a short time, till he should be clothed with new power. For he had not yet been enjoined to appear in public for the discharge of his office of teaching, but had only been reminded of his future calling, that he and the others might understand that they had not in vain been chosen from the beginning. Meanwhile, they do what they were accustomed to do, and what belonged to men in private life. It is true that Paul, in the midst of his employment as a preacher, gained the support of his life by his own hands, but it was for a different reason; for his time was so arranged, that the labours of his hands did not withdraw him from teaching. Peter and his companions, on the other hand, give themselves up entirely to *fishing,* because they are not hindered from doing so by any public employment.

And that night they caught nothing. God permitted them to toil to no purpose during the whole *night,* in order to prove the truth of the miracle; for if they had *caught any thing,*[1] what followed immediately afterwards would not have so clearly manifested the power of Christ, but when, after having toiled ineffectually during the whole night, they are suddenly favoured with a large take of fishes, they have good reason for acknowledging the goodness of the Lord. In the same manner, also, God often tries believers, that he may lead them the more highly to value his blessing. If we were always prosperous, whenever we put our hand to labour, scarcely any man would attribute to the blessing of God the success of his exertions, all would boast of their industry, and would kiss their hands. But when they sometimes labour and torment themselves without any advantage, if they happen afterwards to succeed better, they are constrained to acknowledge something out of the ordinary course; and the conse-

---

[1] "S'ils eussent fait quelque prinse de poissons,'—if they had had any take of fishes."

quence is, that they begin to ascribe to the goodness of God the praise of their prosperity and success.

6. *Cast the net on the right side of the ship.* Christ does not command with authority and power as *Master* and *Lord,* but gives advice like one of the people; and the disciples, being at a loss what to do, readily obey him, though they did not know who he was. If, before the first *casting of the net,* any thing of this sort had been said to them, they would not have so quickly obeyed. I mention this, that no one may wonder that they were so submissive, for they had already been worn out by long and useless toil. Yet it was no small proof of patience and perseverance, that, though they had laboured unsuccessfully during the whole night, they continue their toil after the return of daylight. And, indeed, if we wish to allow an opportunity for the blessing of God to descend on us, we ought constantly to expect it; for nothing can be more unreasonable than to withdraw the hand immediately from labour, if it do not give promise of success.

That *Simon Peter* WAS NAKED, is a proof that the disciples had laboured in earnest; and yet they do not hesitate to *cast the net* again to make another trial, that they may not neglect any opportunity. Their obedience to the command of Christ cannot be ascribed to faith; for they hear him speak as a person who was unknown to them. Now, if we dislike our calling, because the labour which we undertake appears to be unproductive, yet, when the Lord exhorts us to steadiness and perseverance, we ought to take courage; in the end we shall obtain a happy result, but it will be at the proper time.

And now they were not able to draw it.[1] Christ here exhibited two proofs of his Divine power. The first consisted in their taking so large a draught of fishes; and the second was, when, by his concealed power, he preserved *the net*

---

[1] In the Latin original of the Commentaries, the illustration of this clause comes before that of the 7th verse; but I have consulted the convenience of the reader, by following the French version, which, in this respect, may be supposed to give us the latest thoughts of the Author, and in which this clause is restored to its natural order.—*Ed.*

whole, which otherwise must unavoidably have been broken in pieces. Other circumstances are mentioned, namely, that the disciples find burning coals on the shore, that fishes are laid on them, and that bread is also prepared. As to the number of *the fishes*, we ought not to look for any deep mystery in it. Augustine enters into ingenious reasonings about the statement of the number, and says that it denotes the Law and the Gospel; but if we examine the matter carefully, we shall find that this is childish trifling.

7. *Therefore the disciple whom Jesus loved saith to Peter.* The Evangelist shows, by his example, that it is our duty to raise our hearts to God, whenever we succeed in any thing beyond our expectation; because we ought instantly to remember that this act of kindness has flowed from the favour of Him who is the Author of every blessing. That holy recognition of the grace of God, which dwelt in the heart of John, led him also to the knowledge of Christ; for he does not perceive Christ with his eyes, but, being convinced that the great multitude of fishes has been brought to him by the hand of God, he concludes that it was Christ who had guided his hands. But, as John goes before Peter in faith, so Peter afterwards excels him in zeal, when, disregarding personal danger, he throws himself into the lake. The rest follow in the ship. True, all come to Christ at length, but Peter is actuated by a peculiar zeal in comparison of the others. Whether he crossed over to the shore by walking or by swimming, is uncertain; but let us rest satisfied with knowing that the act of leaving the ship and going on shore was not the result of folly and rashness, but that he advanced beyond the others in proportion to his zeal.

10. *Bring some of the fishes which you have now caught.* Though the net was filled in a moment, without any great labour on their part, yet the taking of them is not ascribed by Christ to the disciples. Thus, we call the bread which we daily eat, OUR *bread*, and yet, by asking that it may be *given* to us, we acknowledge that it proceeds from the blessing of God, (Matth. vi. 11.)

12. *And not one of his disciples dared to ask him.* It may be inquired, What hindered them? Was it shame arising from reverence, or was it any thing else? But if Christ saw that they were in a state of uncertainty, he ought to remove their doubt, as he had done on many other occasions. I reply, there was no other reason for shame, but because they were not sufficiently certain that he was the Christ; for it is not usual with us to inquire about matters that are doubtful and obscure. The Evangelist, therefore, means that the disciples *did not ask* Christ, because they were afraid of doing him wrong; so plain and manifest were the signs by which he had made himself known to them.

14. *The third time.* The number *three* refers to the distance of time. Christ had already appeared to his disciples more than *seven* times, but all that had been transacted in one day is included in one manifestation. The Evangelist, therefore, means that Christ had been seen by the disciples at intervals, in order to confirm their belief of his resurrection.

15 When, therefore, they had dined, Jesus saith to Simon Peter, Simon (son) of John,[1] lovest thou me more than these? He saith to him, Yea, Lord, thou knowest that I love thee. He saith to him, Feed my lambs. 16 He saith to him again the second time, Simon (son) of John,[1] lovest thou me? He saith to him, Yea, Lord, thou knowest that I love thee. He saith to him, Feed my sheep. 17. He saith to him the third time, Simon (son) of John,[1] lovest thou me? Peter was grieved because he said to him the third time, Lovest thou me? And he said to him, Lord, thou knowest all things; thou knowest that I love thee Jesus saith to him, Feed my sheep. 18. Verily, verily, I tell thee, When thou wast young, thou girdedst thyself, and walkedst whither thou wouldest, but when thou shalt be old, thou shalt stretch out thy hands, and another will gird thee, and will carry thee whither thou wouldest not. 19. And this he said, signifying by what death he should glorify God; and when he had spoken this, he saith to him, Follow me.

15. *When, therefore, they had dined.* The Evangelist now relates in what manner Peter was restored to that rank of honour from which he had fallen. That treacherous denial, which has been formerly described, had, undoubtedly, rendered him unworthy of the apostleship; for how could he

---

[1] " Simon (fils) de Jona ,"—" Simon (son) of Jonas."

be capable of instructing others in the faith, who had basely revolted from it? He had been made an Apostle, but it was along with Judas, and from the time when he had abandoned his post,[1] he had likewise been deprived of the honour of apostleship. Now, therefore, the liberty, as well as the authority, of teaching is restored to him, both of which he had lost through his own fault. And that the disgrace of his apostasy might not stand in his way, Christ blots out and destroys the remembrance of it. Such a restoration was necessary, both for Peter and for his hearers; for Peter, that he might the more boldly execute his office, being assured of the calling with which Christ had again invested him; for his hearers, that the stain which attached to his person might not be the occasion of despising the Gospel. To us also, in the present day, it is of very great importance, that Peter comes forth to us as a new man, from whom the disgrace that might have lessened his authority has been removed.

Simon (son) *of John*,[2] *lovest thou me?* By these words Christ means that no man can faithfully serve the Church, and employ himself in *feeding* the flock, if he do not look higher than to men. First, the office of *feeding*[3] is in itself laborious and troublesome; since nothing is more difficult than to keep men under the yoke of God, among whom there are many who are weak, others who are wanton and unsteady, others who are dull and sluggish, and others who are slow and unteachable. Satan now brings forward as many causes of offence as he can, that he may destroy or weaken the courage of a good pastor.[4] In addition to this, we must take into account the ingratitude of many and other causes of disgust. No man, therefore, will steadily persevere in the discharge of this office, unless the love of Christ shall reign in his heart, in such a manner that, forgetful of himself and devoting himself entirely to Christ, he overcomes every obstacle. Thus Paul declares this to have been the state of his own

---

[1] " Depuis qu'il avoit este lache et desloyal;"—" since he acted the part of a coward and a traitor."
[2] " Simon (fils) de Jona;"—" Simon (son) of Jonas."
[3] " La charge du Pasteur;"—" the office of *Pastor* or *Shepherd.*"
[4] " De tous bons pasteurs;"—" of all good pastors."

feelings, when he says, *The love of Christ constraineth us, judging thus, that if one died for all, then all must have been dead,* (2 Cor. v. 14.) For, though he means that *love* with which Christ hath *loved* us, and of which he hath given us a proof by his death, yet he connects with us that mutual *love* which springs from the conviction of having received so great a blessing. Ungodly and false teachers, on the other hand, are pointed out by him in another passage by this mark, that they *do not love the Lord Jesus,* (1 Cor. xvi. 22.)

Those who are called to govern the Church ought, therefore, to remember that, if they are desirous to discharge their office properly and faithfully, they must begin with the love of Christ. Meanwhile, Christ openly testifies how highly he values our salvation, when he employs such earnest and striking language in recommending it to *Pastors,* and when he declares that, if the salvation of their flock be the object of their earnest solicitude, he will reckon it a proof of the ardour of their love to himself. And, indeed, nothing could have been spoken that was better fitted for encouraging the ministers of the Gospel, than to inform them that no service can be more agreeable to Christ than that which is bestowed on *feeding his flock.* All believers ought to draw from it no ordinary consolation, when they are taught that they are so dear and so precious in the sight of the Son of God, that he substitutes them, as it were, in his own room. But the same doctrine ought greatly to alarm false teachers, who corrupt and overturn the government of the Church; for Christ, who declares that he is insulted by them, will inflict on them dreadful punishment.

Feed my lambs. The word *feed* is metaphorically applied by Scripture to any kind of government; but as the present subject is the spiritual government of the Church, it is of importance to observe what are the parts of which the office of *pastor* or *shepherd* consists. No idle rank is here described to us, nor does Christ bestow on a mortal man any government to be exercised by him in a confused manner according to his own pleasure. In expounding the Tenth Chapter, we have seen that Christ is the only *Pastor* or *Shepherd* of the

Church.[1] We have seen also why he takes this name to himself. It is, because he *feeds*, that is, he *governs* his sheep, because he is the only true food of the soul. But because he employs the agency of men in preaching doctrine, he conveys to them also his own name, or, at least, shares it with them. Those men, therefore, are reckoned to be *Pastors* in the sight of God, who govern the Church by the ministry of the word under Christ, who is their Head. Hence we may easily infer what is the burden which Christ lays on Peter, and on what condition he appoints him to govern his flock.

This enables us plainly to refute the wicked adherents of the Church of Rome, who torture this passage to support the tyranny of their Popery. "To Peter," they tell us, "in preference to others, it is said, *Feed my sheep.*" We have already explained the reason why it was said to him rather than to the others; namely, that being free from every disgraceful stain, he might boldly preach the Gospel; and the reason why Christ thrice appoints him to be a pastor is, that the three denials, by which Peter had brought on himself everlasting shame, may be set aside, and thus may form no barrier to his apostleship, as has been judiciously observed by Chrysostom, Augustine, and Cyril, and most of the other Commentators. Besides, nothing was given to Peter by these words, that is not also given to all the ministers of the Gospel.

In vain, therefore, do the Papists maintain that he holds the highest rank, because he alone is specially addressed; and, granting that some special honour was conferred on him, how, I ask, will they prove from this that he has been elevated to the primacy? Though he were the chief among the apostles, does it thence follow that he was the universal bishop of the whole world? To this it must be added, that all that Peter received does not belong to the Pope any more than to Mahomet; for on what ground does he claim to be Peter's heir, and what man of sound understanding will admit that Christ here bestows on him any hereditary right? Yet he wishes to be reckoned Peter's successor: I wish he were so. None of us hinders him from *loving* Christ, and

[1] See Vol I. p 394.

from taking care to *feed his flock;* but to take no concern about *loving* Christ, and to throw aside the office of *feeding,* and then to boast of being Peter's successor, is excessively foolish and absurd. Now, as Christ, in assigning to Peter the duty of teaching, did not intend to erect a throne for an idol or for a murderer of souls, that by means of it he might miserably oppress the Church, so he stated in a few words, what kind of government of the Church he approves. This removes the mask from all the mitred bishops, who, satisfied with a mere theatrical display and an empty title, claim for themselves the authority of bishops.

16. *Feed my sheep.* Christ does not give to Peter and others the office of *feeding* all sorts of persons, but only *his sheep* or *his lambs.* He elsewhere describes who they are whom he reckons to belong to his flock. *My sheep,* says he, *hear my voice, and follow me; they hear not the voice of a stranger,* (John x. 5, 27.) True, faithful teachers ought to endeavour to gather all to Christ; and as they cannot distinguish between *sheep* and wild beasts, they ought to try by all methods if they can tame those who resemble wolves rather than *sheep.* But after having put forth their utmost efforts, their labour will be of no avail to any but the elect *sheep;* for docility and faith arise from this, that the heavenly Father delivers to his Son, that they may obey him, those whom he elected before the creation of the world. Again, we are taught by this passage, that none can be *fed* to salvation by the doctrine of the Gospel but those who are mild and teachable; for it is not without reason that Christ compares his disciples to *lambs* and *sheep;* but it must also be observed, that the Spirit of God tames those who by nature were bears or lions.

17. *Peter was grieved.* Peter undoubtedly did not perceive the object which Christ had in view, in putting the same question so frequently; and therefore he thinks that he is indirectly accused, as if he had not answered with sincerity. But we have already showed that the repetition was not superfluous. Besides, Peter was not yet sufficiently aware how

deeply the love of Christ must be engraven on the hearts of those who have to struggle against innumerable difficulties. He afterwards learned by long experience, that such a trial had not been made in vain. Those who are to undertake the charge of governing the Church are also taught, in his person, not to examine themselves slightly, but to make a thorough scrutiny what zeal they possess, that they may not shrink or faint in the middle of their course. We are likewise taught, that we ought patiently and mildly to submit, if at any time the Lord subject us to a severe trial; because he has good reasons for doing so, though they are generally unknown to us.

18. *Verily, verily, I tell thee.* After having exhorted Peter to *feed his sheep,* Christ likewise arms him to maintain the warfare which was approaching. Thus he demands from him not only faithfulness and diligence, but invincible courage in the midst of dangers, and firmness in bearing the cross. In short, he bids him be prepared for enduring death whenever it shall be necessary. Now, though the condition of all pastors is not alike, still this admonition applies to all in some degree. The Lord spares many, and abstains from shedding their blood, satisfied with this alone, that they devote themselves to him sincerely and unreservedly as long as they live. But as Satan continually makes new and various attacks, all who undertake the office of *feeding* must be prepared for death; as they certainly have to do not only with *sheep,* but also with wolves. So far as relates to Peter, Christ intended to forewarn him of his death, that he might at all times ponder the thought, that the doctrine of which he was a minister must be at length ratified by his own blood. Yet it appears that in these words Christ did not speak with a view to Peter alone, but that he adorned him with the honourable title of Martyr in presence of the others; as if he had said, that Peter would be a very different kind of champion from what he had formerly shown himself to be.

When thou wast younger. Old age appears to be set apart for tranquillity and repose; and, accordingly, old men are usually discharged from public employments, and soldiers are discharged from service. Peter might, therefore, have promised to himself at that age a peaceful life. Christ declares, on the other hand, that the order of nature will be inverted, so that he who had lived at his ease when he was young will be governed by the will of another when he is old, and will even endure violent subjection.

In Peter we have a striking mirror of our ordinary condition. Many have an easy and agreeable life before Christ calls them; but as soon as they have made profession of his name, and have been received as his disciples, or, at least, some time afterwards, they are led to distressing struggles, to a troublesome life, to great dangers, and sometimes to death itself. This condition, though hard, must be patiently endured. Yet the Lord moderates the cross by which he is pleased to try his servants, so that he spares them a little while, until their strength has come to maturity; for he knows well their weakness, and beyond the measure of it he does not press them. Thus he forbore with Peter, so long as he saw him to be as yet tender and weak. Let us therefore learn to devote ourselves to him to the latest breath, provided that he supply us with strength.

In this respect, we behold in many persons base ingratitude; for the more gently the Lord deals with us, the more thoroughly do we habituate ourselves to softness and effeminacy. Thus we scarcely find one person in a hundred who does not murmur if, after having experienced long forbearance, he be treated with some measure of severity. But we ought rather to consider the goodness of God in sparing us for a time. Thus Christ says that, so long as he dwelt on earth, he conversed cheerfully with his disciples, as if he had been present at a marriage, but that fasting and tears afterwards awaited them,[1] (Matth. ix. 15.)

Another will gird thee. Many think that this denotes the manner of death which Peter was to die,[2] meaning that he was hanged, with his arms stretched out; but I consider

---

[1] " Mais qu'il faloit puis apres qu'ils se preparassent à pleurer et jeuner;"—" but that afterwards they must be prepared to weep and fast "

[2] " De laquelle Pierre devoit mourir."

the word *gird* as simply denoting all the outward actions by which a man regulates himself and his whole life. *Thou girdedst thyself;* that is, " thou wast accustomed to wear such raiment as thou chosest, but this liberty of choosing thy dress will be taken from thee." As to the manner in which Peter was put to death, it is better to remain ignorant of it than to place confidence in doubtful fables.

And will lead thee whither thou wouldst not. The meaning is, that Peter did not die a natural death, but by violence and by the sword. It may be thought strange that Christ should say that Peter's death will not be voluntary; for, when one is hurried unwillingly to death, there is no firmness and none of the praise of martyrdom. But this must be understood as referring to the contest between the flesh and the Spirit, which believers feel within themselves; for we never obey God in a manner so free and unrestrained as not to be drawn, as it were, by ropes, in an opposite direction, by the world and the flesh. Hence that complaint of Paul, " The good that I would I do not, but the evil that I would not, that I do," (Rom. vii. 19.) Besides, it ought to be observed, that the dread of death is naturally implanted in us, for to wish to be separated from the body is revolting to nature. Accordingly, Christ, though he was prepared to obey God with his whole heart, prays that he may be delivered from death. Moreover, Peter dreaded the cross on account of the cruelty of men; and, therefore, we need not wonder if, in some measure, he recoiled from death. But this showed the more clearly the obedience which he rendered to God, that he would willingly have avoided death on its own account, and yet he endured it voluntarily, because he knew that such was the will of God; for if there had not been a struggle of the mind, there would have been no need of patience.

This doctrine is highly useful to be known; for it urges us to prayer, because we would never be able, without extraordinary assistance from God, to conquer the fear of death; and, therefore, nothing remains for us but to present ourselves humbly to God, and to submit to his government. It serves also to sustain our minds, that they may not altogether faint, if it happen at any time that persecutions make us tremble. They who imagine that the martyrs were not moved by any fear make their own fear to yield them a ground of despair. But there is no reason why our weakness should deter us from following their example, since they experienced a fear similar to ours, so that they could not gain a triumph over the enemies of truth but by contending with themselves.

19. *Signifying by what death he should glorify God.* This circumlocution is highly emphatic; for though the end held out to all believers ought to be, to glorify God both by their life and by their death, yet John intended to employ a remarkable commendation for adorning the death of those who, by their blood, seal the Gospel of Christ and glorify his name, as Paul teaches us, (Philip i. 20.) It is now our duty to reap the fruit which the death of Peter has yielded; for it ought to be imputed to our indolence, if our faith be not confirmed by it, and if we do not keep the same object in view, that the glory of God may be displayed by us. If the Papists had considered this end in the death of the martyrs, that sacrilegious and detestable invention would never have entered into their minds, that their death contributes to appease the wrath of God, and to pay the ransom for our sins.

And when he had said this. Christ here explains what was the design of that prediction of a violent death. It was, that Peter might be prepared to endure it; as if he had said, " Since you must endure death by my example, follow your leader." Again, that Peter may the more willingly obey God who calls him to the cross, Christ offers himself as a leader; for this is not a general exhortation by which he invites him to imitate himself, but he speaks only of the kind of death. Now, this single consideration greatly soothes all the bitterness that is in death, when the Son of God presents himself before our eyes with his blessed resurrection, which is our triumph over death.

20 And Peter, turning about, seeth the disciple following whom Jesus loved, who had also leaned on his breast at the supper, and had said, Lord, which is he who betrayeth thee? 21. When, therefore, Peter saw him, he said to Jesus, Lord, and what shall he do? 22 Jesus saith to

him, If I will that he remain till I come, what is that to thee? follow thou me. 23. Then this saying went forth among the brethren, that that disciple would not die; yet Jesus had not said to him that he would not die; but, If I will that he tarry till I come, what is that to thee? 24. This is the disciple who testifieth of these things, and wrote these things; and we know that his testimony is true. 25. There are also many other things which Jesus did, which, if they were written every one, I think that even the world itself would not contain the books that would be written.

20. *And Peter, turning about.* We have in Peter an instance of our curiosity, which is not only superfluous, but even hurtful, when we are drawn aside from our duty by looking at others; for it is almost natural to us to examine the way in which other people live, instead of examining our own, and to attempt to find in them idle excuses. We willingly deceive ourselves by this semblance of apology, that other people are no better than we are, as if their indolence freed us from blame. Scarce one person in a hundred considers the import of those words of Paul, *Every man shall bear his own burden,* (Gal. vi. 5.) In the person of one man, therefore, there is a general reproof of all who look around them in every direction, to see how other men act, and pay no attention to the duties which God has enjoined on themselves. Above all, they are grievously mistaken in this respect, that they neglect and overlook what is demanded by every man's special calling.

Out of ten persons it may happen that God shall choose one, that he may try him by heavy calamities or by vast labours, and that he shall permit the other nine to remain at ease, or, at least, shall try them lightly. Besides, God does not treat all in the same manner, but makes trial of every one as he thinks fit. As there are various kinds of Christian warfare, let every man learn to keep his own station, and let us not make inquiries like busybodies about this or that person, when the heavenly Captain addresses each of us, to whose authority we ought to be so submissive as to forget every thing else.

Whom Jesus loved. This circumlocution was inserted, in order to inform us what was the reason why Peter was induced to put the question which is here related; for he thought it strange that he alone should be called, and that John should be overlooked, whom Christ had always loved so warmly. Peter had, therefore, some apparently good reason for asking why no mention was made of John, as if Christ's disposition towards him had undergone a change. Yet Christ cuts short his curiosity, by telling him that he ought to obey the calling of God, and that he has no right to inquire what other people do.

22. *If I will that he remain.* It has been customary to take this sentence as detached, and to read the former clause affirmatively, *I will that he tarry till I come;* but this has been done through the ignorance of transcribers, not through the mistake of the translator; for he could not have been mistaken about the Greek word, but a single letter might easily creep into the Latin version, so as to alter the whole meaning.[1] The whole sentence, therefore, is a question, and ought to be read in immediate connection; for Christ intended to put his hand on his disciple, in order to keep him within the limits of his calling. "It is no concern of yours," says he, "and you have no right to inquire what becomes of your companion; leave that to my disposal; think only about yourself, and prepare to follow where you are called." Not that all anxiety about brethren is uncalled for, but it ought to have some limit, so that it may be anxiety, and not curiosity, that occupies our attention. Let every man, therefore, look to his neighbours, if by any means he may succeed in drawing them along with him to Christ, and let not the offences of others retard his own progress.

23. *Then this saying went forth.* The Evangelist relates that, from misunderstanding Christ's words, an error arose among the disciples, that John *would never die.* He means

[1] CALVIN here throws out a conjecture, that the clause originally stood in the Vulgate, SI *eum volo manere,* and that, by the addition of " a single letter" to the first word of the clause, some ignorant transcriber altered it to SIC *eum volo manere.* He declares it to be impossible that the word *Sic* should have found its way into the verse in any other manner, because the translator could not mistake the meaning of "the Greek word" ἐάν. —*Ed.*

those who were present at that conversation, that is, the Apostles; not that the name *brethren* belongs to them alone, but that they were the first-fruits, as it were, of that holy union. It is also possible, that, besides the eleven, he refers to others who were at that time in company with them; and by the expression, *went forth,* he means that this error was spread in all directions; yet probably it was not of long duration, but subsisted among them, until, being enlightened by the Holy Spirit, they formed purer and more correct views of the kingdom of Christ, having laid aside carnal and foolish imaginations.[1]

What John relates about the Apostles happens every day, and we ought not to wonder at it; for if Christ's disciples, who belonged to his family and were intimately acquainted with him, were so egregiously mistaken, how much more are they liable to fall into mistakes, who have not been so familiarly instructed in the school of Christ? But let us also observe whence this fault arises. The teaching of Christ is useful, and for edification; that is, it is plain; but we obscure the light by our wicked inventions, which we bring to it from our own views. Christ had not intended to pronounce any thing certain or definite about John, but only to affirm that he had full power to decide about his life and death; so that the doctrine is simple and useful in itself, but the disciples imagine and contrive more than had been told them. Accordingly, in order that we may be safe from this danger, let us learn to be wise and to think soberly. But such is the wantonness of the human understanding, that it rushes with all its force into foolishness. The consequence was, that this very error, against which the Evangelist had expressly warned them to be on their guard, continued notwithstanding to gain currency in the world; for a fable has been contrived, that he ordered a ditch to be digged for him, and went down into it, and that next day it was found empty. We see, therefore, that we shall never cease to err, unless we unreservedly receive what the Lord hath taught us, and reject all inventions of men.

---

[1] "Toutes imaginations charnelles et extravagantes rejettees."

24. *This is that disciple.* Having hitherto mentioned himself in the third person, John now declares that it is himself; that greater weight may be attached to the statements of one who was an eye-witness, and who had fully known all that he relates.

25. *There are also many other things that Jesus did.* Lest any one should view his narrative with suspicion, as if it had been written through partiality, because *Jesus loved him,* he anticipates this objection, by saying, that he has passed over more than he has written. He does not speak of Christ's actions of every kind, but of those which relate to his public office; nor ought we to think that the hyperbole is absurd, when we bear with many figures of speech of the same kind in heathen authors. Not only ought we to take into account the number of Christ's works, but we ought also to consider their importance and magnitude. The majesty of Christ, which by its infinity swallowed up, if I may so speak, not only the senses of men, but heaven and earth, gave a miraculous display of its own splendour in those works. If the Evangelist, casting his eyes on that brightness, exclaims in astonishment, that even the whole world could not contain a full narrative, ought we to wonder at it? Nor is he at all to be blamed, if he employ a frequent and ordinary figure of speech for commending the excellence of the works of Christ. For we know how God accommodates himself to the ordinary way of speaking, on account of our ignorance, and sometimes even, if I may be allowed the expression, stammers.

Yet we ought to remember what we formerly stated, that the summary which the Evangelists have committed to writing, is sufficient both for regulating faith and for obtaining salvation. That man who has duly profited under such teachers will be truly wise. And, indeed, since they were appointed by God to be witnesses to us, as they have faithfully discharged their duty; so it is our duty, on the other hand, to depend wholly on their testimony, and to desire nothing more than what they have handed down to us; and especially, because their pens were guided by the sure providence of God, that they might not oppress us by an unlimited mass of narratives, and yet, in making a selection, might make known to us all that God knew to be necessary for us, who alone is wise, and the only fountain of wisdom; to whom be praise and glory for ever. Amen.

TABLES AND INDEX

TO THE

COMMENTARY

ON THE

GOSPEL ACCORDING TO JOHN.

TABLE I.

OF PASSAGES FROM THE HOLY SCRIPTURES,
WHICH ARE QUOTED, OR INCIDENTALLY ILLUSTRATED,
IN THE COMMENTARY ON
THE GOSPEL ACCORDING TO JOHN.

GENESIS.

Chap	Ver	Vol	Page	Chap.	Ver.	Vol.	Page
i.	1	i.	26	xxvii.	38	i	304
ii.	2	i.	196	xxviii.	12	i.	81
xvii.	5	i.	407	xxxii.	30	i.	54
	7	i.	347	xlviii.	22	i.	145
xxii.	2	i.	156				

EXODUS.

Chap	Ver	Vol	Page	Chap.	Ver.	Vol.	Page
ii.	12	i.	156	xx.	8	i.	375
iii.	12	i.	69		12	ii.	232
	14	i.	362	xxiii.	12	i.	375
xii.	46	ii.	240, 241	xxv.	40	i.	225
xix.	6	i.	347	xxxi.	18	i.	319
xx.	5	i.	366	xxxiii.	23	i.	55

LEVITICUS.

Chap	Ver	Vol	Page	Chap.	Ver.	Vol.	Page
vi.	30	ii.	225	xxiii.	34	i.	282
xvi.	27	ii.	225				

NUMBERS.

Chap	Ver	Vol	Page	Chap.	Ver	Vol	Page
ix.	12	ii.	240, 241	xxiii.	7, 8	ii.	198
xxi	9	i.	121	xxv.	7	i.	156

DEUTERONOMY.

Chap	Ver	Vol	Page	Chap	Ver	Vol	Page
iv.	7	ii	117	xvii.	8	i.	315
vi	5	i.	220	xxi.	23	ii.	225
viii.	3	i.	232	xxvii.	26	ii.	114
xii	8	i.	158	xxix.	4	ii.	43
	14	i.	158	xxx. 12, 13		i.	248
xiii.	3	i. 106, 221, 291		xxxii.	34	i.	194
	5	i.	417	xxxiv	10	i.	54
xvii.	7	i	320				

JOSHUA.

vii	19	i	383

I. SAMUEL.

ii.	30	i.	356

I. KINGS.

xvii	1	i	57

II. KINGS.

Chap	Ver	Vol	Page	Chap	Ver	Vol	Page
v	10	i	188, 371	xvii.	27	i.	154
	14	i.	188, *n* 1	xviii.	4	i.	122

TABLES.

JOB.

Chap	Ver	Vol	Page	Chap.	Ver	Vol	Page
xv	25	ι	223				

PSALMS.

Chap	Ver	Vol	Page	Chap.	Ver	Vol	Page
ιι	4	i.	449	lxix.	9	ι	94
	6	i.	233		22	ιι	234
	7	ι.	272	lxxviii.	24	ι	246
	10-12	ιι.	210		39	ι.	45
	12	i.	202, 358, 449	lxxxi.	10	i.	444
xιι	2	i	78	lxxxii.	6	i.	419
xvi.	10	ii	253	xci.	11	i	428, 453
xix.	10	i.	170	civ.	22, 23	i	368
xxii.	19	ii.	229		24	ι	115
	22	ii	229, 260		29	ι.	197
xxiii.	4	i	402	cx.	1	ii.	253
xxxv.	19	ii.	129	cxvi	10	i	167
xxxvι	9	{ i.	207, 455	cxviii	25	ii.	18
		ιi.	85	cxιx.	105	ιi.	156
xli	9	iι.	65	cxxxviii.	8	ιi.	35
lv.	22	ι	301				

PROVERBS.

xv	8	i	386	xxi.	2	i.	102
xvii.	15	ιι	214	xxviii	9	ι.	386

ISAIAH.

i.	3	i	40	vι.	9	{ i.	392
iι.	2	ι	121			ii	42
	3	ι.	72, 160	viii	6	i	371
	4	i	407		14	ι.	277

VOL. II.

Chap	Ver	Vol	Page	Chap	Ver	Vol	Page
viii	16	i.	278	liii.	5	i.	65
ix.	6	i	120			ii	115
xi.	4	i	313		7	ii	196
		ii.	192		8	ii	253
xix.	18	i.	407	liv.	13	i	258
xxviii	11	ii	156	lv	1	i	307
xxix.	11	ii	100		3	ii.	252
xl	3	i	59		6	i	305
	6	i	45	lix	21	ii.	132
xlii	1	i.	267	lx.	19	ii	39
	3	i	67	lxi	1	i.	166
xlv.	19	i	221	lxiii	10	ii	242, *n*. 1
xlix.	8	i	305, 331	lxv	1	i.	148
l	8	i.	299			ii.	158
liii	1	ii	40	lxvi.	1	i.	445

JEREMIAH.

i	5	ii	120	xxiii	24	i.	67, 445
vii.	11	i	423			ii	163
xvii	9	ii	220		29	i	270
	21	i	190	xxxi	34	ii	152
xx	7	i	299				

EZEKIEL.

xviii	20	i	366	xxxvi	26	ii	158
xxxiv	12	i	399				

DANIEL.

ix.	25	i	98	ix	25, 26	i	72

JOEL.

iii	2	i	347

MICAH.

Chap.	Ver	Vol	Page	Chap	Ver	Vol	Page
iv	2	i	160, 407	v	2	i	298

HABAKKUK.

ii	3	i.	183

HAGGAI.

i	4	i	98

ZECHARIAH.

Chap	Ver	Vol	Page	Chap	Ver	Vol	Page
viii	23	i	407	xii	10	ii	242
ix	9	ii	22				

MALACHI.

Chap	Ver	Vol	Page	Chap	Ver	Vol	Page
ii.	7	i	280	iv	2	ii	39, 97
iii	1	i	66		4	i	186
iv	2	i	57, 135		5	i	57, 60

MATTHEW.

Chap	Ver	Vol	Page	Chap	Ver	Vol	Page
i	23	ii	21	iii	17	{ i / ii.	199, 409 / 112, 185
ii.	2	i.	88	v	13	ii.	261
iii	9	i.	42		14	{ i / ii.	37 / 261
	11	i.	111				
	14	i	68				
	16	i.	88		39	ii	202

TABLES.

Chap	Ver	Vol	Page	Chap.	Ver	Vol	Page
vi.	10	ii.	20	xx.	19	ii.	207
	11 {	i.	250	xxi.	1	ii	16, 21
		ii.	286		13	i.	92, 423
	21	ii.	262		15, 16	ii.	21
	33	i.	231, 240		25	i.	67
vii.	7	i	291	xxii.	42	i	388
	8	i.	221	xxiii.	2	i.	403
	16	i	209, 275		24	ii.	205
viii	11	i.	407		37	ii.	109, 174
ix	15	ii	293	xxiv	14	i.	106
x	5	i	146	xxvi	2	ii.	10
	6	i.	323	7 {		i.	425
	27	ii.	201			ii.	10
	41	ii	231		8	ii.	11
xi	9	i.	57		16	ii	10
	14	i.	57		27	i.	265
	28, 29	i	413		38	ii.	242, n. 1
xii.	39	i	245		44	ii.	191
	50	i	284		49	ii.	52
xiii	11	ii	156, 201		52	ii.	195
	12	ii.	98		74	ii.	203
	13 {	i.	33, 96, 329		75	ii.	204
		ii.	41, 157	xxvii.	35	ii	229
	16	ii	279		45	ii.	224
	17	ii.	279		48	ii	234
	58	i	444		51	i.	162
xiv.	26	i	236		57	ii	243
xv	14	i	374	xxviii	1	ii.	248
xvii	2	ii	255		2	ii	255
	5 {	i.	80, 358, 409		3	ii.	255
		ii.	185, 267		9	ii	258
xviii	11	i	391		18	i	201

MARK.

i	10	i	88	ix.	13	i.	57
ii	16	i.	376	xi	1	ii	16, 21
vi	49	i	236	xiv	1	ii.	10

TABLES.

Chap.	Ver	Vol	Page	Chap.	Ver	Vol	Page
xiv.	3	ii.	10	xv.	25	ii.	224
	4	ii.	11		33	ii.	224
	71	ii.	203		36	ii	234
	72	ii.	204	xvi.	1	ii.	248
xv	23	ii.	234		9	ii.	232, 261
	24	ii.	229		20	ii.	281

LUKE.

Chap.	Ver	Vol	Page	Chap.	Ver	Vol	Page
i	53	i.	307	xvii.	21	i,	204
	77	ii.	271			ii.	210
ii	8	i.	88	xviii.	13	i.	445
	34	i.	126			ii.	164
iii.	16	i.	111	xix.	29	ii.	16, 21
iv.	27	i.	188, *n*. 1	xxii.	61	ii.	204
	30	i.	363	xxiii.	19	ii	213
vi	44	i.	209		34	ii	172, 229
vii.	22	ii.	158		36	ii.	234
	37	i	425		44	ii	224
viii.	2	ii.	232, 261		50	ii.	243
x	24	i.	360	xxiv.	10	ii.	248
	30	i.	205		10, 11	ii.	249
	38	i.	424		12	ii.	249, 252
xi.	27, 28	i.	284		16	ii	256
xii	13	i	323		22	ii	248
	47	ii	127, *n*. 2		49	ii	269
xiv	26	ii	231		51	i	80

ACTS.

Chap.	Ver	Vol	Page	Chap.	Ver	Vol	Page
i	8	i.	213	vii	55	i.	48, *n*. 1, 80
	9	i	80	x.	10	ii.	264
ii	3	i.	67		30	ii.	255
		ii.	269	xiii.	34	ii.	252
	27	ii.	253		35	ii.	253
	36	ii	242	xvii.	27	i.	32
iii.	15	i	267		28	i.	32, 197
vi.	5	i.	48, *n* 1	xxi.	14	ii.	196
	8	i.	48, *n*. 1				

ROMANS.

Chap	Ver	Vol	Page	Chap	Ver.	Vol	Page
1	4	i	272	viii.	10	i.	308, 357, 436
	5	ii	120				
	16	i.	21, 127, 278		11	i.	98
		ii	180		15	i.	254, 386
	28	ii	71, 193, 219		22, 23	ii.	151
ii.	12	ii	127		26	ii	160
iii	27	i	245		34	ii	157
iv	11	i	247		36	i	253
	17	i	407	ix.	4	i	343
		ii	158		31	i.	304
	25	ii	140	x.	4	i.	385
v	1	ii	23		6, 7	ii	117
	8	i	123		6-8	i	248
	10	i	123		8	ii	131
		ii.	96, 116, 159, 186		10	ii.	45
					15	i	154
	14	ii.	127		16	ii.	40
	19	i	410		17	ii	131
vi	4	ii.	146, 240, 241		20	ii.	158
				xi.	36	i.	30
	4-6	i	61	xii	12	i.	40
	6	i	203		18	ii.	124
		ii.	146, 269		20	ii.	71
	10	ii.	169		21	ii.	202
vii.	19	ii.	294	xiii.	1, 2	i.	420
	24	i	342		10	ii.	76
viii.	1	ii	113	xv	3	i.	95
					11	i	359

I. CORINTHIANS.

Chap	Ver	Vol	Page	Chap	Ver	Vol	Page
i.	3	i.	231	i.	30	ii.	146, 159, 181
	22	i	180				
	27	ii.	248	ii.	2	i.	397

TABLES.   311

Chap	Ver	Vol.	Page	Chap	Ver	Vol	Page
ii	8	i	251	vii.	31	ii	209
	12	ii	130	x	3	i	122, 247, 260
	16	i	120				
		ii	120	xii	3	ii.	267
iii.	5	ii.	183	xiii	5	i	103
	7	ii	122	xiv.	23	ii	139
	18	i	120	xv.	20	ii.	10, 246
iv.	4	i	353		24	ii	102
	5	i.	299		26	i	204
v	5	i	387		36, 37	i	115
	7, 8	ii.	241	xvi.	22	ii	289
vi	12, 13	ii	133				

II. CORINTHIANS.

Chap	Ver	Vol.	Page	Chap	Ver	Vol	Page
i	20	i.	159	v.	7	ii.	279
ii	15	ii.	43		14	ii	289
	16	i	331		16, 17	ii	96, 148
		ii.	273		17	i	284
iii	6	ii	138		18	ii.	271
	14	i	217		19	i.	279
	18	i	330		20	i	21
		ii	185			ii	272
iv.	3, 4	i.	379		21	ii.	226
		ii	156	vi.	2	i.	331
	6	i.	369	x.	6	i.	127, 391
	16	i.	436			ii.	273
		ii.	28		18	i	359
v.	4	i.	97	xi	2, 3	i	135
	6, 7	ii	148	xii.	12	i	107

GALATIANS.

Chap	Ver	Vol.	Page	Chap	Ver	Vol	Page
i	15	ii.	120	iii.	13	ii	226
iii.	1	i.	122		24	ii	145
		ii	144, 279		27	ii.	269

312   TABLES.

Chap	Ver	Vol	Page	Chap	Ver	Vol	Page
iv.	1, 2	i	173	iv	19	ii.	250
	6	i	386		29	i.	344
	9	i.	162, 407, 414	vi.	5	ii.	296
		ii	258		15	i	284

EPHESIANS.

i	3	ii	32	iii	4	ii.	83
	4	ii.	186		18	ii.	144
	5	i	123	iv	3	ii	183
	10	i.	455		4, 5	i	408
	13, 14	ii.	131, 145		7	i.	140
	14	i	172		10	ii.	140
	22	ii.	20		11	ii.	266
ii	1	i.	206		11-16	ii	183
	3	i	142		17	i	206
	4	i.	41	v.	2	ii	116, 223
	12	ii.	158		8	i.	37
	14	i	158, 407		20	i.	231
	17	i.	177, 303		26	ii	180
	19	i	81		30	i	134
iii	2	ii	83				

PHILLIPIANS.

i	6	i.	241	ii.	7-10	i.	207
	20	ii.	295		9, 10	ii	244
ii.	6-8	i	281		10	i	327, 358
	7	i	256, 267, 446			ii.	90, 169, 277
		ii.	169, 262		11	ii	90
				iv	12	i	88

COLOSSIANS.

i	12	i	42	i	18	ii	246
	16	i	187		28	ii	118

TABLES. 313

Chap	Ver	Vol.	Page	Chap.	Ver	Vol	Page
ii	3	{ i	395	ii.	16	i.	195
		ii	144, 146		17	i	52
	8	i.	401	iii	1	ii	259
	9	{ i	363		3	{ i.	204, 253
		ii.	21			ii	28
	14	i.	338		10	ii	168

I. THESSALONIANS.

iv.	13	i	441

II. THESSALONIANS.

ii	8	ii	192	ii.	12	i	221
	9	i	106, 221				

I. TIMOTHY.

ii	1	ii	172	iv.	4	i.	230
iii.	16	{ i	25, 98	vi.	13	ii	219
		ii	242		16	i	54

II. TIMOTHY.

i.	12	i	416	ii	15	i	277
ii	13	i	299, 336	iii	17	ii	144

TITUS.

i.	12	i.	178	ii.	14	i.	210
	15	ii	205	iii	5	i	61
ii.	11	ii	117				

HEBREWS.

i	3	{ i	29, 31, 54,	i	6	i.	358
			197	iv	15	i.	145
		ii	21				

TABLES.

Chap	Ver	Vol	Page	Chap	Ver	Vol	Page
v.	4	i.	133	xi	27	ii	47
vii	25	ii.	157	xii	17	i.	304
viii.	5	i.	225		25	i.	137
ix	1	i	162			ii.	88
	27	ii.	196		26	i.	225
x	22	i.	149	xiii.	8	i	362
xi.	1	ii	279		12	ii.	226

JAMES.

i.	1	i.	305	ii	20	i	101
	18	i	43		26	i.	101
ii	17	i.	101	iv	12	ii	53

I. PETER.

i.	1	i.	305	ii.	24	i	65
	8	ii.	280	iii.	21	i.	61
	12	i.	174	iv.	17	i.	365
	23	i.	44, 204,	v.	7	i.	301
			357, 436		8	i.	351
ii.	7	i	126				

II. PETER.

i.	13	i.	97	i.	19	ii.	156

I. JOHN.

i.	1	ii.	132	iv.	10	ii	96, 152
ii.	1	ii	157		14	ii	158, *n.* 1
	19	i.	400	v.	6	ii	240
	23	i.	160, 202				

REVELATION.

i.	5	ii.	269

TABLE II.

OF GREEK WORDS EXPLAINED.

	Vol	Page		Vol	Page
αἴρειν,	i	65	ἐκείνου,	ii.	238
ὁ αἴρων,	i	65	ἐλέγχειν,	i	353
ἀληθῶς.	i.	78		ii.	139
ἀμὴν,	i	107	ἐμφατικὸν,	i.	124
ἄμπελος,	ii.	106	ἐμφατικῶς,	ii.	127
ἀνέβη,	i.	92	ἐν,	ii.	73
ἀντὶ,	i.	51	ἐν τῇ διασπορᾷ,	i.	305
ἀνακεφαλαίωσις,	i.	220	ἐνθουσιασμοὺς,	ii.	131
ἀνακόλουθον,	i.	238	ἐξ αἱμάτων,	i.	43, n 1
ἄνωθεν,	i	109	ἐξουσία,	i.	41, 207
ἀξένους,	i	15	ἐπὶ τὸ πολὺ,	i.	178
ἀξίωσις,	i.	41	ἐσκήνωσεν,	i.	47
ἀπέστειλε,	ii	203	ἔσται,	ii.	31
ἀπολέσει,	ii.	29	εὐαγγέλιον,	i.	20
ἀποφθέγματα,	ii	155	ἤδη κέκριται,	i.	127
ἀρχὴν,	i.	334	ἱκανότης,	i.	42
ἀταξία,	i.	441	κακοζηλία,	i	156
ἀταξίας,	ii.	141	κασίγνητος θανάτου,	i.	430
αὐτόπιστος,	ii.	278	Κέδρων,	ii.	190, n 1
βασιλικός,	i.	179	κεφαλή,	i.	73
γενέσθαι,	i.	362, n. 3	κλήματα,	ii.	106
γέγονεν,	i.	30, n. 1	κρίνω,	i.	126
διὰ τοῦτο,	i.	295	κρίσεως,	ii.	141
ἐάν,	ii	297, n 1	κρίσις,	ii	36
ἐγκαίνια,	i.	412	Κύριε,	ii.	257
εἰμί,	i.	362, n. 3	λαλία,	i.	176
ἐκείνῃ,	ii	238	λόγος,	i	26, 28

	Vol.	Page		Vol	Page
λόγχη,	ii.	239	προσεκύνησεν,	i.	389
μαρτυρεῖ,	i.	49	πρόσωπα,	i.	29
μημαρτύρηκε,	1	216	προφήτης,	i.	57
μεταβέβηκε,	i.	204	πρῶτον ὑμῶν,	ii.	123
μετεμψύχωσις,	i.	366	πρῶτος,	ii	124
μετρητής,	i.	86	ῥῆμα,	i.	28
μιᾷ,	ii.	249	συμπαθεία,	i.	83, 439
ὁμοούσιος.	i.	417	τετέλεσται,	ii.	235, n. 4
ὄνου σκιὰ,	ii.	22, n. 3	Τί ἐμοὶ καὶ σοί,	i.	84
ὅτι,	i	335	τόπον,	ii.	274
παλιγγενεσία,	i.	111, 112	τύπον,	ii.	274
πάντες ὅσοι,	i.	398	ὑποζυγίου,	ii.	22
παρεπιδήμοις διασπορᾶς,	i	305	ὑπόστασις,	i.	29
περιττολογία,	i.	31	ψυχή,	ii.	29

TABLE III.

OF HEBREW WORDS EXPLAINED.

	Vol	Page		Vol	Page
אהד	ii.	249	יהוחנן	i.	36
אשד	i.	185	מן	i.	246
גבח	ii.	223	משל	ii	155
גבתא	ii	223	משלימ	ii.	155
גלגל	ii	227	משפט	ii	36
גלגלתא	ii.	227	פרושים	i.	105
גלל	ii. 227, *n* 1		שם	i	42
הושיע־נא	ii.	18			

INDEX.

∗∗∗ *The references are to the Volumes and Pages.*

ABIDE, to, in Christ, ii 109.
  in the love of Christ, ii. 112.
Abraham is the father of the whole church, i 360
  Christ existed long before, i 362.
  seed of, the Jews foolishly boasted of being, 1 342, 345.
  children of, who ought to be accounted, 1. 347.
  joy of, 1 361.
Abuse of religious instruction reproved, i. 214.
Afflictions not accidental, but punishments of sin, i 193
  our slowness in deriving benefit from, i. 194.
  compared to medicinal draughts, ii 196
  believers are exposed to many, ii 162
  the severity of, ought to be traced to our obstinacy, i. 193
  for Christ's sake, ii 132.
Alms are an acceptable sacrifice, ii. 15
Ambition always accompanies hypocrisy, i 222.
Ambition, considerations fitted to restrain, i 133.
  hinders many from believing in Christ, i. 223.
Anabaptists, what they imagine Christ to be, i 46
  falsely maintain that baptism administered by a wicked minister is vitiated, i. 145.
Andrew, Simon Peter's brother, i 71.
  Peter was brought to the knowledge of Christ by the agency of, i 72.
Angels, how they are said to ascend and descend on Christ, i. 80.
  why they are called *gods*, i. 419
  why they appear clothed in white garments, ii. 255.
  why they are called *principalities* or *powers*, i. 187.
Anointing of Christ at Bethany, ii. 10.
  had a reference to his burial, ii. 13.
  practice of, described by Pliny, ii 11.

INDEX.

Anointing, expense of, ii 12
Apostacy of many of the disciples of Christ, i. 276
  not complete, i 277
Apostles, the, represented under the character of reapers, i 172
  invincible courage and magnanimity of, i 359.
  would do greater works than Christ had done, ii. 89
  what was the amount of the ignorance of, ii 157.
  were too much attached to the visible presence of Christ, ii 136.
  were not taught anything else by the Holy Spirit than what they had learned from the mouth of Christ, ii 156.
  the calling of, and of Christ is the same, ii 180.
  Christ breathed on, ii 268
  the Papists frame idols for themselves out of, i 358
Arians, cavils of, about the word *beginning*, i. 26.
  the madness of, refuted, i. 198, 420
  argued that Christ is some sort of inferior God, ii 102.
Arius refused to acknowledge the eternal divinity of Christ, i 29.
  maintained that the Son of God is inferior to the Father, i 198
Arm of the Lord, the, denotes his power, ii. 41.
Articles, three, of faith, ii. 168.
Ascend into heaven, what is meant by, i 120.
  and descend on Christ, why angels are said to, i. 80.
Ass, why the prophet describes Christ as riding on an, ii 23
Augustine addicted to the philosophy of Plato, i 31
  opinion of, about hirelings, i 404

Augustine, speculations of, about the word *sleep*, i 430.

BAPTISM, Christ abstained from the outward administration of, i 144.
  is not vitiated by being administered by a wicked man, i 145.
  women ought not to be allowed to perform, ii. 261.
  was administered by plunging the whole body beneath the water, i 130
  of John the Baptist did not differ from that of Christ, i 61.
Barabbas, a robber, demanded by the Jews, ii. 213.
Bath, or firkin, contents of the, i. 86, n 2
Bed, why the man cured of lameness was commanded to carry his, i. 189.
Beginning, the, what is meant by, i. 26
  from, meaning of the phrase, i 334.
Behold, to, the glory of Christ, meaning of, ii 187
Believers are freed from condemnation, i. 127.
  pointed out by good works, i 209
  how to distinguish hypocrites from, i. 341
  encouraged to render honour and reverence to Christ, i 359
  why it is said that they shall never die, i. 436.
  in what sense they do not believe in Christ, ii 48.
  always have Christ present by his Spirit, ii. 94.
  the obedience of, is the effect, and not the cause of, the love of Christ, ii 113.
  in what respect they are clean, ii. 59

INDEX.

Believers are enjoined to cultivate brotherly love, ii 116
  cannot make progress in the gospel till they have first been humbled, ii 140
  in what consists the safety of, ii 178
  are exposed to many afflictions, ii. 162.
  are kept by Christ in the present day not less than formerly, ii. 176.
Believing on Christ, what it is that hinders men from, i 221
  is denoted by *coming to* him, i. 250.
  why said to be only begun in the disciples, i. 90.
  how it is said that the Jews cannot believe, ii 40
  is the work of God, i. 244.
Belly, water flowing out of the, i. 308
Bethabara, where John baptized, situation of, i 62.
Bethany, situation of, i 432.
  anointing of Christ at, ii 10.
Bethesda, meaning of the name, i. 185
  miracle performed by Christ at, i 189
  reasons why miraculous cures were effected at, i. 186.
  two reasons why the man was asked if he wished to be made whole, i. 189.
  a lesson of patience taught us by this example, i. 190.
  the amazing gentleness and condescension of the Lord manifested in, i 194.
Bethlehem predicted by Micah to be the birth-place of Christ, i 298.
Bethsaida, why it is mentioned as the birth-place of Philip, i. 74.
  was on the same coast with Capernaum, i 236
  was half-way between Tiberias and Capernaum, i 238
Blasphemy, two kinds of, i. 418.

Blasphemy, Christ was accused by the Jews of, ii 217, *n*. 1.
Blind, all unbelievers are, i. 390
  from his birth, miraculous cure of a man, i 363.
  ingratitude of the parents of, i 380.
  freely acknowledged Christ to be a prophet, i 378.
Blindness, the, of men arises solely from their wickedness and obstinacy, i 219
  of the Jews was voluntary, i. 379.
Blood, the, of Christ is truly drink, i 267.
  born of, i 43.
  and water flowed out of the side of Christ, ii. 239.
Born of water, i 109
  mistake of Chrysostom concerning, i. 110.
  of the flesh, i 112.
  of the Spirit, i 111.
  again, necessity of being, i 108.
Bosom of the Father, i. 55
Branch, a, that beareth not fruit, ii. 108.
  withers, ii 110.
Brazen serpent, the, erected by Moses, i. 121.
  why Christ compares himself to, i. 122
  does Christ pronounce it to have been a sacrament? i. 122
Bread, Christ is the true, i. 248.
  of heaven, the manna was called, i. 247.
  of life, Christ is, i 249.
Breathed, Christ, on the Apostles, ii. 268.
Brethren of Christ, the, who were, i. 92.
  did not believe in him, i. 284.
Bridegroom, the, and bride, i. 134.
Brotherly love is called a new commandment, ii. 75.
  it is the will of Christ that believers should cultivate, ii 116

Brotherly love, whence arises the neglect of, ii. 60
Bucer, appropriate quotation from Moses made by, i 69
Budæus, computation of, i. 229.

CAIAPHAS, why called the high priest of that year, i 453, ii. 197
  prediction of, why God caused to be uttered by so wicked a man, i. 454.
  ridiculous inferences of the Papists from, i. 454
  deposed by Vitellius, ii 197.
  interrogates Christ concerning doctrine, ii 200.
Calling necessary in the teachers of the Church, i 36.
  of Christ and of the Apostles is the same, ii 180.
  of God is like the light of day, i. 428
  is profitable and efficacious among the elect alone, ii. 170.
  effectual, illustrated by the case of Philip, i. 74.
  the image of, is exhibited in Christ, ii 114.
  every man ought to attend to his own, ii 296
  in Mary we have a lively image of, ii 258.
Cana of Galilee, where situated, i. 82.
  the first of Christ's miracles performed at, i. 88.
Capernaum was on the same coast with Bethsaida, i 236.
Celibacy, the diabolical system of, i. 323
Cephas, or Peter, a name given by Christ to Simon, meaning of, i. 73. *See* Peter.
Ceremonies, the reason why God enjoined, ii 205
  repeal of the Law so far as relates to outward, i 158.
  without the word, are dead, ii. 246.

Ceremonies, the Papists have buried the Church under a huge mass of, i 157.
Charity, Christ is the strongest bond of, i 411.
  whence arises the neglect of, ii. 60.
Chastisements, our slowness in deriving benefit from, i. 194.
  ought to be imputed to our sins, i 193.
  sometimes are only trials of patience, i 365
Christ, meaning of the name, i 52.
  eternal Divinity of, asserted, i. 25.
  is called *the Speech*, and why, i. 26.
  is called *life*, i. 31.
  and *light*, i 32
  created all things, i. 29.
  testimony of John concerning, i 35
  is called the *only begotten*, and why, i 47.
  was full of grace and truth, i. 48
  is called the Sun of Righteousness, i 57
  was made flesh, i 44
  glory of, beheld by those only whose eyes the Holy Spirit opened, i 47.
  was acknowledged by Nathanael to be the Son of God, and King of Israel, i 79.
  gave demonstration of his divine power by his miracles, i 89
  drove out of the temple those who made merchandise in it, i. 90
  why he declares himself to be the Son of God, i. 92.
  claims for himself the glory of his resurrection, i. 98.
  knew all that was in the hearts of men, i. 102.
  apparent harshness of his reply to his mother, i. 83

Christ is the proper object of faith, i 124.
  asks drink from a woman of Samaria, i. 146
  the work of, i. 170
  attempted nothing but by the command and direction of the Father, i. 211.
  faithfully executes the command of the Father, i 220
  distinctly maintains that he is equal to God, i 198.
  is the Eternal Word of God, ii. 169
Church, the, small and low beginning of, i. 76.
  God alone preserves and defends, ii. 20
  what ought chiefly to be desired in the government of, i. 402.
  the elect alone are the true children of, i 258.
  Zion was the habitation and abode of, ii 23
  inquiry into the claims of the Papists to the title of, ii 217.
  how it can be restored, i. 258
  the unity of, is founded on nothing else than the authority of Scripture, ii 230.
  Christ by his example lays down a general law for, i. 336
  has had no enemies more inveterate than the members of, ii. 66.
  calling necessary in the teachers of, i 36.
Circumcision, argument from the writings of Moses concerning, i. 296
  comparison between, and the cure of the paralytic, i 295.
Clean, in what respect believers are, ii. 59.
Come, to, in the name of the Lord, meaning of, ii. 20.
  to Christ is the same thing with believing in him, i 250.

Comforter, the, the Holy Spirit is called, ii. 92
  will teach the Apostles all things, ii. 130.
  could not have come, if Christ had not left the world, ii. 137
  the name is applied both to Christ and to the Spirit, ii 92.
Commandment, brotherly love is called a new, ii. 75.
  of Christ, they who abide in his love, ii 113.
Communion, the, of saints is a preparation for eternal life, i. 455.
Condemnation, believers are freed from, i. 127.
  of unbelievers is just, i. 128.
  of Thomas, two remarkable clauses in, ii. 277.
Confession, faith is never unaccompanied by, ii. 45.
Conscience, a bad, sign of in Judas, ii 191
  whence arises peace of, ii. 114.
Conversion, healing is the fruit of, ii 44.
Convicteth, import of, i 353
Convince, two ways in which the Holy Spirit will, the world, ii 138.
Co-operation of human power with divine grace, the doctrine of the Papists concerning, ii. 109.
Courtier, a, who entreated Christ to cure his son, i. 178.
  the rank of, i. 179.
  apparent harshness of Christ towards, i 180
  ignorance of, i. 179.
  astonishing kindness and condescension of Christ to, i 181.
  effect of the faith of, i 182
Created, all things were, by Christ, i. 29
Cross, many take offence at the degradation of the, i. 76

Cross, how shameful will it be if we are deterred from following Christ by the dread of the, ii 232.
Cyprian vindicated, i. 405.
Cyril, opinion of, i 109.

DANIEL exclusively appropriated to the Redeemer the name of Messiah, i 72.
Darkness, to walk in, i 325; ii. 39.
Day, the calling of God is like the light of, i. 428
  denotes the time which the Father had fixed, i 368.
  sometimes divided by the Romans into twelve hours, i. 71, 427.
  and sometimes into four hours, ii. 224.
  and night, Christ borrows a comparison from, i 428.
  of Christ, Abraham desired to see the, i 360
Dead, the, shall hear the voice of the Son of God, i. 206
Death ought not to be dreaded by believers, i. 204.
  compared to sleep, i. 430.
  we ought to be prepared for, ii. 196.
  advantages yielded to us by Christ's dread of, ii 32.
  believers have already passed from, to life, i 204.
  to see, i. 356.
  to taste of, i 357.
  spiritual, Christ raises from, i 205.
  of martyrs, God is glorified by, ii 296
Death of Christ, the, is a voluntary sacrifice, i 410
  is compared to sowing, ii 28.
  we behold a magnificent triumph in, ii 164 .
  what we ought chiefly to consider in, ii 32.
  why so carefully mentioned by all the Evangelists, ii 237.

Death of Christ, the, was the full restoration of the world, ii 36 and resurrection, are the two pillars of our faith, ii. 159.
Deceit, what Christ meant by, i. 78.
Dedication, the feast of, origin of, i. 412.
Defilement, two faults committed by the Jews in abstaining from, ii. 205.
Denarius, value of a, i. 229
Denial of Christ by Peter, ii. 200.
  indirect, is not a venial sin, ii 47
Devil, a, Judas Iscariot was pronounced by Christ to be, i. 280.
  to have, meaning of, i. 294, 355.
Devil, the, is the father of ungodly men, i. 350.
  is a murderer, i. 351.
  put it into the heart of Judas to betray Christ, ii 55
  did not enter essentially into Judas, ii. 71
  is the father of falsehood, i 352.
  is called the prince of this world, and why, ii 104.
  how we ought to meet the attacks of, ii. 182.
Disciple whom Jesus loved, the, John the Evangelist was called, ii. 69.
Disciples of Christ, the, beloved in Christ, i 89.
  Christ washes the feet of, ii 56.
  apostacy of many of, i. 276.
  reproved for having made so little progress, ii 88.
  who are the true, i. 341.
  Jesus stands in the midst of, ii 264.
  by what mark Christ distinguishes them from the world, ii. 97.
  first-fruits of faith in, i 90.
Divinity, eternal, of Christ asserted, i. 25
  proved by his knowledge of the hearts of men, i. 275.

INDEX. 325

Divinity of Christ denied by Arius, i. 29
   was more powerfully displayed after his ascension, ii. 89.
Doctrine, miracles prepare the way for, i. 178
   the temple was a sanctuary of heavenly, i 91.
   what is the chief design of, i. 75
   the mark by which we may know, i. 292
   the contempt of, gives great uneasiness to the godly, ii. 125.
   Christ is interrogated by Caiaphas concerning, ii. 200.
Doctrine of Christ, the, is a stone of stumbling to unbelievers, i. 277.
   came from the Father, i 289.
   what was the design of, ii. 156.
   will be a hammer to unbelievers, i. 270.
Door, Christ is the, i. 397.
Dove, the Holy Spirit appeared in the form of a, i. 67.
Drawn, how men are, by the Father, i 257.
   only out of free grace, i 276.
   by Christ, who are, ii. 37.

EAGER desire of the people to hear Christ, 1 227.
Earthly things, what is meant by, i 119.
Eating the flesh of Christ, meaning of, i. 261.
   effect of, i 268.
   debates of the Jews about, i. 263.
Effectual calling, illustrated by the case of Philip, i. 74.
   in Mary we have a lively image of, ii 258.
Elect, the, alone are taught by God, i. 258.
   the gift of heavenly wisdom is peculiar to, ii. 168.

Elect, the, belong to the peculiar flock of Christ, ii. 165
   the salvation of, is certain, i. 416
   none profit by the grace of the Spirit but, ii 170.
   the calling of God is profitable and efficacious in none but, ii. 170.
   none are the true children of the church but, i 258.
   are distinguished from the reprobate by pure grace, ii 170.
   God restrains by a secret bridle, ii. 276.
   the Spirit of God works secretly in, ii. 250.
Election, the eternity of, ii. 170.
   the perseverance of the saints ascribed to, ii. 63
   without faith, would be imperfect, i 254.
   two kinds of, ii. 64.
   ordinary and special, ii 119.
   we ought to be aroused to earnestness in prayer by our knowledge of, ii 173.
Elijah the Tishbite, why John the Baptist was compared to, i 57.
Enon, where situated, i. 130.
Erasmus very properly substituted *Speech* for *Word*, as the translation of λόγος, i 28.
   translates improperly the adverb ἄνωθεν, i. 109.
Essenes, the, a sect of the Jews, i. 105
Eternal Divinity of Christ asserted, i. 25
   denied by Arius, i. 29. *See* Divinity.
Eternal life, the manner of bestowing, ii 166.
   is promised universally to all who believe in Christ, i 125
   the communion of saints is a preparation for, i. 455.

Eternal life is to know the Father and the Son, ii 166.
is bestowed on the elect alone, ii 168
Eternal Word of God, the, Christ is, ii. 169
Eucharist, the, or Lord's Supper, young children forbidden to partake of, i 265.
why Christ added the cup in, i 267
Exalt, a term employed by Christ to point out his own death, i. 337.
Example of Christ, the, ought to be followed by all shepherds, ii 193
in giving to the poor, ii 72
Excommunication arose out of the most ancient discipline of the Church, i 380
has often been wickedly abused, i. 381
ought to be the sinew of holy discipline, ii 46
must be brought back to its true and lawful use, ii. 134
is a dreadful judgment, i. 381.
of the Pope, we have no reason to be alarmed at, ii. 134.

FAITH denoted by *receiving Christ*, i 40.
we become the sons of God by, i. 41.
in the name of Christ, i. 42.
is regeneration preceded by? i 44
is not common to all, i 125.
first-fruits of, in the disciples, i. 90.
Christ is the proper object of, i. 124; ii 81.
is distinguished from all doubtful and wavering opinions, i 138
is founded on the word of God itself, i. 176.
is called the work of God, i. 244

Faith, why and how it bestows life upon us, i 125.
proceeds from the knowledge of Christ, i 255
is a remarkable gift of the Spirit of God, i. 276
is a precious sacrifice in the sight of God, i. 138.
what is the true and lawful profession of, i 359.
is never unaccompanied by confession, ii 45.
disputes of Popish divines about the object of, ii 81.
persecution is a touchstone to try, ii. 161.
the feeble beginnings of, ii. 250.
flows from the predestination of God, ii 170.
the power and nature of, ii. 278.
ought to rest exclusively on the promises and word of God, ii. 281.
election would be imperfect without, i 254.
sometimes inaccurately put for a sort of preparation for faith, i 340
three articles of, ii 168.
is a spiritual resurrection of the soul, i. 436
Falsehood, the devil is the father of, i 352
Fanatics disdain the outward preaching, ii. 131.
Father, God the, governs the world in the person of his Son, i. 201.
how Christ desired to be glorified with, ii. 169.
bosom of, i. 55.
in what manner the Son is loved by, i 199.
attested Christ by miracles, i. 215
testified concerning his Son under both dispensations, i. 216

Father, God the, Christ faithfully executes the commission of, i. 220.
we are given to Christ by, i. 252
what is the will of, i 253
how men are drawn by, i. 257.
the doctrine of Christ comes from, i. 289
Christ is called the image of, i. 329.
how the Son is known by, i. 405
why the Son is loved by, i. 409
in what sense the Son is one with, i. 416.
how Christ was sanctified by, i. 420
gave all things into the hands of the Son, ii. 55
Christ is in, ii 88.
the Holy Spirit is the gift of, ii 92
is in us by the efficacy of the Spirit, ii 95
the Holy Spirit proceedeth from, ii 131.
Christ came out from, ii 159.
the reprobate are subjected to Christ by, ii. 165
the will of Christ did not differ from the will of, i 212.
Christ was regulated entirely by the will of, i 339
in what sense he is greater than Christ, ii 102.
wishes to be acknowledged and worshipped in the Son, i 201
Christ attempted nothing but by the command and direction of, i 211.
why Christ informed the disciples that he returns to, i. 159.
distinction between the person of Christ and of, ii. 169.

Fathers, the, did not worship God *spiritually* under the law, i. 161.
beheld Christ, though darkly, under shadows, i. 202.
were not accustomed to pray without a Mediator, ii 153.
the condition of, after death, before Christ ascended to heaven, ii. 82
Papists are vain of an uninterrupted succession from, i. 348
four faults committed in copying, i. 155.
Feast of the Passover, two reasons why Christ celebrated, i. 92.
of Pentecost, i. 184.
of Tabernacles, i. 282.
of Dedication, origin of, i. 412.
Feet, the, metaphorical meaning of, ii. 59.
of his disciples, Christ washeth, ii 56.
Finished, it is, import of, ii 234.
repetition of the word, ii. 235.
Firkin, or bath, contents of the, i. 86, n 2.
Flesh, Christ was made, i. 44.
contrasted with the Spirit, i. 112, 273
various meanings of, i 45.
to judge according to, i 327.
power over all, Christ declares that he has, ii 165.
the will of, i 43.
of Christ, to eat, i 262.
sometimes denotes the outward appearance of a man, i. 327.
Fold, meaning of, i 406.
there shall be one, i. 408
Food, rules to be observed concerning, i 169.
which perisheth, i. 240.
which endureth to eternal life, i. 241
why Christ refused to partake of, while conversing with the woman of Samaria, i. 168.

Forgiveness of our sins by God is unconditional, i. 204.
Forty-six years spent in building the temple, i. 98
Free, how the truth makes us, i 341.
  the Jews falsely boasted that they were, i 343
Free grace, men are drawn by God only out of, i. 276.
  the elect are distinguished from the reprobate by, ii. 170.
Free-will, allegorically and foolishly compared by the Papists to the man who was left half dead on the road, i 205
  the doctrine of the Papists about, overthrown, i. 258.
Friends, how did Christ die for? ii. 116.
  the Apostles were not servants, but, ii 117
Full of grace and truth, Christ was, i 48.
Fulness of Christ, the, how we receive out of, i 50
  who they are that receive out of, i. 51.

GABBATHA, meaning of, ii 223.
Galilee, why Christ sojourned for a time in, i 281.
  erroneous opinion that Christ had come out of, i. 312.
  sea of, why called the sea of Tiberias, i 227
Gennesareth, the lake of, is called the sea of Galilee, i. 227
  extent of, described by Pliny and Josephus, i. 236.
  is called the sea of Tiberias, i. 227
Gentiles, the, calling of, i 406.
  how the Jews came to be associated with, i 407.
  the reconciliation effected by Christ is extended to, i. 455
Gerizzim, Mount, a temple had been built on, by Manasseh, brother of Jaddus, i 155.
Giants, wars of the, i 223, n 1

Gift of God, what is the, i 148
Giveth, Christ, himself to us, various meanings of, i 263.
Glorified. how the Son of Man is, in his death, ii. 72.
  how God is, in Christ, ii 73.
  how Christ desired to be, with the Father, ii. 169
Glory to be sought from God alone, i 222.
  of men, what it is to love the, ii 48.
  to give to God, a form of administering an oath, i 382.
Glory of Christ, the, displayed in his miracles, i. 89.
  beheld by those only whose eyes the Holy Spirit opened, i. 47.
  Isaiah saw, ii. 44.
  what is meant by beholding, ii 187
Glory of God, the, a miracle is called, i. 444.
  the death of Lazarus, was for, i 426.
God is invisible, i 53
  in what manner he was seen by the Fathers, i. 54.
  and by Moses, i 55.
  contains in himself the fulness of life, i 207
  is the fountain of truth, ii 144.
  Christ is the lively image of, ii. 87.
  alone preserves and defends the Church, ii 20.
  takes, as it were, a visible form in the sacraments, i. 216.
  Christ distinctly maintains that he is equal to, i. 198.
  is a Spirit, i. 164.
  to give glory to, i. 382.
  what is the gift of, i. 148
Gods, angels are called, i 419
  magistrates are called, and why, i 420.
Golgotha, meaning of the word, ii 227.
Good works, what are justly accounted, i. 210.

Good works, believers are pointed out by, i 209
  eternal life is not suspended on the merits of, i. 210, 242
Gospel, the, in what manner hypocrites assent to, i 100
  the superiority of, to the Law, i. 172.
  the publication of, was a new and sudden resurrection of the world, i. 206.
  how a man becomes prepared to obey, i 222
  twofold advantage of, i. 401
  is not hidden or obscure except to the reprobate, i 379.
  Christ is said to be lifted up by the preaching of, i. 121
  the last judgment will be a ratification of, ii. 52
  the principal object intended to be accomplished by, ii 271.
  eagerness of the Papists to extinguish, i 302
  why it is called a harvest, i 172
  why so few believe, i. 276
  the fruit derived from, i 341.
  the chief difference between heathen philosophy and, ii 271.
  the preaching of, is called Christ's descent to us, i. 303
Government of the Church, what ought chiefly to be desired in the, i 402.
Grace, Christ was full of, i. 48
  for grace, i 51
  and truth contrasted with the law, i. 48
  of Christ, the, is a true resurrection from the dead, i 206.
  free, the elect are distinguished from the reprobate by, ii. 170.
  of the Father, why Christ promises to his disciples, ii. 179.

Gratitude due to God for his gifts, i. 192
Greeks, the dispersion of, i. 305.
  were those Greeks who came to seek Jesus Gentiles or Jews ? ii. 26
Gregory Nazianzen, observation of, about the three Persons in the Godhead, i. 29.

Harvest, comparison drawn by Christ from the, i. 170.
  why the gospel is called a, i. 172.
Hateth Christ, he who, hateth his Father, ii 128.
Healing is the fruit of conversion, ii. 48.
Heart, the, various meanings of the word, ii. 43.
  of Judas, the devil put into, to betray Christ, ii. 55.
Heathen philosophy, the chief difference between the gospel and, ii 271.
Heaven, coming down from, two things implied in, i 248.
  mansions in, prepared by Christ, and how, ii. 82
Heavenly things, meaning of, i. 119.
Heavens opened, i 80
Heel, to lift up the, a metaphorical expression, ii 66.
Herod, the temple at Jerusalem completed by, i 99.
Hirelings, who are, i 403.
  opinions of Tertullian and Augustine concerning, i 404.
Holy Spirit, the, is the only Author of a pure and upright nature, i 114.
  why he appeared in the form of a dove, i 67.
  faith is a remarkable gift of, i. 276.
  water an emblem of, i. 309.
  had been given, though less abundantly, under the Old Testament, i 310
  is the gift of the Father, ii 92.

INDEX.

Holy Spirit, the, two ways in which the world will be convinced by, ii 139

Christ says that he is *seen*, when he dwells in the disciples by, ii. 148.

is called the Comforter, ii. 92.

is the Spirit of truth, i. 93

testifies of Christ, and how, ii 130

proceedeth from the Father, ii. 131.

did not teach the Apostles anything else than what they had heard from the mouth of Christ, ii. 156.

the world cannot receive, ii. 92.

the elect alone profit by the grace of, ii. 170.

believers always have Christ present by, ii 94

works in the elect in a secret manner, ii 250.

was not given by measure to Christ, i. 139.

what men can do when deprived of the protection of, ii. 94.

the gifts of, the reprobate are sometimes endued by God with, ii 64.

are all contained in *life*, i 200

Hosanna, meaning of the word, ii. 18.

Hour of Christ, various meanings of the, i. 85.

why the Evangelist tells us that it was not yet come, i 301.

sometimes refers to the publication of the gospel, ii 27.

Hours of the day, the, were generally reckoned to be twelve, i. 71, 427.

but sometimes were reckoned to be four, ii. 224.

House of God, the, why the temple was called, i 92.

Human passions, Christ was subject to, i. 439

but took them upon him without disorder, i. 441.

Humility, the true and only rule of, ii 56.

Hyperbole, a figure of speech frequently employed by heathen authors, ii 299.

Hypocrisy detected, i. 221.

is always ambitious, i. 222.

presumptuously shelters itself under the name of God, i 349.

is always proud and cruel, i. 373

has always been full of venom, i 392.

faults connected with, ii 205.

Hypocrites deceive themselves by poor disguises, i. 450.

how to distinguish believers from, i 341.

always resort to flattery to deceive themselves, ii. 135.

in what manner they assent to the Gospel, i 100.

I AM, import of, i 362 ; ii 66

I, it is, effect of these words in comforting the disciples, i. 237.

effect of, on the soldiers who came to apprehend Christ, ii 191

Image of God, Christ is the, ii 87.

Impiety is ingenious in obscuring the works of God, i. 372.

Incarnation of Christ, i. 44.

Intercession of Christ, the, no prayers are heard but through, ii 85.

danger of indulging in carnal imaginations about, ii 157.

for whom it is offered, ii. 172.

Invisible, God is, i 53

Isaiah, allusion to a passage in the prophecies of, i 307.

predicted that very few would believe the gospel, ii 40.

saw the glory of Christ, ii. 44

predicted the resurrection of Christ, ii 253.

INDEX. 331

Israel, Christ is acknowledged to be King of, i 79.
    why Christ reminded Nicodemus that he was a teacher in, i 117.

JACOB, ladder in the dream of, alluded to, i 81.
    example of, blindly and ignorantly followed by the Samaritans, i 157.
Jerusalem, triumphal entrance of Christ into, ii. 12
    high privileges enjoyed by the inhabitants of, ii. 17.
Jews, the, had been adopted into the family of God, i. 40
    in rejecting Christ showed base ingratitude, i. 39
    points of agreement and of difference between us and, i 162.
    falsely boasted that they were free, i. 343.
    the blindness of, was voluntary, i 379
    how the Gentiles came to be associated with, i. 407.
    the predictions of Scripture did not lay necessity on, ii. 39.
    salvation is from, and how, i. 159.
    superstitions of, about washing, i. 87
    how it is said that they could not believe, ii 39
    Barabbas was demanded by, ii 213.
    accused Jesus of blasphemy, ii 217, n. 1.
    origin of the disagreement between the Samaritans and, i. 146.
John the Baptist, import of the name of, i 36.
    testified concerning Christ, i. 35. and how, i 69.
    was not the true light, i. 37
    surrenders his office to Christ, i 49.

John the Baptist, why he is compared to Elijah, i 57.
    why he is called a voice, i. 59.
    was before and yet after Christ, i. 49, 62
    prepared disciples for Christ, i 70.
    what knowledge of Christ he had before his baptism, i. 68.
    question among the disciples of, about purifying, i 131.
    declares that he was the herald or forerunner of Christ, i. 133.
    was a prophet, i 57.
    and yet differed from the other prophets, i 58.
    is pronounced by Christ to have been a burning and shining lamp, i 212.
    his instructions were wickedly abused, i 214.
    performed no miracle, i. 423.
    the baptism of, did not differ from that of Christ, i 61.
John, the Evangelist, is called the disciple whom Jesus loved, ii 69.
    is appointed by Christ to be his substitute in taking care of his mother, ii 232.
Joseph of Arimathea unites with Nicodemus in burying the body of Jesus, ii 243.
Josephus, extent of the Lake of Gennesareth described by, i 236.
Joy of believers, the, ii 114
    is greatly enhanced by its perpetuity, ii 151
    is both Christ's joy and ours, ii. 115.
    Christ is the Author, cause, and pledge of, ii. 178.
    the sorrow of the disciples would be turned into, ii. 149.
Judas Iscariot is pronounced by Christ to be a devil, i. 280.
    murmured at the anointing of Christ by Mary, ii. 11.

332   INDEX.

Judas Iscariot was a thief, ii. 12.
 the devil put it into the heart of, to betray Christ, ii 55.
 why Christ gave a dipped sop to, ii. 70
 was the son of perdition, ii. 176
 sign of a bad conscience in, ii. 191.
 the devil did not enter essentially into, ii. 71.
 did he receive the body of Christ as well as the other Apostles ? i 268
Judas, (not Iscariot,) question put by, ii. 97.
Judas Maccabæus, the temple again consecrated by, i. 412.
Judge, a, Christ laid aside for a time the office of, ii. 50
 to, is sometimes put for to condemn, i 126; ii. 51
 we ought not, according to the appearance, i 296.
Judgment, the Holy Spirit convicts the world of, ii. 141.
 sometimes denotes authority and power, i. 201
 sometimes denotes the punishment inflicted on unbelievers, i 389.
 of this world, meaning of, ii. 36.
 the last, will be a ratification of the doctrine of the gospel, ii. 52.

KEDRON, meaning of the name, ii. 190.
King, the multitude intended to make Christ a, i 233.
 of Israel, Christ is acknowledged by Nathanael to be, i 79.
 Christ was publicly saluted as, ii 24.
Kingdom of Christ, the, what was the nature of, ii. 209
 is it lawful to defend it by arms? ii 210

Kingdom of God, the, what it is to see, i 108
Knowledge distinguishes faith from erroneous and false opinions, i 279.

LADDER in Jacob's dream alluded to, i. 81.
Lamb, the paschal, was a figure of the true and only sacrifice, ii. 241.
 of God, Christ was called, and why, i 63, 69.
Lame man cured at the pool of Bethesda. *See* Bethesda.
Lamp, a burning and shining, John was, i. 212
Law, the, contrasted with grace and truth, i 48.
 yet did not want grace and truth, i. 52
 repeal of the worship and ceremonies of, i. 161
 the superiority of the gospel to, i. 172.
 all the doctrine of the prophets was but an appendage to, ii. 129.
 what is the peculiar office of, ii. 140.
 reason of the ceremonies contained in, ii 205.
 the fathers did not worship God spiritually under, i. 161.
 summary of, given by Moses, i 220.
 injunction of, concerning witnesses, i. 330.
 the sacraments differ widely from the ancient figures of, ii. 241.
Lazarus, the brother of Martha and Mary, i. 424
 Christ offers thanksgiving to God at the grave of, i. 445.
 is raised from the dead, i 447.
 consultation of the Jews about killing, ii. 16.
Lent, or forty days' fast, the Papists falsely plead Christ's example for, ii. 61

INDEX. 333

Liberty, what kind of, is bestowed by Christ, i 342.
Life, how Christ is the, i 31, 436.
 God contains in himself the fulness of, i. 207.
 three degrees of, i 269.
 why the word of God is called, i 274.
 what it is to hate and to love, ii. 29.
 to see, is put for enjoying, i. 142.
 believers have already passed from death to, i 204
Life, eternal, is promised universally to all who believe in Christ, i. 125.
 the manner of bestowing, ii. 166.
 what is contained in, i 200.
 is attained by hearing the word of Christ, i 203.
 the communion of saints is a preparation for, i 455.
Lifted up, how Christ is said to be, i. 121, 336, ii 37.
Light, Christ is called the, i. 32.
 is a name which belongs properly to Christ alone, i 37.
 children of, who are, ii 39
 in the Lord, all the godly are, i 37.
Loaves and fishes, miracle of the, i 230
 meaning of, i. 231
Longinus, a soldier so called, childish fable of the Papists about, ii. 239.
Lord's Supper, the, little children forbidden to partake of, i. 265
 celebrated sometimes daily and sometimes only on the Lord's day, i 266.
 why Christ added the cup in, i. 267
Love of Christ, the, the obedience of believers is the effect and not the cause of, ii 113
Love of God, the, is the first cause of our salvation, i. 122.

Love of God, was founded on the purpose of his will, i. 123.
 flows through Christ to the members of the Church, ii. 112
 the habitation of the Holy Spirit in believers is an exhibition and pledge of, ii. 185
 comes in order before our love of Christ, ii 96.
 we ought not to judge of, from our outward condition, i 427.
Love of God, our, put for all religious feelings, i. 219.

MAGISTRATES are called gods, and why, i. 420.
Mahomet agrees with the Pope in denying the perfection of Scripture, ii 101.
 the religion of, collected from wicked additions to the word of God, i. 165.
Malachi prophesied concerning John the Baptist, i. 57.
Malice, the, of men, alone hinders them from believing in Christ, i. 218.
Manasseh, brother of Jaddus, built a temple on Mount Gerizzim, i. 155
Manicheans, absurd tenets of the, i 350, ii 104.
Manna called the bread of heaven, i. 246.
 comparison between Christ and, i 247.
Mansions in heaven prepared by Christ, and how, ii 82.
Marriage, the institution of, highly honoured by the miracle at Cana of Galilee, i. 89
Martha, the sister of Lazarus, i. 424.
 faith of, i 434.
 honours Christ by calling him Master, i 438.
 distrust of, reproved, i. 444
 excessive timidity of, i. 434.

334 INDEX.

Martyrs, the Papists frame idols for themselves out of, i. 358

Mary, the mother of Jesus, one of the guests at the marriage in Cana of Galilee, i 82.
apparent harshness of the reply of Jesus to, i. 83.
obedience and modesty of, i. 86.
disgraceful superstitions of the Papists concerning, i. 85, 284.
Christ's affection for, was worthy of admiration, ii 231

Mary, the sister of Lazarus, i 224.
distinguished from the woman who was a sinner, i. 425
reverence of, for Christ, i. 439.

Mary Magdalene was one of the witnesses of the resurrection of Christ, ii 257

Mass, the wicked sacrilege of the, ii 263
condemned by the exclamation of Christ on the cross, ii 236.

Measure, the Holy Spirit was not given to Christ by, i 139

Mediator, the, two errors committed concerning, ii 91
the grace of, was common to all ages, i. 312.
the fathers were not accustomed to pray to God without a, ii. 153.

Medicinal draughts, afflictions compared to, ii 196

Messiah, the, a Hebrew word, signifying anointed, i. 72.
the Samaritans held some principles taken from the law relating to, i 164
and entertained strong expectations and desires of, i. 173
the fulfilment of prophecies proved Jesus to be, ii. 17.
Daniel was the first who exclusively appropriated to the Redeemer the name of, i 72.

Micah, remarkable prediction of, concerning Christ, i. 298.

Miracles prepare the way for doctrine, i 178.
reasons why they were performed at the pool of Bethesda, i. 186.
God sometimes permits false prophets to perform, i. 376.
twofold use of, i. 448

Miracles of Christ, the, were proofs of his Divinity, i. 89.
were the Father's attestation of him, i. 215
it is of great importance what we keep in view in, i 240.
Nicodemus had profited aright by, i. 106.
were not all recorded, ii. 299.
of turning water into wine, i. 88
of driving the buyers and sellers out of the temple, i 95.
of curing the nobleman's son at Capernaum, i. 179
of curing the lame man at the pool of Bethesda, i. 189.
of loaves and fishes, i. 230.
of raising Lazarus from the dead, i 447.
of entering into a room while the doors were shut, ii. 264.
of a large draught of fishes, ii 285.
of walking on the sea, i 236.
of curing the man who had been blind from his birth, i. 363.

Monks, shocking crimes of, i 293

Moses erected the brazen serpent in the wilderness, i. 121.
striking quotation from the writings of, i. 69
summary of the Law given by, i. 220
argument drawn from the writings of, concerning ceremonies, i 295.
in what manner God was seen by, i 55

INDEX. 335

Moses wrote concerning Christ, i. 224.
  the woman of Samaria prefers Christ to, i 165
Moses, the ministry of, was inferior to that of Christ, i 52.
  lasted till the time of Christ, ii. 129.
Mountain, why Christ went up into a, i 228
Murderer, the devil is a, i 351
Murmuring of the Jews against Christ, i 255
  two ways in which we thus sin daily, i. 256.
  of Judas at the anointing of Christ by Mary, ii 11.

NAME sometimes denotes *power*, i 43
  and sometimes *authority*, i. 100
  in his own, i 220.
  of Christ, to pray in the, i 154
  of the Lord, to come in the, ii 20.
Name of God, the, was manifested in the preaching of Christ, ii 170.
  the end of all things is the sanctification of, ii. 90.
  false prophets arrogantly boast of, ii 21
  hypocrisy presumptuously shelters itself under, i. 349
Nathanael informed about Christ by Philip, i 75
  is pronounced by Christ to be a true Israelite, i 77.
  and to be free from deceit, i. 78.
  acknowledges Christ to be the Son of God, and King of Israel, i. 79.
Nazareth, foolish prejudices against, i 76
Nestorius, argument of, about the body of Christ being called *a temple*, refuted, i. 97
Nicodemus, a ruler of the Jews, i. 103
  why it is mentioned that he was a Pharisee, i 104

Nicodemus, why he came to Jesus by night, i. 105.
  had profited aright by the miracles of Christ, i 106
  was imperfectly acquainted with the grace of regeneration, i 109
  why Christ forbids him to wonder, i. 112
  acts in the Council as a neutral man, i 316.
  false pretences of resembling, i. 317.
  why Christ reminded him of his being a teacher in Israel, i. 117.
  unites with Joseph in burying the body of Jesus, ii 245.
Night, day and, Christ borrows a comparison from, i 428.
Nobleman, miraculous cure of the son of a, at Capernaum, i. 179.
Nonnus, a Greek writer, quotation from, i. 334 *n* 5

OATH, form of administering an, i. 382.
Obedience is the foundation of true worship, i 234.
  the fruit of, i 203.
  illustrious example of, in the blind man, i 370.
  instance of, in the mother of Christ, i 86.
  as the ransom of our righteousness, Christ offered his, ii. 106.
  Christ by his own example instructs us to perfect, ii 234.
  the, of believers is the effect and not the cause of the love of Christ, ii 113.
Object of faith, Christ is the proper, i 124, ii 81.
Offences, why the greater part of men give way on account of, ii 177.
Office of Christ, summary view of the nature of, i 200.

INDEX.

Officers sent to seize Christ, i. 313
Ointment, precious, vast expense of, stated by Pliny, ii. 12.
Only-begotten, why Christ is so called, i. 47.
   this word magnifies the fervour of the love of God towards us, 1 124.
Orphans, who are so called, ii 94.

PAPISTS, the, hold out a phantom in the room of Christ, i 76
   gross and disgraceful superstitions of, concerning the Virgin Mary, 1. 85
   effrontery of, in pretending to have relics of the *water-pots* employed in the miracle at Cana of Galilee, i, 87
   absurd canons of, forbidding the clergy to attend a marriage, i 89.
   declaim about the fathers, but allow no place for prophets and apostles, i. 155.
   have buried the Church under a huge mass of ceremonies, i 157.
   object of the pretended miracles of, i 90.
   have collected their religion from wicked additions to the word of God, 1. 165.
   endeavour to support free-will by comparing it to the man left half-dead on the road, i 205
   confound the distinction between the Jewish and Christian religion, i 162
   false inferences of, about good works, 1 210.
   their wicked sacrilege in the mass, i. 263
   break out into horrid blasphemies, i 271
   disfigure the worship of God by gross and singularly carnal pomp, i. 163.

Papists, are vain of an uninterrupted succession from the fathers, i. 348.
   idle and foolish slanders of, i. 375.
   absurd ceremony of washing the feet of twelve men, ii. 62.
   put forward their own inventions as the oracles of God, ii 142
   have no authoritative guide but the traditions of the Church, ii 182.
   torture the words of Christ to prove their doctrine of transubstantiation, ii. 280
   frame idols for themselves out of the apostles and martyrs, i 358
   foolishly maintain that we ought to pray to departed saints, ii 27
   disputes of, about the object of faith, ii 81.
   their doctrine about the co-operation of human power with divine grace, ii 109
   inquiry into the grounds of their claim to the title of The Church, 11 217.
   falsely plead the example of Christ for Lent, ii. 61.
   are not less eager than the Pharisees were to extinguish the gospel, i 302.
   the diabolical system of celibacy held by, i. 323
Parable of the vine and the branches, ii 106
   sophisms of the Papists concerning, ii 109
Parents, the sins of, sometimes punished in their children, i 366
Passions, human, are not in themselves sinful, i 440.
   Christ was subject to, i. 439.
Passover, feast of the, two reasons why Christ celebrated, i 92
   the lamb of, was a figure of the true and only sacrifice, 11. 241.

INDEX. 337

Pastors, who are the faithful, i. 396.
Patience taught us by the example of the man cured at the pool of Bethesda, ı 190.
 chastisements sometimes are only trials of, i 365.
Peace, what Christ means by, ii. 101, 265
 of conscience, whence arises, ıı 114
Penelope's web, allusion to, explained, i 320, *n* 1
Pentecost, the feast of, ı 184
Perdition, Judas Iscariot was the son of, ii 176.
Persecution is a touchstone to try faith, ıı. 161.
Perseverance of the saints, the, ascribed to election, ii 63.
 the method of, ii 113.
Person of Christ and of the Father, distinction between the, ii. 169
Persons in the Godhead, distinction of, denied by Sabellius, i. 28.
 the fathers had good reasons for using this term, ı. 29.
Peter was brought to the knowledge of Christ by the agency of Andrew, his brother, i. 72.
 brief summary of faith given by, i. 270.
 reproved for refusing to have his feet washed by Christ, ii. 58
 his denial of Christ foretold, ii. 79
 the foolish zeal of, ii 195
 denies Christ, ıı 200
 is guilty of profane swearing, ii 203.
 a striking mirror of our ordinary condition is to be found in the life of, ii. 293
 uncertainty as to the manner of the death of, ıı 294
 the Pope falsely claims to be the successor of, ıı 290

Pharisees, the, whence the name was derived, i 104
 were held in higher estimation than the Essenes, i. 105.
 were filled with rage against Christ under the pretence of godly zeal, ıı 145
 opposed Christ more bitterly than all the other sects, ı. 302.
 had a reputation above others, both for knowledge and holiness, i. 314.
Philip called by Christ, ı. 74
 modesty of, appears in his conversation with Nathanael, ı. 75.
 why Bethsaida is mentioned as the birth-place of, i 74
 made two gross blunders in speaking about Christ, ı. 75
 and yet, unlike the Papists, he held by the true Church, i. 76
Piety, the first maxim of, i. 211
Pilate acknowledges that there is no guilt in Christ, ii 214
 foolish boasting of, reproved, ii 221.
 delivers Jesus to be crucified, ii 225
 without knowing it, proclaims the gospel in three languages, ii 228
 we behold an image of a proud man in, ii 220.
 the example of, instructs us to be steady in defending the truth, ıı 228
Plato, Augustine addicted to the philosophy of, ı. 31
Plautus, an expressive idiom taken from, ıı 218, *n* 2
Pliny, practice of anointing described by, ii 11
 extent of the Lake of Gennesareth described by, i 236.
 price of ointment stated by, ii 12.

VOL. II.   Y

Plural number, why employed by Christ in speaking of himself, i. 117.
  in speaking of the prophets, i. 258.
Poor, the, Christ giveth to, ii 72
  pretended care of Judas about, ii 12
Pope, the, boasts of being Christ's deputy or vicar, i 220.
  falsely pretends to a right of excommunicating, ii. 47
  sacrilegiously binds souls by his inventions, ii 53.
  agrees with Mahomet in denying the perfection of Scripture, ii 101.
  we have no reason to be alarmed at the excommunications of, ii 134.
  falsely claims to be the successor of Peter, ii. 290.
  the court of, is filled with Epicureans, i 293.
Porch, Solomon's, why so called, i. 396.
Power to believe put for right or claim, i. 41.
Prætorium, meaning which the Romans gave to the word, ii 204.
Praying, what is indicated by lifting up the eyes in, ii. 163.
  aright, what is the rule of, ii. 111.
  we ought to begin with, whenever we take food, i. 230.
Predestination, vain attempts to overturn the doctrine of, i 254.
  faith flows from, ii. 170.
  danger of indulging in curious inquiries about, i. 254
  is manifested to us in Christ alone, ii 171.
Prediction of Caiaphas concerning the death of Christ, i. 453.
  of the resurrection of Christ by Isaiah and others, ii. 253.
  of Malachi concerning John the Baptist, i 57
Prediction of Micah concerning Christ, i. 298
  of Christ concerning his own death, ii 207.
Pride, the chief and most dangerous of the vices of men, i. 285
  hypocrisy has always been full of, i 392.
Priests, the, why questions were put to John by, i 56.
  tyranny exercised by, i 286.
  boasted of their knowledge, i. 316
  monstrous blindness of, i 449.
Prince of this world, the, Satan is called, ii. 36.
  cometh, ii 104.
  shall be cast out, ii. 36.
Principalities, why angels are called, i. 187.
Profession of faith, what is the true and lawful, i 359
Prophecies, the, Jesus was proved to be the Messiah by the fulfilment of, ii. 17.
  the course of events ought not to be ascribed to, ii 177.
Prophet, a, Christ is acknowledged by the multitude to be, i 311.
  sometimes denotes any teacher, i 178.
  hath no honour in his own country, a proverb, i. 177.
  John the Baptist was, i 57.
Prophets represented under the character of sowers, i. 172.
  invincible courage and magnanimity of, i 359.
  the whole doctrine of, was but an appendage to the law, ii. 129
  why mentioned in the plural number, i. 258.
Prophets, false, are sometimes permitted by God to perform miracles, i 376.
  arrogantly boast of the name of God, ii. 21.

INDEX. 339

Proteus, a king of Egypt, fabulous accounts of, ii. 256, *n* 1.
Proverb about a prophet, i 177.
Proverbs, to speak in, ii. 155.
Providence of God, the, striking display of, in the conclusion of a meeting of the Sanhedrim, i. 318
punishments inflicted by, three ways in which we commonly err concerning, i. 364.
Purifying, meaning of, i 132.
Pythagoras, the transmigration of souls, taught by, i. 366.

Rabbi, various meanings of the term, i. 70.
Rabboni, meaning of, ii. 258.
Rashness of men in the things of God, i. 287.
Reapers and sowers, illustration taken from, i 172.
Receiving Christ is put for *believing* in him, i 40.
Reconciliation, the, effected by Christ, is extended to the Gentiles, i. 455
Redemption, in the order of time goes before salvation, i 126
Regeneration, absolute necessity of, i 108
does it precede faith? i 44.
Nicodemus was imperfectly acquainted with the grace of, i. 109
Reprobate, the, are not moved by promises any more than by threatenings, i 357.
by their unbelief draw down on themselves a new death, i. 142
are sometimes endued by God with the gifts of the Holy Spirit, ii. 64.
are subjected to Christ by the Father, ii 165
the gospel is not hidden or obscure but to, i 379.
the elect are distinguished from, by pure grace, ii. 170.

Reprobate, the, how God punishes the contempt of his grace in, i. 304
Reprobate mind, given up to a, ii 43.
the most evident sign of, i 354.
Rest of God on the Sabbath, nature and design of, i 196.
Restored, how the church can be, i. 258.
Resurrection, why Christ calls himself the, i 435
of Lazarus, i. 447.
of the soul, faith is a spiritual, i. 436.
Resurrection of the dead, why Christ so frequently connects with eternal life, i 266.
why mentioned by Christ in connection with his own death, i 253.
Resurrection of Christ, the, plainly showed him to be the Son of God, i. 272.
predicted by David and Isaiah, ii. 253
why women were chosen to be the principal witnesses of, ii. 248
was not full and complete till he sat down at the right hand of the Father, ii 259.
himself claims the glory of, i. 98.
agreement of the Evangelists with each other in relating, ii 248.
is our triumph over death, ii. 295
the death and, are the two pillars of faith, ii. 159, 247.
Righteous Father, why Christ called God, ii 188.
Righteousness must be looked for through the satisfaction made by Christ, ii 225.
the world must be convicted of, ii 140
the Sun of, Christ is called, i. 57

340 INDEX.

Righteousness, spiritual, in what it consists, i. 53
   why Christ makes it to consist in his ascension to the Father, ii. 140
Rulers, many of the, believed in Christ, ii 44
   general character of, ii 45

Sabbath, the, nature and design of the rest of God on, i. 196.
   two reasons why Christ healed the lame man on, i 190
   was purposely selected by Christ for curing the man who had been blind from his birth, i 374.
   the Jews falsely charged Christ with violating the sanctity of, i 191.
   the keeping of does not interrupt or hinder the works of God, i 196, 375
Sabellius denied the distinction of Persons in the Godhead, i 28.
Sacraments, the, a twofold manner of speaking about, i 61.
   differ widely from the ancient figures of the law, ii. 241
   whence is derived the efficacy of, ii 269.
   God takes, as it were, a visible form in, i 216.
   it is not in the power of any man to institute, i. 67.
   contrived by men are nothing else than absolute mockeries, ii. 270
Sacrifice, the death of Christ was a voluntary, i 410.
   alms are an acceptable, ii 15.
   faith is a precious, in the sight of God, i 138
Saints, the communion of, is a preparation for eternal life, i. 455
   departed, the Papists foolishly maintain that we ought to pray to, ii 27.
Salem, where situated, i 130

Salvation, the source or first cause of our, i 122.
   in the order of time, redemption goes before, i 126.
   is declared by Christ to be common to the whole world, i. 176.
   the, of the elect, is rendered certain by the power of God, i 416
   how it is from the Jews, i 159.
   how much it cost the Son of God, ii 32
   in the person of Christ God testifies how much he cares for our, ii 116
Samaria, a woman of, Christ asks drink from, i 146.
   is convinced that Christ knew fully her wicked life, i 152
   prefers Christ to Moses and all the prophets in the office of teaching, i 165
Samaritan, Christ was reproachfully called a, i, 354
Samaritans, the Jews held no intercourse with, i 147.
   falsely boasted of being descended from the holy fathers, i 150.
   were Cutheans by descent, i. 151.
   shielded themselves by the example of the fathers, i 155
   held some principles taken from the law, relating to the Messiah, i. 164.
   entertained strong expectations and desires of the promised Messiah, i 173
   origin of the disagreement between the Jews and, i. 146.
   astonishing success of the gospel among, i 177
Sanctification, the means of, ii 179
   common to all believers, i. 420.
   the word of God is the instrument of, ii 109.
   is not instantly completed in us on the first day, ii 180
   includes the kingdom of God and his righteousness, ii. 179

Sanctification of the name of God, the end of all things is, ii 90.
Sanctified, how Christ was by the Father, i 420.
Sanhedrim, or supreme council of the Jews, meeting of, i 314
  Nicodemus acts in, as a neutral man, i 316.
  singular conclusion of the meeting, i 318.
Saviour of the world, Christ is the, i 176
Schism is a highly pernicious evil in the Church of God, i 377.
  arises solely from the wickedness of men, i. 411
Scriptures, the, Christ cannot be properly known but from, i. 218
  how pernicious the mangling of, i. 298
  the Pope agrees with Mahomet in denying the perfection of, ii. 101
  we are commanded to seek Christ in, i 218.
  Christ was eminently distinguished by his knowledge of, i 289
  cannot be broken, i. 420.
Sea, Christ walked on the, i. 236
See death, to, what it is, i 356.
  life, is put for enjoying, i 142
  the kingdom, i 108.
  and hear, contrasted with doubtful rumours, i 137.
  sometimes expresses the certainty of faith, ii 86.
Seek, ambiguous signification of the word, i. 303
Serpent of brass, the, erected by Moses, i. 121.
  why Christ compares himself to, i 122.
Servants, the Apostles were not, but friends of Christ, ii. 117.
Servetus denied the Eternal Divinity of Christ, i 26.

Sheep, the, various allegorical meanings of, i 399
  hear the voice of Christ, i. 408.
  they who do not obey the gospel are not, i 415.
  why unbelievers are sometimes called, i 406
  why believers are called, i. 415.
Shepherd, Christ is the only, i. 401.
  is the good, i. 402.
  in protecting his flock, discharges the office of a good, ii 193.
Shepherds, who are the good, i. 395
Sichar, where situated, i. 145.
Signs, wickedness of the Jews in asking, i. 245 See Miracles
Siloam, the pool of, i. 370.
  meaning of the name, i. 371.
Simon received from Christ the name of Cephas, or Peter, i. 73 See Peter
Sin, there is but one method of taking away, i 64.
  all the evils which we endure ought to be ascribed to, i. 193.
  forgiveness of, is unconditional, i 204.
  the degrading slavery of, i. 344
  with what abhorrence it is regarded by God, ii. 226.
  the Comforter will convict the world of, ii 139.
  what it is to die in, i 332
Sinner, often denotes a person of immoral conduct, i. 376.
Sinners, how God heareth not, i. 385
Slave, how a son differs from a, i. 344.
  he who committeth sin is the, of sin, i 343.
Slavery, the, of sin is voluntary, i 344.

342 INDEX.

Slaves of sin, all men by nature are, i 344.
Sleep, why death is compared to, i. 430.
Solomon's porch, why so called, i 412
Son of God, the, Christ is acknowledged by Nathanael to be, i. 79.
    why he declares himself to be, i. 92.
    why the Father loveth, i. 409.
    in what respect he can do nothing of himself, i 198, 210.
    is one with the Father, and in what sense, i. 416, ii 174.
    the Father gave all things into the hands of, ii 55.
    is the object to which our faith ought to be directed, ii 81
    the dead shall hear the voice of, i. 206.
    did not ascend to heaven in a private capacity, ii 82.
Son of Man, the, why Christ calls himself, i 120.
    why angels are said to ascend and descend on, i. 80
    how he is glorified in his death, ii 72
Sons of God, we become by faith, i. 41.
    by adoption Christ communicates to us the honour of, i 124.
    difference between, and the reprobate in dying, ii 237
Sop, a dipped, why Christ gave to Judas, ii 70.
Sowers, comparison drawn by Christ from, i 172
    were philosophers or profane writers included in the number of? i 173
Sowing, Christ compares his death to, ii. 28.
Speak from himself, Christ does not, i. 292.
Speech, and not *Word*, is the proper translation of λόγος, as a designation of Christ, i. 28

Speech, why Christ is so called, i. 26.
    put for talkativeness, i. 176.
Spirit, God is a, i 164
    what it is to worship God in the, i 163. *See* Holy Spirit.
Spiritual, why the worship of God is called, i. 161.
Steps, five, to be observed by us in considering the words of Christ in his agony, ii. 33
Stoics, the tenets of, set aside by the example of Christ, i. 441.
Stones, the Jews took up, to throw at Christ, i 363.
Stooping down, intention of Christ in employing the attitude of, i 319.
Suetonius, anecdote about Vespasian related by, i. 376.
Sun of Righteousness, Christ is called the, i. 57.
Superstitions of the Jews about washing, i 87.
    of the Papists about the Virgin Mary, i 85, 284.
Syllogism, the accusation of the Jews against Christ reduced to the form of a, ii. 217, *n* 1.
Sympathy of Christ, i. 439.

Taking away sins, there is but one method of, i 64.
    spurious rites of, derived from a holy origin, i. 65.
Taste of death, to, i 357.
Taught by God, the elect alone are, i 258.
Teaching, God has two ways of, ii. 101.
Temple, the, Christ drives out those who transacted merchandise in, i. 90.
    was a sanctuary of heavenly doctrine, i 91.
    completed by Herod, i 99.
    inquiry about the forty-six years spent in building, i 98.
    why Christ taught in, i. 288.
    the treasury was a part of, i. 330.

INDEX. 343

Temple, the, why called the house of God, i. 92.
　sometimes denotes the whole worship of God, i 94
　why the body of Christ is called a, i 97.
Tertullian, opinion of, about hirelings, i. 404.
Testaments, the Old and New, distinction between, i. 53
Testimony of the Father concerning Christ, i 215
　of Christ, all do not receive, i. 118.
　of John the Baptist concerning Christ, i 35
Thanksgiving to God offered by Christ at the grave of Lazarus, i. 445
Theology, the principal articles of, ii 212
Thief, Judas was a, ii. 12.
　why Christ chose as a steward one whom he knew to be a, ii 13
　and robber, who is, i. 394.
Thirst, descriptive of an ardent desire of salvation, i 306
　allusion to the use of the term by the prophet Isaiah, i. 307.
Thomas, called the Twin, Christ reproves the unbelief of, ii. 274
　monstrous stupidity of, ii 275
　two remarkable clauses in the confession of, ii 277
　faith of, had not been wholly extinguished but choked, ii. 276
Tiberias, Bethsaida was halfway between Capernaum and, i. 238
　the sea of, why the lake of Gennesareth was called, i. 227.
Time of Christ, the, various meanings of, i 284.
Traditions of the Church, the Papists have no authoritative guide but the, ii. 182

Transmigration of souls, the doctrine of the, held by many of the Jews down to the present day, i 366.
Transubstantiation, the Popish doctrine of, ii. 280.
Treasury, the, was a part of the temple, i 330
Trinity of Persons in the Godhead denied by Sabellius, i. 28.
　observation of Gregory Nazianzen concerning, i. 29.
Triumphal entrance of Christ into Jerusalem, ii. 16.
　not understood at that time by the disciples, ii 24.
Troubled, Christ's soul was, ii 31.
　five steps to be observed in, ii 33
　was it unsuitable that the Son of God should be ? ii 32
　in spirit, import of, ii 68
Truth, Christ is the, ii 84
　of the worship of God consists in the spirit, i 163
　God is the fountain of, ii 144.
　is not to be found anywhere else than in the word of God, ii 180
　what it is to be of, ii 212.
　question of Pilate concerning, ii 212.
　how we are made free by, i 341.
　the Holy Spirit is the Spirit of, ii 93
　grace and, Christ was full of, i 48
　to do, meaning of, i. 129.
Tyranny, exercised by the priests and scribes, i. 286.

UNBELIEF is the source and cause of all evils, i 333.
　hinders God from approaching us, i. 444.
　of Thomas, reproved, ii. 274.
Unbelievers are already condemned, i 127
　are guilty of the greatest insult that can be offered to the Son of God, i. 138.
　are blind, i. 390.

Unbelievers, the doctrine of Christ is a stone of stumbling to, i 277

Union between Christ and believers, what is the way of knowing the, ii. 95.

Unity of the Church, the, is founded on nothing else than the word of God, ii 230

VENIAL sin, an indirect denial of Christ is not a, ii 47

Venom, hypocrisy has always been full of, i 392.

Vespasian, supposed miracle of, related by Suetonius, i 376.

Vicar, or deputy of Christ, the Pope boasts of being, i. 220

Vine, Christ is the true, ii 106.
three things chiefly to be observed in, ii. 1, 7.

Vinegar is given to Christ, ii 235.

Virgin Mary *See* Mary

Vitellius, Caiaphas deposed by, ii. 197.

Voice, why John the Baptist is called a, i 59.

Voice of Christ, the, what is meant by, i 209
the sheep hear, i. 408
how alarming will be, when he cometh to judge the world, ii 192

Voice of God, the, a metaphor, i 216.
the efficacy which Isaiah ascribes to, ii 192.

Vulgate, corruption of a passage in the, ii. 297, *n.* 1.

WALK, to, in darkness, i. 325; ii 39.

Wars of the giants, i 223, *n* 1.

Washing of the feet of the disciples by Christ, ii 56
intention of Christ in, ii 60
absurd imitation of, by the Papists, ii. 62
how Christ washes us, ii 58.

Water, what it is to be born of, i. 109.

Water, an emblem of the Spirit, i 309.
flowing out of the belly, i. 308
what we are taught by the troubling of, i 189.
living, what it is, i 149
there flowed from Christ's side blood and, ii. 239.

Way, Christ is the, ii 84

Will of the flesh, the, means the same thing with *the will of man*, i 43.

Will of Christ, the, did not differ from the will of the Father, i. 212

Will of God, the, how we may know, i 290.
ought to be placed by us in the first rank, i 212.

Will, to, is put for to desire, ii 187.

Wind, comparison taken from the, i 114.

Wine, miracle of turning water into, i. 88

Witnesses, injunction of the law concerning, i 320
of the resurrection of Christ, why women were accounted the principal, ii 248

Wolfius, marginal German readings quoted by, ii. 105, *n* 1.

Woman taken in adultery, the, brought before Christ, i 319.
false glosses on the passage by Popish theologians, i 323

Women ought not to be allowed to administer baptism, ii 261.

Wonder of the Jews concerning Christ, of what nature it was, i. 288
why Nicodemus is forbidden to, i 115

Word of Christ, the, astonishing efficacy of, i 417
why it is called life, i 274.
officers sent to seize Christ are vanquished by, i 313.

Word of God, the, faith is founded on, i 176.
the truth is not to be found anywhere else than in, ii 180.

INDEX. 345

Word of God, ceremonies without, are dead, ii. 246.
  the unity of the Church is founded on nothing else than, ii. 230.
  is the instrument of sanctification, ii. 109.
  the religion of Mahomet is collected from wicked additions to, i. 165.
Word, the eternal, Christ is, ii. 169.
Work of Christ, what was the, i. 170.
Work of God, faith is the, i 243.
Works of God, the, manifested in the cure of a blind man, i 367.
  impiety is ingenious in obscuring, i. 372.
  are not subjected to the judgment of men, i. 188.
  men do not immediately see the result of, ii. 24.
  all do' not derive equal profit from, i. 101.
  how great is the indolence of man in considering, i 283.
  in what sense Moses says that God put an end to, i. 196.
Works, good. See Good Works.
World, the, was created by Christ, i. 39.
  Christ taketh away the sin of, i. 64.
  is the universal term employed to show that all are invited to partake salvation through Christ, i. 125.
  why Christ was hated by, i. 285.
  Christ is the light of, i. 324, 368.
  cannot receive the Spirit, ii. 93.
  why believers are hated by, ii 124.
  why Christ came into, i. 126.
  Christ hath overcome, ii. 162.

VOL. II.

  the monstrous madness of, ii 182.
  Christ does not pray for, ii. 172.
  the death of Christ was the full restoration of, ii. 36.
  the publication of the gospel was a new and sudden resurrection of, i 206.
World, two ways in which the Holy spirit will convince, ii. 139.
  by what mark Christ distinguishes his disciples from, ii. 97.
  the bodily presence of Christ was the true and remarkable day of, i 369.
  all who are not regenerated by the Spirit of God are called, ii. 124
  sometimes includes all that is opposed to the salvation of believers, ii. 162.
  why Christ's brethren desire him to show himself to, i. 283
  why the devil is called the prince of, ii 104.
  ingratitude of, i. 38.
  the judgment of, what is meant by, ii. 36.
  the death of Christ was a passage from, to the heavenly kingdom of God, ii. 54.
Worship of God, the rule for the, ii. 214.
  ought to be spiritual, i. 163.
Worshippers of God, who are the true, i. 163
Worshipping, meaning of, i 389.
Wrath of God, the, abideth on unbelievers, i 142.

ZEAL to be kept within proper bounds, ii. 195.
  when accompanied by hypocrisy, is a dangerous plague, ii 46.

z

Zeal, foolish, of Peter, ii. 194.
Zeal of Christ, the, for the house of God, i. 94.
Zechariah, prophecy of, concerning Christ's sittting on an ass, ii. 22.
Zechariah, inquiry whether or not he literally refers to Christ in another prediction, ii. 242.
Zion was the habitation and abode of the Church, ii. 23.

THE END.

www.ingramcontent.com/pod-product-compliance
Lightning Source LLC
Chambersburg PA
CBHW050332230426
43663CB00010B/1830